The Pogues

'The Best Night Out In Town'

by Calum Bruce

Typeset in Meta Serif and Archer

Editing, design and publishing by UK Book Publishing

www.ukbookpublishing.com

ISBN: 978-0-9926433-8-6

Wishing you every success
with your book, Calum

Love,
Shane MacGowan
&
Victoria Mary Clarke

xxx

Foreword from James Fearnley

After our first gig on the October 7th 1982, it took just a few weeks for the Pogues to spark what grew into a fire of fanaticism which, over the past 30 years, has sometimes licked our heels, scorched us now and again, but above all has warmed us. The tinderbox ignited at the Pindar of Wakefield in Kings Cross and spread from there, up the country, jumping the Irish Sea, sending embers across the North Sea to Scandinavia, over the Channel to Europe, across the Atlantic to North America. In such a short time, it seemed, Pogues' fans crammed pubs from Brixton to Camden, Hammersmith to Harrow. A year later it was the same thing in Newport and Birmingham, Dublin and Glasgow.

The first couple of gigs in the capital were local, the audiences comprised of our neighbours, friends and relatives. The gigs we did outside London seemed local and intimate too, and just as impassioned. The further afield we went, and as our popularity – or our notoriety – grew, the stories our audience could to tell, about how far they had come to meet us, and the experiences they had on the way, increased too.

Each band has its fans, who will go to any lengths, travel any distance, endure all hardships – impecuniousness, the weather, mishaps, the vagaries of public transport, sometimes interminable car journeys – overcoming all manner of obstacles which ill-luck can throw in their paths, but still they came, to sit in wait for the tour bus to pull up behind the concert venue, to race across the empty hall to latch their arms over the barrier to secure a place at the front, to stand in rain, snow, sleet, to say greet us after a gig, stop one of us in a conversation for a minute or two, get a record signed. It's a thankless job, but someone's got to do it.

Calum Bruce's story of his life as a Pogues' fan is a work of dedication, a chronicle of penury, injury, devotion, death, marriage, self-denial, stupidity, the vaulting of seemingly insurmountable obstacles, dare-devilry, drunkenness, comradeship, and random acts of kindness.

It's de rigueur, nowadays, for the rock and roll musician to write a memoir or an autobiography. I think memoirist musicians could do no better than to read such a one, but of the rigours of being one of their fans.

James Fearnley, The Pogues

Foreword from a Pogues fan, Paul McCluskey

One chilly autumn night in 1996, I was sitting at the bar in the legendary Filthy McNasty's, Islington, London. Beside me, holding court was Shane MacGowan. A discussion was afoot regarding Shane's musical output. I'm damned if I can recall what point was up for debate. What I do remember distinctly was Shane's antennae picked up on something I said. He turned toward me and exclaimed to the assembled company, "Now, there's a man who knows his Pogues records." I'd be lying if I said I didn't feel proud at that moment.

I've been a fan of The Pogues since the early days. Their intoxicating blend of folk music, punk, Irish music, and whatever you're having yourself, had me hooked from the off. I'm now in my early forties. I have seen The Pogues play live in their original incarnation, during Joe Strummer's stint as lead vocalist, with Spider Stacy as front man, and latterly when the original band reformed for a raft of successful shows. I've also been to gigs by assorted Pogues in their solo guises.

I've amassed a large collection of official and bootleg recordings. Then there are magazines and press cuttings. These reside, carefully boxed, collecting dust, in my attic. Occasionally, when nostalgia bites, I'll haul these down and thumb through The Pogues in print.

Yes, you could say, I'm a certifiable Pogues head case.

Finally, there are the books. These include two officially sanctioned biographies of the band, an unauthorised biography of Shane, the autobiography of band member James Fearnley, and the unforgettable 'A Drink With Shane MacGowan', written by Shane and his girlfriend Victoria Mary Clarke. This is probably my favourite. Its rambling nature enables the book to cover a vast number of often intriguing subjects. These books all have one thing in common though: none of them are written from the perspective of the 'ordinary punter'. The tale of the ticket buying fan rarely appears in print. Even on the internet, most concert reviews are written by wearied hacks who typically regurgitate the same material.

In April this year, I was in Shane's company in Dublin when I was politely interrupted by a man who it transpired was Calum Bruce.

This genial Scotsman told me he was writing a book. When Calum mentioned it was Pogues related I was naturally interested. As we talked, it transpired Calum wasn't an established writer. He wasn't approaching The Pogues from an angle other than that of a fan. His aim was to tell his story and how The Pogues impacted upon his life. I asked him would he be so kind as to send me a sample of what he had written. He obliged. About a week later the initial chapters arrived by post. They were wonderfully entertaining reading.

Calum and I have remained in regular contact and I have been fortunate to read more of his writing. As I write this, his book is nearing publication. I, for one, can't wait to read it.

Paul McCluskey

This book is dedicated to the memory of the following:

Philip Chevron

Jackie Ford, William Smith, Bob Davidson, Robert Priest, David Simpson, Allan Black

Les 'Reg' Rennie

And my dear mother,
Roselle Wilkie Bruce

Introduction

All right? Thank you for buying my book, or, if you're still thinking about it, I'll try and tell you briefly what lies in store in the forthcoming pages. That may help you make up your mind.

It's about being a fan of The Pogues, for many years. I've been to a ridiculous amount of their live shows, with many stories to tell – a night with The Pogues is never a dull, or a straightforward affair.

Read about how, after a Pogues gig, I narrowly escaped the ultimate. Death. Read how I blagged my way backstage at an early Shane MacGowan and The Popes concert in London, and, more recently, how I managed to manoeuvre myself on stage at The Pogues open air concert in Greenwich, to give Shane a cuddle!

I've been a chef for almost all my working life. This wasn't dull either, with some of the most amazing characters and situations I've come across, perhaps hitting a peak when, along with my wife, I ran my own bar and restaurant for five years.

There's a bit of everything here, from suicide, gay blind dates and even how a greyhound called White Paws turned me into a gambler! I'll tell you about a little red skirt that used to drive me lustfully wild! Companionship and friendship have always been important to me, as has my football team, Hibernian FC. I've had a few interesting adventures following them too; my Hibs mates have been there or thereabouts through everything. We have a special bond. See how I turn the Pogues line up into a team of Hibernian footballing marvels!

And then there's family. I recently lost my dear mother. The Pogues actually helped me get through that heartbreaking experience. I tell it how it is, a lot of the time making myself look none too clever.

There's some choice language, probably something to do with small man syndrome, and hopefully I'll manage to make you laugh now and again. The Pogues and Shane MacGowan in particular, have been a huge part of my life; the music they've created can reach the very nerves of emotion, it has brought me out of some dark places and made me happy, it's even made me cry at times – that's how strong it is.

I'm very lucky that they are still around and doing live shows, but I never take this for granted. That's why I go out of my way and have been very selfish at times, to get to these shows. I'll tell you about one of the highlights of my life, when, in Dublin, I was able to tell The Pogues vocalist himself, exactly what his music meant in my personal world, and how he reacted to what I had to say.

I was born in February 1966, a terrible year for any Scotsman to be born! Ian Brady and Myra Hindley had just been jailed, and a certain Shane MacGowan would be just eight years old.

This is my story – hope you enjoy it. Be careful getting out of that taxi. Cheers.

DAVO'S POOL TABLE

I first came across The Pogues in my mate's bedroom one night. I had met Paul Davidson (Davo) at the beginning of secondary school, and after a short time we became good pals. The lucky bastard had a good size pool table in his bedroom, and naturally was shit hot. I, on the other hand, wasn't. So whilst Davo was slowly crucifying me at pool, in the background he was playing some sounds on his stereo. "WHAT THE FUCKIN HELL IS THAT?" were my exact words. At the time I was listening to heavy metal and punk mostly, and hearing this Jimmy Shandesque, hiddledy-diddledy nonsense was way over my head. I even had the cheek to question Davo's sanity – I thought he was having a laugh! Davo and I shared a love of music. Not all the denominators were common re our musical tastes, but we certainly respected our sometimes differing opinions. But THIS?

So Davo, to answer my ignorance, tells me that it was a band called The Pogues and the singer is a geezer called Shane MacGowan. I must have looked at him in utter bewilderment – where the fuck did THAT come from? THIS had a banjo, a tin whistle and an accordion in it. I could only initially relate it to the Scottish Country dance music my father listened to regularly. I couldn't take to Dad's love of Scottish music, I really couldn't. And it's not as if I didn't give it a chance – he used to play it in the kitchen of the family home daily. You also got it rammed down your throat at school, when you had to pick a girl to dance with, the more hesitant boys being left with the ugly birds at the end, doing absolutely nothing for either party's self esteem.

There's no doubt I got my love of music generally from my father though. One of my earliest memories was of me sitting on my potty with a bare arse, my father trying to encourage me to 'go'. The deal was if I did a number one then he would put two singles on to play on the record player, but a dirty shit was the jackpot with TEN singles promised. This exercise was clearly to prevent me from stinking out my breeks or nappy or whatever whilst we were out. Christ, I pushed hard, my little veins must have been sticking out. I even remember Mum getting on at my dad, when she realised the ways of his dodgy deal. Looking back on that now, if he had the record player turned on, then he was probably going to play the records anyway – what a con!

Me and my father's differing views on the subject of music were so far apart as to be almost competitive. On a Saturday teatime we used to listen to the football results on the radio. After this and after we'd had our meal, Dad and I used to wash up the dishes, and this horrendous programme commenced with the Scottish Country sounds – fucking awful. It did nothing to enhance my weekend, especially if Hibs had been gubbed earlier in the day.

For some inexplicable reason, the next time I found myself at the end of another hiding in Davo's room (yes, at pool) I was asking him to put on the hiddledy-diddledy song again, so I could have a go at him and question his normally reliable musical sanity. Davo was, quite rightly reluctant to put it on, and who could blame him really, but I kept on and on and on about it, until eventually he had to give in to my vociferous demand. I was asking him a load of questions about The Pogues, one after the other; as usual Davo was well clued up about it all and actually had not one, but TWO albums of this stuff at his disposal.

He showed me the sleeve of the first Pogues album, entitled 'Red Roses For Me'. None of the band members of The Pogues were smiling. They were all scary looking fuckers; you certainly wouldn't buy a car off any of them. In fact you wouldn't buy anything off any of them. They had big grey coats on and looked as menacing as fuck. They looked the type of people that would take the piss out of you in a minute without compassion. They all looked like they needed a hose down with hot water and a shave. One of the band members was a girl. She looked scary too. One got the impression that a sub standard sexual performance with her would not be tolerated. Perhaps she needed a shave too. I have a spare sleeve from that album today; it's in my garage, on the door of the electric meter. We've never been troubled by mice!

So, when Davo put the music on again, I found myself to be very interested all of a sudden. They didn't play the instruments the way they were played in the Scottish music my Dad listened to. The Pogues made it altogether more aggressive and ultimately more acceptable to a teenager who was serious about his music. The other obvious difference between The Pogues and Dad's stuff was the fact that the band were playing their tunes with a most definite Irish flavour. The green thing fitted in perfectly with the love of my football team, Hibernian FC, who have Irish origins. Somehow it might not have been right to fall for a band that were, shall we say, all Rangers fans. Wet, Wet Wet were not for me!

Then there were the lyrics to consider and of course the singer delivering them. Shane MacGowan's voice was aggressive too; it was utterly addictive actually. He sung about drinking, fucking, pimps, whores, junkies, psychos and shithouse poets. Even his name 'Shane MacGowan' was interestingly Irish, and he had the looks to go with it. Big ears and hellish teeth, a polished pop star he was not, but who the fuck wants one of them? Davo showed me a 7 inch single called 'Boys From The County Hell'. On the sleeve there was a quote that said "lend me ten pounds and I'll buy you a drink" – sounded fair enough to me.

This was indeed the kick up the arse my musical taste needed. It was so new to me and very refreshing, very different to the stuff I had been listening to. Back in those days you were supposed to be into this type of music or that type. Rocker (or greaser), mod or punk. Only the absolute wallies would admit to being a new romantic. You were expected not to like other sounds outwith your chosen category. Davo told me a wonderful story, years after the actual event, where he skulked in the vicinity of a local record shop one Saturday morning, for quite a long time trying to buy a copy of The Specials' 'Too Much Too Young'. Problem was, he didn't want anyone to see him, as Davo was a punk, so if someone spotted him from school, making his guilty purchase, then he was in for a serious stewards' enquiry in the form room, first thing Monday morning; it would be vigorous, that's how it worked.

In a way, The Pogues broke down this particular barrier for me; it was time for my musical tastes to mature, because how on earth could you put The Pogues into a category? It was so unique, new, and as I mentioned earlier totally addictive. I'm so grateful to Davo that he brought The Pogues to my music turntable as it were.

There was lot of swearing on the record – again this made it more real, acceptable and likeable. However there was another side to this band too. It wasn't all blood and guts, swearing and aggression. They did slow numbers as well which were equally as appealing. Shane's voice was emotional, the playing of the instruments interesting and fresh sounding; it made you pay attention... addictive, addictive, addictive! On the faster tempo songs, he howled and he wailed and he screamed, as did all of the band at the end of the track 'Down in the ground where the dead men go'. The songs had strong melodies, brilliant rhythm and powerful toe tapping beats.

It wasn't long at all until I was pestering the pool king for a shot of his albums, so I could take them home to play and investigate further. Against his better judgement he lent me a copy of 'Rum, Sodomy & the Lash', the band's second album, and I gratefully carried it up the hill that stood between his house and mine. That probably makes the area between our houses sound somewhat idyllic, so I must point out that the hill is concrete and it links one council scheme to the next. The artwork on this album had a nautical flavour to it, with the band dressed as vintage sailors – still needing a wash I may add. MacGowan in one picture looked like he was positively ill, rather than merry, with drink. The band members were all still looking scary, and there was an addition: a guitarist. His name was Philip Chevron. The albums were made up of mostly Shane MacGowan-penned originals and traditional Irish based songs that the band had very much put their own anarchic take on.

After my initial outburst of ridicule, I can only imagine that Davo was pretty pissed off with me doing a turnaround and securing his precious vinyl on a loan deal that didn't really benefit him in any way.

So with the record secured, the first time it was laid on my turntable, in my part of Struan Road, Perth, is the stuff of legend. It was a hot, summer afternoon, and in Scotland these don't happen too often, so there were a lot of folk out in their gardens taking advantage of the beautiful weather. These days, I find it amazing that nobody really knows their neighbours like they did years ago, but then, in my neck of the woods everyone got along ok and were very familiar with each other. My bedroom was situated high enough, looking over the gardens that I could see most of the people nearby that were outdoors that sunny afternoon. When the sun is scarce, and you're out relaxing under it, the last thing you need is some arsehole polluting the air with loud music. Well this arsehole had his bedroom window open, and I provided the residents with high numbers in Struan Road with exactly that! My parents were no exception – they were in their garden too, and the look on my father's face in particular was priceless, as 'The sick bed of Cuchulainn' kicked into life.

However, the amazing thing was he didn't tell me to turn it off, turn the volume down, shut the window – nothing! Yes, you could tell that he felt under pressure to restore order, but there must have been an inner voice stalling him, and his judgement proved to be spot on. Bearing in mind that the album was almost totally new to me, I wasn't really aware of the choice language contained on the first two tracks of this classic album. Shane's voice is really clear on this record and my father's face was even more of a picture as the record progressed; my mother was pissing herself laughing! And what of the neighbours I hear you ask? Well, for me, this was an early lesson into the massive appeal of the mighty Pogues. Everyone within earshot of the album's opening track was clapping their hands, tapping their feet or whatever. Our elderly neighbour Aimee, who was as daft as a brush (in a great way) was going fucking berserk! The music felt so powerful, feelgood and uplifting that I think everyone got swept along with the whole thing.

I let side one of the album continue naturally and in order, the next track being 'The Old Main Drag' which is much slower than its predecessor, but just as coarse if you like with more colourful lyrics all to do with the 'everyday' subject of rentboys. Still there were no objections from parent or neighbour, and the album did what it intended to do in the first place and entertained the nation. I was personally becoming hooked in a massive way; the more I heard, the more I was drawn to the whole thing – it was so different and unique in a really refreshing way. The songs were really clever. I'd never considered anything like this before when listening to music, and now that I was over the hurdle of "WHAT THE FUCKIN HELL IS THIS?" I couldn't get enough of it, and was very eager to find out and listen to more. Remember, Davo owned TWO albums, so there was definitely more to be had.

That afternoon in Struan Road's back gardens is actually quite significant. My mother spoke of that day often whenever conversation flirted with the subject of The Pogues or even just the subject of music. Aimee, whenever she was in our house, often asked "for that wonderful group" to be put on the record player. The Pogues' faster tunes suited her personality perfectly. She lived life to the max, lived until she was 99 years old and was actually doing full cartwheels in her garden when she was well into her 80s. There was a real mixture of people in the gardens that day, both young and old, and the fact that everyone was digging the sounds speaks volumes for the band's general appeal.

I think, after a good listen, the majority of folk become a fan in varying degrees. My mother took to the band instantly, a lot quicker than I initially did. She also liked the fact that the band members looked rebellious with the strong hint that they just might like a drink or two. My father was more reserved, but I just knew he liked it, really loved it in fact. He wasn't the type to dish out praise for anything. He didn't recognise in vocal terms that I was getting along all right with my chosen career, he absolutely slated my favourite football team and he was never going to say that he agreed with my musical taste. Dad's thing was cassettes – he loved to make compilation tapes and had so many of them, when he played them back, he really didn't know what was coming on next; that was the whole point he'd tell me, and this process would keep him entertained with his music for many years. But later on I caught him out a bit, because he had indeed been in and about my records and had recorded The Pogues onto his precious cassettes. Don't you get into trouble for that? Naughty Daddy.

I was reluctant to give Davo his album back, but I did of course. I then started sniffing around his copy of The Pogues' first album 'Red Roses For Me' that he had played to me in his pool table bedroom. He didn't take the hint though, and I can't say I blamed him, as I reckon he missed the album he lent me for 'the garden party'.

Buying an LP album in those days, for ordinary folk really was a big deal. I want to state, here and now, that I did not have a hard luck story upbringing – I had a very happy and loving one, an only child in a working class family, but there were no hardships as such. Money was not exactly flowing, like the 'Streams of whiskey' Shane MacGowan sang about, so when it came to buying an album with your cash, you just had to get it right. Buying an album that failed to live up to expectations was nothing short of a fucking disaster! CDs, downloads etc are very easily had these days, and you can also pick up music on the cheap in charity shops, car boot sales and on sites like ebay. It's amazing to think now that none of these things were available in the mid eighties. So when a piece of music was purchased, it really was for playing many, many times.

Well, I had no hesitation whatsoever investing my LP pennies in the two Pogues albums that were available, and was very safe in the knowledge that I knew they would both be stonewallers, sure fire winners. And so I became familiar with 'Red Roses For Me' which was most enjoyable, and I found myself becoming more and more engrossed in the whole thing. As I learned the lyrics and digested the music it was just a real feeling of excitement, it really blew me away. The Pogues package just seemed so consistently different and I was eager to learn all about them. I'd always loved music, and followed various groups and artists over the years – different trends came and went, nothing unusual in that, but this was right outside any of those boxes though. At the time, I really had no idea that The Pogues were going to be forever present, and have such a big impact on my life itself.

SAD TO SAY, I MUST BE ON ME WAY...

I had left school at 16, and got my first proper job as a commis chef in a seasonal hotel in Pitlochry. I managed to survive the summer and then did a year full time at college, which I really enjoyed. The lecturers in the catering department at Perth College were very competent at passing their knowledge on, and I had met some great people among my classmates.

College, however, does not really prepare you for life as a chef, which is not for the faint hearted. Nevertheless, I was lucky enough to secure employment after college in The Station Hotel, Perth. The head chef was Philip Borthwick, but I referred to him as THE CHEF when I worked for him in his kitchens. He remains a very close friend to this day. He was hard but fair, which is more than I can say for some chefs I've come across in my career. Professional kitchens can be scary places, but I've always hated bullying in the workplace.

In my early days at The Station Hotel, I would be doing well if I avoided being bawled at, for fucking something up; the aim was to get through a shift without a bollocking. If a bollocking is dished out, then that's fine if it's deserved and relevant to the kitchen business going on at that time. But, on occasion, I have seen bullying take place on a personal basis by a couple of individuals, The Station Hotel had one such individual, and it made me think to myself that if I managed to progress at this chef thing, then I would never be like that to the staff under my command. And I'm glad to say that I did progress in the Chef's kitchen, and spent three very enjoyable years in The Station Hotel in Perth.

The Chef was heading off to pastures new, to Ilkley, in West Yorkshire, and I was delighted when he asked me and another chap to accompany him to assist with his new venture. I travelled down to Ilkley before we were due to start for a look around at the hotel and the area; the whole opportunity seemed a really exciting prospect. Ilkley itself was a small, but beautiful place. The majority of the buildings were made of a very distinctive, characteristic soot-coloured stone. The town was near Leeds which could provide a bit more variety in things to do.

The Craiglands Hotel was bigger than The Station Hotel, but it was a bit tired food-wise, so Philip Borthwick's services were secured to give the place a boost. There were a few people we knew who worked there already, so they showed me round, and took me out for a beer at night. On my way back to Perth after my 'look around' I had to change trains at Leeds and I had a bit of time to kill. Leeds town centre seemed huge, and as I passed the Virgin record shop, I saw a massive promotional display plugging The Pogues' 'Poguetry in Motion' EP. It looked like a quality product. There were four tracks on it, so I handed over some good Scottish money and nursed it home on the train, being careful not to damage the sleeve.

What an outstanding EP this turned out to be. The single getting the airplay from this EP was a track called 'London Girl', a MacGowan penned number, high tempo with manic accordion and as always, solid, interesting lyrics. However, two other tracks on the EP turned out to be a couple of my all time favourites, namely 'Rainy Night in Soho' and 'The Body of an American'. The former a slower, ballady type of song that gives me goosebumps, an absolute classic; the latter being a mid tempo beat with tremendous imaginative lyrics sandwiched between a two part instrumental. Yes sir, this Shane MacGowan chap really was the dog's bollocks when it came to writing a tune!

A little while later in the year, when everything was finalised, our notice had been worked, and the odd night out was had to say our cheerios, it was time to leave the warmth and security of my family home in Perth. I didn't realise what a big step this was for me, to fend for myself away from the love of my mother and father. I started to realise, very quickly, how much I had taken for granted – talk about a perch out of its pond! It was dawning on me what life was really about – where, for example, were my next pair of clean underpants going to come from, etc etc etc.

It was now summer of '86, the summer when Maradona scored THAT goal, the one that knocked England out of the World Cup. It always takes time to adjust to a new kitchen, in a different hotel, with new staff to get to know. I was quite homesick, but I acquired a small record deck for my live-in accommodation, which was a small room on the third floor of the hotel. Pogues sounds resumed as normal, which certainly helped.

We inherited a flock of bandits, staff-wise, The Chef had a bit of a hard time with the hotel's employees helping themselves to various foodstuffs that were going out the back door as it were. We met an interesting lad in the kitchen, Keith Clifford Williams. Keith was a little bit older than me and hailed from Shrewsbury in Shropshire. In years to come, he became a very close friend, and indeed a Pogues stalwart considering the amount of gigs he's been to. It wasn't always like that though. My position in the kitchen was Sous chef, which basically means I was second in command to Mr Borthwick. I don't think Keith was impressed with me, probably because I'm a small chap, though Keith himself is no jolly green giant either! So I made a mental note that I would be 'sorting him out'!

Initially Keith struggled to come to terms with Philip Borthwick's regime, and he appeared to be quite aggressive. We had a big waste skip for kitchen rubbish, just out of view of the restaurant – however, our Keith made sure the diners got a good view of the skip one evening when he set it ablaze with some paraffin and the dog end of his fag, probably to release some of his tensions. It was definitely a new take on dinner by candlelight!

I met a local girl, Victoria White (Vikki), who worked in the hotel. We didn't get off to the best of starts, just like with Keith. I didn't fancy Keith though! One night I was at the local nightclub 'Travs'. Unsurprisingly, this place was a regular haunt of the hotel staff –

nightclubs usually are for hotel workers who finish their shifts at unsociable times. Vikki's parents were on holiday, and there was to be a party at her gaff. I wasn't invited, but her pal Laura was a big Pogues fan and we'd been chatting at Travs about the most exciting band that we'd seem emerge for a while. Laura said I could tag along to Vikki's party with her, and who was I to refuse? There was never anything going to happen between me and Laura; she was really tall and as I've stated earlier I'm just a wee chap. We would have looked ridiculous as a couple, but we were enjoying talking about The Pogues.

At Vikki's large impressive house (definitely not council) Laura and I sat listening to Vikki's copy of 'Red Roses For Me' – she was clearly a fan too. We were in one of the rooms on the ground floor when Vikki came in and asked Laura if there was something going on between us – which she answered with a no, and I thought nothing more of her question.

The main party as it were was going on in the living room; there were a lot of bodies in there. But I couldn't help thinking a lot of the blokes at Vikki's party were Hooray Henries. Not my cup of tea at all, so I stayed put with Laura, listening to The Pogues. As the party drew to a close, a lot of the goers went home, including Laura. My problem was, I didn't really know where I was in relation to the Hotel, which apparently was quite a considerable walk away, and the prospect of this didn't really appeal to me. So I looked around for a place to lay my head, and quite fancied the couch that Vikki had settled down on, so I invited myself, without words, to that very attractive location. The party host and I had a kiss and a cuddle, much to the horror of one of the Hooray Henries who, I later found out, had a massive crush on Vikki. He pretty much stared at the couch all night, as me and my new companion succumbed to sleep. Whenever I turned in the night and opened my eyes, old Henry's stare was still present.

In the morning, I left without fuss and bother, and tried to locate the direction of the Hotel. Luckily for me, a milk lorry took me there after I asked the driver for directions. I washed, changed into my whites and went down to work, absolutely fucking knackered. We were working long hours at this time, trying to settle into a system at our new workplace. When it came to finish time, about ten at night, I gratefully sloped into my bed upstairs and closed my eyes. Next day at work, I came face to face with Vikki again. She was a real looker, dark brown hair, lovely figure and a very pretty face. She asked me why I had made such a rushed getaway in the morning after our brief couch liaison. I told her that I didn't really think nothing of it, leaving the way I did, so she asked if the kiss and cuddle on the couch meant anything to me. I didn't know whether to throw my hat into the ring, as it were, or not. But we arranged to meet after work for a drink. We got on really well, and very quickly became an item. It was probably the first time I ever fell properly in love, with our relationship blossoming into something more than just physical.

Vikki had an older sister and a younger brother. Her mum was nice, but her dad was wary, a canny Yorkshireman – he gave very little away regarding his feelings over his daughter hooking up with me, a jock after all.

In December of that year, the first opportunity came up to go and have a look at what The Pogues were all about. The Pogues were playing a gig at Leeds University. Vikki, Laura and I bought tickets to see them; only problem was that December is obviously a very busy time in hotel kitchens and it was touch and go to get time off, but at the eleventh hour, a night off was secured, and off we went on the train to Leeds.

Once in the concert hall at the University, and with the support band out of the way (Light a Big Fire they were called), I got chatty to a fellow who had obviously seen the band live a few times. When I told him it was my first time, he laughed and said "you won't know what's hit you mate". I thought the crowd were quite sombre and civilised, then BANG, on came the Pogues, MacGowan and all, and the audience instantly turned into a mass of one, swinging back and forth.

The band's line up had changed slightly since I first saw their mugshots on the record sleeves. The lady had been replaced by a geezer called Darryl Hunt. He was apparently the roadie and general band supporter, in lots of ways. Now he'd been promoted to the stage, to take over bass guitar duties from Cait O'Riordan. He was spectacularly clean shaven. It really was survival of the fittest and unfortunately my girlfriend didn't make it and had to be pulled out by the bouncers to a more quiet area. That left me and her pal, right in the thick of things, right at the front, and I wasn't moving for all the tea in China!

The band were absolutely mind blowing. I'd been at a good few concerts by this time, but nothing had quite the same affect on me as this one did. They looked really cool and confident in their somewhat traditional style clothing. There were no jeans; it was all proper trousers and shirts, and there was the odd hat thrown into the mix. Their clothing all had a second hand look about them, but they made their gear appear trendy rather than thrifty. They even looked as if they may have had a bit of a wash! They still looked scary though.

The sound was fantastic; they sounded just like they did on record, and played all the songs I was hoping to hear from the two albums they had released. Hearing the instruments that were 'new' to me as far as concert going was concerned, really broadened my appreciation of live music – the accordion, the banjo and the tin whistle all of a sudden sounded amazing.

A beer tray appeared and was bashed ferociously off Spider, the tin whistle player's head! Shane MacGowan even handed me a tin of his beer, which went down a treat. I did give the people around me a swig, but made sure I got the tin back in the end. Even in those days, Shane used to go off for a break at the side of the stage during instrumentals etc, and during one of those breaks I shouted at him "Oi! Shane!"; he looked around and I howled at him "get back on that fuckin' stage!". He laughed and to my utter amazement, complied with my demand and went back out to his position on stage. I stupidly gave him a very uncool thumbs up, which he quite rightly ridiculed me for, putting his own thumbs up back to me with a Doh! Like face, but I didn't mind. I remember after the show, James Fearnley talking to someone at the side of the stage for a while; I would have liked to have said hello, but concentrated on reuniting with my girlfriend, and we all talked about the Pogues, with excitable enthusiasm, all the way home.

I was totally hooked now. I wanted to find out more about this band; they sounded amazing, they looked amazing, they were really hip and totally unique. The whole experience of seeing them live and surviving within their audience was FUCKING AMAZING!

By now Keith and I were getting on a lot better. Keith's hotel accommodation was in fact a cottage, on the grounds of the hotel, right on the edge of Ilkley Moor. The chap he was sharing with moved on, so I took his room and moved into the cottage; it was a more attractive deal than my small room on the third floor of the hotel. Keith's record collection was desperate. He was definitely what I would call a 'charts man'. He told me that all the dodgy discs he owned like Dead or Alive's 'You spin me round' belonged to a series of ex girlfriends. There was a lot of real suspect vinyl in his record box; the man was clearly a stallion! It's a wonder he didn't have a handbag at the side of his records, to put on the floor and dance round whilst he played his teenage girl music.

My parents came down to England; they were visiting an antiques fair and they drove over to Ilkley when they were done, to see their wee laddie. I introduced them to Vikki, and also to Keith. My mother was never good with my girlfriends. I think she may have seen them as a threat to our relationship – it's just the way it was, but it made things a tad uncomfortable for me on many occasions. Keith was different, however, as I wasn't sleeping with him, so he was treated to breakfast with our small family, in Betty's Tearoom no less, just down the road, on Ilkley's main street. Overpriced, but very nice, they didn't have ketchup for your back bacon, but fresh tomato relish was available, served by waitresses dressed up like something out of 'Upstairs Downstairs'.

I worked in Ilkley for about a year, and visited home when I could and saw Davo and the boys. Around that time there was a nightclub in Perth called The York House that had three different areas; one of them was an alternative room, which was upstairs. An excellent DJ was resident here on a Saturday night – Hugh used to play some brilliant sounds with plenty of punky stuff and regular Pogues tracks. Most of the punters were the same faces every week, a good bunch, and these Saturday nights were much missed by me when I first left home. When the Pogues came on a load of us would get on the dance floor and we would have a right old jig, linking arms and burling each other round, playing 'air drums' just before the chorus of Sally MacLennane. One of my close friends, Les Rennie, would regularly end up on his arse whilst playing these very air drums.

Unfortunately, Hugh's alternative disco ceased to exist, and if we fancied a late drink on a Saturday, it was back to the usual shite music that courting couples danced to at the weekend. Not to be outdone, a few of us started pogo-ing to the manic beat of George Michael's 'A different corner'. If you are not familiar with this song, check it out, it's a real hellraiser of a track. Needless to say we were all thrown out, for inappropriate behaviour. PAH!

Meanwhile, back in Ilkley, things were about to change again. The Chef was never really happy there – it was a lovely place, but the hotel just didn't float his boat, and an opportunity came up at a large conference centre and hotel in Surrey, on the border of Windsor Great Park. He was kind enough to ask me to go with him again. My performance in his kitchen in Ilkley was sub standard if the truth be told – I was concentrating more on my relationship with Vikki, and at first I didn't want to go to Surrey and leave her behind. My parents got involved though, and pointed out that I would be passing up a fantastic opportunity for an alternative of very little in the way of career prospects if I stayed behind in Ilkley.

And so, I decided to go. We were on the move again, even further 'down souf'. There were a good few of us going down there, and it proved to be a masterstroke as the majority of us turned out to be really happy at this place; indeed, The Chef is still there to this day.

The move was far from ideal when it came to my relationship with Vikki. It was going to be difficult moving away, but I did manage to visit her back in Ilkley, and she me down in Surrey. I was able to visit after my first week working at the new hotel, in fact. I travelled by train, and it was the first time I can remember being on the London underground. Fuck me, I just couldn't believe the enormity of the escalators. I really thought some bugger was having a laugh, they reminded me of big scary rides you get at theme parks. I'm not fantastic with heights, and they were so steep, but I mountaineered my way to King's Cross, clinging on to the moving banisters for dear life, and on to the train to Leeds for my connection to Ilkley, this particular connection made without the use of Matterhorn escalators!

Vikki was waiting for me at Leeds station, making my whole

escalator experience more than worthwhile. Eventually, she did come down to stay permanently, once we found a suitable place to live, which, in that neck of the woods was a tall order, unless you were on mega money, which I was not. Initially, before Vikki's arrival, I had lived in a very modern, comfortable staff flat, in Staines, Middlesex, that I shared with two other chaps, and this worked out very well indeed. An old couple lived on the floor underneath us, and were regularly telling us to "Fuck off back to Glasgow". I don't think they appreciated their new neighbours, our musical tastes and the odd hours we were keeping working in the hotel, but we did try our best to be good boys most of the time.

It wasn't long before the opportunity to see the Pogues came up again. They were due to play Finsbury Park, in North London, and the gig was being staged in a big tent! This gig was to go down in the Pogues' history as one of their best and memorable to date. There were two lads in the kitchen that had caught the Pogues bug, through listening to them in my flat – with, I may add, many similarities to my experience in the days of Davo's pool table. At first they were appalled almost, but they soon couldn't get enough, just like I had been with my introduction.

Anyway, we all wanted to go to Finsbury Park, but I couldn't get the time off work and I was gutted. I had to listen to the two fuckers when they got back, telling me how fucking wonderful their night had been. I was so jealous and pissed off that I had missed out.

In another bizarre twist, I almost caught a Pogues show in the most opportune of circumstances. Just down the road from the new hotel I found myself working in, stood the majestic and imposing building of The Royal Holloway College. Local word was that at the students' annual bash, The Pogues were actually appearing to provide the dear boys and girls with some live musical entertainment, just to see the jolly old evening along. Also on the bill at the college were The Damned and Tom Robinson.

I was working in the kitchen that night with scouser Jimmy, one of the attendees at Finsbury Park, and a local lad called Alex. Alex was a big fan of rap music, so much so he wished he'd been born black. Alex knew all about The Royal Holloway College, his opinion of the place was entirely about the posh totty there that were apparently 'dying' for some local dick! Well, that's all well and good, but I wanted to get into this bash of theirs and see the Pogues.

After our shift had finished, Alex drove us down there in his bright orange Volkswagen Beetle. We got as far as a security guard, who looked out of his depth, but nevertheless wasn't letting us in. Alex looked towards some unsavoury looking characters that were approaching – thank fuck he knew a couple of them. They were all skinheads, really menacing looking and they WERE going into the ball, no matter what the security bloke was saying. Alex had tipped me and scouse Jimmy off, just not to speak. Jock and scouse accents would not have gone down well at all, so we kept quiet. The security guard was threatened and received a couple of slaps for his trouble, then he quite rightly retreated to hell out of the dangerous situation he found himself in.

So this particular barrier was now clear and in we all went: me, Alex, Scouse Jimmy and the scary skinhead geezers. Again, we got so far, to a glass door, and we could see The Pogues on stage; MacGowan had a black t shirt on and the band were belting out 'The Body of an American' to what appeared to be a courtyard of male students with dinner suits and dickie bows, and the posh totty girls that Alex was telling us about, with their expensive party frocks. There were a few security guys on this door, and they wasted no time in getting aquainted with the skinheads and a mini, very dangerous riot commenced. Neither party was fucking about, Jimmy receiving an unwelcome stray slap to his coupon. It really was time to go, the cop sirens were evident in the distance, and as much as I dearly wanted to see the band, I didn't want mixed up in the skinhead's battle with security and the polis. Alex, Jimmy and I made our way out into the grounds, and walked slowly back to Alex's trusty Beetle. Whilst we were doing this 'The Sick Bed of Cuchulainn' was belting out into the slowly darkening summer evening air. What a tease, but it really was time to go.

I made up my mind that next time they played, I'd definitely be there, but I had no idea what lay in store, when they did indeed, play in London again – boy was I in for a shock!

TAXI! TAXI!

Everyone was enjoying working in their new surroundings. The place had a weird name – it was called 'The Anugraha Hotel and Conference Centre'. It was owned by a religious group called The Subuds. They often met at the hotel, in the grand hall to do their religious chanting and what I can only describe as 'slow dance movements' posturing, making shapes out of their bodies, and all this without even laughing! It was funny watching them though.

When Vikki joined me in the South, we moved into a bedsit in Hounslow West. It was far from glamorous. Vikki came from a well to do family, and I hadn't exactly had a rough time of it either, but this place was a bit of a hovel. Still, we got on with it. There was an Indian family living on the ground floor, and very disturbingly, both the husband and the son used to regularly beat up the wife/mother. I'm no Rocky Balboa, far from it, but I went down one night to see if I could help her. The lady pleaded with me to go and leave them alone, which I did, but I felt lower than a snake. I was learning more about life and the sometimes unpleasantness surrounding it, compared to the sheltered one I had led up until then.

My girlfriend secured herself a really good job at Toshiba, in the clerical side of things. This at least took her attentions off the terrible digs we had found ourselves in for a while.

I didn't have to wait too long for another Pogues gig to come along. One day as I was mooching around London, I went into a ticket agency office and randomly asked if the Pogues were playing anytime soon.

Much to my surprise, I was in luck. They were doing a one-off show at Camden's Electric Ballroom. I secured two tickets and was as pleased as Boy George in a dildo factory. The date wasn't that far away, so my choice of company on the night was limited. Vikki didn't fancy it after her experience in Leeds, and I ended up going with a workmate, big Howard, who wasn't really interested in the band, but was up for a night out. And what a night it turned out to be!

I'm a great believer in what goes around, comes around, and the day of the concert is memorable to me for all the wrong reasons. In the afternoon, before we set off for Camden, I played a quite nasty prank on the hotel we had left behind in Ilkley. The chef that was taking over after Philip Borthwick and his team had left was a right prick. There was a handover period where we worked with this new head chef for a week. One day me and him had a bit of a set to, when he stopped me putting some salad in the bin. It was wilted and the lettuce had gone brown. I told him I wasn't using it and he could dish it up himself, if that's the kind of standards he had. This, of course, didn't go down too well, but apart from that incident, I didn't have many dealings with him, so my shennanigans on him was pretty much undeserved on his part.

I could remember the telephone numbers of the hotel's suppliers, and decided, wickedly, to order them a whole load of stuff for the following morning, that they certainly would not need: eight turkeys, six whole sirloins, six best ends of lamb... the list goes on and on. The sheer inconvenience this would have caused doesn't bear thinking about! And the suppliers must have thought they were in the money! It was a laugh at the time, bravado and showing off after a few drinks, but ultimately it was a stupid thing to do, with hellish consequences for the poor buggers having to sort out the mess the next day.

Anyway, with the skulduggery completed, Howard and I made our way across London and had an absolutely brilliant night in the bars of Camden Town near the ballroom, and got caught up in the whole experience. It was obvious there was a great excitement in the North London air, surrounding this band; everyone was just so enthusiastic about them, it reminded me of football supporters pumped up in the boozer before a big, important match. We both blew all the money we had on us, and had nothing to show for it bar slurred speech and lots of steam on various urinals.

The Pogues were supported by two bands that night, and the whole evening seemed to be running very late compared to the norm for gigs. I clearly remember the second support band going down like a lead balloon, and a quite nasty atmosphere developed with a very impatient audience wanting a square go with the band – and, believe it or not, an angry band wanting a go at the audience! When all this died down, eventually the Pogues appeared and proceeded to strut their stuff. I personally thought they were a bit disappointing this time. The set seemed short to me and they were not nearly as tight as I had remembered them at Leeds University, but I still very much enjoyed the occasion.

Joe Strummer of The Clash made an appearance, as did Lynval Golding of The Specials, and joined the Pogues for a few songs taken from their own groups. I actually saw this as an inconvenience, as I wanted to hear more of the Pogues' own material played – I suppose you can't please everyone! In much later years, I read in James Fearnley's book 'Here Comes Everybody' that his accordion actually stopped working that night, it was soaked so much in his own sweat. So maybe my judgement of the gig not sounding so good was correct after all.

After they'd finished and the lights went up, we discovered that we had long missed our last train home, so decided to hang around for a bit. It wasn't long until Shane appeared, just at the side of us, talking to someone. I totally interrupted his conversation, saying something really uncool no doubt. He told me to wait a minute, then when he finished I gave him a hug which was certainly not reciprocated. To be fair to him, he did listen to what I had to say, which was to ask him why they didn't play this song or that – a few favourites of mine that I was disappointed I didn't hear on the night. He didn't really answer my question, and my 'mate' was taking the piss out of me behind my back (I caught the bugger!).

Shane shook our hands, bid us both a very goodnight, and even told us to take care. Oh, how I wished I had listened more to that last piece of advice!

As I said earlier, we had spent all our money on the demon drink, so no self sympathy there. The Pogues came on really late, the last train whilst not forgotten about entirely, was not high on the list of my priorities, and by the time we were done at the Electric Ballroom, all the public transport in London had long gone to bed. What I'm about to reveal has never been fully disclosed to many people, especially my boss, the Chef, so I apologise humbly sir, in advance, for the following events of sheer stupidity.

So we were fucked, basically, as far as getting home was concerned. We were both working the next day, so I had no hesitation in suggesting we take a taxi to my gaff, in Hounslow. Howard lived in Staines, my place was nearer, so he could crash at mine. The distinct lack of cash to pay for the taxi was no problem at all, as we would do a runner. All my idea, I may add!

I've read a lot of books, a lot of them being autobiographies, and I always find that you build up an imaginary rapport with the author in your mind. There's been a few where when I've finished the book I actually find that I don't like or respect the person as much as I did previously. I hope you don't give up on me just yet, but I have to tell the truth or this book is pointless.

I hailed a black cab on Camden High Street. The cabbie agreed to take us on our long journey, then we engaged in the usual cabbie/passenger conversation. For some strange reason, I thought I'd be extra 'fly' and put on a very badly done, see through cockney accent, all part of my pathetic cloak and dagger 'adventure'. What made matters even worse was the cabbie chappie was a genuine good lad; how decent he was will become crystal clear.

Howard and I hadn't even discussed a plan for our getaway, nothing; he was actually quite a big fellow and carried a lot of weight, so I wasn't even thinking how he would get on when it came to the chase. A wee bit before we reached the location of my digs, I asked our friendly cabbie to stop, which he did, and we got out and I made a dash for freedom from the outstanding taxi fare that we didn't have. Before I knew it, I was staggering about on the road, my brain trying its damndest to send signals to my legs to take me out of there – all to no avail.

As I got out of the cab I'd been hit by a passing car, travelling at speed, and went right over the top of it. I must've jumped slightly at the time of impact, thus the force of this obviously took me over the top as opposed to the car mowing me down on the spot. That wee jump certainly saved my life. It doesn't do for me to think about this too much as it actually freaks me out and troubles me to this day.

As I lay there, crumpled on the tarmac, it began to sink in very slowly what had actually happened. What a fanny! The taxi driver then proceeded to show how much class he really had (unlike his latest passengers) by helping me to the safety of the pavement. The car that hit me didn't stop (wonder if he was at the Pogues gig too?); however the police arrived in no time, swiftly followed by an ambulance.

The police quite rightly showed me no sympathy whatsoever, and tried everything in their persuasive powers to get the taxi driver to press charges against me. But to his eternal credit, and to my eternal gratefulness, he had decided in his mind that I had been punished enough and repeatedly refused to press charges much to the police officers' disgust. He wasn't interested in charging my mate either. Instead he followed the ambulance to Isleworth Hospital, where I was to be treated, waited around for absolute ages, then when I was discharged he drove us both to Staines, where my mate lived. He was presented with a cheque for the fare and his troubles, and he then made a no doubt weary journey back into London, just before the rush hour kicked in.

What an absolute diamond geezer that taxi driver was, one in a million for sure. I doubt very much if he'll come to read this, but if so then words could not explain how grateful, sorry and indebted to him that I am. Thank you.

Rewind back to the hospital: I'd discovered that I had a broken ankle, dislocated and badly bruised shoulder and had a deep cut in my forehead. Pretty lucky methinks compared to what might have happened. I was also understandably concussed. The doctor kept asking me questions to no doubt assess where my mind was at; later I was told that the only question I got right was to tell him who the prime minister was at the time, the lovely Mrs Thatcher! I kept thinking about the video for the Pogues song 'A pair of brown eyes' where a poster of her gets the works with some spray paint.

I was signed off work for the foreseeable future, and we were heading for that busy Christmas period that I keep referring to (and, oh how the Pogues will affect this in future years for me!). The Chef was livid with me; he's no fool, and he definitely knew something wasn't quite right regarding my accident. To be honest, I think I was very close to receiving my books.

After my accident, I was lying on the bed at Hounslow, feeling sorry for myself, when I caught the news on the TV. The story dominating the news that night was of the hellish King's Cross fire at the railway station. A lot of poor souls lost their lives that night, and sometimes it takes things like this for you to realise how fortunate you are compared to some. A work colleague of mine missed that fire in King's Cross by the skin of his teeth, as he was travelling home to visit his folks in Scotland. He would have been in the very place, coming up from the Piccadilly line tube, where the fire was, just moments before the chaos unfolded.

I made a decision to travel home to Perth, to recover from my self-inflicted accident, in my parents' house. Vikki certainly couldn't have looked after me; she could hardly take care of herself. Cooking, cleaning etc just wasn't her bag at all, so I thought it better to not burden her with all this, on top of having to deal with a self pitying lump lying around the place. I really didn't fancy being cooped up in that bedsit all day either.

To be fair to him, the Chef took me to Heathrow airport for my flight home. The airport authorities had been informed of the state I was in and very helpfully provided a wheelchair for me to get me smoothly through security and on to the aircraft. I felt like a V I fuckin' P! I was well looked after on the flight (not really deserved since I had just wreaked havoc on a Yorkshire hotel and tried to screw over a London cabbie). My folks met me at Edinburgh Airport where they first clapped eyes on me in the wheelchair as I came out of a lift, looking a right fucking mess. My dear mother said to me, almost instantly, "You are no' goin' to see that band again!" Just the sort of thing mothers say I suppose, but in future years, whenever I was going to a Pogues concert, she always thought of the night I got run down.

She fed me like a king, and the attention I received during my recovery was second to none. It's actually just as well I went home, as the doctor in Isleworth had made a mess of the plaster cast round my ankle, and after it had been checked in the local hospital it had to be removed and set all over again.

Vikki came up to spend New Year at the family home. She seemed to be doing well enough down South without me. It was good of my mother to agree for her to come up, but she wasn't exactly accommodating towards her, after she had arrived. She never really coped with the fact that her wee boy had a partner! Despite the plaster, which went right up to my knee, and an over inquisitive mother hovering, I did try to be 'romantic' with Vikki during her visit, but these attempts ended in fits of laughter at the hopeless situation. My mother and the plaster were formidable opponents!

And so, the message from this whole episode of near disaster is actually very simple. For me, the big man up the stairs paid me back for being a prick that afternoon, in ordering all that stuff for my previous hotel, and certainly for being a one hundred percent tosser to that taxi driver. I will never forget how kind you were to me pal, to someone who tried to screw you over. I'm ashamed to say that I would not have been as gracious as him. Would you have been?

A VIDEO STAR
AND A T-SHIRT

The Pogues' third album 'If I Should Fall From Grace With God' had been released by now. It sounded a bit different from the first two albums, but it didn't take long at all to realise what a monster of a record it was. By all accounts, the band had a few long term issues with their record company, thus delaying the release of If I should fall – this must've given them a bit of extra time to perfect it, and it really shows. Steve Lillywhite, the album's producer, gets a really good, refined sound for the quality songs that the band were unleashing on the music world. The material on this album took The Pogues to yet another level; the songs were just fantastic. The two previous albums were hard acts to follow, but, in my opinion, they surpassed them both with this one, and I believe this was The Pogues at their peak.

The opening track, 'If I Should Fall From Grace With God' is short and very sweet with classic MacGowan lyrics, and a customary howling roar just before the instrumental piece in the middle which gives your body hairs an erection. 'Turkish Song of the Damned' has a very Eastern Mediterranean feel to it, concentrating on the ghosts of a shipwreck. This one has a very uplifting, melodic chorus, with a rousing instrumental finish. I find it to be very easy on the ear. 'Bottle of Smoke' is a rip roaring tale of having a good day at the races, with the added bonus of a 25/1 winner, something I couldn't do, even if my life depended on it. MacGowan is on fire with his songwriting, comparing the horse getting to the finish line first, to "a drunken fuck on a Saturday night". 'Metropolis' is an instrumental. There are a few instrumentals on their first two albums, but again, this one was different to what they had done before with a really new 'jazzy' sound, incorporating a strong brass section into the mix. Indeed, the playing of the instruments appear to be less aggressive as time went on for the band, 'Metropolis' having an almost polished finish to it.

Philip Chevron, the Pogues guitar man, contributes the next track, 'Thousands Are Sailing'. It's the story of Irish folks venturing across the Atlantic Ocean, to seek better fortunes in America. The track is a Pogues classic, a real favourite at live shows. Shane sang this one on the album, but latterly Philip Chevron himself provided live vocals. The majority of The Pogues fans seem to prefer Philip singing his self penned masterpiece rather than Shane; however, I firmly believe Shane's voice enhances the song to its full potential – just my opinion though. The lyrics to the song are very original, and are accompanied by real strong melodies musically; it's just brilliant – top marks to you Mr Chevron!

We need to flip the record over now, as we're on side two. Enter 'Fiesta'. How on earth do I describe this one? Fast and furious, with Spanish influences. Lots of brass instruments involved again. However, it's actually not one of my favourites. It was released as a single by the band, and is very much a live favourite, these days getting saved for the last number of their set. Once again, I'm definitely in the minority here, as The Pogues fans lap up the song, beer trays are getting clattered off skulls, and the stage turns into a mêlée of streamers and general chaos. I'm usually doing an 'old firm supporter' when they play the song live, and take an early exit, to avoid the mass of audience all leaving together.

The album, for me, gets back on track with the next one, 'The Recruiting Sergeant/Medley'. Mr Terry Woods joined the band before this album was recorded. A mate of Frank Murray The Pogues manager, Terry, an older member than his new band mates, brought more to the table instrument wise, with his cittern and mandolin. He opens the vocals with this one, singing a conversation with Shane, declining his invitation to sign up for the army. The medley bit is a collection of traditional Irish tunes, played at the pace of a Ferrari tearing up the outside lane, brilliant!

We now enter into the first time that the band have flirted with the politics of being 'Irish influenced'. 'Streets of Sorrow/ Birmingham Six' is all about the Birmingham pub bombings of the seventies, and tells the tale of the travesty of justice that occurred, with the people being wrongfully convicted of the crimes. The law would support Shane's views/lyrics in years to come, as the convictions were quashed. It's quite a powerful song, and I just love the singular horn at the end of the track that sets up the next song on the album perfectly.

'Lullaby of London': my favourite ever Pogues track. This is a slower number, with beautiful lyrics about ghosts howling round a house at night, and of haunted graves. It describes stones dancing on tides and of winds sighing. Shane MacGowan's lyrics really hit my spot here, no mistake. The accordion playing is mesmerising, as is the banjo near the conclusion of the song. There's two verses, no chorus – it's just the dog's bollocks. I most definitely want this played at my funeral. If there's anyone there, my wish is that they pay attention, and listen to this sheer work of art. Shane's singing on this track is also spot on, his voice even croaks ever so slightly, just at the right moment. To fully appreciate the sheer brilliance of this Shane MacGowan masterpiece, I would strongly recommend the following as the perfect way to enjoy it. Go out in the car, just as it's starting to get dark, crank up the volume as far as it will go (without distortion) and tell any passengers you may have with you to refrain from blethering for a while. Let the song wash over you, and I absolutely guarantee that, if not the first time, play it again and the song will 'get' you, stir the very cells of your emotions, giving you a very pleasant, natural rush of feelgood contentment. Of course, be careful and watch the road. Be especially alert, for drunken folk, that may be trying to do a 'runner' from a taxi...! They play 'Lullaby' live quite a lot, but it hardly ever captures, for me, the feeling and emotion of hearing it on the stereo, in the car – it did once, but I'll tell you about that later on (hope that's ok).

After 'Lullaby', we're off again, at breakneck speed with 'Sit down by the fire'. Lyrics about ripping out livers, and giving you the colic for jest, accompanied by music played at a thousand miles an hour, faster than the Ferrari in fact. Disappointingly, I've never heard the band play this one live; I wonder if they ever have?

The final track on this superb album is a track called 'The Broad Majestic Shannon'. Again, it's definitely one of my all time favourite tracks by the band, another MacGowan penned masterpiece, with both music and lyrics complementing each other perfectly. It concentrates on Irish men coming home from the fair, hurley balls and whiskey being drunk on a Sunday. The instrumental piece in the middle is positively dreamy, at live shows, if Shane's in the mood: he turns round to face the band, and conducts the music along by waving his hands from side to side. The conclusion of the song is where the real class of the track is though. The end chorus unexpectedly extends itself, it sounds so natural and flows with really beautiful lyrics about day dawning, small birds singing, and row boats landing, on "The Broad Majestic Shannon", quite clearly a river close to Mr MacGowan's heart, near his homeland in Ireland. The album is finally played out with 'Worms'. Andrew Ranken, the Pogues drummer groans this slimy tale accompanied by a droning melody on Mr Fearnley's accordion. It's very short but not meant to be sweet.

The album is just so clinically good; here you have a songwriter, right at the top of his game, fused with a band of brilliant musicians. Indeed, one of the real qualities of the album is the instrumental breaks between vocal verses; I can't talk highly enough of those – the whole thing is just so consistently superb.

And there we have it, the best album of all time, summarised with my take on it.

I've missed one out though, haven't I? For those of you paying attention, on Side 1, track 4, is the little deal of a song called 'Fairytale of New York'. This track needs, I feel, no introduction or explanation, it's unarguably the band's most famous and well known song, and it truly deserves all the plaudits that comes its way. Shane MacGowan, and my mother's favourite, the banjo mannie, Jem Finer, will probably go down in music history until the end of the world itself with this one that the duo were responsible for writing. Always aired at Christmas, it's probably the biggest singular thing that keeps The Pogues in the limelight to this day.

This album was a significant one for me personally in another way too – Vikki bought me the album on Compact Disc! It was to be the first CD I was to own, and I didn't even have a CD player. However, a player was purchased, albeit a flimsy one of dubious quality. One of my workmates had indeed dipped his toes into the world of CDs with hilarious consequences. Neil, who appears in my story in some significance in a short while, took his CD player and disc back to the shop, and played merry hell that "The fucking thing only plays on one side!" The error of his ways was pointed out, humble pie digested, but it gave me an insight as to what they were all about. A massive bonus, with having the CD of the latest Pogues offering, was an extra track on this format, a cracker of a traditional song called 'South Australia' with main vocal duties carried out by Terry Woods.

Vikki and I managed to escape from our bedsit in Hounslow, moving in with a couple from our respective workplaces, in Ashford, Middlesex. Graham, a real southern geezer, worked with me in the kitchen of The Anugraha, and Shelley worked in the Toshiba office with Vikki – quite a coincidence really, and we were grateful to them both, for providing a bit more quality to our living arrangements. There was a real added bonus, with a resident dog called Bitzer, a cross-bred. Bitzer and I became firm friends.

By this time Keith had come down from Perth to work at The Anugraha. Before that he had left Ilkley behind, to go and work in The Station Hotel in Perth (of all places). He did all right in Perth, and Chef Philip Borthwick obviously thought to himself that Keith may now be a good addition to his team in Surrey; it was great to have him back in the fold. Indeed the staff we had generally got on really well. As I mentioned earlier, there was a healthy Scottish contingent employed at the hotel. A lot of us took supporting our football teams quite seriously, and this one chap, Graham from Edinburgh, was a Rangers fan. Despite this, he and I got on quite well, and he gave me one of my finest, funny memories from my time spent down south. We were walking along Staines High Street one sunny afternoon, and Graham had his new Rangers top on. He was proudly pleased with the latest addition to his wardrobe; I really couldn't understand why. As we went under the railway bridge, a pigeon clearly agreed with me, when it opened its arse, and planted a big, dirty, fresh shite, right on the Rangers badge on Graham's shirt. I couldn't believe it, and was sore from laughing. Of course, Graham was livid, raging even. He looked up at the bridge, trying to locate the very accurate bird. I thought I was going to literally choke laughing, when he shouted, "Dirty Fenian Bastard!"

The Pogues were embarking on a British tour, which included a week's residency at The Town and Country Club, in Kentish Town, followed by a night at Brixton Academy, all of which sold out with ease, such was the popularity of the band with their superb latest album in tow. It was actually a great time to be in the London area whilst the band were so strong and popular. Securing a ticket for one of these shows was to prove difficult, but I did manage to get my mitts on one eventually, a single brief being the best I could do, for the band's Saturday show, at The Town and Country. I had arranged to meet Keith and big Howard, of taxi dodging fame, at Waterloo station on the afternoon of the gig. They had been at an Arsenal v Newcastle match, where a young Paul Gascoigne had scored Newcastle's equaliser in a 1-1 draw. We had a few jars together, but my drinking buddies were not tempted to venture up to North London with me, and perhaps chance their arm to secure a ticket from a tout or a Pogues fan that had a spare. Howard was probably thinking ahead to me hailing a taxi at the end of the gig...

It was time for me to make my way up to Kentish Town on the tube (alone) with much excitement and anticipation. Once there I bought a fucking belter of a t-shirt and made my way right down to the front of the stalls. The Town and Country Club (now the HMV Forum) is a really smart venue, not too big or small, and a viewing choice to suit everyone, with the 'rowdy' bit downstairs, and a balcony with both seats and standing. The Pogues were great that night with guest appearances by Joe Strummer and Kirsty MacColl. I held my own down the front; it was wild but brilliant! You actually felt like you were part of something, and I'd never felt anything like that at a gig before. The fans at a Pogues gig got along like a house on fire, everyone appearing to be a bit tipsy. A bit of beer, spilt here and there, and a stagger from a punter which made them bump into another, was never going to be a problem. During a rowdy number, a whole section of the crowd could fall over; everyone would haul each other back up, the more intoxicated given a bit of extra assistance; it was all good natured, and then it was ready again for the off!

A camera crew were present throughout, and it emerged in later months that I had actually, albeit briefly, secured a place in the Pogues video 'Live at The Town and Country Club'. How fuckin' cool is that! Just after 'The Turkish Song of the Damned', the camera rolls along the front row, and there I am, in my trusty leather jacket, with a full head of hair, looking like I'm having a good time – which obviously I was. What a privilege to be on the Pogues video. Needless to say, I bored everyone to death with this one, play, rewind, play, rewind, a bit like that posh skeleton that used to advertise Scotch video tapes, he was always repeating it too. Look, look, there! THAT'S ME! The video footage of the show failed to capture the wonderful sound of the band, or the amazing rowdy atmosphere of their gigs, but it was great to be on it, recorded in history, for ever! Later on, another Pogues video was released, 'Completely Pogued' which is a documentary type film, and fuckin hell, the same clip is on there too. Boys, I think you may owe me a small fortune for my performances on your films. No? Nah, I didn't think so. In much later years the two videos were released on one DVD, so I make that FOUR performances... now I'm thinking of Oscars and such things!

My journey home from the Kentish Town (just up the road from Camden) went smoothly enough, no broken limbs, no coppers, no hospitals, thank god.

What Vikki and I had been through, with the move from Ilkley, my accident and somewhat dubious accommodation in the South, probably contributed to me and her calling it a day. We were leading quite separate lives socially, we didn't actually fall out or have a big argument, but one night we went out for our dinner and we talked about things. I started the ball rolling by saying I wanted to move out of our accommodation in Ashford, so I suppose it was me that called a halt to our relationship. We didn't manage to finish our meal, and I paid the waiter for the food that we didn't even eat. He thought I was going to complain, and looked totally bamboozled when we left. Vikki ended up going back to Ashford alone and I headed to Keith's staff flat and he very accommodatingly put me up for the night. Mind you, I distinctly remember him being more interested in his soap operas on the TV as opposed to my predicament with Vikki! I think that Vikki and I were probably too young to be worrying about accommodation and such things; we both still had far too much living to do, before settling down.

So I arranged to move out from Ashford, and into a staff flat in Staines again. On the day I finally moved out, Vikki told me she wouldn't be back that evening to see me go, so I gathered my possessions, including my precious music collection and my clothes. Or so I thought. I wasn't interested in the possessions we owned together, but could I find my Town and Country Club t shirt? Could I hell! I turned the place upside down and back again, looking for that Pogues t shirt. Could I find it? No fucking chance. To say I was pissed off would be a huge understatement. I suppose my now ex girlfriend had had the last laugh on me, because she knew how much I liked that t shirt. It later came to light that all my searching was truly in vain as it lay crumpled in her handbag, which she had with her on the day that I left. My only consolation, though a really petty one, was through my desperate searching, I left the place like a tip... and beforehand I'd always been the tidy one between the two of us! So I left t shirt-less, and this wouldn't be the last time a Pogues t shirt would cause me grief.

THE POGUES ARE GOIN TO WEM-BLEY!!!

By this time, I was becoming really 'anorakesque' for all things Pogues. I bought all the singles in their different formats – there were some wonderful things to be had, with stunning picture discs and brilliant picture sleeves that contained the precious music. Such was the quality surrounding this band, their B sides were sheer class as well; now how many bands can you really say that about? As technology has progressed, it's unfortunate I think, that all these different formats of vinyl albums and especially singles, has all but been lost. Of course, quite rightly so, the music itself is by far the most important thing; however I'm sure that I'm not the only one who misses the thrill of obtaining a new record, in a limited edition (when they really were limited).

For example, one of the Pogues' singles, Sally MacLennane, came in three different 7 inch single formats, a 12 inch single, a shaped picture disc and a cassette single. Two of the 7 inch singles came with a wraparound poster sleeve, one of them being a rather fetching green coloured vinyl. Ironically, it's the 'normal' picture sleeve with standard black vinyl that's the rarest one, and it was fun trying to find them all. Again, without trying to sound like a vinyl-sick dinosaur, the records had to be searched for in proper record shops and fairs. Of course, the internet makes that search easy these days, but much less fun than having a good rake in the atmosphere of a quality record shop. The thrill of not quite knowing what you may find in a record shop was utterly addictive. Most cities and towns contained record shops in their shopping areas, and they needed to be located and checked out. Shops that dealt in second hand items and rarities, rather than new releases were generally more interesting (and musty); if you came across a shop that did both, then even better.

The first record shop that I religiously shopped in was Goldrush Records in Perth. Most Saturday mornings, I would usually buy a 7" single, usually from the Punk/new wave box that was situated on the counter. There really were some tasty nuggets to be had in this box of tricks; the earlier you were down to the shop on the Saturday the better, as I was one of many that would be handing over their scarce cash to secure a gem. The punk era was just brilliant for limited editions, coloured vinyls and really wicked artwork on the sleeves of the records. For those of you familiar with frequenting these places, didn't you think it was strange how the music they played in the actual shop always sounded more amazing than it did on your own system at home? The thrill of perhaps finding that elusive item you were looking for always kept you going out of your way to find new shops to browse in. You could get the 'feel' of a record shop by the way it was presented, by the promo adverts on the wall, of the particular type of music the owner of the shop sided with. Usually this gave you a big hint if you were on or not as the case may be, as to whether the shop had potential objects of desire for you. It's understandable, but still a great shame that the majority of our record shops have all but bitten the dust as our world changes.

I saw an ad in The Record Collector magazine (a quality mag to this day), offering a few rare Pogues records I needed for my collection. I replied to the ad and a deal was struck. The seller of this quality merchandise was a guy called Steve, who originally hailed from Ireland but was now based in Stratford, East London. We exchanged some Pogues chat and this led to us meeting for a few pints in The Eagle pub in Camden Town. Steve was quite an intense individual; he had loads of tattoos and despite hailing from Ireland, had a real London geezer accent, and was also a Chelsea fan. He was quite knowledgeable regarding the Pogues, and claimed to have even seen

The Nips (Shane MacGowan's first recording band, that also boasted James Fearnley in their line up for a while.) We had a good night, apart from him giving me a doing at darts. He also talked about politics a bit too much – not my cup of tea at all, the politician bastards are all corrupt, the whole fucking lot of them – it's just not for me. But meeting Steve, and hearing his much more-interesting-than-politics Pogues stories was brilliant – we would meet up at Pogues gigs in the future.

I didn't, however, meet him at the next Pogues gig I attended. The hiddledy-diddley Jimmy Shandesque heroes were headlining at Wembley Arena no less! I had attended a couple of concerts at the Arena before, one of them being Bob Dylan, where a friend and work colleague of mine, David Mundell, had secured two front row tickets. Everyone was asking us if we were from the press, such was the position of these tickets. Tom Petty and the Heartbreakers supported Dylan that night, and they blew me away; I thought Tom Petty was fantastic. Mr Petty even found the time, and the class, to arrange for the security staff to throw out a female heckler, who rudely interrupted him trying to sing a love song – superb, Tom! Mr Dylan, however, went right over my head; he appeared to be extremely uninterested, and thankfully, for me at least, didn't hang around for too long.

I'd not seen the Pogues play in such a big venue, and I couldn't help but wonder how they would sound in such a big arena that held 12,500 punters. Davo was coming down from Scotland for this one. It was on a Saturday and we went to see Arsenal v Manchester United at Highbury in the afternoon (3-1 to Arsenal if you're interested). After the match we met up with two of my workmates, Mark and Keith. I had bought the tickets for the Wembley show weeks in advance, as you do for these things, so my now ex-girlfriend was also in attendance. To be fair, there was no animosity between us, and we did still enjoy each other's company when we met. However, I did quiz her endlessly about a certain missing garment from my sparse enough wardrobe!

Keith's main band, amongst the drivel that he danced around his handbag to, were and still is everything Electric Light Orchestra and Jeff Lynne (more of which later), but he really enjoys a knees up at the Pogues. So we oiled our throats at the Bonapartes bar at Waterloo station, before making our way north, to the vicinity of the home of

English football. The company, although mixed, all knew each other, so we were getting along just fine; the problem, as it always is, was the ale! Davo and I had had a few already, followed by a few more at Waterloo, followed by a wee carry out for the longish tube journey to Wembley. The lads in the company were having a jolly old time, a good sing-song, and spirits were certainly high, anticipating seeing the Pogues at such a large and well known venue. I think we may have even had a wee pogo along the way – wonderful.

Then the mood changed very suddenly as far as my ex was concerned. One of us (I honestly can't remember who) was slapping the big willie type thing that was hanging from the roof of the tube carriage for people to hang on to, and it smashed into one of the lights with glass going all over the place. Nobody was hurt or cut, but it wasn't clever. Vikki by this time had enough of the high jinx, so when the train stopped at the next station, she very coolly got off the train, and took a seat at the southbound platform waiting for the next tube to take her back to central London and eventually home, far far away from us! It was all over in seconds and suddenly our little throng was down by one. There were a couple of other lads that had joined us for a sing-song and one of them didn't have a ticket for the gig, so as I was holding the tickets for me, Davo and Vikki, I was able to provide one for our ticketless new comrade – he was understandably delighted at the events of the evening so far!

The train was busy, and the non-Pogues attending public were no doubt very pleased at our alightment at Wembley station. Mark and I were accidentally separated from Keith and Davo as we made our way out of the station and towards the arena. In front of the venue, a full highland dressed pipe band were present and strutting their stuff. Of course, this being a bit of a red rag to a bull for a drunk Scotsman in London, Mark and I were right in the middle of them in no time doing our very own highland fling. The band handled our somewhat unwelcome presence well; however, very soon we were indeed reprimanded by no other than Frank Murray, the Pogues' manager, who was not overly impressed. I think he recognised however that we meant no harm and were just over excited at the prospect of the evening's entertainment which was about to unfold. For some strange reason, I remember him telling us that the first song would be The Broad Majestic Shannon, and could we let the pipe band get on with it without our 'help'. He shook our hands warmly, told us to enjoy the concert and scurried off into the venue to do whatever he does on gig night.

I got to my seat in the 'wings' of the arena before Davo and was really chuffed at the view we were going to have. It's always been important for me to have a good viewpoint at something so dear to me and being a wee chap, there's nothing worse than standing behind some beanpole with a huge head, and dancing about behind him on tiptoe trying to see what's going on. We really did have a perfect view, and when the band came on they sounded amazing, and were right at the top of their game.

There was quite a lot of 'bother' that night at Wembley during the gig. I think the actual occasion was so massive, the band were on fire, and naturally as a result of these things, the audience were going nuts, especially the section directly in front of the stage. I really think it was a case of the faithful throng not used to seeing their heroes in such a vast arena as headliners. I remember a chant going round, like it would at the football, of "Wembley is shit, Wembley is shit!". Spider was doing his very best to restore order, giving the ticketholders a bit of a bollocking. There were a few seats flying about by this time, and he announced to the over-excited masses that "they" were going to turn off the electricity if calm was not found. Whoever put ten shilling pieces in the Wembley lekkie meter decided the evening would indeed continue, thank God!

I remember when the band played 'Dark Streets of London' treating their fans to an extended remix-type version, and they also played an instrumental of sorts called 'Japan' with Spider to the fore with his whistle for this one. At the end of the gig Spider thanked everyone after his earlier reprimand, telling us all that we weren't that bad after all – aahh, nice chap! What a fantastic gig. I read with interest in Shane MacGowan's book, written with his girlfriend, Victoria Clarke (A Drink With Shane MacGowan) that when he stepped out on stage at Wembley that night, it kind of dawned on him how big this band were. I think that sums the whole thing up perfectly, from their somewhat humble origins of playing in pubs, the band had made it, in their own right, to the cup final at Wembley, and they had won the match in some style. Shane went on to comment that he thought playing Wembley was a mistake – well Mr Mac, that show was one of the highlights of my concert-going life, it was just fucking magic! The whole Pogues thing was just so powerful, I needn't have worried about how they would sound in Wembley Arena – the sound was loud and clear, from a real top drawer band that took the whole occasion very naturally in their stride. This gig remains one of my favourites; it was just a truly awesome occasion. At nights like this I genuinely feel privileged to have been lucky enough to be there.

Somehow, Davo and I were reunited with Mark and Keith somewhere in the London tube network. Bearing in mind that they were in the 'mêlée' downstairs, it was hardly surprising really to discover that Mark had had his glasses broken for him. Keith had a big gash in his leg and was black from head to toe. We had to get a taxi part of the way home, but, aha, relax, this one was paid for, all above board. Keith and Mark did have a 'small discussion' re their cash contributions towards the fare (Keith being a little short of sovereigns). An absolutely fantastic night was had by all; the Pogues had conquered Wembley – it was just fucking brilliant.

I couldn't resist giving my ex a hungover phonecall next morning, just to tell her how good it was, and what a night she had missed. Pretty childish really! However she didn't miss me when she explained how she felt re our behaviour on the tube train. Ah well!

The night after the Pogues date at Wembley, Chris Rea was performing in the same arena, and a couple of chaps that I worked with at the hotel went to see him. I asked them how it went and they said it was good, but the arena was in some state, even the floor was sticky. When they told me this, I felt strangely very proud.

DIESEL THE DOG AND VICTORIA CLARKE'S ASSETS!

I settled in well to the staff flat in Staines' Moormead estate. There were a lot of similar flats for the hotel's workers nearby, so a booze up and a party were never hard to come by.

I really enjoyed mooching around Central London on my days off from work. A quick walk to Staines railway station, a purchase of a brilliant value for money travelcard and half an hour later the train rolls into Waterloo. The travelcard takes you anywhere you like, on the tube, bus or overhead train, within the confines of this wonderful capital city. I'd often do this just by myself, with only my Walkman for company. I'd search the record shops for Pogues goodies, and generally just walk around. I really liked going to Camden and would go there quite often. I genuinely had no idea at the time how significant the area was to the members of the Pogues. Rock On record shop, next to the tube, on Kentish Town Road was always worth a look – they even had a Pogues section in the shop which was always of interest. There's a video clip of Philip Chevron, the Pogues' guitarist, serving a punter in this very record shop, hassling him for the correct change, then launching himself into singing 'Thousands are sailing' whilst playing an accompanying guitar.

Davo came down from Perth again for a visit; this time we were going to see an England v Scotland football match at Wembley Stadium situated next door to the Arena that the Pogues had conquered previously. We had a good enough day out even if England did win the match 1-0. We saw lots of people we knew from Perth, and had a good old sing-song in Trafalgar Square. I have to admit that I've never quite got into the Scottish national football thing in any great way, but it was a good crack all the same and we met plenty of characters and chancers, I can tell you.

On the tube journey up to Wembley, Davo truly excelled himself. He asked me, with a very pale face, where the toilet was on the tube train. I gave him the news he was probably expecting when I told him there wasn't one. An inner sense of calm must have descended on Davo at this moment as he managed to locate an empty carrier bag, and promptly spewed the day's ale consumption thus far into the unfortunate receptacle. The exercise was carried out with a great deal of accuracy and dignity considering the difficult situation he found himself in.

After the match, Davo's stomach had recovered sufficiently to join me for a memorable meal in Chinatown, before we headed up to Camden to spend the evening. We were sitting outside this pub, on a lovely summer's night and got chatting to a very interesting lady and her company. Carmel was a wee bit older than me and Davo, and it turned out she was a school teacher (infants). She was very interesting to talk to; her personality fitted Camden Town perfectly in my opinion, where anything goes regarding trends and fashions. Our conversation was flowingly comfortable, and the subject of the Pogues reared its head, as it inevitably would in Davo's and my company. Carmel then announced that she shared her flat with Victoria Clarke, Shane MacGowan's girlfriend no less! She was busy telling us how pissed off she was, as Shane had apparently ruined one of her carpets with paint. The way she described it was that it wasn't an accidental drip or two, more like a full on Picasso moment using the carpet as a canvas! Naturally we found this hilarious but Carmel was not amused; she must have liked that carpet, or clearly didn't rate Shane's latest masterpiece. This particular outlet of Shane's artistic prowess, however, was from far the last I was to discover through Carmel.

Anyhow, a short time later, Victoria actually came by outside the pub where we were sitting and stopped to chat to Carmel. We were introduced. Victoria was both stunning and charming. I'm not usually one for noticing jewellery, but couldn't help noticing a huge oval, black onyx ring that she wore. As quickly as she had appeared, Victoria disappeared into the night as it were. Davo and I were left with Carmel and her fella Paul, and we had a really good night just chatting, mostly as you can imagine, about all things Pogues. However Carmel was also very interested in us, and she asked me what I did for a living. When I told her I was a chef, I got the usual reaction of "Oh you must cook me a meal". Naturally I agreed, as people do when they've had a few beers, and so we exchanged telephone numbers and addresses (no emails or mobiles then remember). We had a parting glass of something nice and we bid farewell, and I decided that next time I was in Camden Town, where the cold North winds blow, that I would definitely look her up.

And so a few weeks later, I found her flat; I duly pressed the buzzer and a very accommodating Victoria let me in to wait for Carmel who was still at work. We exchanged small talk, and she told me that Carmel was due in at any moment. She was busy doing something when I arrived, and asked if I minded amusing myself whilst she finished whatever it was that she was occupied with. Amuse myself? I think I knew what she meant, but I'm sure she didn't realise that she herself would be providing my 'amusement'! She ended up crawling about on the floor looking for something, she had a loose top on, but nothing in the way of modesty or support (not that it was needed) and I copped a more than generous eyeful of her womanly wares! Very impressive they were too, amusement indeed!

Carmel duly arrived, and seemed genuinely pleased to see me which was cool. She announced that there was no booze in the house, so I volunteered to go and get some, from the local off-licence. Enter Carmel's dog, Diesel. Diesel was told by Carmel to take me to the local off-licence on Kentish Town Road as I wasn't 100% sure where it was, and quite simply and most brilliantly, Diesel did exactly that! I followed her out of the flat. She was very 'London Cool' and she took me, with the absolute minimum of fuss to the off-licence, sat on her arse until I came out with beer and wine, then took me back. Fucking brilliant. What a hound! Diesel was a collie and had a very obvious, sky high, doggie IQ.

In Carmel's living room of the flat, I was privileged enough to be able to view, with my own eyes, some of Shane's art. In the corner, stood proudly, one of Shane's modern art exhibits, in the shape of Carmel's lamp that he had turned into a 'Blues Brothers' figure, very cool, complete with shades. It was an utterly brilliant specimen (see pictures). Was there really no limit to this man's talent? Apparently not.

Carmel's boyfriend, Paul, I felt, was wary of me. I suppose I can't really blame him. I liked Carmel but not in 'that' way, and I'm quite sure she felt the same about me, but there was definitely a touch of the green eyed monster about her Paul. Apart from being a little uncomfortable at being on the receiving end of some dodgy looks from Paul, we had a nice evening, talking about all sorts. There were lots of visitors in and out of the flat; Carmel had told me previously that her humble abode could be like Euston Station at times. At one point, the door buzzer went. Someone desperately wanted in, as their finger was constant on that button that relayed the head-frying tone of someone that was really badly needing attention. A general comment went round the room of "Oh, that'll be Shane for sure" and naturally I was quietly, but very excited at the prospect of him entering the flat. Alas, false alarm. I can't remember who it was, but it certainly wasn't Victoria's poet boyfriend.

Later in the week, I wrote Carmel a wee letter, telling her how much I enjoyed myself, and included the fact that I had very much appreciated Victoria's 'show'. She wrote back to me saying Victoria was mortified at my revelation, HA!, and that she had received considerable ribbing about showing off her own ribs. Carmel also said that if I was ever up town again, if she wasn't in her flat, she'd be in the Devonshire Arms alehouse or Molly Malones in Stoke Newington, her two favourite refreshment hostelries.

I was to see Carmel and Victoria periodically, but the times when I was in the flat, Shane's presence was proving to be somewhat elusive – he was always busy with the band. It's a shame that I didn't manage to see him at Carmel's. Victoria's tits were also now elusive, never to be seen again. In the flesh. I always saw Diesel though, and she would still take me for a walk; when we were out, she was kind enough to never put me on a lead. I've never again, in my life, come across a hound that was as intelligent as Diesel was. If only there was 'Doggie Mastermind'!

There was a time when I didn't venture up to Camden for a good while, but I did go to Molly Malones on a number of occasions, but didn't run into Carmel. In Molly's they had on display a number of Pogues silver discs presented to Spider for record sales. On one of my visits there I had a crack with the actor Sammy Johnson, who played 'Stick' on the TV series Spender with Jimmy Nail playing the main character. It was a programme I had enjoyed on the box, set in Newcastle. 'Stick' was telling me how he was hacked off that Jimmy Nail got to snog all the nice looking actresses, where he was not nearly as good looking or as streetwise as his character. He was a nice chap and was a big admirer of The Pogues, but sometimes I struggled to understand his thick Geordie accent, which he clearly had scaled down whilst on TV. Sadly, he's no longer with us today, passing away before his time, a good few years ago.

Another time in Molly's I was very lucky to see Andrew Ranken, the Pogues drummer, have a bit of a sing-song on the tiny stage in the pub. He was part of what seemed to be a makeshift band. I thought it was pretty good actually, and after their first number I gave them a deserved, hearty round of applause. The pub was pretty quiet, but I was the only one to show any appreciation. Londoners really can be quite miserable and ignorant at times, not nearly as cool as Diesel the dog though, eh? Mr Ranken had put everything into his vocal display and deserved recognition for his efforts. I enjoyed the song he sang at Pogues concerts, 'Star of the County Down' and here he was singing in a pub – brilliant. I managed to get a quick word with him at the end of the set. I had bought a Pogues CD earlier that day and he was happy to sign it for me. I asked him what Shane was up to. He just said, "Oh yeah, Shane, he is some man him!" In much later years, reading Carol Clerk's most excellent book about the Pogues, Andrew Ranken is quoted as saying something like, "I was fucking well fed up, y'know, people asking me about Shane all the fucking time!" Maybe I'm just normal then, or more possibly, a wee bit pathetically predictable!

The next Pogues show in London, after the fantastically wild night at Wembley, was at Brixton Academy. They used to have a big black screen on the stage that hid the performers, just before they were about to unleash their wares to their adoring audience at the venue. It had seen better days for sure, and was full of holes, so much so that you could actually see what was going on behind this screen. I was down the front with Chelsea Steve for this gig – man it was wild and a huge effort had to be made to hold your position. The audience were packed in like sardines and the mass just swayed this way and that constantly – and that's before the ropey curtain went up! I can remember Philip Chevron blowing smoke from his fag through one of the holes in the screen and having a giggle to himself. There was always tobacco aplenty within The Pogues' stage. Shane appeared to be a seasoned chain smoker, Spider not far behind, but I liked James' improvisation when it came to having a snout while he was working. He actually had some apparatus on his accordion, a holder of sorts, to harbour his smouldering bolt, until it was time for James to have his next drag – brilliant! After the events of Wembley Arena, and the crowd reaction, a subtle opener was chosen by the band for this gig: the very slow tempo, but brilliance of 'The band played Waltzing Matilda', to keep the adoring punters calm? Aye right! First song over, and the literally heaving masses got into gear very quickly, albeit with a little more order than previously at Wembley. Perhaps the slow opener just added to the foreplay, before the crowd went nuts. Steve's attention on the band was being distracted however, by the gorgeous creature directly in front of him, that he was very pleasantly close to due to the audience being squashed together. His hands were wandering, then he got the shock of his life when the gorgeous creature turned its face round, and it was indeed a hairy geezer, albeit with shiny long blonde hair. Funny thing was though, he certainly wasn't complaining! Steve is a stocky bloke; he didn't hang around, managing to manoeuvre himself a wee bit away from the site of his fondling exploits.

The enthusiasm and commitment to the band from the audience was clearly huge; you could feel the buzz of the punters. It was a very exciting time to watch the band live. I guess Waltzing Matilda kept the fans simmering but the pot duly came to the boil soon enough. The band were really playing out of their skins. Steve and I survived down the front and enjoyed the whole evening's entertainment immensely. You certainly got your money's worth at a Pogues concert. Happy days indeed!

FOR SHANE, VICTORIA, CARMEL... AND DIESEL

Where the towns of Kentish and Camden Shack

Lies an oasis amongst Matterhorn concrete, Torbay Court, Carmel's gaff

Here you'd find Shaney Mac and his girfriend, Victoria Clarke

A big white pad, and a biro, never far from her lap

Shane with his finger on that damned buzzer, relentless, open the door...

Diesel's ears prick, he knows who it is, clever dog, he knows the score

*Carmel's in, she's back from the school, you just can't
miss the shiny bright red lacquered lips*

Her fella Paul, glassy eyed, would look lustfully to her hips

*Victoria, crawling around on the floor, giving strange
Scotsmen a flash of her... (large, black oval, onyx ring)*

*Out on the balcony, the dubious, exotic fumes,
hanging over dear Camden Town*

*Diesel's bark, Shane's manic laugh, in that flat, so
it seemed, half of London came round*

*Yeah, Diesel and Shane, two trendy geezers,
wise, talented, human and canine*

Away to the off-licence, beer, cigs, rolly papers and white wine

Later on in the night, a trip to the Dev'

Or maybe the Falcon, or Dingwalls instead

Spider would show, very sure to add spice

He'd order the drinks, but did not have the price.

Or maybe an evening up at Molly Malone's

A good bet that the jukey would be playing The Pogues

Spider's shiny silver discs, displayed high on the wall

He can pay for them drinks, and chasers an' all!

Change it comes, life goes on, but Carmel stayed put

Diesel sadly has gone, but she has a new pooch

Torbay Court, Camden Town, carefree crazy days

We look back in time, with great memories unfazed.

CAMDEN TOWN, A BIG SPLASH AND JEM FINER'S SCARY EYES!

On one of my many jaunts exploring London, I came across an absolute cracker of a record shop, in a road just at the back of Oxford Street. The bloke that ran the place, Alan, was a massive Pogues fan, and there was always gold, frankincense and myrrh to be found when it came to the 'P' section of the records on sale. It was here that I saw a copy of The Pogues' VERY first single, 'Dark streets of London', the white label version, with the harp sticker on the plain white sleeve. Not much to look at, but a real diamond in the Pogues' catalogue, no mistake, more than enough to cause a twitch in your groin. It was £18.00, a small fortune to me at the time, so I gave it a miss. But it bugged me. We've all been there at some time or other. So, I phoned Alan at the shop, a day or so later. The record was still there and available, so I reserved it, and went in to London as soon as I could and bought it. I felt like I'd just bought the crown jewels right enough of Pogues discs. I believe there were a total of 237 copies of this record pressed, and considering they were sold at early gigs, quite boisterous affairs no doubt, one wonders how many originals are actually still intact and in existence today. Purchasing this piece of music history kind of put the cherry on the cake so to speak on my Pogues collection, as I had practically everything else released by them on a wide range of formats.

I'd also started collecting Shane MacGowan's former band's records. They came into the music world as The Nipple Erectors, but later shortened their name to The Nips – this was less offensive, apparently, to radio stations and the like, the dear sensitive souls that they are. The band had a good few changes to their line-up, but Shane and his on-off girlfriend, Shanne Bradley, were mainstays. As mentioned previously, it was through the Nips that a certain James Fearnley came into Mr MacGowan's world, as a guitarist with the band – thank God he did! Their songs were fast and furious with a vein of rockabilly or punkabilly running through it; they were actually very well written with plenty of humour present, and Shane was certainly not scared of a controversial lyric or two. In his song 'All the time in the world' he sang of a picture of a desired female, and how he used to "cream" himself over it – brilliant! There were two albums to be had, one of them a live one, the latter containing hilarious banter between tracks of MacGowan introducing the songs to the audience in an over the top cockney accent. The band also released a handful of singles; they were all crackers, with brilliant artwork on the sleeves.

Possibly The Nips' most famous song was 'Gabrielle', a slower, catchy, melodic song; it was very accomplished and was unlucky not to do better than it eventually did in the charts. If it was plugged properly, it might have had a chance to have put the group more in the limelight. You could tell through this track alone that Shane was destined to become a master musical poet all right. I found all The Nips material to be really good. Their records certainly didn't come cheap however; their value is still rising to this very day – well, it's early Pogues history after all. There was something original about The Nips, something that attracted you to their package. Shane plays down his time with The Nips when asked about it in interviews. His talent was evidentially there, and I personally find The Nips part of Shane's story to be quite uplifting, but he clearly blossomed into the songwriter he eventually became through The Pogues.

I kept my records in date order, neat and tidy, like a true musical librarian would. I also collected music paper articles on the band, and had started a compilation video tape of their appearances on TV. Sometimes it would get out of hand and bordering on the ridiculous.

One day I was looking at the pages on Ceefax and found an article about The Pogues. On one of the pages, there was a Ceefax picture of Shane MacGowan's head, basically made up of thousands of dots. I wondered how I could collect the image to keep. But short of taking a photo of the TV screen, this just wasn't possible; perhaps I was taking things just too far! On one of Davo's visits, I was proud to let him inspect my Pogues collection. He told me after his viewing that it was the best record collection he had ever seen. Well what could I do, but agree, wholeheartedly with my pal? The music, most certainly, was the best, that's for sure.

In the flat I lived in at the time in Staines, I shared with three other lads. My room was the biggest, and it's most unlike me, but I reluctantly volunteered my room to be the lounge. So if I wasn't sleeping, entertaining, ahem, myself or if I got luckier than that, then the residents of the house could come in with their coffees and watch TV etc. I was visiting my folks back in Perth one time, and my flatmates decided to have a bit of a party one night, my room being the venue (celebrating my absence?) and some bright spark had the idea of putting on the Pogues video, the one in which I had starred in for about two seconds. They had to find the video first. Whoever was rummaging to find the video obviously had had a few by then, so they were less than careful in going through my Pogues collection to find it. When I got back and saw the state of my Pogues gems, I was fucking livid; there was no real damage done, but the dishevelment of my collection was just not on. I told everyone in no uncertain terms that if it happened again then I would be permanently entertaining MYSELF in my room, and there would be no entry for them anymore. It would be sore, but necessary!

One of the lads that I shared the flat with was gay. I say on record here and now that I don't have a problem with this at all; we all got on really well in the flat. One night we were all in the kitchen having a chat, and the subject got round to blue movies. Bear in mind we are going back a few years here, the gay thing is much more openly common now and accepted; back then it's fair to say that it wasn't as advanced, shall we say, as it is nowadays. I asked the gay chap if he had blue movies to suit his taste. He said, "Oh yeah, of course, but you lot wouldn't be able to watch it for five minutes." We all replied that we thought we could, no problem. So, into my room, video machine clicking into life, and away we go. He was right. None of us lasted more than two minutes, never mind five. Except for one chap. Neil, who you may remember for double-sided CD fame, was a good bit older than the rest of us and a law unto himself in lots of ways. When I clicked the stop button on the video to halt proceedings as it were, Neil, disappointed said "Aawh, just wait till you see the next bit!" None of us could believe our ears – he'd just rumbled himself, with the fact that he was having a bit look when the rest of us were out of the flat. Dirty bastard!

The gay chap told me one day that he had a blind date organised for that afternoon, after answering an ad in the London Evening Standard. I was going into London that day, and after it emerged that the liaison was happening at our local railway station, Staines, I asked my flatmate for a lift in his car. I was also being nosy, obviously. I asked him how he would know who his date was. His potential partner was to stand by the bus stop with a newspaper in his hand. He would also be wearing a fawny coloured raincoat. All very Columbo-esque! On our arrival, in the car, at the railway station, we clocked the guy straight away. I don't think my flatmate was too impressed. He was hinting that he was going to drop me off, then just drive away. I told him not to be so hasty. Before he could even answer me, I was out of the car like a bullet out of a gun, over to yer man at the bus stop, and with a pointed finger told him, "there he is mate, he's all yours!" My flatmate's look was a mixture of disgust for me, and a very lukewarm and half hearted smile for his new chum. I made a rapid exit, and headed for the ticket office in the station, and so on to the platform for my train to Waterloo. The next day, I was in the kitchen of the flat, when I got this horrible recollective feeling of the incident at the station that I had manufactured. I heard my flatmate's footsteps heading towards the kitchen, dreading the bollocking I was about to receive. But no, he seemed quite happy, in fact, old bus stop Charlie was currently in his bed! Probably a bit sticky, but 'C'est la vie'!

At the Wembley Arena show, I had bought another tour t shirt; it wasn't a patch on the one I had 'lost' previously to my ex, but it was still not bad at all. One day, I had a real shit day at work, when I just couldn't get anything right. The Chef was not impressed with my performance and wasted no time in telling me. Anyway, about half past three, I finished my shift, and Vikki was coming round to mine for dinner. We had kept in touch. She didn't hang around when it came to finding a new partner, which was just as well as she needed looking after for sure. I on the other hand was enjoying pleasing myself.

My bad day intensified though when we argued really badly that night, and she left my flat quite early. I thought, since I had the rest of the evening to myself, I would catch up on my chores, which included the exciting prospect of doing my washing. I'm actually not too bad at this for a bloke. So, it was the whites first, with the coloureds aside for the next wash. I noticed, to my horror, that my Wembley Pogues T shirt was missing. OH NO! I hunted high and low for it without success, I looked fucking everywhere. I even looked in the kitchen bin, thinking this was maybe my ex doing the sequel to the first T shirt episode, since I had clearly pissed her off earlier that evening. When I put my hand in the bin, I cut my hand open, on a tin of Heinz tomato soup with the lid proudly standing to attention. Fuck! What a day!

Thinking I was organised (as well as being good at the washing) I went to the medicine box for a bandage or a few plasters, only to discover that I was kidding myself, as I had nothing like a bandage or a plaster even. I went across the road, knocked on the door of another staff flat, to ask for a bandage, but they didn't have one either. Back to my flat, and I'd locked myself out! I did, however, manage to scrape through an open window to Neil's room, and just about ripped my balls to smithereens in the process. I'd had enough. It was still quite early, the sun was still shining, but I wrapped my hand in a towel and went to bed – my thinking was nothing else could possibly happen to me whilst in there. And it didn't.

For the record, my T shirt was mixed up in Neil's washing, yes him of CD and now gay video fame, and for the record, Neil was not into separating whites from coloureds when he was doing his washing – but I got there in time. Neil got a clip round the lug hole for his troubles; he was a real domestic nightmare. For example, if the kettle was broken, he would try and fix it, removing parts from the toaster perhaps, making his way round the kitchen until nothing fucking worked! So, t shirt reunited with owner, all's well that ends well, but what a shit day that was, never to be forgotten.

My father's theory on life is very simple: have a good day. That's it! One night I was speaking to Dad on the phone, and he told me he'd seen the results of a survey that rated the best parts of the UK to live in and also, obviously, the worst parts. This survey took all sorts of points into the equation, such as air quality, crime figures, house prices etc. Perth came out on top, and way down the line, Staines actually turned out to be the worst of all. My father congratulated me on how I had got things so 'right' regarding where I had ended up living! I really do wonder if he made up that well known cheesy line of "have a good day".

On a further trip into London, I was in a clothes shop in Camden and listening to 'Billy's Bones', a rip roaring track from The Pogues' second album Rum, Sodomy and the Lash' on my Walkman. I experienced the most weird sensation of looking round and seeing Jem Finer, his wife and one of his bairns in the same shop. In the days of Walkmans, you could sometimes hear the distant sounds of whatever someone nearby was listening to, and I really felt that Jem was recognising what was on mine. He was just looking at me; his eyes were fucking scary. Maybe he was dreading the fact I would go over and speak to him, to tell him what I was listening to, blah blah blah. Well if that's what he thought, then it worked, as I didn't have the nerve to speak to him, especially as he was with his family, so I just left the shop and left him to it.

Later that sunny day, I was having a sit down near the canal, having a wee cold can of something refreshing, and a read of a music paper. It really was a beautiful day, and watching the world go by (in Camden) was always interesting. I was quite relaxed when all of a sudden there was this huge splash sound. This geezer had hurled himself into the canal with the absolute minimum of fuss, and was making no attempt whatsoever to swim, paddle or anything! Me and this other chap somehow managed to drag him out of the drink. It was a real struggle to get him out without falling in ourselves, but eventually after a short battle, we got him onto dry land. We were fucking knackered and soaking, but the geezer calmly walked away, without even a word. A girl passed by, with a big grin on her face. She said, "Oh, don't worry, he does this all the time!" It could only happen in Camden. I thought it was an amazing place at the time. It's a lot busier these days, just mad with people, but you see it all up in Camden.

They have a famous market selling all sorts. I wanted a long coat, similar to the one Shane MacGowan had worn, on the picture sleeve for the Poguetry in Motion EP. The only one I could find was far too big for me, but I bought it anyway. To say I looked ridiculous in the coat would be a gross understatement – the dubious garment was made for a person probably double my size. On a trip home, when I wore the coat, my mother about choked laughing at my miscued fashion statement; she really thought I was having a giraffe, and couldn't believe I was wearing the coat for real. I also acquired a smart bowler hat, copying the one Shane wore on the record cover and the video for 'A pair of brown eyes'. This suited me a lot more than the coat did, apparently, although I did receive a few comments that it made me look like a thug!

Before I met Carmel, I didn't know that a lot of the band drank in The Devonshire Arms alehouse, one of her locals, just up the road from Rock On records. Or that the Pogues' management office, Hill 16, was somewhere inbetween the two. Anyway, I was too busy saving lives at the canal to be bothering Poguey people in bars, offices or record shops?

The Pogues were doing a lot of live shows at the time. I know now that all was not well behind the scenes, but I must say that was not obvious to us punters; it was one great show after the next. Maybe I missed the bad ones, when Shane wasn't at the races or whatever, but up until that point, I really hadn't seen what I could call a bad gig. Far from it. Quite simply, seeing the Pogues live then, as it is now, is the best night out in town, bar fucking none!

ANYONE FOR SALMON? PEACE AND LOVE!

I had been thinking for a while of a move back to Perth to live with my parents again. Although I had kept in touch with Davo and my Hibs mates, I missed going to the football with them and all the carry on that went along with it. I finally made the decision, and northbound it was for me. I was lucky enough to be given a very memorable leaving party from my workmates. We had a meal in The Staines Steak House, the very restaurant where Vikki and I had discussed going our separate ways. I was presented with a cracking Rotary watch and the latest Walkman on the market at the time (of obvious still limited technology). I was totally humbled by my leaving gifts and by the number of people that turned out for the meal. I had met a lot of really wonderful work colleagues, hailing from all over the UK and beyond, and I was starting to wonder if I was doing the right thing in resigning from my job.

Philip, the head chef, came into Staines that night and we had a quiet drink in The Greyhound pub with my mate Mark Alexander. When Mark and I got together, life was anything but quiet; we used to get up to all sorts of shenanigans and mischief. Mark was a chef at the hotel too, and it got to the stage where our boss had to put us on separate shifts, and keep us apart. Tonight though we were on our best behaviour in his company; it was good of him to go out of his way to spend a bit of time with me, and again, I started wondering what potential employment in Perth would be like without his guidance. The training Philip Borthwick gave his staff, especially in organisational skills, was second to none; over the years he gave a lot of young hopefuls a brilliant platform to launch their careers in the catering industry.

My leaving party continued in several of the staff houses and went on all night. I didn't go to bed at all, lots of 'sherries' were consumed and The Pogues were naturally to the fore, keeping the good folk in The Moormead estate from their sleep that night in Staines. Keith was going through a wee bit of a hard time financially and had been working on his days and nights off from the hotel in a local French restaurant. He had been working there the night of my shindig and had been paid in cash, quite a considerable sum by the proprietor, for his troubles. Keith headed for the Party, possibly listening out for The Pogues sounds to locate where the sherry tasting was taking place. He caught up with things quickly – the poor bugger was knackered and fell comfortably asleep on a setee. Unfortunately, and tragically for him, some twat relieved him of his hard earned cash while he was snoozing. We all had our suspicions but couldn't prove anything – perhaps not all my workmates were quite so wonderful after all.

The next day, I was due to board a train at King's Cross that was going to take me and my gear home. Two of my pals accompanied me into London. We didn't go straight to the station; instead we made a small detour, at my request, to Camden, so I could buy another record that had been 'bugging' me. It was a copy of The Nips' 'Gabrielle' and was signed on the sleeve by the band's vocalist, simply 'Shane', so I relieved Rock On records of that particular stock item. My two buddies helped me on to the train with all the stuff I owned, except for my precious Pogues collection. That was to be delivered to my parents' house in the near future, by a very reliable character who was driving to Scotland, and was willing to be a courier for me.

For the first time in my working life, I settled into a routine job, set hours every week, off every night and every weekend. I was head chef at Dewar's Whisky distillery in Perth, looking after the canteen for the workers and the small, fine dining restaurant, where they were selling the precious, golden liquor to major buyers. The River Almond flowed nearby, and I was full of fairytales for the diners of how their salmon had been swimming in the river that very morning, before being landed by a local angler, just so I could poach a piece of the majestic river knight, for their absolute pleasure! Not the most accurate of tales, but never mind, they seemed to lap up my tall stories as well as their nosh!

I went to the football every Saturday, midweek matches, friendly matches, the lot. I drank far too much beer and gin, ate like a lord on my mother's most excellent cooking (without the bullshit of fish in rivers), I played in a pub pool team every Thursday night (still badly – Davo was also in the pool team, and still shit hot). It was nice to be home, with Mum and Dad and close friends, but I did miss the South, as I expected to, and especially missed the buzz of my previous job – maybe the routine hours just didn't suit me.

Up to this point, I had never seen The Pogues live in Scotland, and for the six months or so I was at home, this was not to change, as there were no scheduled shows at this particular time. What did happen though, was the release of The Pogues' fourth album 'Peace and Love'. The album was first released in 1989; it had a picture of a young boxer on the front cover, and one of his hands boasted five fingers and a thumb, a convenience that enabled the words 'Peace' and 'love' to be displayed on his clenched fists. The record was dedicated to the memory of the Liverpool football fans who lost their lives at Hillsborough. Two of the group, Philip Chevron and Darryl Hunt, had actually attended that very match, where the disaster unfolded before their eyes. I can say now, that it's The Pogues album that I listen to the least, out of them all. Obviously, a lot was expected after the sheer brilliance of 'If I should fall from grace with God', and for the very first time, I felt a bit disappointed with something that the band had released.

I was actually due to travel south, on the train, to visit my old hotel comrades on the day the album was released, so I first bought the cassette version so I could play it on my new fancy Walkman. Hearing an album from a band that you adore, for the first time, is a really exciting prospect, so I got comfortable and settled down to it, this time without Jem Finer's scary stare. The standout track on the album at the first listen was 'White City', a MacGowan penned song about the long ago demolished Greyhound Stadium in West London, a short track with a catchy tune and superb lyrics. There's a line in the song that goes "The torn up ticket stubs, from a hundred thousand mugs" – well that line certainly applies to me, Shane! As we'll find out about later... The rest of the album contained some songs that I knew would grow on me; however there were a few that I found totally un-Pogue like, one of which was utterly embarrassing! 'Blue Heaven' was composed by Philip Chevron and Darryl Hunt. It's the worst Pogues track in history in my opinion. It sounds like Philip and Darryl have been hanging out with the Wham boys for this one, and really, if they were feeling creative, they should have left this song firmly in their camp camp.

Unbeknown to us fans, I think it would be fair to say that The Pogues' main songwriter, Shane MacGowan, was, by all accounts, not firing on all cylinders any more, hence the other members of the band contributed more to this album than they had with the previous three. This record felt less Irish than the others and certainly felt over produced.

As I played the album more though, a few other classics shone through. 'Misty Morning, Albert Bridge' had been released previously as a single, written by 'scary' Jem Finer; it's a real classy piece of music. There was a 12" vinyl promo single of this superb song released in colourful Hibs emerald green vinyl, with a shamrock on the label – very nice indeed. The song is a tale about how Jem misses his wife Marcia whilst on tour; it's a cracker. I actually managed to sneak a pre release listen of this track. A music paper had published a phoneline that you could ring, for a ridiculous price per minute, so you could have a listen to the Pogues' latest offering. I had one of those phonecards (remember them?) and to use the credit up, I phoned up for a listen of the forthcoming single. The sound on the phone, of course, did the song no justice whatsoever – what did I expect? At least there was no heavy breathing provided by the likes of Terry Woods, the band's mandolin player, or him telling tall tales of working in a pet shop and stroking all the pussies...!

'London You're A Lady', the last track on the album, written by Shane is a favourite of mine; the lyrics are clever, comparing London to a woman. I've read on occasions how certain people think this song is disappointing which intrigues me somewhat – there's plenty of disappointing stuff on this album, but for me not on this track.

'Boat Train', again by Shane, tells the hilarious tale of a journey from London up to the ferry at Holyhead at typical Pogues breakneck speed. 'Gartloney Rats' by Terry Woods is a toe tapping rammy with a lot of Irishness present this time – most welcome.

The album, I suppose, was just not so easy on the ear as their previous ones. It was the first time I found myself skipping tracks that I didn't care for too much, a problem I'd never encountered before when listening to The Pogues. As I stated earlier, even the B sides of the singles were outstandingly good. The band, however, do not turn into a crap one overnight. Their strength in versatility is somewhat amazing, in their career they've probably covered every type of music you could classify, such is their collective strength as musicians. I personally think that they have a unique sound, something that makes them recognisable in their own right.

Also, let's be positive: a new album would ultimately mean a tour, new singles released in all their differing formats for me to track down and collect, and lots of coverage in the music and national press. Mind you, I remember reading an article in a music paper, regarding a Pogues concert I'd been to, and the writer of the article telling the nation that Shane might have been drunk and consequently the gig was awful! Shane? Drunk? Surely not! This article made my blood boil, the quill-dragger in question must've got his dick caught in his zip that day, he really should have gone to review an Erasure concert or something like that. The gig I was at was a huge success, band and audience as one; this tit head's opinion was not the end of the world, but annoying just the same, a real injustice to the boys indeed. These sort of reviews were never far away from Pogues concerts – you'd think that if it wasn't the reviewer's cup of tea, then he or she might gauge the audience reaction for a wee bit of guidance, perhaps.

Shane's looks at this time had taken a goofy change for the worse, what with a crap beard and, even worse, acid house shirts that he was wearing. I'd much preferred his big coat and bowler hat look that I'd tried to copy, with mixed results.

I had a great time visiting my old muckers in Surrey, and was still a bit confused when I travelled back to Perth, in regards to where my future lay. There was another wee trip looming though...one to really look forward to.

PENNY WHISTLE IN SZEKESFEHERVAR

During my time at home, I experienced a wonderful adventure, when three of my friends and I had decided to follow Hibs to the away leg of their first match in the UEFA Cup that season. Eddie 'the Gazelle, beer belly' Edwards, Gavin 'Useless C' Black, Davo (yes, him again) and I had decided that wherever the Hibs were playing, we'd be going, no excuses. On the day of the cup draw I was at work. I made my way to the public telephone and called Davo, who had been listening to the radio for the draw.

"Videoton," he said.

"What's that?" I replied – didn't know what to expect for an answer, but I thought he might be randomly talking about something to tape programmes off the TV on, or to play Pogues videos, that, incidently, I starred in – did I tell you about that? He tells me that's who Hibs are playing, and they come from Szekesfehervar, that's in Hungary. Fuckin' hell! Hungary. I knew nothing about Hungary and have to admit that I grabbed a map and had a look to see where it actually was. A deal's a deal though – it was confirmed amongst my comrades that indeed we would be going, no matter what it took.

We decided to travel from Perth to Budapest by train, all apart from negotiating the Channel at Dover, that particular hurdle being overcome by ferry. Beginning our journey with an overnight train to London, a few of the other Perth Hibees gave us a rousing boozy send off from the Railway Tavern, and off we went, ready for our great adventure.

I took with me a penny whistle, the kind that Spider Stacy from the Pogues has made famous. I'd been dabbling in trying to play the damned thing; I was trying to master Spider's classic instrumental 'The Repeal of The Licensing Laws'. I could play the first part of the tune no problem; however the fluidity of my playing soon petered out, rather miserably, so I just played the bit I knew, over and over, when the notion came over me to do so.

Spirits were sky high on the night train to London, plenty of sherries were consumed, and amongst the dubious in-carriage entertainment we supplied for our no doubt unappreciative fellow travellers was a game of solo sing-song. Each of the four of us had to stand up, hic, and sing a song from start to finish. Ed the gazelle sang 'Yesterday', that very famous well known song by those well dodgy, one hit Liverpudlian legends The Cockroaches. Davo sang a catchy punk song by the Mow Mows, Gavin attempted something by the Stone Roses and I sang the absolute worst version of The Pogues' 'White City' that you've ever heard in your life! Clearly, no one in our vicinity was getting any shut eye. We reached London early morning and went for a wash in the Station lavvies. Tube to Victoria, train to Dover and the ferry over to Oostende.

Gavin was by this time almost matching my standard on the penny whistle. I wanted to keep it that way, so the whistle was hidden for a while, just in case he could progress further. Gavin was a good bit younger than the rest of us; when we drank, Gav used to start like an express train, always finishing his first two pints before everyone else, then calling us all pussies for drinking so slow. He was soon blootered though, yes, long before the rest of us, he was legendary for fucking things up, and this was always followed by a wee song from his pals. It went like this: "Pee pee pee pee pee pee pee pee pee pee, pee pee pee pee pee pee, P, pee pee pee pee pee, P, pee pee pee pee pee, pee pee pee pee pee pee, P P pee pee pee pee pee, pee pee pee, pee pee pee pee P pee!" What on earth is that all about? Well, it's actually meant to be the theme tune from 'Some mother's do 'ave 'em' the one with Frank Spencer, who always fucked things up, played by Michael Crawford, him that used to say "Oooh, Betty!".

The ironic thing is that Gavin, to be fair, has probably outshone all his Perth Hibs mates when it comes to career and earning capacity. He's a nurse on the oil rigs and is doing very well, thank you. Mind you, his cousin, Andy Thompson, once told me that all the 'nursing' duties he performs on the rigs, for the big hairy bears, is to tend to the cuts they all seem to have at the end of their penises. Don't worry Gav, your secret's safe with me – I don't believe what Andy said anyway!

The train at Oostende was taking us all the way into Budapest, scheduled to arrive lunchtime, next day. All in all, the journey from Perth to Budapest was to take us 39 hours. We travelled through Germany, it was getting dark, and at one of the stations we stopped at, this dodgy looking geezer got on, and settled in our carriage quite near to where we were sitting. He looked just like a baddie out of a James Bond film, thick glasses, raincoat, briefcase, and clearly not happy. We started a game of fantasy, that he was out to get the Hibs fans, before they got to Hungary, and before long we'd whipped ourselves up into a total state of self inflicted terror! We'd decided that he must have been a colleague of Hitler's, who was quite obviously a Hearts fan, but no worries, 'Good' would prevail in the end, scary Bond baddie, Hitler and Hearts would all be defeated! And indeed, Bond baddie saw sense, bowing out at some station further east, in Germany, sensing defeat with his task, and leaving the four Hibby warriors to support their team in the forthcoming European battle that was before them.

We had booked some sleeping accommodation on the train; these were called couchettes. The guard showed us to our sleeping quarters, which consisted of a berth with six beds, each side having like a triple bunk arrangement. We took up, obviously, four of these bunks in a couchette – the other two were already occupied – and we 'settled' down for the night. Except Davo and I never settled. We never do in situations like this. Davo was on fire, telling us and the so far two unknown couchette sleepers that we would be all rounded up any time soon, our 'papers' would be demanded for scrutiny AND if things didn't go well, we would be put before Hitler's Bond baddie's firing squad, and they would sort us out! Hardly a fuckin' lullaby, but very entertaining; Davo was in his element.

Eventually, we succumbed to a wee bit of sleep – clearly, our papers were ok. I think Davo and I had a total of about four hours' sleep between the night train from Perth and our arrival in Budapest. We awoke in the morning, somewhere in Austria. Much to our surprise, the other two sleepers in the couchette were ladies, one of them a young one. She was very confident, the way she changed her clothes, in front of us four guys – you could have heard a pin drop! We ventured out back into the seating carriages for the final furlong of our journey into Budapest.

Davo, Gav and I had a common interest in finding some female company, if we were lucky enough to come across some, whilst we were on our adventure. To be fair to the Gazelle, he stated clearly, that he would be "merely browsing". Towards the end of the journey, two young lassies got on the train and sat next to us. We were like flies round a honey pot. They were both lookers, so, without further ado, it was out with the tin whistle (the REAL one!) and Repeal of the Licensing Laws, first part, was played for the new audience. There was no reaction. I wondered what they would have thought if Spider had been playing? We assumed that the two girls were Austrian or Hungarian, so they wouldn't understand what we were saying. So, led by Gavin (God's gift to women, didn't you know, except that he just isn't!), we started talking about what we liked about them. The girls didn't bat an eyelid, so the conversation continued, and ultimately went downhill. A short time later we heard the two girls talk to each other, in yep, you've guessed it, perfect English! They actually thought we were pretty funny, as well as pathetic, and were not fussed too much about what we were saying... I must state though, they were not up for anything!

Once the train shuddered over the border, into Hungary, the police came on board, to see that, indeed, our passports and visas were all in order. The police chappies looked the business, so we were on our best behaviour now. However, we did hear a story, from a Hibs fan we met later in the week, that when their train crept over the border, one drunken hibee reached for a policeman's gun, took it from the actual holster and then had a pretend moment or two as James Bond himself! Remarkably, the policeman was laughing, taking it all in his stride, almost enjoying this particular game of high jinx. One can only assume that the safety catches on the pistols were of the ultimate highest quality.

Eventually, we arrived in downtown Budapest. It seemed like any capital city really, busy busy, traffic, people, and of course, at the entrance to the station, taxis. We approached a taxi, Gazelle leading the way, to take us to an agency of sorts, that provided information about accommodation for visitors. The taxi driver was an old man, string held up his trousers, and he gratefully accepted our journey to this agency. Stringy Breeks' taxi was rattling all over the place, but he got us there. When Gazelle asked what the fare was, we were pleasantly surprised that it was very cheap, considering the relatively long time we were in his vehicle. Stringy Breeks received a good tip for his troubles, everybody happy then. After we got our accommodation sorted, we ordered another taxi to take us to our digs. We discovered early in this second journey that, much to our surprise, we weren't even one minute away from the railway station! Stringy Breeks had managed to put one over the ignorant tourists. We all agreed though, fair play to him, and it was still cheap; however, this taxi we were in now took us even further and was even cheaper. I'm convinced that Stringy Breeks dined well that evening.

Our accommodation turned out to be a large room in a Hungarian family flat. It had a couple of beds and a couple of sofas which suited us just fine. I think it's funny how when you're younger, digs like this are no problem at all, yet in later years, your standards go up, almost becoming snobbish about where you lay your head – that's true in my case anyway! Once we settled in, we headed off in the hunt for some local sherry. We were all pretty knackered so we didn't stray too far from our digs, and settled in a boozer that was like a wine bar. We had a couple of hours in the gaff, then headed back to have a kip. We were all starving – our own fault I may add, food being way down on the list of our priorities – so we decided that we would raid the kitchen of our new digs, no mistake. It was very disrespectful of us to think this way, especially when we discovered what the crack was in our newly acquired abode. The family we were staying with had actually given up their living quarters, and were sleeping on the hard kitchen floor because of this. I found this out to my cost, when trying to get into the kitchen, to be met by a locked door and angry grunts coming from the other side of this very door. The Hungarian family had made way for us 'wealthy' Westerners; the whole episode was a sobering thought, quite literally. We found it very sad that the Hungarian family had to do this in their own home to make ends meet; they were truly wonderful people who made us very welcome, despite our excitable and boisterous behaviour.

We did manage to go for a slap up meal the next day, at a place called The Berlin Bar. They had an extensive menu, with about 40 main courses to choose from. Our waiter was eyeing up our bright green Hibs tops – we couldn't give them away, but we did present him with a Hibs hat, and we saw him show his new trinket to the chef. Back to the menu, out of the vast number of main courses, in fact only three dishes were actually available, but it was all good, a brilliant experience; we wined and dined for the rest of the evening for about a fiver a head. Next night we tried somewhere else. Gavin had the phrase book on the go for this particular menu and was giving us a wee lecture about how good the Hungarians were at pastries and desserts. Very impressive, Gav! Davo and Gav are vegetarians. The fantastic dessert that Gavin had sussed out was ordered, presented, and found to be a revolting curd like substance, with big fuck off pieces of bacon right the way through it! After three: pee pee pee pee pee pee pee pee peee pee!

On the day of the match, we travelled by train from Budapest to Szekesfehervar, about an hour's journey, with the locals. In our emerald green Hibs tops we stuck out like the proverbial sore thumbs; every man and their dogs found us quite fascinating, their stares focussed on us with much curiosity. Everything in Hungary outside Budapest was grey and drab. When we got off the train at our destination, however, we were met with the unmistakable sound of screeching tyres, coming from a Lada that appeared into view, containing three Hibs supporters clearly under the influence of something nice, having a whale of a time in a probable easy-hired vehicle, fucking hilarious!

We made our way into town, and settled in a hotel bar that only had the Hibs Squad residing at this very establishment! As the day wore on, the Hotel bar swelled in numbers with more supporters enjoying the occasion and also, for sure, the unorthodox location we all found ourselves in. We enjoyed a bit of banter with the Hibs team, Paul Kane in particular, a Hibs player that us Perth boys knew personally – he was indeed the president of our supporters' branch, 'The Perth Paul Kanos' if you don't mind! We had a banner with us for the match which read: "PERTH PAUL KANOS, PERTH TO SZEKESFEHERVAR...WE MADE IT!" When 'Kano' first saw our banner, he was clearly delighted, and rounded up his team mates to view our graffitied cloth. Happy days. On to the match, and for once, our team did not disappoint, winning the game by three goals to nil. Having travelled so far to be there, it really was the stuff of schoolboy dreams.

After the match, it was back to the same hotel. There was a nightclub down in the basement, where fans and team congregated as one – what a night we had! At one point, Davo and I were dancing with the German referee from the match. He had sent one of the Videoton players off during the game, and he gave me the red card he had used for this task, kindly signed it for me, then got stuck into his beer and his manic dancing – mental!

Later on, players and fans went out of the hotel, for a wee recce of the town. Both parties were very well lubricated at this point, but there was no abrasion present whatsoever. Now, I thought that football fans had a bad reputation for travelling abroad and getting up to mischief of varying degrees. Nah! I think that the Hibs fans were somewhat angelic compared to the players and their behaviour. The Hibees players were openly swigging out of champagne bottles, whilst trying to negotiate walking over parked cars and pulling off the odd windscreen wiper on the way, just to maintain balance, of course. It has to be said that us supporters thought all this was just brilliant; it was definitely a case of all naughty boys together, on tour. Was it was like that with the Pogues – without the football obviously – what was their behaviour like on tour, I wonder?

We were hanging out with the likes of Andy Goram, Steve Archibald, John Collins (who incidently pissed on Davo's jeans in the bog!). Keith Houchen was also in attendance, he of 'diving header for Coventry City in the FA Cup Final against Spurs' fame. Davo and I gave him a new nickname of 'Brown bottle' – this from the Viz comic character. Brown bottle was the hilarious story of a Geordie (like Keith Houchen) who turned into a nightmare drunk when partaking in too much Newcastle Brown, saying things like "I love ya, yer me best mate". Naturally all of this went over his head, but he was happy to sign our match programmes as per his new name, being quite amused, even if blissfully ignorant, of the whole brown bottle thing.

As our memorable night drew to a close, a taxi was sourced to take us back to Budapest, and to our dwelling room within the family home. The journey took about an hour, like the train, and cost next to nothing, even if the driver did go round the block a few times in Hungary's capital city to boost the fare. After all, we were fair game for sure, so no problem there; the cabbie got his 'tourist rate' tariff on the go, everybody happy, and what a night, a brilliant time was had by all – probably one of the most enjoyable experiences I've ever had at the football, in such a way out location.

Next day, I had a massive hangover, so decided to try and revive myself by having a bath. It didn't work; in fact, the hot water didn't agree with me at all, I was in even bigger trouble when I started uncontrollably spewing, whilst still in the bath! My stomach was out of control; it was one of those times when the spewing was going all the way to the bile, fucking awful, even if self inflicted. To make matters considerably worse, I really thought I was hallucinating when two young girls passed right through the bathroom I was in, to witness me retching and spewing. I obviously hadn't locked the door, and, unbeknown to any of us, there was a further letting room at the back of the flat, where the two young lasses were staying, and they had to venture through the bathroom to get to their digs. I don't know what nationality they were, but they gave me a polite wave and "hello". I just sat there, in my vomit infused bathwater – a right fucking sight I must have been right enough! When I eventually sorted myself out and got back to our room, the lads were howling with laughter at my bathroom frolics.

Talking of hangovers, me and Davo in particular didn't exactly help ourselves. We were in a bar in the centre of Budapest and decided to have a go at various colourful optics displayed on the wall of the hostelry. We weren't really communicating very well with the barman, except to point at the particular brew we wanted to try. God knows what we were drinking, but it was all going down the hatch with the minimum of fuss. One of the optics we pointed to though made the barman look at us with some concern. We could understand well enough that he really, strongly did not recommend this particular potion in the bottle, so, of course, this made us more curious and determined to give it a try – that's usually how it works, isn't it? Our barman friend tried again to put us off; however a couple of shots of this stuff was eventually poured and served. I went first... JESUS! I felt every single drop of this stuff go all the way down to my must-have-been-crapping-it stomach! Firewater as a description doesn't even come close. Of course, my face must have said it all regarding how I felt about my experience – I had turned into an expert gurner! The barman's face had a "I fucking well told you so" expression on it. Davo's turn next, same again, a bit of horror on his face as the molten liquid hit the spot, then Davo brought the house down by asking for "another one"! None of us were expecting that. I politely declined joining him, but Davo had earned the barman's respect, big style – what an alkie! The stuff in question turned out to be Slivovitz, apparently a local plum brandy of sorts, except this was a special one, designed to knock you into the middle of next week. Davo was so impressed by this latest alcoholic discovery that he sourced a bottle in a shop, to take home to bonnie Scotland with him. Hmm. I just wonder what a certain Shane MacGowan would have made of the Slivovitz adventure?

Our journey home was pretty straightforward; we did sample some neat Russian vodka however, courtesy of some Hibs fans we met up with on the train. This was rough as well, but nothing even close to the fare being served up in THAT Hungarian bar!

We were all back home, in Scotland, by the Saturday, to welcome our Hibees heroes when they took to the pitch in the home game v Dunfermline, to applaud them for their European exploits. It was so ironic though, that the fans that were present in Hungary during the tomfoolery, drinking and windscreen wiper raping escapades, were expecting the team to be modern, professional footballers again. Aye right!

A few weeks later, I'd been at the football again, this time at an Edinburgh derby, Hibs v Hearts. When me and the boys got back to Perth and partook in the usual Saturday night boozing, I very suddenly got a sense that I just wasn't enjoying this lifestyle bubble that I was in any more. I was sick of the routine that the drink had become, week in week out, whether it was at the football, at the pool nights or whatever else was on the go.

My contract at the whisky factory with its fictional Salmon fish was up. I had previously hoped it would carry on beyond its six month period, but it didn't, and in the end I was glad, as I wasn't really progressing in my career as such. So, back to the night in the pub, after the Hearts game, I decided there and then that I was leaving Perth, hopefully to head back down south and join Philip Borthwick's kitchen brigade once again, get my head down and get on. It would be a wrench to leave Mum and Dad for sure; my mother actually saw it coming – when I told her she wasn't surprised at all. Luckily for me, Mr Borthwick did agree to take me back. There would probably be more chance of seeing The Pogues in London again, it had been a while, and I was definitely needing a fix of this kind. Also, living with Mum and Dad, and the predominately male company I was keeping, limited my opportunities in the girlie department.

The following Saturday I was on the train again, except this train wasn't taking me to wherever Hibs were playing that day. It was taking me to London, with a few connections to Surrey, to further my career. After my journey, arrived and settled, I was looking forward to emptying my bags for sure.

WHITE PAWS

On my arrival back at The Anugraha Hotel and conference centre, I was made to feel really welcome. Chef Borthwick took me for a quick pint as soon as I got there, and I told him it was my intention to work hard and try and get promoted, if and when a senior position became available within his kitchen brigade. I stayed in the hotel for a few nights, before moving back into my old flat in Staines, this time into the smallest room, as I was now well down in the pecking order for the best room – I was the 'new' boy after all. I settled in no bother, and really started to enjoy my work again. The hotel catered for large numbers, and the job satisfaction coming from this I always found to be amazing. There had been some fresh faces added to the kitchen staff since my departure – all was good.

There was a Pogues gig looming too, thank fuck, I could sure do with some of that; so I organised to meet Chelsea Steve for their forthcoming show at Brixton Academy. When we were at Brixton for The Pogues, we always arranged to meet at The Wimpy bar. Brixton was still a bit of a scary place back then, so we played safe rather than meeting in a boozer. Steve heartily partook in the fare at The Wimpy, as did I (on a much lesser scale). You don't really see many Wimpys these days. Wimpy restaurants were primarily burger joints, but they did boast waitress service – you got your order taken, your desired nourishment recorded in the waitresses' order pad, that had a pen attached to it with string, traditionally brilliant... sometimes I'm easy pleased! After our bellies were full, we would venture into the venue, we would have a beer then, and get ourselves nicely in the mood for an evening of Pogues magic! And they did not disappoint. It was great to be back down South, back in the thick of things concert-wise. There was always so much more going on in London, especially as far as The Pogues were concerned. Around this time, the band's stage was made to look like a living room, with a big couch, a fridge and various other props; there was no gimmicking about their music though, it was still shit hot quality wise – best night out in town, I'm tellin' ya!

After 'Peace and love', The Pogues' fourth studio album, they had released a single called 'Yeah, yeah, yeah, yeah, yeah'. It was a real one off, a dab at Northern Soul by the band – they really could turn their hand to just about anything. The single was a cracker, backed with a more traditional piece in the shape of 'The Limerick Rake'. I thought the single would be successful in the charts; it was catchy and not complicated, as my boss pointed out to me when he said "Have you heard that new song by that band you are mad on? It's called yeah, yeah, yeah, yeah, yeah, yeah, yeah, yeah, yeah, yeah..." The single didn't really trouble the top 40 though, peaking just outside, but hey, at the end of the day, that doesn't really matter, as the charts target young girls, most of whom Keith has shagged, the stallion.

Steve meanwhile, really enjoyed telling me that he actually appeared on the video for "Yeah, yeah...". There was an announcement on the radio one day, telling any Pogues fans who were in the vicinity of a certain location, to get down there pronto, and help them make this video. Psychedelic dress was recommended, so Chelsea Steve and a couple of his mates answered the call so to speak, and got himself on the video for the single. He appears right at the end, swaying about trendily to the tune, looking like something out of the Top of the Pops audience of old; he had shaved his coupon, brushed his hair, looked like a nice boy, probably even smelt nice, smoothie Steve! I'm actually just fucking jealous, as I was oblivious to the whole episode regarding the Pogues video, but of course, I HAD appeared on one previously...

I managed to get home for Christmas. This was a real bonus, as us chefs are usually working on Shane MacGowan's Birthday (yes, it really is). My mate Les, who was staying in The South at the time, kindly offered me a lift up the road with him and his wife Lorraine, and with Roxy, their boxer dog. Roxy and I were in the back, and Roxy was not for a quiet overnight journey home – I was fucking knackered by the time we hit Perth, but I'm glad to say that my bags were still intact!

My mother in particular was disappointed that I had gone back down south, so it was nice to spend Christmas with her and Dad, and see the boys of course. I still knew though that my decision to move back was the right one.

Back to work after the festivities, this time on the train (without Roxy) and on my return I got together with a girl called Paula. Paula hailed from Northampton, and worked in the same kitchen as me – hardly an ideal situation I suppose, but we handled it ok. Paula lived in a staff flat just round the corner from mine; she was a resourceful girl and even had a little Peugeot car – very handy indeed. Her mum and dad back in Northampton had divorced, and I got the impression Paula had to look out for herself quite early in life, but she was clearly doing all right – she knew the right side of a five pound note, that's for sure; she even had a little system of charging folk a small sum if she gave them a lift in the motor. The Chancellor of the Exchequer didn't have a look in with Paula!

So, with my luggage now suitably settled, all was well. Paula and I enjoyed many days out, thanks to her car, and yes, I had to pay my share of the petrol, of course. Her music taste was extremely limited though; her favourite band was Erasure, Jesus! Paula and her pal had bought tickets to go and see the Erasure 'concert' take place at The London Docklands Arena. I had to give this one a miss, but her pal's boyfriend Derek and I did accompany the girls to their gig on London Transport, departing to a nearby boozer for the evening whilst they watched the Erasure singer swinging his hips. Whilst Derek and I were in the pub, a ticket tout came in and wasted no time in trying to punt two premium tickets for the huge sum of £1.00 each. This offer was enthusiastically turned down, as was the second offer, two for £1.00. The frustrated tout geezer took a seat with us, and explained that he'd had his fingers severely burnt that evening, hardly shifting any tickets at all. Ah well, there's got to be some justice in there somewhere for true fans and concert goers. Couldn't wait to tell Paula though, that the tickets were going for a quid – she'd paid way over the odds for her one at face value, she almost screamed more than she had watching the Erasure singer gyrating, JESUS!

The Chef called me at my flat one late morning and told me that he'd be picking me up in ten minutes. I thought I was in trouble. I was dressed in a pair of jeans and a green 'Ordnahone' t shirt – this was a Pogues fan club t shirt, fucking smart it was too. Chef pulled up outside my flat with David Mundell – he was manager of the hotel we worked in at the time, and had been present in both The Station Hotel, Perth and in Ilkley. David was driving in his smart BMW, there was a receptionist, Amanda, also in the car, and they were all dressed as dapper as the sparkling BMW. As I got in the car, I realised straight away that I was not so sparkling, even if I thought my t shirt was the dogs. We drove into central London, more specifically to Kensington High Street. I didn't have a clue what was going on, and when I asked, they just laughed and said not to worry about it. I was initially worried as I was scheduled to start work early that afternoon and I just wasn't going to make it time-wise, but, I thought, the head Chef was in the car and so was the Manager, so surely, surely, I couldn't get into trouble for being late for my shift.

The BMW was parked, and we walked a while in the brilliant sunshine, and turned into Phillimore Gardens, just off the High Street, and into a bar/restaurant called Sticky Fingers. The four of us went to the bar, Chef started ordering up drinks; I still didn't know what was going on, so he ordered me a pint of Budweiser on my behalf. I didn't drink lager, or light coloured beer, so I wasn't really looking forward to this draught Budweiser. I had a gulp, then another – it was cold and absolutely fucking delicious. I got the shock of my life with how gorgeous it was; it slipped down an absolute treat. Proper draught Budweiser back then was really quite something when it came to quality, leisurely refreshment; hardly anyone does it right nowadays, which is very unfortunate.

We had quite a few more tall fizzy glasses of this very easy to quaff stuff, and whilst nothing was still being said, it was clear that I wasn't going to work, so I relaxed nicely into the balmy afternoon in Kensington. Sticky Fingers was Bill Wyman's place, he of Rolling Stones bass-playing fame. There was some amazing

Stones memorabilia on the walls of the place, good sounds being played, with plenty of Stones numbers of course, and this wonderful draught Budweiser. We went through to the spacious, air conditioned restaurant, and we ordered food, the full works: starter, main and sweet. The food was as good as the beer, typically American fare, ribs, steaks, burgers and a few house specialities. I had ribs to start, followed by a steak, and a sticky pudding to finish. The meal was faultless; this was some place that Mr Wyman had. Chef and David had treated me and Amanda to a day out, with a few beers and a scoff; they did this now and again for certain staff members as a thank you for services at the hotel. I must have been doing something right, it was a nice touch, and discovering this brilliant establishment started something of a national treasure for a lot of hotel staff. We still go to Sticky Fingers to this day.

I had made another discovery. However, this one was not to be so sweet, savoury or as thirst-quenchingly good as the one nestling just off Kensington High Street in London. Paula and I were downtown in Staines. We had this notion of going into a William Hill bookies, to have a bet. I really can't recall what made us do this, I'd no idea at this time how to put a bet on in such an establishment, but the second that I darkened that bookies' door was to have a huge bearing on my future, even if I didn't realise it just then. There was a greyhound race almost ready for the off, Brough Park was the venue; the event was televised in the bookies' shop.

We looked at the names of the canine athletes about to perform. We liked 'White Paws', he was number 6. The odds were 3/1 for White Paws to win the race; he was the favourite. It all sounds so simple. And it was. Me and Paula put a tenner on each, for White Paws to win. I checked with the bloke behind the counter if our betting slip was ok and he rattled it through the till and took our cash without batting an eyelid.

When the hare at Brough Park started running, a bell rang in the bookies to signify no more bets. The traps opened up, and White Paws emerged like a streak of lightning, hit the front and he stayed there, on the outside, all the way round, in front, right to the finish line and beyond! Fuck me, that meant that we'd won, won the bet, we were going to get good money for White Paws' superb exploits at Brough Park that afternoon. After a short, almost nervous wait, Mr Bookie did indeed give us 80 of Lizzie's folding vouchers for the slip we'd filled in earlier, with White Paws' name on it. Fuckin' easy, this betting lark, fuckin' easy! The buzz of the magnificent hound that we had backed, crossing the line first was really tremendous. I could understand, clearly, what all the fuss was about, in Shane MacGowan's lyrics in his brilliant song 'Bottle Of Smoke' when his nag came in at twenty fuckin' five to one, and Spider telling it to hurry along, "C'mon you bastard!"

We walked out of the bookies and I actually found it hard to believe that the guy really gave us the money; it felt brilliant. And before you could say "Stewards enquiry", that was me hooked. Not so brilliant! The bookies' office gradually became a regular haunt of mine, usually on my own, so nobody could see what I was up to. I was to quickly learn, and realise to my cost, that it was not, indeed, easy at all, this betting gig. One Saturday afternoon, I finished work and headed straight to the bookies, the bets were getting serious, and any lucky touch I thought I may have had, was proving to be somewhat elusive to say the least. I lost a lot of money that afternoon, about a fortnight's wages. I was really lucky that my digs came as part of my salary with my job, but it was a long two weeks until pay day came along again. I was dining mainly on cornflakes in the flat, feeling very sorry for myself; it was all part of my bookies controlled diet! I never again bet quite to the extent I did that afternoon; it was real mug punting stuff, trying to recoup your losses. If it's not your day, then it's not your fucking day right enough, a hard lesson to learn.

Paula thought my betting habit was outrageous – understandable considering how much she liked cash – but she enjoyed the White Paws experience to a certain extent, so much so that we started to go to the occasional live Greyhound meeting, on our days off. We went to just about every London Greyhound track there was, and also went to meetings at places like Ramsgate, Bristol, Oxford and Hove. I really enjoyed the live racing, trying, not always successfully, to be a good boy with my stakes and not put on too much. Of course, now and again this betting thing did actually work...

My parents often holidayed in the Merseyside town of Southport.

My dad came across Southport when he attended a course there with his work, and liked it so much, he took Mum for a break there, staying in a holiday flat right on the seafront with an amazing panoramic view – one of his smarter moves. I would describe Southport as an upmarket seaside town. It boasts a pier and a funfair, and the town centre has a canopied main shopping area, Lord Street. There's a market hall, and just behind this, there was a quality record shop that unfortunately has since bitten the dust. The bars and restaurants were hosted by friendly Lancashire local folks. Southport deservedly attracted lots of holidaymakers and was invaded by Scousers mostly at weekends, when the weather was good. Mum loved Southport, especially the Gala Bingo Hall; she would always say that it was more "big time" than the bingo at home.

I first visited Southport to spend some time with my parents when they were down for a visit. With me down in Surrey, Southport was almost a halfway meeting point for me, and them coming down from Perth. Alex, the mate from work (who you might recall had some local skinhead mates and were at the college) and his orange Volkswagen Beetle, were taking me to Euston to catch a train to Liverpool, then onto a connection to Southport. Alex was a brilliant and daring driver in Central London, but we were running late (through no fault of his, that was all my doing) and even with the odd one-way street negotiated the wrong way, I didn't have a hope in hell of catching my train. So I got the next one, but when I arrived in Lime Street station in Liverpool, I discovered that the last train to Southport, from Central Station just down the road, had gone, without me. What to do? Have to be a taxi then!

I had the grand sum of £15 on me, but I did not even think about doing a runner from a taxi – as if I would do that! I really had no idea how far Southport was from Liverpool, but I started talking to this old boy, who was waiting for a fare in his taxi, on the station rank. I told him I was going to Southport and asked how much it would cost. He said it would be "about" £25. I said to him that I only had £15. Quick as a flash he said "Get in!" As the diesel engine of the Black Taxi grunted into life and we rolled out of the Station car park, it did cross my mind if this would indeed be 'the revenge of the taxi driver' since I had been previously a nuisance, to say the least to that particular profession. I needn't have worried though; the cabbie was a great bloke with a real thick Scouse accent and a personality to match. It was a rainy night (but we weren't in Soho) and it became apparent that my £15 was indeed taking me a long way in this taxi.

We got to the outskirts of Southport, and Scouser Sammy asks me, "Where do you want dropped off?"

Erm, well, I didn't bloody know, did I? I'd arranged for Mum and Dad to meet me at Southport Railway Station at an approximate time. Fuck me, how DID we survive before mobile phones? I did manage to remember that their holiday flat was overlooking the seafront, so the cabbie headed for that area – it was a start. Unbelievably, luckily, amazingly, when we reached the start of the seafront, I looked up at the first whitewashed building, and right on the top floor, I saw my mother, looking out of the window, no doubt looking for her travel time unreliable son. What a welcome sight that was; lady luck was shining on me that dark night, that's for sure! The cabbie was genuinely happy for me, he got his fifteen squid – yes, I did pay him – and my mother came down and met me at the front communal door of the flats. I enjoyed Southport as much as my parents did; it was a real vibrant place, and was to become, over the years, a really special location for my family.

A great thing Paula did was to push me to learn to drive. I passed my test, and we bought a car together, 50/50. It was a Black Suzuki Swift, with fancy headlights, and we got our money's worth, it was a great car.

My first real journey of any note in the Suzuki was travelling up to Southport again to spend some time with Ma and Pa. I set off after my shift finished in the afternoon, but made a detour to the bookies' shop before I started the journey proper. Keith and I had discussed a bet that we were intending to partake in. It was a treble on the football, in the English league cup. We wanted Arsenal to beat Leicester City, Crystal Palace to beat Hartlepool and Sheffield United to beat Wigan. Keith placed the bet before he came to work, the day I was leaving after my shift for Southport. The stake was a ridiculous £300 shared between the two of us. The odds for this treble to come up were evens. I couldn't resist a fly visit to the bookies for a bet on the last horse race of the day, before my journey – this proved to be a winner, a good omen for the football bet, then? Hope so!

I set off for Southport, enjoying some sounds on the car stereo – a real perk, I think,in travelling by car, as music in this intimate environment is just the best, it just hits the spot perfectly – just the way I feel about it. However. A little later on in my journey, as I was driving on the M6 through Birmingham, I tuned into the radio and the football, the programme keeping its listeners updated with the latest scores, and ultimately, news of the bet that we had taken the plunge on.

Arsenal were doing all right, winning their game, Crystal Palace were out of sight, murdering Hartlepool. The problem was Sheffield United. No goals at their game with Wigan, which was no fucking use to me and Keithy. Ironically, my team Hibs were playing at Ibrox that night, against my favourite other team, Rangers (aye, right!) and were doing rather well, as I recall, winning by two goals to one. I have to admit, that for once, the Hibs performance was secondary to the investment that was made in Morris Road branch of William Hill's in Staines that afternoon.

As I neared my destination, I picked up a local radio station that was concentrating on Wigan's performance that evening. I'd missed the fact that Sheffield United had indeed scored in their match, winning one-nil, thus meaning, as things stood, that Keith and I were, indeed, in the money, honey! The game, however, was not finished yet. This radio station was providing live commentary on the last five minutes of the match, and I was about five minutes away from Southport town centre.

The last attack in the cup tie that would map out my mood for the rest of the evening was described with great passion on the radio: "And Wigan come so close from the corner, the downward header from (Wigan player not remembered) hits the post." Fucking Hell. "And there goes the final whistle." Yeeeaaaaahhhhs! The relief, more than anything, was immense! Keith and I had won the battle with the Morris Street bookie. As I drove into Lord Street, Southport, it was my duty to phone Keith, who I knew would be at work. I parked the Suzuki and got some change out for the phone box, dialled the hotel number, and asked for the Chef's office. The extension rang a few times, then Keith Clifford Williams gingerly answered the phone: "Hello".

I said "Who the fuck do you think you are, Lionel Ritchie?"

"Calum, just tell me what the fuck happened in the football tonight, please?"

I said, "WE WON!" The earpiece of the phone was distorted for a few seconds, such was the ferocity of Keith's roar. It was a great feeling to tell him that we were in the lolly, for a wee while at least. For the record, Hibs actually lost their game 4-2, but that didn't do hellish much to spoil how I was feeling.

My folks were staying in the same holiday flat that I had fortuitously found on my previous visit to Southport, and I had arranged to meet them in a traditional pub that they liked, situated just round the corner. I parked the Suzuki and walked excitedly towards the pub door, eager to see Mum and Dad, mood buoyed further by the win at the bookies. As I walked through the door, I saw my parents straight away. They looked pleased to see me, and as if that wasn't enough, the jukebox was giving it big licks, about halfway through 'The body of an American' which just happens to be performed by my favourite band. If Carlsberg did car journeys to Merseyside...

For someone who had a wee problem with betting, the money from the football win was predictably, steadily, fluttered away, back to where it came from. Between White Paws the greyhound (I won on him a few times) and my weak willpower, I was to be under Mr Bookies' spell for quite a while.

WEMBLEY REVISITED, VIA HELL'S DITCH

My gambling gig was not too clever, that I readily admit; however, I didn't really get into major debt or start to mug old ladies to feed my habit. I was chasing my tail financially though – by that I mean when I got paid, fortnightly, it was already gone, to pay my credit card off, then I started again. I had no savings to talk of, but fuck it, I was young, and enjoying masen; plenty time for saving and thinking of my future later on.

One Saturday, Keith and I had a rare day off together, the hotel being unusually quiet. We launched into a two-man betting marathon, and duelled against each other covering everything, all the sport the television could throw at us – horse racing, football, cricket, rugby, you name it. Sometimes we even bet on how many letters we would get in the post! We took things to extreme levels early evening of that Saturday though, when we found a channel showing a disabled basketball match! "That'll do, I'll pick the team in red!" Before you knew it Keith and I were howling at the TV, 'encouraging' our respective teams to do the business. Ridiculous, I know. Keith came out on top, as he often did when we bet against each other, and yes, I think he was victorious with the disabled basketball.

We would often travel to a greyhound track in the evening, if we had a few bob in our pockets; we'd take turn about at driving. If we were going to Wembley, and Keith was at the wheel, around the North

Circular Road, there were always geezers hanging around the busy traffic light junctions with a bucket of water, and a widow wiper thing. I would secretly try to get the attention of these boys, so they would come to Keith's car, and give his windscreen a once over. Keith's car was always clean – he is actually a very good housekeeper in lots of ways – so his windscreen wasn't needing a wash. It was hilarious watching him waving his hands to try and put Mr Wiper off, but it was always too late, as the soapy water sploshed onto the glass, and Keith would be cursing, as he fumbled in his pockets looking for £1.50, calling me foul and dirty names.

Paula, of course, didn't see the fun side of gambling at all, like I did through my turf accountant tinted glasses. One day we drove down to Crayford dog track in Kent, did the civilised thing of having lunch, then I proceeded to lose some money on the live performing (not mine though) greyhounds. One key thing that gambling punters do is chase their losses – the next bet can bring you back on song, perhaps even put you a little bit in front. Not very often though. Once the Crayford meeting was over, and I was going through that familiar losing feeling, I told Paula that I wanted us to go to the evening greyhound meeting at Walthamstow, due to start in a few hours' time. Walthamstow was my favourite track; alas, it's no longer in use these days. I loved Walthamstow, the atmosphere there was electric. Lots of London geezers attended 'The Stow', especially on a Saturday night. Some of the bets you would see placed would probably be enough to buy a small family car! All this on a doggie who just might not be in the mood!

I always loved driving in the London area; there was always so much to see, so many different areas to go through that all ran into each other; there wasn't much green space in between. When darkness fell over Greater London, the endless lights just seemed to go on forever and ever, just like Shane sang about on his track 'London you're a lady': "Your headdress is a ring of lights, but I would not follow them". Maybe he was trying to tell me something, but the journey from Crayford to Walthamstow was negotiated, a withdrawal was made from a cash machine (a credit card withdrawal) and we were set for an evening's racing and speculation at Walthamstow, – me with notes,

Paula with coins.

I was off to a flyer, first two races done and dusted, two winners, one of them at a very good price. And that was that! No more winners for the TEN remaining races, and I took a financial pounding. On the long drive home, I realised that I really did have a bigger problem with the betting than I may have thought. It was high time I took off those tinted glasses and removed myself as a member from Shane's 'Hundred thousand mugs' in 'White City'. I spoke to Paula about this problem in the car, with the conclusion that I would have to stop betting, and generally not spend any unnecessary money, so I could get back to base, so to speak, with my finances. And I actually managed to do just that, for a good while.

The Pogues were releasing their fifth album, 'Hell's Ditch'. I was naturally really excited about the prospect of this latest offering from MacGowan and Co hitting my turntable. Paula pointed out to me that buying The Pogues' album was an extravagance. Eh? Buying The Pogues' album was a fucking necessity! This is not Erasure we are talking about; a new Pogues album being released should be the first announcement made before the 'Doiyng' on the 10 o'clock news!

So it was down to Our Price (remember them?), the only record shop in Staines, first thing in the morning when the shop doors opened. Vinyl secured, and a walk back to my flat, checking out the artwork of the album on the way. Not the most striking of covers for the record: a map of sorts on the front, with the tracks of the album providing the various locations marked on the map. I don't think many of the album covers actually did the group much justice to the delights that were contained within, with the exception of 'If I should fall from grace with god', where we have a fantastic picture of the band with their instruments, around some antique luggage. The boys look like they've had a bath (and a shave) before this photo shoot; they just ooze cleanliness! You'd still be wary of them though. It's a classic photo, one of my favourites, as are the individual band photos done on the same shoot. I also very much liked the artwork for the single 'A pair of brown eyes' where the band are captured by the lens in very traditional style, MacGowan in big coat and bowler hat (?) with the addition of a powerful doggie, that would have your balls off in a second, under

Spider's grip on his lead.

So, the needle on the record, and the first thing I noticed when 'Sunny Side of the Street' kicked into life was a deterioration in Shane's voice. It wasn't terrible by any means, but it was noticeably weaker than before. Once you heard it a few times though, a Pogues fan can get over the fact his voice is weaker, and you hear it for what it is, enjoy it for sure. I've spoken to many Pogues fans over the years on this very subject, and the vast majority agree with me here; it's just like a short period of readjustment, to where his voice is, at that particular time. The album impressed me though, I knew I would grow to enjoy it more than its predecessor, 'Peace and Love'.

There was a distinct Thailand flavour to this album; apparently, yer man, the vocalist, had discovered the various delights of this particular country and had taken to write a few songs about it all, with fantastic results I would say. 'Sayonara', the second song on the album, was one of those Thai influenced numbers, and it was a cracker, with the immortal line towards the end of the song: "So mother fucker kiss the ground". Basically I thought Shane's songs on the album really stood out, but there were a few that were easily skipped, written by various other members of the band. I really don't want to appear biased or disrespectful to the various contributions made by them, but remember, as I said before, I had no idea at all of what was going on behind the scenes. In Carol Clerk's book, 'Pogue Mahone', which was written and released many years later, the hassles the band were going through with Shane is very well documented. He was disillusioned with the music industry in general and was sick of the very heavy touring schedule the band were undertaking. He wasn't co-operating at all with the rest of the group; it was like a big divide, them and him, and by all accounts, he had lost his passion for The Pogues in a big way. Everything was hard work and pretty negative, especially for his band mates who needed him to be more channelled to make a new album. Her book is an incredible piece of work, her attention to detail, and her insight into what would interest the reader is really spot on. I was gutted when I learned of her death – it would have been a great honour to have been able to tell her personally what I thought of her book, but sadly she was taken from us prematurely by breast cancer.

Of the other notable tracks on the album, 'Summer in Siam' stands out for sure, a slow number punctuated by James Fearnley going down the scale of the piano keys, with a jazzy background; the lyrics are sparse and simple but effective, a dreamy smoocher! The title track, 'Hell's ditch' has a long instrumental intro, before the very graphic description of life in a jail, with its howling, screaming and, er, fist fucking. Nice. If MacGowan wasn't playing the game with his comrades, there was certainly nothing wrong with his writing; it was all really good, imaginative stuff, even if it had a slightly different direction to his previous work.

'Rain Street' was another standout track penned by MacGowan, brilliant melody and lyrics, again with Thai flavours. The album bows out in a whimper with a very insignificant track by Terry Woods; 'Six to go' is just an album filler in every sense – this was not what The Pogues were about at all, what a waste of album space, especially, again through Carol Clerk's book, once you know that there was quite a bit of much stronger material available. I wasn't too keen on Terry Woods' other track either, 'Rainbow Man'. Jem Finer had written a track called 'The Curse of Love'. Sung by Shane (he must've approved), it's a brilliant song with great lyrics, head and shoulders above the Terry Woods track that was stuck on by Frank Murray, the band's manager, for what must've been royalty reasons rather than artistic... not good for the fans though, eh Frank?

Overall, I would say the album was a winner, the general sound a lot clearer than the sound achieved on 'Peace and love'. Joe Strummer produced 'Hell's Ditch' and I think he did a good job.

Of course, a new album means gig time again, and I almost wet my knickers (almost!) when I found that they were doing a return date at Wembley Arena, fucking marvellous! I had enjoyed their Wembley show so much the time before – could it be that good again? There was a mini crew of us going to this one: Me, Paula, 'Geordie' Jane (Paula's pal that had not long started working at the hotel), Keith, big Les, and his lovely 'fork and knife' Lorraine was also in attendance. Les, or Reg as we often affectionately called him (as in Reggie Kray) enjoyed life to the full and was very much the main man in my group of friends, all Hibs supporters – that was the common bond – however, most of us were fond of The Pogues too, in varying degrees.

I managed to buy tickets for the same spot as I had been at Wembley before, but this time we were all together. As the date for the gig got nearer, the excitement levels mounted. I was looking forward to this one, as much as George Michael would be, when he's about to start sooking the Armitage Shanks porcelain in a public lavvie! Keith, the girls and I made our way from Staines railway station to Waterloo, and had a fantastic booze fuelled party to ourselves on the train. The journey was only about 40 minutes, but Keith and I made the absolute most of the time, and got seriously stuck into some whisky and gin respectively. We made our way up to Baker Street, where we were meeting Les and Lorraine in The Globe pub, a well known haunt of English football hooligans I believe. We all sat outside the pub on wooden benches. It was busy, early evening, and quite a lot of punters were enjoying a well deserved drink after their work hooters had told them they were free to go.

Keith and I were considerably more 'well on' than the others, a result of the refreshments on the Waterloo train. However, when I know in the back of my mind that there's something to look forward to later in the evening, then there's no chance of me flaking out through the ale, and it doesn't get any bigger for me than a Pogues gig, especially at Wembley Arena. Keith and I were having a little push and shove with each other, as we often did, and before you knew it, we were squaring up to each other, playfully, for a bout of Sumo wrestling. What's more, we had a captivated audience: the pub's customers. I was getting the better of Keith at the Sumo thing, managing to skip his lunges toward me, helping him on his way, thoughtfully, to the ground in the process. All of a sudden, I got the shock of my life, when he floored me with a slick move, putting me right on my arse, not that far away from the stairs of the subway which I scrambled to avoid. Keith received an almighty cheer from our audience for his troubles; he was victorious, and I was beat – there was no return from that! I got all paranoid about it, asking my friends what was so fucking funny. I think everyone to a man enjoyed Keith's victory at the Sumo bout.

After I was over my paranoia crisis, we shuffled ourselves back onto the tube and made our way to Wembley, got settled into our seats at The Arena with supplies of plastic bottled, unchilled Hofmeister lager to quaff during the gig. The lad that I had sold Vikki's ticket to on our last visit to Wembley was sat right next to us. He had thought the seats were in a great viewing position too, and, like me, had secured the same again. It was good to see him. We reminisced about our night there previously, and spoke about how much we had enjoyed our night and of how lucky he was to get Vikki's ticket. There was a fantastic attendance, and they had removed the seats from the floor in front of the stage, creating a standing area to about halfway back – at least that saved the fans from removing them themselves this time, all above board and everyone happy. Spider would surely have an easier time of it tonight, and not have to struggle with the masses to keep order.

The start of the gig was both fantastic and also very dramatic. They opened with Terry Woods' brilliant 'Battle March Medley' an instrumental with a subtle slow beginning, building up, steadily, to a furious finish. The stage featured the band appearing gradually to adoring cheers from their frenzied fans, all their cakes were iced in a flash when MacGowan appeared, in a red checked shirt, leather strides and his customary shades. It was just a truly magical beginning, to set up the evening's entertainment. Our little group wasted no time in getting into the swing of things – there was nowhere else in the world that I would rather have been, the gig was just the berries! Paula was troubled though. I asked her what on earth could possibly be wrong. She shouted in my ear that her underwear down below was irritating her; she had a basque thing on that had a clip at the honeypot area and it was uncomfortably digging into her. I told her, unsympathetically, to just take the damn thing off! This advice was not received with any gratefulness whatsoever, but, aha, when she was dancing to the fabulous music something must have adjusted itself, and her leisure centre was comfortable again!

The Pogues were belting out their songs and the new material from Hell's Ditch was very well received. When they played 'Rain Street' and it came to the fast instrumental bit in the middle, the standing crowd downstairs went nuts, a mass of swirling bodies with bobbing heads. Keith, the victorious Sumo warrior, was very impressed, and kept telling us to look down at the clearly delighted punters. This

Wembley gig was eclipsing the last one for me, and that's really saying something!

I'm not proud of the next part of the Wembley story, but nevertheless it must be told. Keith and I desperately needed a piss. I wasn't going anywhere, I didn't want to miss anything, no fucking chance. So I carefully pissed into one of my empty plastic lager bottles. Keith followed suit. The plastic bottles' new contents could probably have given the original product a run for its money – our piss might even have been colder! It seemed like a good idea at the time, really it did, when the bottles with our poison were thrown over the side, and onto the bottom floor of Wembley Arena. We laughed, and accepted reluctantly, the wrath of Paula and Geordie Jane, and giggled some more. Yes, an immature thing to do with possible disgusting consequences, but I'm sure no one died. About two minutes later, a member of the Wembley staff appeared in our row with a torch – he was like an usherette that you used to get at the cinema years ago, except he was an ugly twat (I always thought the usherettes were hot) and he wasn't the brightest spark either. He came to me and said, "Who threw them bottles downstairs?" Ehh, as if I was going to say, "Oh aye chief, it was me, take me away from this absolutely wonderful gig right now!" I jokingly tried to blame Geordie Jane, but Twat wasn't having it. However, without an admission of guilt we were at a stalemate, so away he went. Just as well or Keith would have 'sumoed' him! Geordie Jane would have been stunning as an usherette... pity she didn't need any help adjusting the clips on her undergarments!

The concert was flowing along superbly. A real nice touch was when the band were halfway through one of their familiar songs, when all of a sudden, they redirected into The Temptations' famous song 'My Girl'. The whole thing appeared effortless and brilliant – a really memorable moment to cherish.

And then they were gone. It was a fantastic occasion: the set the band played was perfect, the sound was really good, just the right volume, as close to heaven as it gets. All good things come to an end unfortunately, and we made the long journey back home through Central London and beyond. Everyone in our posse enjoyed their night immensely. Geordie Jane, in her fantastic accent, told us that she wasn't sure what she was letting herself in for, not knowing much about The Pogues, but she had had one of her best nights out for a long time – she was blown away by the music, the crowd and the whole atmosphere. The Pogues just have such a persuasive way about them, they win people over so easily, even, ahem, for those dead against them at the first listen! I often wondered how the band themselves felt after a monumental performance such as this Wembley gig – did they feel the adoring love from their audience? Or was it just another day at work? For me personally, it was right up there with the best Pogues gig I'd ever been to, and that probably still stands to this day.

So much for the band being in turmoil regarding Shane MacGowan's reluctance to 'play the game'. I'm quite sure the vast majority of the delighted Wembley hordes that night had no idea whatsoever what was going on behind the scenes with the band and their politics. For quite a while now, I was starting to become familiar with some of the London Pogues audience. This one chap seemed to have a different, dramatic hairdo for every show. We always gave each other an "All right?" but I didn't even know his name; it didn't matter though – we were both feeling the vibe of the majestic Pogues. They were just beyond superb, out of this fucking world. It was starting to dawn on me, that it was indeed a pleasure and a privilege to be there to witness a night like this, the first time I'd felt like that at any concert. Didn't The Pogues just reach the parts that other bands didn't? You fucking bet they did!

A DEATH IN AFTERNOON

Life in general kept rolling along merrily – or did it? Maybe life itself shouldn't be taken for granted, a lesson I learned at extremely close quarters one Saturday in Staines.

The hotel had employed a courting couple from the Newcastle area, John and Dawn. They lived in a staff flat together. All the staff flats in Staines were in close proximity to each other; it was almost as if the staff were a small community within a community. I didn't really have much to do with the couple, my social circle was just outwith theirs I suppose. John resigned from his under manager role in the hotel, and travelled back North, but Dawn stayed put; she was a receptionist. They were a nice enough couple, she was always upbeat and chatty, but he was a little bit deep – conversations with him, even at work, could be a bit weird to say the least, but there seemed to be no malice with him.

When he returned North, word was that Dawn had not heard from him, not a dicky bird. She had tried to get in touch with him, without success, so she assumed that their liaison could be over, history. In the meantime, a chef work colleague of mine, Derek from Dundee, saw his opportunity with Dawn, and made his move – which she gratefully accepted. Derek was a bit of a boy with the women. Dawn was about a foot taller than him, but it's all the same lying down I suppose!

Somebody must have been in touch with John though, as one

day he arrived, without notice, back in Staines. It was a Saturday. I had been to the town centre to get some bits and pieces (yes, and no doubt to the bookies!) and was making my way back, up the lane that took you from the High Street to the Moormead estate, where the staff houses were. I could see John in front of me, walking straight in my direction. When we got closer to each other, I greeted him and stopped to ask how he was doing, all the while in the back of my mind thinking that dirty Derek was spending his evenings playing 'Monopoly' with Dawn. John seemed weirder than ever. He asked me where Derek was, and was clearly not in the mood for small talk. He was really agitated, shaking, and spoiling for some serious bother.

I would never have predicted what was about to unfold that Saturday afternoon, just another day really, in Staines. I told him that I hadn't seen Derek, made my excuses and went back to my flat, which was quite close by. After a while, I ventured out again to try and find Derek, to tell him that he was a wanted man, but I couldn't find him in any of the obvious places. When I got back to my flat again, my doorbell was red hot, with hysterical Anugraha staff. They were saying that John was in the flat on the opposite side of the road. His search for Derek had proved to be fruitless, and someone had let him into the flat and then left him there, alone, to his own devices. Fucking 'ding dong' my kitchen was now full to bursting point – everyone who could get to the window was looking over the road. Apparently, John had a gun! He was a member of a gun club back home in the North East, he'd been seen waving a 'piece' around when he was enquiring about Derek's whereabouts, but not, obviously, when he asked me. I couldn't really take all this in. I didn't really buy the story that he had a gun – this wasn't downtown Chicago, this was bloody Staines, a very unremarkable place at the best of times.

The frenzied speculating throng in the kitchen were silenced in a second, when we heard a loud BANG! Fucking Hell! Surely John hadn't got a hold of anyone and shot them? Derek was still nowhere to be seen, the speculation among the staff was now at fever pitch, but there seemed to be still an underlying feeling that no one really *had* been shot. Gregor, who was the bar's manager at the hotel, had a calm head on him, when he did the only thing that could be done in the circumstances and phoned Old Bill. They arrived pretty quickly, first coming into my flat, for a bit more information, before crossing the road, and entering the flat opposite and into the unknown.

A short while later, plod was back out in the street, talking to Gregor. When the conversation finished, Gregor came back in to face the staff. You could have heard a pin drop when he stopped talking. John had taken his own life, putting the gun into his mouth, and blasting his own brains all over the wall of the room he had chosen to take his last breath in. Unbelievable. No one could comprehend what had happened. There was a certain amount of relief that he hadn't actually killed someone else (Derek springs to mind). An ambulance arrived soon after. Looking back on it all now, I'm amazed they took the body away so quickly – normally, you'd have thought, they would leave the incident scene as it was for Bill to do tests etc. One can only assume that they were clear enough with what had unfolded that afternoon.

Derek arrived on the scene at last, with Dawn, after things had settled down. It was them who went to identify the body.

I didn't know John well at all, but it must have been a nightmare for his family back in the North East when they learned of his death. God knows what John himself must have been feeling, for him to carry something like that off. The whole episode was really sobering and sad, it showed how life can be precious, but also precarious at the same time. I for one felt extremely lucky that he didn't have a pop at me when I passed him on the lane – maybe if I'd come out with a smart remark (which would have been typical of me) or looked at him the wrong way, then things might have worked out very differently. And what of Derek? He was one lucky, lucky dude, that he wasn't about in Staines that day – whatever location he found himself in, whatever he was doing, almost certainly saved his life.

The staff frequented the local pub, The Garibaldi. It was the nearest one to their flats and houses, but that, for me anyway, was the only thing the fucking place had going for it. The landlady at the time thought she was everybody's mother, far too controlling and judgemental. I always tried to drink in a couple of bars that I much preferred a wee bit further down the road. I just didn't get on with this pretend 'Babs Windsor' at all. But the blackness of the night that followed the afternoon when John shot himself, I thought it would be the right thing to do, to go to the 'staff pub' – folk would be upset, and it would be good if we could all stick together and get over this terrible tragedy. I needn't have worried. When I opened the door of The Garibaldi, what took me by surprise was the fucking noise! The place was full of staff, and the atmosphere was far from the serene one I was expecting. The Proclaimers were on the jukebox, '500 Miles', and everyone was singing along passionately. It's a wonder that 'Babs' was allowing this, but I suppose the till was going Ker-ching! plenty enough to keep her in bleach for her barnet. Yes, life goes on. I was still a bit shook up by the day's events, but the vast majority were getting on with things with ease. Derek and Dawn weren't there though, they must've been feeling awful, relieved and no doubt lots of other emotions.

*

There was to be a development at work. Roger Halford, the second sous chef, was leaving for pastures new. Roger was a real one off, hard as the hardest nails. His heart was in the right place, but you'd be a fucking idiot to be against him. He had a rare talent in the kitchen, superb at sugar work and ice carvings, the more artistic parts of kitchen duties. He was loyal and not a lot or anyone fazed Roger. I've never seen anyone drink bottles of Newcastle Brown Ale like he did, in abundance, quickly and with absolute ease. The tab he had lit to accompany his brown ale never left his lips until it was finished, right at the cork.

The drink is one thing, but Roger's eating habits, in particular, on one night, really is the stuff of legend. Roger was in London, he was pissed, and he was hungry. He negotiated his way into a Kentucky Fried Chicken joint, and ordered himself up one of those buckets they do. They usually comprise about 10 bits of chicken, multiple portions of fries and various other bizararries in the form of side orders. On his way back home, on the train, Roger ate the lot. Probably not in the way that you are thinking though. Roger ate everything bar the packaging;

in particular, the chicken bones, he ate the fucking lot, and that's a lot of bones, with 10 or so pieces of the Coronel's fowl. Roger went home, slept it all off, and his digestive system coped with the bones without a problem. If you knew Roger like I do, then you would find this story to be very matter of fact actually, all down to his individuality.

I got on well enough with Roger, but his departure meant that his position was up for grabs, and I wasted no time in telling the head chef that I was the man for the job. Luckily for me, he agreed. I was over the moon with my promotion; it meant a lot to me, as I felt I had knuckled down since returning South. It's nice when your hard work can be rewarded measurably, but I had no plans to follow in Roger's footsteps and eat any bones. There was a small wage rise, but that wasn't important – the bloody bookie would be the beneficiary anyway!

Talking of the bookie, Paula and I were in Windsor one afternoon. I always got bored with the shops, so the Ladbrokes sign drew me in, just for a change, and Paula reluctantly followed me up the stairs and into this particular Windsor branch. I had a £20 bet on a horse, over the jumps, at odds of 5/1. My horse was doing ok until, inevitably, near the finish, he appeared to be running out of steam. There was only one other horse in contention at this point, the favourite; when the two horses reached the last fence, the animal I backed barged the favourite away from the fence, and off the actual racetrack – a most definite case of foul play. With the favourite gone, my horse trotted up to the finish line, pretty much alone, and the commentator, quite correctly, called him the winner! I knew though that my horse would be disqualified after a stewards' enquiry, and probable objection, however I was up at the payout counter quicker than you could say "and they're off!" where a naive but obliging lady paid me out anyway.

The £20 notes came over the counter agonisingly slowly, as time was not on my side, but we got there, £120 tucked into my pocket. I literally grabbed Paula and told her to move, sharpish, as the office filled with the sound of "Stewards' enquiry, stewards' enquiry, this horse is certain to be thrown out!" Paula fancied a bet herself that afternoon, but she wasn't on I'm afraid; she was almost manhandled down the stairs and out on to the street, much to her anger.

The bookie had made a mistake paying me out, but my thinking was that Ladbrokes could handle it, they wouldn't have to resort to budget brand buying just yet – besides, they'd had enough of my dosh over the past wee while, since White Paws came on my scene. When I got home, I checked on Ceefax, and indeed my horse was disqualified and thrown out, but as far as I was concerned, just like in 'The Bottle of smoke' my horse had won, and I had the lovely folding vouchers in my hand to prove it.

Another event that I really enjoyed, still on the gambling theme, was a game of cards. I actually had a little bit of 'previous' with cards, when I first started travelling through to Hibs games. I was 14 years old, but all my Hibs mates were older than me, so they had a good bevvy and a game of pontoon, for cash. I didn't partake in the ale, but I loved the card games they played – it was never for too serious amounts though. So that experience perhaps prepared me slightly, as now and again, on a pay day afternoon, a few of us would go to a pub in Staines called The Three Tuns where the landlord would turn a blind eye to the card school we had. These could last for hours, going on until late in the evening. We always played the one game, three card brag, and I simply loved those card schools. I had two rules that I applied to myself during those brag marathons: be patient, and don't get too drunk. Being drunk and gambling are a poisonous combination that usually ends up being a disaster.

Generally speaking, I fared very well in the card schools, though I didn't win all the time. I particularly remember Graham Parker, the Southern Geezer that I shared a flat with previously, giving me a good hiding at brag one evening, when I was lucky to leave the table with the shirt on my back! By and large though, I managed to win quite a bit of money at cards, and on one occasion at The Three Tuns I had an absolutely brilliant day. After a slow start, I won a small fortune. I remember going back to my flat that evening, and I seemed to have money in every pocket of my clothing.

Some members of the card school didn't know when to stop. A bloke from Newcastle ended up skint, and was doing IOUs. To cut a long story short, he was in to me for his whole next paypacket, which was two weeks away. The next morning, as I thought about his situation, I wondered if I should just tell him to forget it. But I reckoned that if things were the other way round, he'd be looking for his money, so I stuck to my guns, and to be fair, the man paid me in full. Mr Borthwick, the head Chef, was waiting for me, when I arrived at work the following afternoon after my big win. The stories had been doing their rounds in the morning, and as usual in hotels, the stories had grown a few arms and legs, whilst going through 'the manufacturing process'. Someone had told my boss that I had LOST a heap of money the day before, and he was concerned that I'd got out of my depth and could have been in trouble. I furnished him with the real facts, and he started laughing, although I think he was surprised at the amounts involved. I was rich, but, as usual, just for a wee while. Good fun though. My win at the cards was perfectly timed, as The Pogues were coming back, to Brixton Academy again... happiest of days!

I was meeting Chelsea Steve and big Les 'Reg' Rennie for this one, at our usual place, the Wimpy on Brixton High Street. It wasn't that long since the Wembley show that followed the sumo bout at Baker Street, but the frequency of the gigs did nothing to dampen any enthusiasm for the band's fans. As we ventured into the Academy, there were the usual advertising posters all around the place, and there were one or two for The Pogues, which I assumed were for the show we were about to see. When I checked with a little more concentration, the advert was for yet ANOTHER gig, a matter of a few days away – fuckin' hell, it felt like Christmas! A quick conflab between the three of us, and it was straight to the Academy box office, who were selling tickets for the forthcoming gig, being held at The Electric Ballroom in Camden. Aye. The place I was at before getting into that taxi, when I was skint... Les bought an extra ticket, for his wife Lorraine. It was a great feeling going into the stalls for this gig, knowing there was another one to look forward to in the very near future, brilliant!

When they came on stage, Brixton's Academy appeared to be bursting at the seams, with a mass of enthusiastic Pogues followers heaving backwards, forwards, sideways, excitement levels off the scale. When Shane MacGowan appeared, he had a mini zxylophone instrument in his hand, gave it a rattle into his microphone, followed by his customary giggle, KKkrrrrrcccchhhhhhhh! The gig was up to The Pogues' usual high standards. I had seen them quite a few times now, but their gigs were never stale or boring, oh no, I couldn't get enough. They played their tunes to the delighted masses. The audience was so manic and wild on this occasion, that Les, Steve and I lost each other in the crowd, never to be reunited that night, but it didn't matter, as we'd already made our arrangements for Camden.

The concert at The Electric Ballroom seemed a bit mysterious. We couldn't really understand why they had decided to play again so soon after two major headlining shows at Wembley and Brixton – we certainly were not complaining though! We met at the obvious boozer in Camden, The Devonshire Arms, a place very familiar with various members of the band. Les had come straight from his work; alas, Lorraine didn't make it, so he had a spare ticket. So we got on with it. I mean, it's a hard life, a game or two of pool, in a quality boozer that had plenty cold beer on tap followed by a night being entertained by the greatest band that ever played music, oh yes, life was hard.

An added bonus was that Jem Finer and Darryl Hunt all of a sudden appeared in the pub. Jem wasn't so scary this time, his eyes didn't appear to be so big and so wide, we all exchanged "hellos" and "all rights?" and they were gone, as quickly as they had appeared – pity really, I would have loved to have taken Jem on at pool... We made the very short walk to the Ballroom, all the while listening out for anyone that needed a ticket for the show. This proved to be difficult, more difficult than I had imagined; the band were so popular, and were playing in a small venue in their own back yard so to speak, but unless you start screaming like the touts did, how could you sell your spare ticket, unless some opportunism fell into place, like it had previously on the tube to Wembley? So big Les had to sell his brief to one of those touts, for a crap price, under the face value, but at least we could get ourselves into the venue now, and grab, ahem, another cold refreshing drink.

The Ballroom was as busy as we expected. We were in the bar upstairs, looking down at the small stage. It was exciting to think of the forthcoming entertainment, being held in such intimacy, compared to where I'd seen the band more recently. Steve and I wanted to go right down to the front of the stage and get into a good viewing position for the band coming on, but Les wasn't up for this at all – he'd had a hard day at work and still had his bag on him that earlier in the day had contained his sandwiches etc. As I've stated and will continue to do so, when it comes to Pogues concerts, I'm afraid I'm pretty selfish – the way I see it is you can't come back tomorrow and do it again, see the band at The Electric Ballroom, so you just HAVE to make the most of it and regret nothing.

So Steve and I went down the front, and left the big man, my mate, in the bar, on his own. Charming! The band came on; the crush at the front was crazy but just about manageable. There were some youngish girls near to us, they were struggling a bit with the crowd, the place was packed to the rafters by now, and Spider, one of my heroes of course, gave me a right bollocking for 'pushing' the young girls, he upset me no end! I literally couldn't move, I wasn't shoving the fucking girls, but that didn't stop our tin whistling grumpy mannie from giving me utterly filthy looks for the next wee while. If that wasn't bad enough, the guilt about leaving Les had started to kick in some more, I looked up at the balcony bar, and he was gone. Les had left the venue altogether and was on his way home, his mates having deserted him. Wonder what Spider would've thought of that? He'd have probably smacked me over the heid with his whistle!

And what of the actual gig itself? Well, it was sheer pleasure, it was fantastic to hear all the songs from their latest album 'Hell's Ditch' and seeing them so close up. Spider had forgotten about me, so it seemed (thank fuck), and I was able to relax a bit and survive the crammed, swaying crowd. I've very rarely encountered trouble at a Pogues gig amongst their following. The enthusiasm of the punters mixed with the alcoholic beverage intake of most of them, means inevitably that there will be plenty of incidents like falling down on yer face or yer arse; it's never usually a problem though, as there's always someone around to lend a helping hand to the more fragile members of this big happy family that are watching the band.

One of the punters though was giving Shane a hard time, heckling him between songs. This was not tolerated for long: Shane himself even offered his agitator outside with his hand signal for him to 'come ahead'. The prick doing the heckling was reprimanded by various members of the audience and order was restored, and thankfully,

Shane was left to sing out the rest of the magnificent set in relative peace. The band were so tight that night, their performance was clinical, they were really talented musicians, a real unit. Their growing catalogue of songs had a bit of absolutely everything –it didn't matter if they played an old song or a new one, their adoring audience loved it all.

They were a special 'team' all right. If I was the Hibs manager, I'd have signed up all the band members in a flash, on rewarding contracts, to play for the magnificent green machine, from Easter Road. You have Andrew Ranken, the drummer, the trusty goalkeeper, with a very safe pair of hands, the last line of defence. His distribution being exceptional. Left and right backs, Philip Chevron and Darryl Hunt, guitarist and bassist respectively, defending the very rhythm of the band and their sounds. Jem 'scary eyes' Finer, the dependable centre half, his banjo keeping the whole thing very real, now and again though, retiring to the back of the stage to keep the brass section going – such a masterful, demonic geezer should surely wear the captain's armband. Word is, if someone needs sorting, or a quiet word in the lug hole, then Jem's yer man; he would bite the very legs of a rival centre forward! Terry Woods: a classier midfielder would be very hard to find, with his creative mandolin and cittern, a fine header of the ball, his bonce tilting from side to side as he loses himself in the music.

Which brings us nicely to Mr James 'maestro' Fearnley, the jinky winger, marauding up and down the very front of the stage, with that squeeze box of tricks hanging round his frame, hugging the touchline, full of magic, trickery and devilment. Between his anarchic accordion and piano playing, a diving header each match, jumping off the stage at 'Repeal'. And what of the temperamental vocalist and lyricist centre forward? Enter, Sir Shane MacGowan, scoring a goal, a top corner job, every fucking time – well, when he's in the mood! Missing an open goal now and again is not beyond him. But hey, he knows he's good, he always bounces back, attempted overhead kicks, sometimes landing himself on top of the monitors, is all in a day's work for Shane. The darling of the fans, whatever his performance.

Finally, Spider Stacy. And his whistle! Well he's head of security didn't you know, the fucking referee, a very unpredictable, temperamental one at that, keeping order with the crowd, and yellow carding, as well as bollocking, poor, innocent Scotsmen in the audience that were NOT pushing young girls. Spider is always blowing that damned whistle. Why do refs always have to be so controversial? I was probably lucky not to receive a red from Spider at The Electric Ballroom.

Steve enjoyed roaring in my ear during 'Sick Bed of Cuchulainn' the bit where Shane sings "Now you sing a song of liberty, for Blacks and Packs and JOCKS!", him trying to be funny, I suppose. The gig had to end unfortunately, but what a night, just fantastic, no other band I'd ever seen made me feel as totally entertained as The Pogues had (best night out in town, I tell you!). We found out afterwards, that the show had been some kind of benefit gig, to do with Frank Murray, the band's manager. Much later in years, and again, due to Carol Clerk's book, I learned that the gig was actually for his daughter who unfortunately ended up paralysed after an accident. So that was good of the band, I thought, to support their manager during a difficult time for his family, and of course, even better that the place was full on the night of the gig.

I thought the band would continue to go from strength to strength; the sky was the limit for them. It was all very, very different though, the next time that I went to see them.

"SO, YOU WANNA BE A CHEF?"

As I mentioned previously, the first kitchen I worked in was at Pitlochry, right after leaving school. I even remember the very first, delicate, culinary task I was asked to negotiate. The grumpy chef/ owner told me to cut a load of cold, shelled, hard boiled eggs in half – these were for the salads to be served during dinner. Piece of piss, I thought to myself, so I started cutting them, only to get the shock of my life a few moments later. Grumpy puss walked by, picked up two halves of egg, that were admittedly quite a bit out when it came to being the same size, and threw them in the bin, along with all the other eggs – the ones I had cut *and* even the ones that were still whole. He went berserk! After the eggs were dispatched, I thought it a minor miracle that I didn't join them in the fucking bin. This bloke was a head case, but, at least working with him taught me what kitchens could be like in terms of being scary. That's about all I learned in Pitlochry really.

After my full time stint at college, the first proper kitchen environment for Bruce junior was at Perth's Station Hotel. On my first day there, I was told to go in the larder area to work, and was introduced to a fella called Matthew Defranco. He looked me up and down, and his opening line to me was the immortal line: "So, you wanna be a chef?" I spluttered my way through a reply, trying to justify my choice of career. Matthew just looked at me and slowly shook his head, his body language suggested that he had a doughball standing in front of him! You meet a lot of tossers in the catering industry, so called chefs who never tire of telling you that they can do this or that, but in reality very few of these mouthpieces can walk the walk. Matthew Defranco could most certainly walk. I found myself very quickly wanting to be like him; he had a real natural flair for everything he was doing in the kitchen, and once we were over "So, you wanna be a chef" I really enjoyed working with him. I was learning more in a few weeks than I'd learned in a year at college.

Then I got another of those 'shocks'. Matthew told me one day that he was going to work on the vegetable section, leaving me, alone, in the larder. JESUS! The next few weeks were what I can only describe as Hell. It was a matter of survival, every night during dinner service. The head chef would be 'encouraging' me to go faster, to keep up with service. The sheer magnitude of what was required to keep up, and to maintain standards was unbelievable. Some nights, when service was over, I was so relieved, I was actually close to tears. But slowly, things began to get a bit easier, and I would find that the chef wasn't on my case as much. Philip Borthwick was a very hard man to work for, but he was always fair. Again, as I mentioned earlier, there was a bully in the kitchen, and he certainly wasn't fair.

I remember one day, when I was on a breakfast shift, I was due to finish at 3pm, which was handy as I was planning to go through to Edinburgh when I finished to cheer on my beloved Hibees against Rangers in the League Cup. My train was around 4 30pm, plenty time to get ready and away to the football – magic! Bully chef had other ideas. At 3pm on the dot, he turned and said to me: "Right, last job, make me 100 portions of crème caramel, make large ones, for buffets." What a cunt! He knew I was going to the match, I had done my work, was all up to date, and then he hits me with this. There was absolutely no question of not doing it, you didn't say no to authority in the kitchen. Bully boy would often pull stunts like this.

Anyway, I got to it; maybe I would make the train and meet my pals after all. Now, I have to admit that desserts have never been my strong point (something that Philip Borthwick never tires of reminding me) and I thought I would take a wee short cut, just to speed things along. When making the caramel part of the dessert, you must boil sugar, until, yes, it caramelises. Well, I didn't have bloody time for all that, so I made a syrup of dissolved sugar and water, and carefully added blackjack, otherwise known as gravy browning. My improvisation looked the part, and actually tasted ok. I was really pleased with myself, and managed to get my train with a bit to spare. Hibs had a bit to spare too, defeating Glasgow's blue team by two goals to buff, the delectable Ally McCoist even missing a penalty. What a brilliant outcome to a potentially difficult day.

Next morning, whilst getting changed into my whites at that hotel, I got the feeling that something wasn't right. As I gingerly entered the kitchen, a full welcoming committee had assembled and had been anticipating my arrival. I was invited to turn out one of my crème caramel desserts onto a serving platter. Which, nervously, I did. Fucking Hell. The 'custard' part of the dessert was fine; trouble was the caramel part had literally disappeared. The caramelised brown colour that the gravy browning had been a substitute for did not survive the cooking process, leaving a very bland, unappetising clear coloured liquid instead. The ten large desserts I had made were all the same, and couldn't be used. My God, was I popular. After my shift finished, I had to stay behind and do it all again, bully boy reading me the riot act. Mr Borthwick was not best pleased with me either, but he got over it quickly, as he always did, and moved on. Bully boy never moved on though. I saw him give other young lads, one in particular, a lot harder time of it than I got, bullying for the sake of it.

There were lots of pranks played on the younger members of kitchen staff. Right in the middle of service, things were hectic, and someone would roar at a junior, "Go to the freezer and get me a box of chicken lips, NOW!" The puzzled looking victim was told again, this time the demand's decibels rising considerably. "Yes Chef" and off junior would go, frantic, in the freezer looking for chicken lips, all the while getting more and more anxious, as the chicken lips were proving to be somewhat elusive. Of course, it would cross their mind, "Chicken lips? C'mon!" They would return to the fire of the kitchen, with no chicken kissers. "FUCKING CHICKEN LIPS!" yelled at them again, back to the freezer for an even more anxious, fruitless search. Of course, the scene would come to an end with a very embarrassed junior, very red around the face, just above their own lips.

Another trick was when making Hollandaise sauce. You add

clarified butter to egg yolks over heat, and junior would be told that they had to whisk the butter and eggs, but only in a clockwise direction, or the sauce would turn green. Half way through, someone would call junior away for a second, meanwhile a spot of green food colouring would be slipped into the sauce. On junior's return, to their absolute horror, the sauce would turn green and then the fun would start. "I never, honest." "You fucking must have, useless cunt, do it again, CLOCKWISE!"

There was a huge boiler in the kitchen, a large intimidating stainless steel tub, and every fortnight one of the worst jobs in the kitchen needed done. Boiling a load of ox tongues, cooling them, then peeling the fuckers, before pressing them in aspic jelly. I hated this task, it was rank, bogging; only fun thing was putting a tongue up to your face and pretending you were in the rock group Kiss. The prank, however, came right at the beginning. Junior would be shown first how to light the gas boiler – this would mean getting right down on the floor, holding a lit taper to a pilot light for about 10 seconds, all the while keeping a valve pushed in. Once you let the valve go, if the pilot was hot enough then the boiler would light. Now it was junior's turn. So down he got, hand shaking with the taper, only when it was time to let go of the pilot, ignition time, some cunt would be right behind him with a load of silver serving flats, that make some racket when dropped on the floor BANG! Junior would get the fright of his life. Then, the icing on the cake, a little later there were the tongues to peel, fucking JOY!

One of the funniest kitchen stories I heard concerned a kitchen porter (a rarer breed of employee would be hard to find!). This poor chap, apparently, was discovered in the early hours, in a big walk in fridge, by one of the chefs. As the chef entered the fridge, he was met with the alarming sight of matey, having full sexual intercourse with a raw turkey. I don't know all the ins and outs but there's a thought for you, when you're next tucking into your Christmas dinner!

Humour was forever present in well run kitchens. I've also worked in a few though, where the order of the day is just to be aggressive, pretty much for the sake of it, usually instigated by pathetic, insecure individuals. Yes, when the heat's on, and you're in the middle of service, there's a lot of raised voices and passions are running high, but that's how to get the job done, and get the kitchen brigade through it. The job satisfaction in a busy kitchen, when things go well is immense.

The wages at the Station Hotel in Perth were atrocious, the hours were unsociable, but to be fair, never long in Philip Borthwick's kitchen anyway – he always saw you all right for time off. You were effectively paying for your training, and at the time, there was no better than the British Transport Hotels had to offer.

As a nation, we have a hearty interest in TV chefs. A lot of the programmes on the box are unrealistic, especially when celebrities are put into so called kitchen environments. It takes time to master a busy kitchen service, not two minutes as is often portrayed.

I don't have too much time for these sorts of programmes, but I do have a soft spot for a certain Marco Pierre White. I think the man is a touch of class. He wouldn't need to start howling and swearing whilst on camera (someone springs to mind, but I just can't recall who?) I heard a story about Marco not being happy with the cheese trolley one evening in one of his restaurants. Apparently he stood and threw the large slabs of various cheeses, one by one, splat! up high on the wall of the kitchen. The staff started scurrying round, away to clean up the mess, but Marco told them, in no uncertain terms, to leave the cheeses be. They were there for days, before eventually he gave the signal to clean them up. The cheese trolley was never wrong again! Brilliant Marco. Also, if a punter was 'playing up' in his restaurant, and he felt it was unjust, he would summon the waiters to gather round the punter's table, and they would totally strip the contents of that table, right in the middle of service, and ask the occupants to leave. The place would fall into a heavy mixture of bewildered silence and embarrassment. Later on, you'll read about my restaurant – well I wish I'd had the bottle to do a 'Marco' table shuffle at times, but I didn't.

Of the other TV chefs? I really like Nigel Slater. He doesn't feel the need to bastardise good food. We are awash with quality ingredients here on these shores, and sometimes there's just no need to turn them into a mess. His programmes are based on true wholesome recipes; watching his way with food genuinely make you feel hungry, he's a natural, and I would also highly recommend his book 'Toast' – but not until you've finished this one. Thank you.

I'd like to see Shane and Spider on Masterchef... I tell ya, I'm on to something here – think about it, it would be real compulsive viewing. Can you imagine that twat with the bald head and the specs telling Spider his risotto was not up to scratch? And as for Shane, well, the thought just brings a big smile to my face. He'd have the place in uproar, going about with his fag and would look sheepish when the Calvados and Grand Marnier were posted missing!

I must state, here and now, that I am far from being a superstar in the kitchen, (something that Philip Borthwick never tires of reminding me) but I don't try to pretend to be something I'm not. I see myself as an experienced centre half, I'll rely on my own judgement, and will not take on an overhead scissors kick, if I feel out of my depth. But I just about manage to clear my lines through organisation, a skill I learned from the master, Mr Philip Borthwick. My Yorkshire puddings are not great (something that Philip Borthwick never tires of reminding me) but I've stayed behind, after training, and my Yorkshires are actually all right now. I've never been into and I've never been a fan of egotistic 'shock factor' food. You can keep your parcels of cheese made with mongoose milk, cooked in a live snake's belly, with an accompanying reduction of brandy, infused with toe nails, collected from people that live near Crystal Palace!

Matthew Defranco, on the other hand, went on to great things after the Station Hotel. He won a gold medal at Hotelympia in London, in a first class live cooking competition for professional chefs. I was personally gutted when he left The Station Hotel to go and work at The Old Course hotel in St Andrews. His career peaked when he achieved the position of premier sous chef at The Dorchester Hotel in London. Matthew walks with a swagger, and he knows he's good. It was a pleasure to work with him in those very early days. I have very fond memories of my time with him both in the kitchen and socially. We still keep in touch.

HIBS FOR THE CUP

I had a trip booked to go home to Scotland. In fact, I had a function booked: Hibs were in the final of the League Cup, at Hampden Park. And I was never going to miss that! The match was on a Sunday, so I did my usual when visiting home, and travelled up on the Thursday, finishing my early shift at work at approx 4pm. The normal train I caught to take me North of Haddy's Wall was the 1800 from King's Cross to Edinburgh. I actually struggled to get gone from work this day, but managed to get a lift to Staines station, getting there a wee bit later than I would have liked. Still, I thought all would be well in the end. The train from Staines was delayed just before it reached Richmond. Fuck! I was struggling now. I eventually got to King's Cross, via Waterloo and Leicester Square, and with seconds to spare, got myself on the train to Edinburgh; the mannie on the platform blew his whistle, and all of a sudden the train was mobile, thankfully, with me just about on it! I was knackered, from running through the tube network, to get on the train, but hey, I was there, maybe a bit sweaty and dishevelled, but I had made it.

Once I composed myself, I started walking through the carriages to find the seat I had booked for my journey, ready to relax, and think of the weekend that lay ahead of me, and all the carry on that went along with it. I found the seat. There was a geezer sitting in it, he had a suit on, and even looked familiar somehow. I politely pointed out to him that he was indeed on my seat, the one I had reserved at the time of booking my ticket. He told me, politely, that it was his seat. The train was busy, I was still hot under the collar from my efforts to make the train on time, and I certainly wasn't in the mood for this twat! I told him, less politely, that he was in my seat, and could he please remove himself from it, as soon as was possible. He wasn't for shifting, and the tone of our conversation started rising, rapidly. There were another couple of rounds of "You're in my fucking seat" before the suited geezer asked to see my ticket reservation. No fucking problem. I said, "Here, see for yourself, if you don't believe me!" The suited gentleman very calmly pointed out that my seat was in fact opposite him, and at present, was still vacant, and waiting for its occupant. Me. JESUS!

I really did feel like throwing myself out of the window, I was so embarrassed. I was totally wrong, and had managed to get myself into a ridiculous situation. Of course as the volume of our argument escalated, there were plenty of eyes watching us, which just added to the shade of my beetrootesque puss! Suited geezer had a female companion with him – she was very attractive and one couldn't miss her ample cleavage in a far too tight blouse, but she was not impressed with me or my performance though – her scowling looks towards me more than confirmed this. What to do? I got as comfortable as I could, and settled into my real seat, carefully removed my four pack of McEwan's Export from my bag, and did the decent thing, and offered the suit a can, which he gratefully accepted. He was brand new about the whole seat thing, seeing the funny side of it; big tits however, was still scowling, no McEwan's Export for her then. They were both travelling as far as Newcastle. I had a decent crack with the boy, but she sulked all the way to Tyneside, which actually made her less attractive, big bazookas or not.

A few weeks later, the geezer in the suit's familiarity was confirmed – he was in fact a TV weatherman. I howled with laughter when I saw him on the box, and told him to get out of ma seat! I explained to my flatmates how I knew him, but when I told them the story, they were more interested in the tart with the tits!

When the train rolled into Edinburgh's Waverley Station, there was just enough time for a pint of Scottish beer from the tap, lovely, before catching my connection to Perth, where my father would be waiting for me at the station – really good of him, as by the time my train arrived, it was already way past his bedtime. It definitely wasn't passed my mother's bedtime though, and she had a pot of stovies on the go for my arrival in the family home. Stovies, for those of you that don't know, is a traditional Scottish delicacy. My mother made stovies north style, made from the remnants of a roast (beef or lamb); the fat and the gravy went in the pot with sliced tatties, a diced onion and a little gravy salt, cooked under cover very slowly, then mixed with a wooden spoon after cooking for about an hour and a half. Serve with thin oatcakes, fucking magic!

Now you have a classic recipe, don't be tempted to put some of the awful ingredients in stovies that I've seen over the years in lesser versions, eg corned beef or even baked beans – do me a favour! If I'm sounding like a stovie snob, then it's purely intentional. So with me tucking into my stovies, Mum would tuck into her sherry and a fag, whilst updating me on all her news, and there was always plenty of news. The second night of my visits home was Mum's night. I always took her out, whatever she wanted to do was fine by me, and the routine never changed, it was always the same: a night at the Bingo, followed by a visit to a Chinese restaurant, just across the road, for a wee bit of supper. Dad wasn't being shut out, but the Bingo was certainly not his scene, whereas I didn't mind it at all (it's gambling isn't it?). Now and again one of us would get a shout – we were a team and always shared the mini pot of gold we came into.

Saturday of course was football day usually, though not on this particular visit, the final being played on a Sunday. However, a normal Saturday going to watch The Hibees with my mates was always a big hoot, never a dull moment, all accompanied by plenty of liquid refreshment. The football itself, more often than not, would let us down; Hibs were big underachievers in comparison to the fabulous support that they have.

The Hibs boys liked a party though, which brings me nicely to a tale about one of my pals: enter Mr Jimmy Duthie. Jimmy worked in the Forestry Commission at the time, but on this particular day, Jimmy really fancied a temporary change of career. To kick start his new potential employment, Jimmy displayed his gymnastic skills. We were all on a train platform, Edinburgh Haymarket if memory serves me correctly, when a train arrived, slowly, temptingly, to Mr Duthie anyway. It wasn't our train, because it didn't actually stop; however, Jimmy managed to get himself on the moving vehicle, even open the door. He roared out to his comrades with delight that he'd found "a smoker!". As the train gathered a bit more speed and was running out of platform, Jimmy sussed that he was actually the only person on the train. Cooler than a beer that's been in the fridge for a week, Jimmy hurled himself onto the almost diminished platform, with a bit to spare – the whole movement and execution of his landing was a perfect 10! Jimmy was quite suitably marinated at the time, making the whole scenario even more impressive.

These days all the train doors lock automatically, and there's absolutely no 'smokers'. I wonder if, with his antics, our James instigated those changes on our railways... Once our proper scheduled train arrived (and stopped so we could get on) it became apparent that Jimmy had no ticket to ride. His way round this small problem was nothing short of genius. Jimmy disappeared for a while, and next time we saw him, he arrived in our carriage complete with guard's jacket and hat, shouting "Tickets please!" He really looked the part, modelling the railway threads with some considerable style. Whilst we were falling about laughing, it was amazing to see so many people fiddling in their pockets etc, looking for the tickets that Jimmy was demanding. The real guard eventually caught up with his impostor, and once he overcame the struggle to retrieve his uniform, he asked Jimmy for his ticket. Jimmy said he didn't have one, so the guard asked him where he got on the train. Jimmy asked the guard, "Where was the last stop?" The guard said "Kirkcaldy", so Jimmy told him "Well that's where I got on then!" Brilliant stuff from our James – nobody got hurt, all good clean amusing fun.

Supporting Hibs from a footballing point of view, is not easy, but the camaraderie and days out we had following our favourite team, kind of made up for the fact that we've never had much joy on the park. I would never change my support for another team, ever. Most young boys are persuaded into supporting the team of their father's, but that wasn't the case for me. My old man was an Aberdeen fan; all his and my mother's family are from Aberdeen. We used to go there for family holidays. I had two cousins, Billy and Michael, and we were watching the football highlights, late at night. The date was 1ˢᵗ January, 1973, and I was approaching my seventh birthday. Seventh. Hearts were playing Hibs, and my cousins were arguing about who would win, as none of us were aware of the score, the game having obviously been played earlier in the day. Michael, who I idolised, was supporting Hibs; Billy was going for Hearts. As the game progressed, there seemed to be a goal every minute. Hibs destroyed Hearts on their own ground by SEVEN goals to nil. That's SEVEN! Naturally, Michael was delighted; the Hibs captain, Pat Stanton, was his hero. Billy meanwhile had not much to say for himself – brilliant. So that was that, I became a Hibby, my Uncle Iain, Mum's brother, also had a love of the Hibees, who were playing some fantastic football at the time, and presented me with an emerald green Hibs strip, which I fell in love with. I wore it everywhere, my loyalty to the cause of Hibernian FC, was now set in stone.

I really enjoyed seeing my mates at home. We always managed to turn a day at the football into an enjoyable social occasion, and a 'Jimmy Duthie-esque' adventure was never far away. But there was an element of seriousness to this particular match, as it was the League Cup final, and we had a good chance, up against Dunfermline Athletic, Hibs having already disposed of Glasgow Rangers in the semi final. The day before the big match, Scotland were playing England in the rugby world cup. None of us were big rugger fans, but it was a good excuse to go to the pub early and get nicely in the mood for our match on the Sunday. The thing I remember most about the rugby match against the old enemy was a relatively simple kick that Gavin Hastings made a right mess of, him missing this conversion was the difference, or so it appeared, between a Scotland victory or a defeat – a defeat it was then. No worries though, the rugby was not a big deal compared to the Hibees being in the cup final.

We all had a good crack though. The boozer we were in, The Railway Tavern, had a geezer on later in the night with a guitar and a microphone, belting out a few well known tunes to keep the punters entertained. Davo and I temporarily increased his numbers from solo to trio, when we volunteered our services (free of charge I may add).

The slightly apprehensive axeman had a conflab with us as to what we were going to perform. First number was a shambolic attempt at the vintage Pogues track 'Sally MacLennane'. Davo and I did ok with remembering the lyrics; we maybe weren't much in tune though, and the guitarist wasn't overly familiar with the song – fucking hell, he didn't realise what he was missing then! We asked him for one more chance, as we just didn't get any reaction at all from the otherwise occupied punters in the bar; even our pals just kept talking amongst themselves. This was it then, shit or bust! We attempted 'The Wild Rover' next. The Pogues had recorded this one too as a B side, and axeman was familiar enough with this traditional song. We produced a rowdy but altogether more professional performance – people were watching, even our mates. At the conclusion of our piece, we were rewarded, like proper buskers, with currency. We made 4p: one 2p coin and two 1p coins, one of which was bounced off my head! Applause is cheaper, but sadly this was also in very short supply. We made a group decision that as a trio, we should perhaps call it a day, and the guitarist chappie got on with his duties unhindered and, no doubt, relieved.

Sunday came, cup final day, here we go then. We hired a bus and a driver, the deal being that he took us through from Perth to Glasgow for the match, and on to Edinburgh (the home of the Hibees) if we managed to come out victorious and win the cup, then back to Perth after the celebrations were finished. The driver was well paid and he turned more than a blind eye to the absolute party we had on his bus that day. Because Celtic or Rangers weren't involved in the final, it was decided, by the chiefs of Scottish football, that the fans could just turn up to this match and pay cash at the gate to get in rather than the usual scenario of buying a ticket. Hibs had a massive following through to support them, and unfortunately a few thousand of them didn't manage to get in, as our end was more than full before kickoff. There wasn't much room, it made for uncomfortable viewing, but hey, I had some good experience of swaying crowds at Pogues concerts. The Dunfermline end was far from full, a wee bit more thought and organisation could have seen all the Hibs supporters safely inside Hampden Park that day; unfortunately the clowns that run the game in Scotland possess neither thought nor organisation, and sadly that's always been the case.

The Perth lads all got in safely though. A nervy match unfolded throughout the afternoon, and the mighty Hibees emerged victorious winning by two goals to nil. Fuck me, we'd won the League Cup. The only major trophy my team had won since I was born was back in 1972, also winning the League Cup. I was only six years old then, and as this was just before the Seven-Nil game against Hearts, it was just before my time, and I wasn't able to celebrate that win like I would this one! We were all thrilled when we watched Murdo MacLeod, the Hibs captain at the time, lift the trophy high up above his head in the middle of the Hampden stand.

Back to the bus, with the news the driver was probably dreading, and to Scotland's capital city we were now headed, and boy did we party on that journey! There was a massive fleet of supporters' buses heading east to Edinburgh that Sunday evening, but I can honestly say that our mobile function suite seemed by far the rowdiest. Obviously the overwhelming majority of the Hibs support hailed from Edinburgh, but they had loyal numbers in Scotland's other towns and cities, notably Perth, Glasgow, Inverness, Dunblane, Aberdeen and Fife. All the 'out of town' supporters got to know each other through chance meetings travelling on the trains, and we all got on really well, shared a drink or twelve, and were up for a good time and a carry on for sure.

We got back to Edinburgh in good time, to get into Easter Road stadium, the Hibs ground, to welcome home our victorious heroes, who duly paraded their recently acquired silverware in front of their delighted faithful. I physically cried with joy. It was very emotional inside the old stadium that night, the same sort of emotion that I would experience in later years at the best Pogues gigs. Our team's exploits were even more amazing if you consider that the season before, they came close to extinction, thanks to an arrogance that was better known as Wallace Mercer, who tried in vain to combine his own club, the enemy, Hearts, with our club, thus trying to kill off our great name – no chance, Mr Mercer! Overall, it was just a fantastic day, one I'll cherish forever, spent with my closest Hibee friends – fabulous!

Next day, I travelled back down to the smoke, with a very happy but slightly sore head. At the train station, I bought a copy of every different newspaper they had available that day, to read, and re-live the Hibees' triumph in Glasgow. On the train, when I walked to the toilet or the buffet car, it was obvious that a large number of my fellow travellers were actually at the multiple newspaper thing too, the papers bearing joyous news for a change. There were Hibs colours everywhere, and lots of happy punters, all comfortable, sat in the proper seats they had booked! When I got back to work, everyone was talking about the fuckin' rugby. I suppose not many people in the south would be that fussed about the Scottish League Cup final, but the rugby talk did not take the shine off the fine trophy being displayed in the Hibs' trophy cabinet.

A FINSBURY FARCE

I bought the odd music paper on an occasional rather than religious basis, usually the NME or Sounds, both of which had regular articles about The Pogues. Indeed the band always fared well in their polls for best live band and the like, such was their popularity in the serious music world. I noticed a competition, with a couple of tickets being offered as a prize, to The Fleadh, an open air Irish music festival, being held in Finsbury Park in North London in June. The question that needed answering was about The Pogues, who were headlining the festival that year (1991), as is the norm with these types of competitions. The question was an easy one, so on to the phone I went and stuttered my way through the automated instructions, before hanging up. A few weeks later, a very pleasant surprise found its way through my letterbox in the shape of two briefs for The Fleadh – a competition winner I was then! The tickets had quite an expensive face value, as far as concert tickets go, so to win two for the price of a phone call was happy days for sure. The other bands on the bill didn't excite to me too much, so winning the tickets, courtesy of music press, gave me the nudge I needed to attend this festival, and to see The Pogues once again.

I decided to invite my sumo wrestling partner, the one who hammered me, Keith, along to Finsbury Park that afternoon, and he said he was happy to accompany me, without giving me a hiding! Keith was becoming a regular at Pogues gigs. His favourite band, The Electric Light Orchestra, had recently reformed, unfortunately without their main man, Jeff Lynne, and were now going under the name ELO Part II. They did a show at Wembley Arena with a big orchestra behind them, so it was only right that I went along to that one with him. Keith was merrily playing air violin and singing along, and the two of us refrained from sumo and peeing into empty beer bottles!

Neither of us had been to a festival before though – the open air thing had never really appealed to me in the past – but with free tickets, and with The Pogues headlining, it was off to Finsbury Park we went.

The event was held on a Sunday, starting early doors in the afternoon, to accommodate a large list of bands and solo artists that were scheduled to perform on the Fleadh's bill, on a number of different stages. Keith and I caught the tube at Hatton Cross, near Heathrow Airport that day, the Piccadilly line taking us direct to Finsbury Park. It was a beautiful sunny day, a real bonus for an open air thing I thought, so we did the clear, logical thing of getting settled in a boozer for a few beers before we entered the park across the road for the festival. The pub was heaving, there was a great atmosphere inside, everyone anticipating the day's events. Most people appeared to be excited to see The Pogues and Van Morrison, who was due on stage just before the headliners as the second major act. In the corner of the pub, there were some folk having an Irish style jam with a number of musical instruments; they were going down a storm, just a wee bit better than Davo and I had fared at The Railway Tavern, many miles away in Perth.

We got ourselves admitted to the park, and it was obvious straight away that there was going to be a massive attendance to see the bands that day. We had a walk around, taking in what a festival was all about. There were lots of stalls, some selling food of all descriptions and some selling hippy type goods. There were plenty of bars too, very handy. On one of the smaller stages, there was an American couple strutting their stuff, dressed in ridiculous banana yellow suits; they truly captured Keith's attention, so we stopped by to watch them for a while. It turned out the couple were actually husband and wife. The husband looked right at Keith and said to him, "Stop looking at my wife's ass!" He then announced, "Right, this next song is called, 'my wife's ass'!" He started strumming his guitar and sang lyrics relating to his wife's farter right enough, looking at Keith all the way through the song, who was revelling in the attention he was commanding from the American husband/vocalist.

We discovered a new band to get excited about that day, in the shape of The Sawdoctors. They attracted me and Keith straight away; they were tight as a band, playing uplifting music in a very Irish way. The vocalist sang with a strong Irish twang, the musicians were talented, the drummer looked really young, not old enough to buy a beer even – he almost confirmed this by sucking a dummy tit during the second half of their set. It was obvious that they had quite a strong following amongst the huge attendance at the festival. To see them play was very enjoyable; they were certainly a band to note. I bought their album "If this is rock n roll then I want my old job back" a short time after the Fleadh and was not disappointed – it was a cracker. The cover of the album had a photo of a band on stage, all the musicians having faces of old boys. The old geezers turned out to be the corresponding band members' fathers – fucking brilliant! Turn the cover over and it's the same shot with the actual band's faces – really good I thought. Their music was great for a party or a sing-along, but it didn't have the depth, musically or lyrically that the Pogues had. Who the fuck did though, eh? Exactly!

Time was rolling on, it was getting nearer to Pogues time, the beer was kicking in, so Keith and I decided to get into position, right at the middle front of the main stage, to await the headliners. We still had Christy Moore and Van the man to perform first, and the crowd at the main stage was swelling like a rancid bum boil in a sauna. I didn't know anything about Christy Moore at the time – his performance went over my head really, which was probably an opportunity missed, as I quite like him nowadays. I knew some of Van Morrison's songs though, but his performance reminded me of Bob Dylan's at Wembley Arena. Van the man didn't look at all interested, despite the obvious love the majority of the audience was affording him. For me and Keith, it was great to get Van the bam and Christy's performances out of the way.

We waited patiently, through some very mediocre music (just our opinions) for the mercurial headlining maestros to grace the stage. The crowd intensified, that bum boil was almost bursting now, everyone highly excited to see The Pogues, in all their glory. There must have been about thirty thousand people there that day, and they roared when the group started to appear from the wings of the stage. As a general rule, they usually came on gradually, rather than as one, with yer man MacGowan appearing last of all. Watching the band members emerge on to the spotlight, I honestly got a strange feeling that all was not well, something just wasn't right – maybe it was the expression on their faces. Keith also picked up on this. After a good while, Shane MacGowan graced us with his presence. Now we could see exactly what wasn't right – he was absolutely fucked, well and truly on another planet altogether, totally finished before he'd even started. It was a minor miracle that he could actually stand up. His first slurred words into his microphone were "Happy Christmas, this is Kirsty" – not bad for the middle of summer!

The band cranked into gear, solid as ever, but Shane couldn't go with them; all we got from him was a whimpering whine. The music continued with very little in the way of lyrics from the frontman. It was a quite unbelievable scenario unfolding before the big crowd: a band headlining such a huge event, with one of the finest songwriters and performers these shores has ever produced, not able to perform. I've a feeling that Shane didn't have the flu. He was certainly under the weather though, with, erm, something or other. It was the first time that I had witnessed the great man's unreliability and lack of respect for his bandmates and the punters who so desperately wanted to see him strut his stuff. I felt so sorry for the rest of the Pogues. They soldiered on, including more songs than usual in the set that Shane didn't do vocals for anyway, and somehow got through it. From a selfish point of view I was so pissed off that we had stood and waited for them to perform, watching and listening to two sets that didn't interest me at all, and for what?

The festival ended, and we made our way back to Finsbury Park tube station, full of punters that were talking of one unified subject – some weren't that bothered, but most were angry about the disappointment Shane had inflicted upon their pretty expensive day out (yes, I know, I won our tickets). We got onto a tube eventually – it's a wonder how the transport system copes after such an event – and we arrived back at Hatton Cross, where a workmate picked us up in his car. First question inevitably, "How was The Pogues then?" Silence. Neither Keith nor I really didn't know what to say. What happened that day was far from the end of the world, but I found it amazing that something so damned good, so brilliant, could so easily be turned into a shambles because of one person. The main person. It had not been the first time, as I mentioned before, that he'd let the band down, it's just the first time that I had witnessed it for myself. You'd have thought an Irish festival in North London, where there's a big London Irish presence in the population, would have been right up his street, and he would've been eager to please. He obviously had other ideas.

Shane having an 'off' day did not dampen my enthusiasm for this band, and very soon there was yet another opportunity to see them live in London. Again, this gig was to be a bit different. Held at Brixton Academy, The Pogues were doing a one off show with The Chieftains, an established Irish band with an acclaimed tradition behind them, who were celebrating an anniversary. Really didn't know what to expect with this one – how would Shane be? Only time would tell. Me and the now Pogues regular Keith, were meeting Steve for this one – back to see the wonderful waitresses at the Wimpy then! As we munched our way through our burgers, it became apparent we had a small problem with our ticket arrangements. Keith and I held tickets for the balcony of the Academy, and Steve had one for the stalls. But I had a plan, one that was to be executed with maximum efficiency. At the entrance to the Academy our tickets were checked, and in we went. You're then free to roam the foyer of the venue with its numerous bars and the merchandise stall. When it's time to enter the actual arena where the concert is held, you have to produce your ticket again, stalls or balcony. We'd decided amongst ourselves that we would try and get Steve into the balcony, so we could enjoy the concert in each other's company. So Keith and I made our way into the balcony area and secured three seats with a good view of the stage. I told Keith to guard the seats with his life, if anyone hustled him for them, then he would have to 'sumo' the dirty devils. I made my way back out to the bar area with Keith's ticket as well as my own tucked into my pocket, met Steve, who was getting the beers in (good man Steve) and so he used Keith's ticket to get past the burly security mannie at the door of the balcony... simplicity in itself!

The lights went down in the Brixton Academy, and Shane MacGowan appeared on the stage first of all, like an Olympic sprinter out of the blocks, like an early paced greyhound out of a trap that had his arse rubbed in Tabasco – he meant business all right! One can only imagine the debates that had gone on between him and his bandmates, and with Mr Frank Murray, the band's manager, regarding his last, recent performance up the road in Finsbury Park. Shane's body language was that of a man who had something to prove, and I thought to myself that tonight was going to be good! At this point, we still didn't know what the format was for the evening's entertainment, but the rest of the Pogues took their positions on stage – no sign of the Chieftains yet – and they blasted us with a fine opener in 'If I should fall from grace with god'. MacGowan was on fire, taking his responsibilities for the night very seriously indeed, fucking great! The rest of the band followed suit; everyone was back in the groove after Finsbury.

The Pogues then departed backstage and The Chieftains came on. Steve knew a bit about them, but Keith and I were ignorant of their history. Having said that, we enjoyed their performance; we very quickly developed a particular liking for The Chieftains' Derek Bell, their percussionist and general multi instrumentalist. He reminded me of an old fashioned school music teacher, moving his head about, almost violently at times, in tune to the various notes of music he was contributing to the Chieftains' performance. After a while, The Pogues joined them on a now very busy stage, and the two bands merged into one mighty fusion of wonderful music.

Of course The Pogues had a bit of experience at this lark of congested stages under their belts, when they had previously joined with The Dubliners to record 'The Irish Rover' and a top ten single was the ultimate result. They proved themselves to be durable and versatile, fitting in with other bands this way. Tthere was TV footage of their performances with the Dubliners and it all appeared to be very natural and comfortable; both bands looked like they were thoroughly enjoying the merger.

This was also the case for tonight's show with The Chieftains. I particularly remember Spider and his tin whistle, having to negotiate a particularly tricky song whilst on stage when both bands had joined together; he looked very humble about the situation, but fair play to him, he delivered the goods in style, to admiring looks from The Chieftains' personnel. And what about Shane? Well he put in a truly vintage performance, as only our sparsely toothed hero could. He most certainly delivered; things seemed so much easier when he did, everything worked, he seemed happy to share the stage with artists he could relate to, and he had redeemed himself to his own comrades after his fuck up in the park. There's only one Shane MacGowan!

So Keith, Steve and I stood up from our seats, as did all the packed balcony that night, and bopped away to the magic music we had come to hear. Keith always liked a bit of rough and tumble at a gig, the rowdier the better, and I think that the upstairs part of the Academy that night, just wasn't quite rowdy enough for him. He was sitting to the left of Steve, and was really trying to encourage him to get rowdier, pulling at his shoulders to the beat of the music, trying to get him in the mood. Steve wasn't in the mood. He'd had a bad day at work, wasn't in the best of fettle, and whilst he was enjoying his night, he wasn't enjoying the attention he was getting from Sumo Keith. I was at the other side of Steve, watching all the developments re Keith wanting a jig, and the expressions on Steve's grimacing face, just adding to the entertainment and great time I was having in South London. Our Oriental, people-shoving sportsman friend did eventually get the hint, and Steve managed to enjoy the rest of his evening in relative unhindered peace. It was a brilliant concert, a mix of Pogues songs, Chieftains songs, and some traditional Irish songs all making a unique enjoyable experience for the Brixton punters.

I didn't, however, realise how significant this concert would turn out to be. Shane MacGowan was one of the main reasons my attention strayed towards the Pogues in the first place: his name, his looks, and, my god, his lyrics and songs! He went against the grain of air brushed polished pop stars, what you saw was what you got (Finsbury Park and all). Shane in my opinion was just totally unique, and obviously so very original. It turned out though that the other members of The Pogues were nearing their wits' end when it came to accommodating Shane, in a working sense. The experience of watching him at Finsbury Park was the tip of the iceberg. I had been lucky up until then. I'd seen The Pogues so many times, all the shows were mesmerisingly amazing, with the possible exception of the first time at The Electric Ballroom in Camden, but Finsbury Park showed thousands of Pogues supporters what it could be like when yer man was NOT at the races.

The Brixton concert with The Chieftains came to an end. Steve travelled home to East London, Keith and I back to Surrey, wondering when we'd see the band next. There was always a next time to look forward to, something would be announced and advertised, and we'd do it all again. The Pogues took off for a while from these shores though, embarking on a tour of Japan. Things came to a head. Things came to an end. Next thing we knew, there was an announcement from The Pogues camp. But it wasn't about their next gig. The news was that Shane MacGowan was no longer in The Pogues – they'd parted with him, or he'd parted with them. Whatever. It was over. The Pogues without Shane MacGowan? How did that work? Well, it didn't, did it?

NIGHT NURSE
TUESDAY MORNING

There appeared to be an air of mystery surrounding Shane's exit from the band. Some reports said he'd been sacked, some said he had just left of his own accord. This actually went on for some time, but really, what did it matter? The band were officially Shane-less, and that was a fact. Word was that the Pogues were going to carry on without him, and as for Shane, well, nobody knew at that point what the near future held for him. The Pogues had recruited old chum Joe Strummer as a temporary vocalist; he didn't record anything with the band, but he sang at their live shows. A popular choice in most quarters, the man is a legend in his own right of course, but he earned that status with The Clash, not The Pogues. Quite simply, no one could replace Shane MacGowan in this band; it just wasn't possible.

Joe Strummer's time with The Pogues came and went. It's reported that the majority of band members were disappointed about his departure. I actually think if he'd hung around, the group would have became 'Joe Strummer and The Pogues'. He would've ended up with the attention, and eventually the live crowds would've been screaming for Clash numbers all night. Yes, Shane MacGowan did receive most of the attention in the Pogues, and I sometimes felt a bit sorry for the rest of the band regarding this, but at least he was part of his own band, the one he formed with his pals back in King's Cross. Joe Strummer was not a Pogue, just a guest now and again. As I said previously, I thought the Pogues were so strong with their own material, that Joe Strummer coming on to do a few Clash songs with the band was an unwelcome distraction, but that was just my opinion, nothing more. I'm well aware that it's a controversial one; it's just how I felt.

Life goes on though, and I was on the move from my flat in Staines, to leafy Englefield Green, to move into Keith's flat. I'd always fancied a move to the green, a room became free, and I was permitted to move. The flat was only about a mile from the hotel, which was handy, as Staines was about six miles away. Englefield Green was a large village, near Egham, Surrey, complete with local cricket team, who played on the actual green. Fucking splendid! Keith's flat was above a paper shop; he had a lovely view of the graveyard from his window! Paula was still living in Staines. In truth, we were more like brother and sister really, our relationship was never of the smouldering passionate kind, and we never moved in together; we both wanted our own space. Keith and Paula were pals, but at times they could bicker for Britain. It used to drive me mad; they were always arguing, usually with Paula winding Keith up, and he'd always take the bait, and then bang, that was it, war. Still, it usually passed quickly enough, and order was restored.

I was back into a smallish room at Keith's gaff. There was a horrific steep staircase from the front door to that of the flat, which needed full mountaineering skills when drunk, but it was a good move for me. I really liked Englefield Green, and still do. The local hostelry that we frequented was The Holly Tree, just a very short stagger from the Mount Everest staircase and the flat. The Pogues, though, were never far away. Steve was in touch, wondering if I wanted to go and see them at Brixton Academy. I replied to him that I would give it a miss this time. I couldn't begin to imagine them without Shane. Steve kept on at me – he was determined to go, we'd been to see them at Brixton quite a few times now, and Steve was probably salivating in advance re the Wimpy. I stood my ground for a while, but eventually gave in. Steve even treated me to my ticket, such was his determination to go to this gig. So we partook in the usual burger and made our way into Brixton Academy; we were in the stalls for this one. Straight away, there was a major difference from the gigs we attended here when the band still had a Shane. The attendance was poor. Brixton Academy's stalls have a massive, swooping sloped floor; it even has football stadium-like metal crash barriers near the front, but rather than the punters being squashed like sardines in a tin, there was plenty of room and wide open spaces in that sloping floor. There was, however, still, a hardcore army of fans, directly in front of the stage; they were certainly up for the cup, even if the punters behind them were somewhat more subdued. I have no recollection of a support band, but when The Pogues came on stage, it was clear that there was not to be a surge of last minute punters flooding through the doors, I think the attendance tells it own story really, it just wasn't The Pogues without MacGowan; interest had waned, I wouldn't have been there if Steve hadn't have been so persistent. Strummer had gone by now – had he been there then I'm quite sure ticket sales would've been considerably brisker – but for now, Spider Stacy was in the saddle for vocal duties.

I didn't know all the circumstances regarding Shane's departure from the Pogues. I don't think a lot of people did at the time, apart from the band and close acquaintances themselves, and I hate to admit, but I did feel some contempt for the remaining Pogues on the stage that night at Brixton, but only through my own ignorance. Spider, I felt, was not up to the job – not for a whole concert. I was really surprised how 'mechanical' the band's performance was; there didn't seem to be much in the way of chemistry on stage. They were at work, doing a job; it would be time to go home soon – that's how it felt. To be fair, musically, the Pogues still sounded as solid as they ever had. Spider was put in an impossible position of trying to sing vintage Pogues numbers that were not 'designed' for his vocals; it just wasn't his bag. I suppose he has to be applauded, for filling the void left by MacGowan.

The situation actually reminded me of when Ian Curtis prematurely said goodbye to the world. His band, Joy Division, soldiered on manfully without him as New Order, with Bernard Sumner stepping up to the lead vocal microphone. I've seen some footage of Bernard's first crack at the singing, and it's so bad it's unbelievable – not his fault though, his courage had to be admired. Spider's vocals were not as bad as Bernard's early performance, but they just didn't work with a Pogues classic. Spider doesn't deserve to be criticised (please forgive me sir), he did his best. It might have been a case of frying pans and fires right enough for The Pogues though, as Spider had major issues with alcohol at the time apparently, and was proving to be difficult to work with. In time, Bernard Sumner somehow managed to grasp and prosper as lead vocalist with the newly spawned New Order. The pressure on Spider must have been horrific. Spider is loved and adored by all Pogues fans, myself included; he was actually on a hiding to nothing really, to stand up there, on centre microphone. Where Shane should have been.

The opening song for The Pogues' set at Brixton was 'Sayonara' a MacGowan song from 'Hell's Ditch'. The hard core at the front showed their enthusiasm and love as they would have back in the day; the rest of us stood and watched and wished for what could have been. Spider's vocals now and again at a Pogues show was fine, his backing vocals were great, but lead vocals for the whole show was beyond him. Even though he had bollocked me at The Electric Ballroom, he was still one of the main men in my opinion in the Pogues set up, always will be; the band would not have been the same without him either.

I went for a piss. You usually had to queue at the Academy, which was a double whammy as you were missing the show and had to hold in your poisonous, steaming waste liquid for a wee while longer than you had anticipated. Debate in the tiled shithouse was enthusiastic; someone had said that Shane was there, and a grand entrance was being planned for him to appear on stage with his band, his family, his friends. It was very easy to believe, you just wanted it to be true, but somehow, you knew it was a load of bollocks. Which it was.

Steve and I left before the end. We went to the tube station on Brixton High Street, and when our tube train got to Victoria, we went our separate ways. Time to reflect. It hit me there and then that The Pogues thing that I dearly loved was over. The Pogues without Shane was just not for me; tonight's show rubber stamped this. I knew I wouldn't be back to see the band with the Shane-less line up – that sounds harsh, but with the very odd exception, Shane MacGowan penned Pogues songs were the best ones, so I wondered what the future would hold, when it came to the band recording new material. I decided that I just wouldn't be bothering to even find out. I was gutted

Shane had left, and, being very ignorant to the facts, I actually blamed the remaining band members for my selfish loss. I still attended music gigs seeing different bands, but The Pogues were my band of choice, and it really was finished. So, I drew a line under The Pogues that night. I suppose, as they say, nothing lasts forever.

Moving to Englefield Green meant that I was obviously spending more social time with Keith, and also with Philip, the head chef. The three of us took up golf, on our own terms, very much fair weather and nineteenth hole stuff! We found two par three courses that we liked at Ascot and Woking. Our style of play was extremely dubious – mine and Keith's gear left a lot to be desired (Philip's was a bit more upmarket) – but I really enjoyed those days. We also started a football team at the hotel. We had a set of GREEN strips (magic) and would play the odd match against bad amateur football sides and against our rival hotel, The Runnymede, just down the road. Big Les and Lorraine came over from their place in Hornchurch, to cheer us on sometimes, when we were playing a match.

On one of those occasions, after the match, we retired to Staines for a wee refreshment, in the Phoenix bar. Spirits were high, it was still quite early in the day and Les introduced us to a drinking game of spoof. Now the spirits were in demand! His version involved tossing a coin. If he said "Heads are in" and you had a head, you stayed in the game, a tail and you were out obviously. The game had three rounds; first round, whoever was left in at the end nominated a drink. But we are not talking gin and tonic here. A good example would perhaps be a Baileys with Malibu and tomato juice! Sometimes the concoctions would curdle. The person left at the end of the second round would go to the bar and buy the particular 'cocktail', and in the third round, yep, the last man/woman would have to neck it, in a oner! The pub was quiet, and the barman seemed happy enough to be serving up these weird and wonderful beverages. However, as the cocktails kicked in, and our volume inevitably increased, he came over to the table and an amazing conversation started. He said to us, "Are you lot drunk?" Erm, well, possibly. "Well if you are, you can bloody get out!" I said to him that it was just as well he didn't run a restaurant – if the punters were full up with their food, he'd be throwing them out an' all! The twat was quite happy taking our money, when we were buying the weird cocktails, and they weren't cheap!

Really, we didn't care though. We made our way along the High Street and to the 'staff' pub, The Garibaldi, where our game of spoof continued, and our speech slurred accordingly. Neil came to join an already blootered company, not the easiest of things sometimes, so we decided to stitch him up and get him in the mood. We would all cheat in the last round of spoof, and take away our coins quickly, declaring ourselves out, until it was just him left in to quaff a bottle of Guinness, a small white wine an' a nip of Southern Comfort, all in a pint glass. It was a lovely colour, and was fragrant from a considerable distance. All was going to plan, but Keith's reactions were waning; Neil escaped the last round, Keith was too slow with his coin and ended up the 'winner'. Like the true sportsman he is, he got through the pint of toxins, but I've never seen anyone be sick like he was, almost instantly – it was like a rapid waterfall coming out of his mouth and it went on for ages. That was us sent on our way from The Garibaldi then, no loss there though.

A new single was to appear on the music scene. It was called 'Tuesday Morning' and it was by The Pogues. I went out of my way to avoid it. I wanted to be uninterested, as a personal, pointless protest. I was in the flat alone one night and the bloody song came on Top of the Pops. I watched for just enough time for the show's host to say something like, "Here's The Pogues with a brand new single, and they've got a brand new front man, this is great". The bastard. Obviously my opinion of Spider being the lead vocalist with The Pogues was not shared by all. He was actually implying that things were better now that Spider was fucking singing – well, that's how I interpreted his introduction. I turned the channel over on the box; there might have been a really interesting documentary about a dating service for single lawnmowers on the other side.

It was an early night for me on this particular evening. I was full of the cold, my nose has never been my strongest body part, my father being the same; we always have hankies on our person, 24/7. Night Nurse liquid nearly always did the trick for me, clearing my cold up. Only downside of this was it made me very hungry and also very, very grumpy. It knocks you out, giving you an amazing sleep, but the next day, you never quite wake up properly, and I was always on a short fuse. Worth it though, to clear up my snottery beak.

Anyway, back to the Top of the Pops night, I went to bed suitably Night Nursed and settled into a comfortable night's kip. That 'Tuesday Morning' thing would be no good anyway, how could it be, without Mr MacGowan? Keith was on a late shift; he was a real creature of habit, and tried to shoehorn a couple or three pints at the Holly Tree before closing time – tonight was no exception. He and Neil ventured up the Everest stairs; they weren't being quiet, and they woke me up from my Night Nurse induced kip. Now we are talking major grumps time! I tried to ignore them, find a comfy spot in my bed and disappear again, into the land of blissful nod. But Keith Williams had other ideas! Being a 'charts man' as I called him, he had taped Top of the Pops on his video recorder, and was in the mood to watch the latest 'hot' tunes that were dominating the charts that he so loved, the same charts that were influenced so much by teenage girls, buying the dubious sounds. I just knew what was coming. My efforts to get back to sleep failed miserably, and I could hear that Top of the Pops presenter introducing The Pogues again. The volume on Keith's TV mysteriously went up more than a notch, his bedroom door wide open for maximum effect. Once 'Tuesday Morning' was played and rewound to play again, several times, Keith was getting into the swing of things; he was now singing along with Spider, giving it large, right outside my fucking bedroom door! I'd fucking well had enough by now, I was up out of my bed, GRUMPY as fuck, opened my door, and screamed at my tormentor, "TURN THAT FUCKING SHITE OFF, NOW!"

Keith was defiant, he was up for some concert style rough and tumble to this song blaring out of his TV set. He'd 'sumoed' me at Baker Street, and now he was tormenting me with the new Pogues single, that he just knew would get my back up. Fair play to him, he genuinely liked Spider's song 'Tuesday Morning'. We often laugh about this night in the flat nowadays, and talking of nowadays, I actually like, no, love the song, especially live. For the record, 'Tuesday Morning' gave the new-look Pogues a top 20 single, it propelled them into the mainstream music scene, and ultimately this did them no harm when they released their album, 'Waiting for Herb'. I took no interest in either the single or the album at the time though. Keith maybe didn't want to give up on The Pogues just yet, where as I was already there. In fairness to him, he still went to see ELO Part II, without Jeff Lynne, so maybe he was more loyal than me; actually, don't think there's any maybe about it.

Talking of ELO Part II, Keith got us tickets to see them at Hammersmith Odeon. An adventure, then, was just around the corner!

KELLY'S HAT

Working in the kitchen of The Anugraha Hotel and Conference centre was, for the most part, all good. The kitchen brigade were a real team, and none of us were competitive or insecure about our work – the Chef wouldn't have allowed any of that. All in all we all got on generally very well; in fact the whole hotel staff did. The majority of the workforce were actually from Scotland or the north east of England, and there were obviously a few locals too. We had quite a few students from various European countries, completing work placements, the kitchen porters were a group of older Indian ladies, so all in all, you could say the staff were from all over the world, which certainly kept things interesting, both at work and at leisure.

Our main market was large number functions; firms, such as car manufacturers, would use the hotel to launch their latest models, and in the summer we catered for lots of couples getting spliced, seeing to their wedding receptions. But there were smaller function rooms within the hotel too, so we could cater for just about anything that was thrown at us. The surroundings of the hotel were beautiful, set in lovely grounds with a lake, next door to a small polo pitch. It was certainly a place to be proud of. Of course, it wasn't sunshine and roses all the time, but when things didn't go to plan, it was sorted quickly, and we moved on; staff morale was generally high, certainly in the kitchen anyway.

We got paid fortnightly, and around payday, a trip to Sticky Fingers in Kensington was never far away. It was a real treat for a few of us to go there for a good slurp of their wonderful draught Budweiser. Between 4 and 5 o'clock, the golden liquor was half price, due to a happy hour. It always proved to be a very happy hour indeed; we naturally got as many in as we could, followed by a meal, and usually a boozy journey home. When you exited Sticky Fingers and went onto Kensington High Street, you turned left for the tube station, or right, as a general rule, if someone was picking us up by car. Keith had an uncanny habit of turning the wrong way and getting lost from the group. However, like a thoroughbred homing pigeon, he always made it back, safe and sound, but often not being able to tell you which route he had taken. Sometimes he would be back well before the rest of us.

It was just me and him, at Sticky Fingers, on the night that ELO Part II were due to strut their stuff, just up the road at Hammersmith Odeon. We'd had a good night so far, a few beers and a quality scoff; the aromas in Sticky Fingers certainly made you want to order food, you could almost taste the sticky sweet barbecue sauce they served, straight from the air. I was in a naughty mood; I was ready for a carry-on. Keith went for a piss when he was finished his grub, and I grabbed the squeezy yellow mustard bottle, that had a very handy fine hole in the top of the lid, for accurate mustarding. I cleared a space where he had been eating at our table, and drew a lovely mustard picture of a house, complete with smoking chimney, straight onto the wooden table. It was a work of art, and I was proud of my creativity. As I saw Keith in the distance, making his way back to the table, I got out of my seat, alerted a waiter, and asked him for our bill. I also apologised to the chap, on Keith's behalf, for the childish act he had committed with the mustard bottle. Then, I carried on, and went for a piss, that I didn't really need. On my return, there was a mini stewards' enquiry going on at the table. I apologised yet again for Keith, and I asked the waiter if he would phone us a taxi – he was more than pleased to oblige, and get us on our way. The black taxi arrived quickly, and we got in, Keith still moaning about the house of mustard. The cabbie asked us where we were going, and before Keith could speak, I said, "Wimbledon Greyhounds please". The cabbie shunted the taxi forward, but Keith was right on his case saying, "No, no, Hammersmith Odeon's where we're going to mate". I've got a feeling the cabbie was crabbit before we'd even stepped into his vehicle; now he was off the scale on the crabbitometer! "Wimbledon Dogs," I roared. The driver stopped the cab. "Where the fuckin' 'ell are ya goin?" I had to pipe down, and settle for our destination being the one that Keith preferred, the crabbit driver hastily, angrily, forced the black cab forward, driving down the main road where Kensington shacks into Hammersmith. On arrival we did the decent thing and gave him a good tip for his troubles; he even managed a little laugh with us, before he sped off, maybe not so crabbit now.

Keith and I headed down to the front of the stalls, ELO Part II appeared and started grinding out their songs. I was familiar with most of them, and they were ok. Keith was lapping it up, but in truth, I was thinking back to the many Pogues shows I'd been to and enjoyed, and realised how shite it was that it was over. I was still, however, feeling naughty. ELO went off, anticipating their first encore; I got a rush of blood to the head, and climbed up on to the stage, ran to the back near the drumkit, and snatched a purple velvet hat that was lying there; it belonged to Kelly Groucutt, the band's bass player. I skipped back into the crowd, and, very proudly, presented Keith with what I thought was a fantastic piece of ELO Part II memorabilia! I don't think Keith could quite believe what had just happened, and what was in his hands. "Kelly's hat," he said.

My naughty mood was showing no signs of let up, so when the band came back on stage to see their adoring fans, I got Kelly the bass player's attention. He was looking straight at me. I was wearing his hat. The realisation of his hat being nicked was written all over his face – he didn't seem to be seeing the funny side of the situation. Suddenly, another encore by the band. I'm not so sure that this one was scheduled to slot in with the set list, but off they went... maybe they were going to add a number or two, how about: "Where did you get that hat, where did you get that hat?" When they came back on, there were no songs about hats, but a security chappie appeared, and he wanted a word with me and Keith. Keith had the hat in his hands at this point, and despite Mr Security saying he would be happy to return it to its rightful owner, Keith wasn't playing, and as the band continued to plug ELO's greatest hits, a mini game of tug o' war broke out with

Keith, security mannie, and a purple velvet hat in the middle of them. Keith lost the battle, and the hat was taken away, presumably to be given back to Kelly the bass player. Perhaps if I hadn't taunted Kelly, by showing him the hat, that mysteriously ended up on my bonce, Keith would've got away with the prized item, but it wasn't to be – sorry Keith! This wasn't to be the end of the purple hat story either!

Paula was driving to Hammersmith to pick us up in the car (for which we would be paying, I may add), so when the band finished, we headed out into the night air to try and find her. As we walked by the side of the venue, a fire door swung open, and a bloke appeared. He was carrying a pile of gig advertisement posters, for the show that we had just witnessed minutes earlier. They were large posters, yellow background with bold black literature, and the bloke was heading for the large bins that were just down the alley. I was over to him in a flash. "I'll have them, mate." He didn't object, and handed the pile over to me, shrugged his shoulders, then disappeared back inside the Odeon. I got into gear quickly; these self praising arrogant Dragons from the Den would've been falling over themselves to make me an offer. I put the posters over my arm and made my way into the middle of the pavement, and into the flow of punters leaving the Odeon. I was battling against the noise of the traffic overhead on the M4 flyover, but, nevertheless, my opportune business venture commenced. "AEEER A POSTIHRS! AEEEER A POSTIHRS! GET YUR OFFISHIAL ELO POSTIHRS HERE! TWO POUN A POSTIHRS!" My kind offer to provide a poster service for the ELO Part II public was appreciated immediately, and initial, early sales were brisk. At £2 a pop, my pockets were soon jingling. Keith was impressed. When the crowds died away, I was still left with plenty of posters. Keith asked me for two, and he had his money out ready. Yes, he really did! We both fell about laughing, but make no mistake, Keith wanted a couple of posters and was quite prepared to hand over currency, to me, to secure them. The silly sausage!

We eventually met Paula, a wee bit later than arranged, due to the poster gig, but at least we had some coinage to pay for the journey home. What a brilliant night, although some of the ELO Part II public didn't agree. Keith had a subscription with an ELO Part II fanzine, and in the issue after the Hammersmith concert there was a review of the night's proceedings, including a report on the Kelly's hat episode. The review mentioned the arsehole that went on stage to steal the hat, but all was well in the end as a 'team' of security personnel waded in and made sure justice was done. Kelly was indeed reunited with his famous, iconic hat, and the arsehole's concert burglary was thwarted. Fantastic. Fame at last! I wonder if the article writer bought a poster from me outside! The article actually made the hat incident a bit more glamorous than it was, but I wasn't going to complain, and I've been called much worse than an arsehole. Keith was, in the future, to meet the person that wrote the article, and was to meet Kelly Groucutt too. I think he kept it firmly shut though, about his arsehole mate, and hat-gate!

I arranged another trip home, back to Perth. Hibs were playing the local side, St Johnstone, in the Scottish Cup, so I negotiated a quiet train journey, and even sat on the correct seat I had booked. Visits home were always superb; my bedroom in the family house had hardly changed at all, even after all this time. Saturday was football day. I remember this day in particular for an event that happened at the actual match itself, and it involved one of the blokes from The Proclaimers. For those of you not familiar with The Proclaimers, they are a band featuring two bespectacled twins, originally from Auchtermuchty in Fife. They actually supported The Pogues many years ago at Picnic in the Park, when they played in the big tent, at Finsbury Park. I mentioned this in an earlier chapter – it was the gig that I couldn't go to because I was working, but was jealous of my workmates who did attend. The bastards! Anyway, the Proclaimer twins are both big Hibs supporters and can be seen at the Hibs matches regularly. I can personally take or leave their music; I think they've released a few good songs, but I wouldn't call myself a fan. The majority of the Hibs supporters love them, and that's fine. They have an emotional song called 'Sunshine on Leith', Leith being the area that Hibs are from, and the song has become an anthem at Easter Road, the home of the Hibees, and I do really like that particular number – it actually became a really emotional song for me and my friends, but that was in the future.

Back to the St Johnstone v Hibs match: a good time, as always, was being had by all. Hibs were one up – happy days then. Half time arrived, with Hibs still ahead, and the punters went about their business, whether it be a piss, buy a pie, catch up with the gossip, or whatever. There was a bloke sat directly in front of me, who had slept and snored all the way through the first half of the game, but he was stirring, and he eventually came to at half time. He had quite clearly overstepped the mark with the drink before the match, and had a wee snooze when he settled into his seat at the stadium.

Now, there was plenty of noise at the game – Hibs had scored a goal after all – and the end of the ground we were in was full, but matey had slept through all this as well; nothing had roused him, but now he was curious! Inevitably, he turned round to face me. "Oi, mate! What's the fuckin' score?" I replied, "It's one nil Hibs, Keith Houchen scored." "Oh, that's fuckin good, aye, good, cheers pal." He was finished with me. I was quite glad.

He started having a look about, slowly bringing himself back into the land of the living, when a monumental moment of recognition descended upon him. One of the Proclaimer twins was sitting near him; our wakened man was squinting his eyes, concentrating hard. He didn't say anything, but his body language was funnily saying, "I know you from somewhere, I fuckin' do!" Still, the penny wasn't dropping, the puzzled staring continued, and he was muttering to himself, tortured that he just couldn't quite put his finger on who the speccy bloke was. He was unaware that he was attracting a small audience; it was hilarious. The Proclaimer bloke could feel sleeping beauty's stare all right, but wasn't too concerned at this point.

Then, all of a sudden, BINGO! yer man was at the races, he'd worked it out. You could almost sense the frustration draining from his body, as he tapped the Proclaimer on the shoulder. "Oi! Mate! Are you one of thae Proclaimer geezers?" To his eternal credit, the Proclaimer was very civil to matey, when he replied, "Yeah, I'm Charlie." There was a measured pause from Charlie's brand new pal, before he delivered a reply that took everyone in the immediate listenable vicinity's breath away – that was. "WELL, YOU'RE FUCKING SHITE!"

Nobody was expecting that. There was no further conversation between the now, best ex mates – surely the quickest best friend relationship in history? Charlie didn't react, lots of eyes were watching developments, and the situation fizzled out, but there was lots of sniggering, giggling and amused faces all around. It was a superbly funny moment; though I wish Charlie and his band no harm, I knew what the bloke meant.

As was usually the case, when it was time to get the train back down South, and leave my parents and friends again, there was always an element of sadness involved. Yes, I loved my job, yes, I more than enjoyed the lure of Central London, with its gigs and poster selling opportunities, but it did hurt saying goodbye to my parents, as it did with my mates. I couldn't have it both ways though, could I? I usually got the sleeper train back to London Euston on the Monday night. Getting the sleeper train back gave me some valuable extra time at home, but I found the whole sleeper experience quite incredible. For a start, when you got on the train, there was a pair of very dubious 'hostesses' there to check your ticket and, erm, greet you. They were older ladies, and would not have looked out of place as top dogs in Prisoner Cell Block H. I'm quite sure that if there was the slightest chance of any trouble brewing in the sleeper carriages, it would have been dealt with, with maximum efficiency by this two!

Unless you had a first class sleeping berth to yourself, you were basically sharing bunk beds with a stranger (of the same gender), and I shared with a few characters over the years. One in particular was a boozy oil rig worker, who had been on the lash all day, before catching the sleeper back to London. I've never been a good sleeper, and this bloke was making sure that it just wasn't happening for me on this journey. To be fair, him on the top bunk offered me a tin of beer, followed by a go at his fish supper, and, incredibly, "a shot" of his dirty magazine. Politely as I could I declined them all. He eventually grunted off into sleep with the worst snoring I've ever heard in my life. I was just grateful that he didn't appear to look at his magazine for too long! I think I may have drifted off around Watford, when I was awoken by the no nonsense dispassionate steward. Matey with the beer, fish and mag had already gone, suitably refreshed no doubt.

I would wearily make my way across London amongst the hustle of the morning rush hour, usually with a heavy heart about leaving my parents behind again. They were getting older, and I was starting to feel that they could have done with having me around. I started to feel guilty, wishing I could be closer and be there to help if they needed me. We were close as a family and kept in touch with religious regularity, but I was always torn between my life in the south and that of home. I decided that I wanted to do something nice for my folks, maybe give them some money for a wee holiday. My cash flow was reasonably all right, but I still had no savings to talk of – the bookie was the main beneficiary of my finances, but I had no real regrets on this score, as I was still visiting the numerous London dog tracks, and really enjoyed this. Apart from a Sunday, there were dog meetings in London every night of the week, so we could just take off in the car and attend one, if time and cash allowed. Sadly, a lot of the tracks we liked going to are now closed – Hackney, Catford, Wembley and Walthamstow were all favourite hunting grounds of ours. Keith and I got into some awful messes with lumps of money going on usually uninterested hounds, but sometimes it came off, we had some great nights, and I always lived within my means, financially.

One night at Walthamstow, a bookmaker told me a wonderful story. For those of you unfamiliar with greyhound racing, the dogs chase an imitation hare round the track, the hare obviously being in front. This bookmaker had chalked up a price for the hare on his list of 'runners' for a race. He had the hare available at odds of 6 to 1. A punter came and put £20 on the hare. Of course, the hare inevitably won the race. When the bloke came to pick up his money, the bookie told him that he couldn't pay him out. He said, "I know the hare won, and so do you, but the judge has called the name of a dog as a winner, and who am I to argue with the official result!" Brilliant. That gives you an idea of the banter at the dogs; you certainly needed your wits about you.

So, with my dog racing nights still at the fore, if I were to do something for Ma and Pa Bruce, then I would have to sell the only real thing of value that I owned. My sparkling, gleaming, clinical Pogues collection. There was nothing else really for me to look for or collect, as I wasn't interested in what the band were doing nowadays without Shane. The fun of the thing was actually looking for the various treasures I had picked up over the years, so if I could turn my collection into cash, then I could send my parents some, and they would be proud of their wee laddie. I wrote to three dealers that I knew would be interested in my collection. I listed everything I had – apart from the band's albums of course; I couldn't do without them, as they were still played regularly, and were still the main attraction at parties.

I received a reply straight away, from a dealer in the Manchester area. He made me an offer, and I was pleasantly surprised at the amount he was quoting. The Pogues catalogue was sought after by serious collectors, the rarer items were gradually becoming more valuable, so it was a good time to sell. The best and most impressive example of this was indeed the very first Pogues white label 'Dark streets of London' single, that I had swithered about for £18 – the Manchester dealer offered me a cool £100 for this particular jewel. I phoned and we struck a deal. I still hadn't heard from the other two dealers, but I was more than happy with the offer I had on the table. We arranged to meet at a service station on the M1.

When we found each other we had a cup of tea and a good crack about music and the football (he was a Leeds Utd fan). The only problem was he didn't have all the money on him. The price we had arranged was quite a large one; he had half the money, and was going to send me a cheque for the remainder in a week or so. This changed the mood slightly, but I made the decision to trust him, and we shook hands. I'm pleased to say that he was true to his word, and a cheque did indeed flop through my letterbox about a week later. He was delighted with his purchase, and I was sure he would do well with it. I did receive another offer from one of the other dealers that I had contacted; the amount was about the same all in all that I had already accepted, although this dealer offered me £120 for 'Dark streets of London', and he was gutted that I had already sold my collection, that single in particular. He was far too slow off the mark though, something that actually really annoys me at times. In certain situations it's only the early birds that prosper, make a decision and live by it. The ditherer usually misses out, and that was certainly the case here.

In time, I thought I might regret selling my Pogues collection, but I didn't. I told myself that I would do it all again one day, but in the meantime I wrote a letter to Mum and Dad, with a nice cheque nestling in the middle of the writing paper. My mother phoned me (far too early in the morning for her), she was in tears, and I felt for the first time in my life that I'd actually managed to do something for them for a change; it was a really nice feeling. Indirectly of course, The Pogues helped me achieve this mature gesture – thanks lads, if the records had been crap or not collectable, then the whole exercise would not have been possible.

There were still no Pogues gigs to go to though, and I'd be a marked man at ELO Part II now, surely. Even though I'd stopped seeing The Pogues without their proper frontman, and sold my collection, I never fell out of love with the superb music they had recorded and released. I just needed something of a tonic on the live music scene to happen. It wasn't long until my prayers were duly answered!

SHANE MACGOWAN AND THE POPES? BACKSTAGE FROLICS

It was time, for Mr Shane MacGowan to, at last, come out of hiding. All had been quiet in his world, apparently, after his exit from The Pogues, but all of a sudden, BANG! An advertisement appeared in the live concerts section of the music press. "Shane MacGowan And the Popes" St Patrick's Day, London, The Grand, Clapham. What the fuck's this? I was very interested, and quickly was on the phone to secure two tickets for myself and Keith. The gig was almost upon us date wise, it was the first time I had booked tickets by credit card, and furthermore I was to pick up the tickets at the venue on the night. I was a bit uneasy about the uncertainty of all this, going to the venue, and the staff saying, "Calum who? Sorry, don't know anything about you booking tickets, so, not tonight son, eh?"

Anyhow, I made the simply awful decision to take the car and drive to this one, Keith being my 'have as much as you like to drink' passenger. The Bastard! Driving on London's South Circular Road was always a challenge; I'd driven on this road a few times previously on the way to Catford, to gamble on the doggies, it was a bugger of a road, with lots of confusing junctions, usually full of impatient Londoners, who were not in the mood for hesitant novices on their road. But, South Circular Road negotiated, we arrived in sunny Clapham in plenty of time for a quick bite and a drink. One drink for me. Great. We settled in a boozer almost opposite the venue. It seemed a bit quiet considering there was a gig on of some significance across the road, and I had my one drink. It was delicious. Keith had his first drink too, followed by several more, and generally relaxed his way into the evening. The Bastard! Fuck me, WHY did I decide to drive?

Anyway, with Keith suitably marinated, we made our way across the road to, I must say, an impressive looking venue, first time for us both, and joined a large queue for the box office. There were lots of folks picking up their tickets, just like us. The mood in the box office area was strangely quiet; I genuinely think the punters really didn't know what to expect, with this Shane and The Popes thing. Enter King Kong's Auntie Bertha! This absolute fucking cow of a security woman appeared, and for some unknown reason seemed to be a bit disappointed that things were so quiet. She was telling everyone to be patient, and to form an orderly queue and various other unnecessary crap that was definitely not appropriate to the punters who were doing exactly that before she turned up. She was proving to be as popular as a doctor in the pox clinic, with an angry facial expression, and a sterile umbrella implement in hand! She really looked the part. Twinkling her bunch of keys, walkie talkie in view, she was huge and had a puss like a bashed in fish box, she boasted facial hair that any teenage lad would have been proud of. It was quite ironic that she was 'working' at a gig, as she looked like she'd just completed her own British tour of 'All you can eat' lunchtime buffets! A real bad case of an insecure jobsworth. She even started having a wee shove, to keep the queue 'in line'.

I had a jean jacket on that night. When it was my turn for her unwelcome attention, she decided to grab my jacket at the bottom, to give me a tug. I could see this coming a mile off, and quick as a flash I grabbed her fat rubbery hand, and shoved it away. She was furious about this, so the witch and I embarked on a healthy debate on the subject of customer service; there were a few comments from our captivated audience, all in my favour I may add, and I appeared to get the better of her as she fucked off back to her hole in the earth. Then I had this terrible thought. It was bothering me big time. I had imagined that she would be back, with a couple of tattooed hairy gorillas, with piercings everywhere. To remove me, hell, even give me a bit of a hiding, all happening under the instruction of Bertha. Thankfully, this all failed to materialise, and I was delighted to speak to a very nice lady in the box office, who produced two tickets for tonight's show. She was watching what was going on, told us to enjoy our night with a wee wry smile to boot. Keith and I were indeed going to the ball, Yeahz!

As I mentioned previously, I had booked our tickets quite late, and we found ourselves way up on the third tier of the venue, in the balcony, along with the pigeons. It was really steep up there, and I'm not the best with heights, so in that respect, it's maybe just as well I was sober. Eventually, onto the stage came the one, the only Shane MacGowan. Accompanied by his band of 'strangers', The Popes. The venue was sold out, so interest in the great man was still there. Shane was looking reasonably well, I thought; he greeted the audience by announcing that he'd won at the bookies earlier that day, picking the winner in the Gold Cup at Cheltenham. So, he was in a good mood then, fucking marvellous!

Shane's new band members were a rough looking bunch. They launched into a set of new songs I'd never heard before and some old Pogues favourites, the obvious numbers if you like. It was very enjoyable; it was actually great to hear Shane singing again. The Popes did not have the craft or style that The Pogues did when it came to playing their instruments, and they certainly didn't knit together as well as a unit, but hey, I was enjoying the concert.

One negative thought did cross my mind. I wondered if this is what a Pogues tribute band would be like, Shane apart, obviously. I could tell that Keith was less impressed than me. I remember him waving his hand from side to side, as if to say "so so". Nick Cave, Shane's new best mate, made an appearance and sang a few numbers. I've never really 'got' Nick Cave, much through ignorance than anything else, as you can't really deny that he's a well respected geezer in the music industry – maybe just not for me. His songs that night made me want him just to finish, and get off, harsh maybe, but that's how I felt. He sung 'Rainy Night In Soho' and fucking castrated the classic song before finally murdering it. He wasn't around for long. Shane and The Popes resumed with more Pogues numbers, did their encores and then departed to no doubt enjoy their rider.

So, the concert ended. Summing up, I had really enjoyed the vast majority of the night's entertainment; Shane playing live had to be a step in the right direction I thought, and maybe there'd be more gigs. If Bertha was still looking for me, then she was unsuccessful. I treated myself to a snazzy black T shirt, with a bold picture of Mr MacGowan smoking a fag on the front. It was a good quality garment and I was really pleased with my purchase. Keith still had about three quarters of his pint to negotiate down his throat; he was well on by now, and was taking his time. The ****!

It was quite a warm night. By this time we were actually out on the street, outside the venue, and Keith had a lot of people joining him in supping up. There were actually still a load of punters in general milling around, and Keith was still in no hurry, so I decided to go back inside the venue, through to the stalls, just to check it out a bit more. It was still busy in there too, there were a load of punters bopping about, to the sounds music venues play before and after gigs. We ventured down to the front of the stage, watching the dancing throng and watching the roadies dismantling the stuff on the stage. I must have got another of my rushes of blood to the head, but with decision firmly made, I ordered Keith to finish his beer sharpish, and to follow me. We climbed up onto the stage with the minimum of fuss, and made our way towards the back, then the side, where we came across a door with one of those combination locks. This was obviously the door that took you backstage proper, to the dressing rooms and all that. No one challenged us or asked what we were doing, and I really had the feeling that something was on for us.

After hanging around the door for a while, these two young lads approached. They stopped in their tracks, paused silently, then ASKED ME, nervously, if they could proceed through the combination locked door! I tried to look composed, 'considered' their request for a moment, then said "Yeah, ok, do you know the door combination number?" "Oh yeah," came the reply, so I 'granted' them permission to continue with their evening. Fuckin Hell! One of the chaps duly punched in the correct numbers, and gave me a "Cheers mate" as they made their way through. Keith and I, as you can imagine, were not that far behind them, trying not to be too obvious that we were just a pair of chancers. If I had drunk as much as Keith, all of this would most definitely not have been possible, but here we were, going up a staircase to what clearly was going to be the area where the band, Mr MacGowan and all, were going to be!

We went down a very narrow corridor at the top of the stairs, and hey presto, there we were, right in the thick of things. Shane looked like he was doing an interview with someone, he appeared agitated with his questioner, but at the same time, really together, and not at all drunk or tipsy even, as he had appeared to be on stage. Keith and I wished Shane a happy St Patrick's Day, which interrupted his concentration somewhat, this agitated him even more for a second, but he changed his tune when I said to him, "That was a great show, you're obviously not missing The Pogues." I got the customary Sssssccccccckkkcccccchhhh laugh, then he was back to the serious matter of his interview. Meanwhile, Keithy boy was helping himself to the vast supply of Stella cans that seemed to be available for the backstagees. I picked one up too, but had to just pose with mine, as I'd had my ration earlier. Did I mention that I was driving?

We grabbed a seat next to Nick Cave, who was sitting with Victoria Clarke, Shane's girlfriend, who I mentioned meeting in an earlier chapter – you will remember she unintentionally showed me her tits, in Carmel's flat in Camden. She had a three quarter length white dress on tonight, and had her tits covered up this time. They seemed to have shrunk. Nick Cave turned out to be a really lovely bloke. I spoke to him for quite a while, whilst Keith was struggling along with Victoria. Keith referred to Victoria as "Shane's woman" which didn't go down well at all; she snapped back, "I'm a person too, you can call me Marilyn Monroe." She absolutely reeked of insecurity; she was so different from what I remembered of her back in Camden, and was trying to tell a very unco-operative Keith about all the things she had done, and that she wasn't just Shane's woman.

Meanwhile, Nick Cave took a bit of a shine to my recently purchased T shirt. At one point he actually asked me if he could have it. Of course, I flatly refused. I actually regret not giving him the T shirt now, for two reasons. Firstly, he was a really cool guy, talking very genuinely to us I thought, considering we were nobodies in the music industry, just a couple of punters who had opportunely managed to get really lucky, and find ourselves in the position we were in now. The second was our Keith actually gave Mr Cave a bit of a hard time. Keith is a bit of a boy when he's had more than a few – I state here and now that I'm not an angel either after I'm suitably refreshed, but you'll have worked that out for yourself by now. Keith's behaviour is very consistent. He has a 'thing' for ears. Yes, ears! He just loves sticking his fingers in your ear holes and pinching the lobes. Then there's beards. Keith loves beards too, he loves pulling them (men's ones I'm relieved to say), providing they are long enough. A new addition to his armoury that night was proceeding to try and strangle the gentle Nick Cave with the various necklaces and beads he was wearing. Nick was actually, still politely trying to get Keith to stop, pushing his hand away etc, whereas a punch in the puss was probably what he was needing! For stopping, Keith was not, and so for that reason alone, I should have given him my sodding T shirt; after all I could have bought another on my way out. Even to this day, I just don't 'get' Nick Cave's music, but at least we were pals, for a wee while.

Whilst all this was going on, I really wanted Shane to sign my ticket for the gig. I was a bit wary of asking him, so I talked to one of the road crew guys who did the business for me and got the ticket signed by both Shane and Nick Cave. Shane signed 'Up the Republic, down the pub' followed by simply 'Shane'. Brilliant! I still have the ticket to this day; it will obviously always remind me of the night we got backstage, at The Clapham Grand, by the skin of our arses.

I was getting the feeling it was probably time to go, considering Keith was probably thinking about debagging Nick Cave by now, so I went over to Shane and wished him well with his new project, and bid him farewell. He shook my hand warmly and wished me goodnight. And off we went, the way we had come, only this time we were subject to a few concerned looks from some of the staff, and even got a "Who the fuck are you?" from a not so on the ball member of Big Bertha's security staff. Too fuckin' late pal, goodnight! By this time, they were turning the stalls of the Clapham Grand into a nightclub. I've a feeling Keith was tempted to hang around for a boogie, but we quit while we were ahead and left.

So it was back out, with happy faces, into the South London air, and yet another joust with the South Circular Road. We duly arrived back home with a signed ticket, stories to tell, and a brand new, most excellent T shirt.

Keith and I joined the pool team in The Holly Tree, our now established local watering hole. I found this to be an enjoyable way to spend our Thursday evenings. It wasn't the only thing I was to find in The Holly Tree!

LITTLE MISS RED MINI SKIRT

My relationship with Paula was coming to an end. We started the ball rolling at work one day. The conversation we had was amicable, sensible and calculated, there was no shouting or mud slinging, but this actually really showed up the lack of passion between us as a couple. Paula (moneybags) bought me out of my share of the Suzuki car, with a negotiated clause that I could borrow it now and again, if I contributed towards the tax and servicing etc. Both of us had wanted to split, but it was weird initially, just because a routine, more than anything else, had been broken. I had a great social life, and was luckily never short of company. I went out mostly with Keith 'the hat' Williams and our boss, Philip, the head Chef. There was always lots on – golf, the pub, pool matches, Sticky Fingers, the dogs, and a new type of gig, for me anyway – we went to see the comedian Roy 'Chubby' Brown, at Hammersmith Odeon of all places. There was no fucking chance though, that I was getting up on his stage! He took the piss out of his audience without any compassion whatsoever. We were in the front row, and I was bursting for a piss. I couldn't wait any longer, so I scooted up the aisle between the seats. He had a good look at me and I knew he was going to destroy me when I came back. Luckily for me, by the time I had finished with the bishop, his set had ended, and he was more concerned with milking his applause, rather than slagging me off, in front of thousands of punters.

Keith, a workmate of ours, Kevin Gerald Bush, and I were regular visitors at Hounslow snooker hall. Kevin drove a Citroen 2CV 'Dolly' car; it was like an upside down motorised pram, but it was always handy and reliable for whatever was on the go. Kevin's snooker matches against Keith were, in my opinion, legendary. As Kevin was driving, Keith and I would partake in the bar service in the snooker hall. Not as much as the Scottish proprietor though. He was always blootered, roaring at the racing on the TV. He used to call Keith "The Incredible Hulk", comparing him to the TV programme, where the bloke got angry and turned into a green monster! Jock would warn Keith that if things didn't go his way, he did not want to see him throw Table 3 out of the window, and down onto the High Street!

Back to the snooker match, we always used to play for a few bob on the side; none of the three of us were great shakes at the game, but Keith and Kevin were ultra competitive against each other. The few bob bet between them always escalated into an amount heading towards serious, which would make viewing the match very entertaining for me. It was actually brilliant, better than anything you would get at that place they call The Crucible. They usually played two frames against each other. Kevin usually won the first one. Keith's snooker would actually improve, the more he partook in the bar products, and by the time the second frame came about, the wager was a high one, and Keith was more 'relaxed'. The frame was usually close, the tension was unbelievable, and, towards the end of the frame, with him behind on points, Keith would play some simply amazing shots, long pots that Stephen Hendry would have been proud of in his day. These shots usually got Keith out of the shit. The margin for error was small, with the money at stake, and of course, pride. If Kevin won, you just didn't hear the end of it. I honestly think I had the best of the deal, watching all this drama unfold before me, just superb.

Shane and the Popes released a single and an album. The single, 'Church of the Holy Spook' was a rocky number, with a heavy guitar riff present throughout; yeah, it was good, but nothing to get too excited about though. The cover of the CD single had images of our Shane, bare-chested, being nailed to the cross. He would've looked fucking awful to someone who was not familiar with all things Shane, but as always, he had a way about him to get away with it, as only he could. The CD was nicely packaged, it opened out to a cross shape with even more images of our 'attractive' hero.

The album that followed was called 'The Snake' At the time, I thought the album was superb; there were a few rockier songs similar to the single, but there was also an Irish flavour throughout, the tin whistle and the banjo were right to the fore, but I missed the inclusion of an accordion. You couldn't help but think what this album would've been like if he was playing it with The Pogues, but let's not be ungrateful, it was really fantastic to have an album of Shane material to get our teeth into. There's a famous story about Shane once actually eating a Beach Boys record, literally, well that's not what I mean by getting our teeth into his latest album; we'll get our ears into it then!

There were a number of standout tracks on the album. 'Donegal Express' contained lyrics that suggested Shane "Might have fucked yer missus, but never fucked yer daughter!" 'Victoria' was another mighty track; obviously, he'd written this about his girlfriend, Victoria Clarke, again, quite a rocky feel throughout, with solid lyrics. 'The snake with eyes of garnet' is a more traditional Irish type track, with a rousing instrumental at the finish. He slowed things down with 'The song with no name', a love song, or a "smoocher" as he sometimes calls them. This one was released as a single, the B-side featuring a fantastic cover version of Neil Diamond's 'Cracklin' Rosie', MacGowan and the Popes really doing this one justice; his voice comes across really well, and there's a catchy banjo outro to finish – it's a cracklin' cracker all right! Possibly the best track on the album was a song called 'Aisling'. Shane's lyrics are brilliant here. Aisling is a girl's name pronounced Ashling – it's a quality track, the toe tapping is on the go again, it's very Irish, with a prominent dose of penny whistle throughout.

Most of the tracks on the album were solid enough; no, it wasn't The Pogues, but the album would keep MacGowan's fans going for the time being. Talking of time though, it's my view that the album is not as timeless as the work he produced with The Pogues. I'm not saying it's a dud, far from it, but Shane's earlier songwriting with The Pogues had set the bar very high in the quality stakes, it's what his fans were used to. So, in that respect, The Snake is not a bad album at all, it just maybe doesn't reach the heights achieved previously. No disrespect to the band members of The Popes, but you can't help but wonder what some of the songs on The Snake would've come out like, with the personnel of The Pogues behind Shane, James Fearnley's accordion and all. It's perhaps wrong of me to think this way – Shane was obviously comfortable with The Popes for a band – but to me it just seemed crazy that The Pogues were making records without Shane, and Shane was making records without The Pogues.

I was enjoying not having a steady girlfriend, doing whatever I pleased. I didn't realise though, that I was about to meet the girl that was going to change all that and turn my world upside down.

The Holly Tree was a decent boozer; the landlord, Paddy, and most of the locals were friendly enough. One thing that the Holly Tree was not, however, was a hotbed of beautiful girls, or even passable crumpet. My boss used to call it the ugly pub, therefore Keith and I would fit in very well indeed. There were two parts to the place: a public bar with a pool table and an adjoining lounge bar, where the shithouse was. One evening when I was in having a drink, the crumpet stakes were about to change. On my way back from the toilet, on my way to the pool table in the public bar, I noticed a cute figure, with strawberry blonde hair, standing near the karaoke machine. I had the feeling, that, being in the Holly Tree, I'd be disappointed when I checked her coupon. She turned round, and wow! The beautiful sight before me was not in the slightest bit disappointing – she looked delicious. Maybe she was in the wrong pub. I wasn't long in trying to get a conversation going with her, but she wasn't for playing. She was smoking a fag, and gave me a very uncomplimentary look, from head to toe, when I started talking to her. She was cool all right, and clearly didn't think I was so cool! Ach well, nothing ventured, nothing gained, so it was back to the pool table for me, leaving the stunner through in the lounge bar, watching the dodgy karaoke show in progress.

Next time I saw her in the pub, I was with Keith. I brought his attention to the new glamorous chick, and Keith, for all his wisdom, said: "Oh yeah, I've seen her, she looks rough as fuck in the mornings!" Knowing Teresa as I do now, I very much doubt that she looked like that on any morning. Keith needed to visit Specsavers, and was actually bespectacled for real, soon after. I quickly established how he was privy to this information – he said that he'd seen her going to work in the morning, and of course, she would not have been as 'glammed up' as she would have been in the pub. But "rough as fuck" was taking it a bit far. I found Keith's assessment quite ironic; he himself had partaken in a drunken sexual liaison with one of the Holly Tree 'dollies' in the romantic setting of the graveyard, opposite our flat! The next time this gorgeous creature saw him in the pub, after their coming together, she cheerfully greeted him with "Hello Brian!"

I wasn't to see the real Holly Tree dolly for a while, and thinking that she wasn't interested in even talking to me, I put her to the back of my mind, and life went along, still merrily. I always kept up to date with the football, especially with what the Hibees were doing back in Scotland. Without the internet then, of course, I had to rely mostly on the Ceefax pages, and the radio. One Saturday afternoon, I was in the flat on my own, I lay down on my bed, half clothed and stuck Radio 5 on, to get the odd update on Hibs' match v Celtic, at Easter Road. Naturally, most of the football commentary and updates centred around the English matches, so I had to be alert to catch the Scottish updates and goals. Alert was proving to be difficult, as I found a comfy spot on the bed and was dozing off into staggered sleep. I must have been sleeping for 20 minutes or so, when I awoke. I realised that there was a swelling in my pelvic region. Seemed a shame to waste the opportunity, so afternoon entertainment indeed took place. Just as the entertainment was reaching its tickly climax, a different voice came on the radio; it was Scottish, it was saying "And Gareth Evans scores for Hibernian, what a goal!" My timing was perfecto, I had scored too, I roared and made a mess all at the same time. I couldn't imagine Gareth Evans, the Hibs striker, in stockings and suspenders but I was physically laughing to myself as I cleaned up after the entertainment drooped off somewhat.

I was in the Holly Tree again one evening, just for a swift one (drink!), before going up to the Hotel to attend a member of staff's leaving presentation. The blonde, object of my desire, was at the bar with two friends, right by the phone that I was about to use, to order myself a taxi to the hotel. I played it cool this time, just doing my best to ignore her. She was looking good though, and I hoped she wouldn't notice me looking at her at every opportune moment. I made the phonecall. Funnily enough the couple that blondie was standing with did engage in conversation with me, just pleasantries – still not a word out of madam though! The taxi arrived, I left, and that was that.

A wee while had passed until I came across her again. It was a Sunday night, the pub was quiet, Keith and I had the pool table to ourselves, no doubt having a bet. Keith got better at pool too with the more he drank; I was the opposite, going downhill steadily, then rapidly, depending on how many I'd had. Dickie, one of the regulars in the pub, came through to the pool table, and asked if he could play me and Keith at doubles. We looked at him, puzzled. Dickie was never usually interested in playing pool, and who was his partner for doubles? He wasn't saying. We told him that would be fine, so he retreated to the lounge bar and soon came back with his pool partner; turned out her name was Teresa. I couldn't believe what was happening – it was the lady that that had proved to be the object of my desires over recent weeks. Suddenly, she had found her tongue, and she was actually speaking! Her very first words to me, her opening line if you like, was "It's like a ghost town in here tonight!" At first I thought to myself, fucking hell, you're talking now are ya? But I was not going to play hard to get; if there was a sniff of an opportunity to get lucky, then I would be there, at the payout counter!

We played pool: me, Keith, Dickie and Teresa. The atmosphere was strange, but I sensed something might, just might, be on. Teresa was now conversing freely, I was 'helping' her when it was her shot on the pool table; she looked at my hands and remarked how clean they were! I wasn't sure what she meant by this at all – surely she didn't know about Gareth Evans? It turned out she thought I might have been a car mechanic or something, so was probably expecting my hands to be mucket. I told her I was a chef, a chef with clean hands; that had to be a plus on my side.

Before you knew it, Paddy was ringing the bell and it was last orders, oh, how time flies. I can't honestly remember how the pool match was going, what the score was, but there was no money involved – Keith would be having a nosebleed! Time to go home. A piece of paper was thrust into my hand. I had a look. The piece of paper had a phone number on it. Oh yes, things were looking up. I was as happy as a pig in shit! Cool. Come on son, play it cool! One of the other locals, Barry, an older gent, had been watching developments with me and Teresa closely. Barry was a super guy, a real creature of habit: he entered the pub just before last orders religiously, every night. He had a really addictive laugh; it was just brilliant when Barry laughed. Barry was watching me when I offered Teresa a cup of tea at the flat (no coffee in our gaff). Well that was it; when Barry heard me offering Teresa an invitation to the tea party, Barry fucking laughed, the laugh of all laughs! Teresa was tagging along with me and Keith then, heading for the Mount Everest staircase (I wondered if I should offer crampons for climbing them) and a nice cup of tea!

Once the tea was brewed, Keith showed remarkable discretion, for him, and retired to his room. I showed Teresa into my room, and shut the door. She headed straight to my CD racks and had a good look at the various titles held within, then she looked at me and said "You're weird!" I actually took this as a compliment – I was no charts man. We talked, and straight away I liked her. She worked at an upmarket nursing home in nearby Virginia Water, and, like me, had just finished in a long term relationship. So, we were both on the rebound. I certainly wasn't looking for anything heavy, but this girl was definitely setting my heart racing. We had a kiss and a cuddle, nothing more, and I did the gentlemanly thing and walked her home. She was back living with her parents after her break-up; they lived on the housing estate, beyond Keith's bachelor pad, the graveyard. I wasn't exactly familiar with the estate, and was wondering if I'd be able to find my way back, but in the meantime I told Teresa I would phone her, and take her out properly. She told me the number she had thrust into my hand earlier was actually her work number, "That's fine," I said, and I arranged to phone her the next day. A goodnight kiss, and then a spring in my step walk back to my flat; navigation wasn't a problem after all.

I phoned the next day, as planned. I knew it was Teresa that answered; she was sounding all official and efficient. Just to be sure I said, "Can I speak to Teresa please?" The reply was: "Who's calling?" I replied by saying, "How many Scottish geezers phone you at your work then?" Ice broken, I asked her when her next night off was, and then asked if she would like to come up to the flat and I would cook her dinner, perhaps get to know her a wee bit better, especially now she found it in her to converse, we could talk about whatever popped up! I did a bit of research, asking if there was anything she didn't like eating. What a waste of time that was. When she did come for dinner, she picked away at her food, playing with it on her plate. I'd gone to a lot of effort and expense. I had thought this would help me hit the bullseye, but it clearly wasn't appreciated; at least she drank the wine. Our evening together was pleasant enough, bullseye missed though, and it was time to walk her home again. I was still keen as mustard, so I thought to myself that if there was another date left in us, then we would do things a little differently! I arranged to pick her up, at her house, on a Friday night, for a hot date – she would not be disappointed! I was feeling, as Shane would say before the track 'Venus in bovver boots', from the live Nips album, "Very roman'ic!"

The date day duly arrived, and Keith and I also arrived, outside Teresa's house, in a red Ford Fiesta that we'd hired for our weekend off. Paula wasn't playing with the Suzuki for the weekend – she was busy, fair enough, and I was also growing tired of her 'fees', so hire the Fiesta it was. Teresa looked gorgeous. Into the Fiesta she got. I was designated driver for the evening, so I drove off. Teresa asked the obvious question, "Where are we going?" while having a sideways look at Keith. She clearly wasn't expecting 'The hat' to be present on our date, but to be fair, she did appear to be cool about going on a mystery trip with the weird CD collector AND his pal!

"Wait and see," I said, always the lover of the control of mystery. I negotiated the M25, hooking onto the M40 and in the direction of central London. We exited at Hanger Lane, destination Wembley Stadium, no less, for a night at the greyhounds! Perhaps I *was* weird. As we gained admission to the old stadium I snatched a look over the car park, to the nearby Arena, and thought of the two truly magnificent Pogues gigs that I was lucky enough to witness in there. The initial shock for Teresa finding herself inside England's national football stadium, watching six athletic hounds, sweeping round the vast bends, was, by her, soon put into perspective. By the time the second race was off, Teresa had a wager on Trap 3. She greatly encouraged the greyhound to win the race by howling "Get a move on or you're in the microwave!" Charming. Trap 3 duly obliged, and therefore avoided a most unsavoury end!

The Wembley dog meeting was another of my favourite haunts. They only opened the central part of the stadium for the greyhound nights – there was more than enough space here to cope with the attendance – and you were free to roam in the best part of this famous old building. You could climb the steps to the Royal Box, turn and face the imaginary crowd, dream, and duly lift aloft the European Cup that Hibs had just won. Hibs were actually the first British side to compete in the European Cup, reaching the semi finals in the fifties, so stop laughing!

We all won a few bob at Wembley that night. Teresa certainly wasn't expecting our 'date' to be anything like this, but she enjoyed being introduced to the excitement in the world of greyhound racing. The night still seemed young, so we went for a drive. Keith and I would often drive around central London late at night, sometimes venturing into the less attractive parts, the dodgy estates – I'm thinking Stonebridge Park in North London and Broadwater Farm in Tottenham. To me, there was always a certain glamour to the dodgy side of estate life; we were always curious, but make no mistake, we were out of there quicker than a Formula 1 driver, if things got too glamorously dodgy! Keith and I would stick out like a sore thumb, if we were clocked by some menacing looking youths; we had no intention of jousting with them, we were merely browsing!

On this particular night, we stayed safe, or so I thought. Our travels took us quite near Stoke Newington, so we thought we'd go to Molly Malones, the pub where I had seen Andrew Ranken, the Pogues' drummer, perform with his other music chums. Once we were outside the pub, I was struggling for somewhere to park, and ended up parking the car in a place that I just knew would attract plod if he was about. We all got out of the car, but my awkward parking position was bugging me. Just as we were wandering over to the pub, I stopped and asked if Teresa and Keith thought I should move the car. Two geezers appeared out of nowhere; they were both black, the size of telephone boxes, and looked liked they'd had a very bad day. They walked right up to us. I really did think our fingers were through the budget toilet paper. We were in the shit! The two geezers stopped; they couldn't have been any closer, you could almost smell their breath. I told Teresa to get in the car. Keith and I are not fighters; if the two blokes decided to have a go or whatever they were intending, we would've been very easy pickings for them, let's make that clear. We would have mustered, between us, as much power as a packet of Poundland batteries! If they were wanting our possessions, then we would've been left in our underpants, if we were lucky.

After a few heart stopping seconds, the two blokes moved away a bit. Not a word had been spoken up until now, but they had begun whispering to each other. Keith and I didn't need asking twice: we were in the car, and I hastily turned the ignition key and got into gear. Bearing in mind how badly the car was parked, I couldn't just drive away. I had to do a few point turning manoeuvres first, and I panicked; I was up on the kerb, the car was jerking about due to my haste, but we did get away. As I looked in the mirror, the two geezers were stood watching us drive away. I don't know what was going through their minds, and was really delighted that we would never find out. I drove for about half a mile, then stopped. My new fear was realised when I discovered that one of the tyres was flat and burst, a result of my aggressive kerbing. Now, I'm really hopeless at changing wheels and likewise tasks, so like the gentleman I am, I let Keith and Teresa change the tyre. Teresa proved to be more than handy in this department, taking over somewhat and making sure we could be on our way. All of this knocked the stuffing out of our night so to speak, so we headed back to Englefield Green.

On the way home, we decided we would go to Bournemouth the next day; the weather was supposed to be scorching, so we thought we'd have a day at the beach. When we picked Teresa up, she looked absolutely stunning, dressed appropriately for the summer. She was wearing a striking red mini skirt, my tongue flopped out, and I just couldn't keep my eyes off her legs. Keith was driving today, so I got in the back with Teresa. I wasn't sitting in the front, and I didn't want her to either, as I needed to see! Teresa and I had not been intimate as of yet, but I was struggling now to keep myself in order.

We had a great day at the beach: Keith and I got our bellies out, and Teresa revealed more of herself in a swimsuit – she had plenty of admirers on that beach, nobody more so than me. After a day soaking up the sunshine, we headed into town for a few drinks and something to eat before heading home. We went to a pub called the Baker's Arms. It was obvious straight away (if you pardon the expression) that the place was a gay pub – obvious, but not to Keith. As time went on, more and more clues presented themselves, and the penny duly dropped. There was an initial element of panic in his face, then an air of calm, when he realised that he wasn't in danger; it was hilarious! As Keith drove us up the M3, I was in the back with Teresa again, and was like an overactive octopus with my hands and fingers. Poor Keith – it must have been a long journey for him. As soon as we got back to the flat, Keith went to the pub. Teresa and I turned the lights out and retired for the evening.

I woke up in the early hours. It was roasting hot and we just had a thin sheet over us, protecting our modesty. In a very ungentlemanly act, I had a wee peep under the sheet, just to inspect the merchandise. Very nice indeed. I did own up to this in the morning; it didn't go down too well, but I think I just about got away with it. Whatever happened to doing the right thing and being honest?

For the record, I'm not one to tell tales, but I accidentally slipped into the conversation one day what Keith had thought of Teresa's 'first thing in the morning' look. Keith's Adam's apple was a rovin' a rovin' up and down his neck, as Teresa looked at him horrified! Also, for the record, Teresa and I did go on dates together, without Keith, and sometimes she wore her little red skirt. She just knew it drove me round the lustful bend!

A CHAUFFEUR
TO THE GIG

My relationship with Teresa was getting seriously steady. Paula, on the other hand, had decided to leave the hotel and move back to her home town, Northampton. She had a leaving party in her flat, and invited Keith, me and my new girlfriend to her bash. Paula's flat was in Staines, so I organised a carriage to take me, Keith and Teresa to the ball. We were having a wee snifter in The Holly Tree when our car duly arrived, on time. Kevin Gerald Bush, and his Citroen Dolly 2CV never let you down. Teresa's pals watched (with envy?) as we got into 'Dolly'!. We all went to Paula's party. Paula told me that she was pissed off, because my new girlfriend was pretty. Wasn't quite sure how to take that, but I wished Paula no harm, and all good, even if she did bad mouth me a bit after we had finished.

Teresa was introduced to the delights of Sticky Fingers in Kensington; she liked it. She, Keith and I enjoyed a wonderful Sunday trip to Greenwich; we had a great day. I particularly remember me and Teresa in the second floor of a junkshop, the book section. She had her little red skirt on again. We were alone, and I was past myself with excitement. I had visions of us getting into trouble as we were kissing, but decency, however difficult, *was* maintained. But there was nearly an extremely messy accident, just between the true crime and erotic section! Everything was going fine, but then I had a wobble.

After my split with Paula, I really didn't want to be serious with anyone, but my relationship with Teresa was going like an express train that was bang on time, and I got cold feet. I was really mixed up, I dearly loved being with Teresa, but I was scared of commitment, so I tried to end things between us. We spent a very uncomfortable night at my place talking, right through to the morning, but I was standing firm. It didn't feel right, but it's what I wanted. In the morning I walked Teresa half way home, and we parted, and that was it. The girl with the wee red skirt was no longer in my life.

Getting predictable now, aren't I? I saw Teresa in the pub, when I was in with The Chef and Keith. She was civil to me, and I just wanted to be with her. She left the pub before me, and after a short while, I ended up walking round to her house, which was shut down in darkness for the night, so I did the obvious thing, of trying to throw little stones at her bedroom window. I found it difficult to get the balance right. The smallest stones were not making enough of an impression, and the bigger ones had a chance of going through the pane – her old man would be out to me, and that was not an attractive option. So I went home. Stupid bastard! I had came to the conclusion that life would not be so good without Teresa, so I phoned her, a day or so later, asking if she wanted to come up for dinner. She reluctantly agreed. I decided to do dinner differently this time: I prepared food, dished it up on serving plates on the kitchen worktop, and let her help herself, buffet style. This went down a lot better, as she only ate very small amounts, and was very fussy. I made a big effort during the evening, to explain that I had made a mistake, and could we rekindle our relationship? Teresa delivered a well deserved lecture, on how I should stop building a wall round myself emotionally, and just go with the flow. She told me in no uncertain terms though, that if I pulled a stunt like I had just done, and finished things again, then that would definitely be that. I had been lucky just to receive a yellow card then!

Of course, it wasn't long before I was round to her family home, for Sunday lunch. I refrained this time from throwing small stones at the windows; instead, I dropped the bottle of wine I had taken round, the kitchen floor all of a sudden awash with green glass and liquid. I'd only been in for two minutes, fucking hell! A few weeks later, I was sitting with Teresa and her folks in the lounge, all was quiet. Teresa's dad was reading the paper, Teresa and her mum were looking at photos together. As I said, all was quiet. I thought I would liven things up a bit with an observation that I was willing to share. "I really like your tits, Mum!" They're reeaallyy nice!" There was understandably a look of astonishment on everyone's faces, but I was standing my ground. "Really nice tits!" Just before I got murdered, I pointed out that I was referring to the ornament of a cluster of blue tits, sitting on the mantelpiece! Bloody Hell. "What kind of house was this?" I asked. "Your minds are all corrupt!"

Along with my lovelife being back on track, there was to be a big change at work. The senior Sous Chef was a chap called Steve Dowell. Steve is a brilliant, talented individual in the kitchen. He was especially good at the finer points of hotel catering. He would be almost over the top with extravagance, but in a really good way, when it came to menus and garnishing. I was next down from Steve authority-wise in the brigade, and he was one down from Philip, The Head Chef. Steve liked a drink, didn't we all, and one night he got involved with one of the young chambermaids at the hotel. The girl must've had a change of heart at the last moment, and made a complaint to the police and the hotel management about Steve. It all ended up with Steve losing his job, although he faced no criminal charges. I thought he was dealt with very harshly; he was a senior member of staff, but there was nothing our boss Philip could do. The police and Hotel Manager took the word of the chambermaid over Steve's, and probably panicked, to Steve's cost.

This meant that Steve's position was now very suddenly vacant. I had a conversation with The Chef, he was sounding me out to see if I thought I could hold the position down. I told him that I would indeed be very proud to be his second in command again, in such a big hotel and Kitchen brigade, but I was really saddened how it had all come about. A lot of us were sad to see Steve go; it just felt like he'd had a bit of a raw deal. So I got promoted, to senior sous chef, and circumstances apart, I was delighted. I had been The Chef's right hand man before, albeit in smaller establishments, and in truth, especially in Ilkley, could've done better. I felt more mature and experienced now, and was well up for the challenge. Keith moved into my old position, so we both got a step up, with a few more bob in our pockets. I'm glad to say, that in later years, with a change of management, Steve returned to the hotel, and enjoyed many more years working there, in the environment of Philip Borthwick's happy kitchen.

How were Keith and I going to celebrate our promotion? A Sunday night gig at the Town and Country Club, Kentish Town, North London, to see Shane MacGowan and the Popes, that's how. We really went out on a limb, when we hired the services of the young breakfast chef, Martin, to be our chauffeur for the evening. Martin was well rewarded for this, and received a gig ticket too, as an added bonus. We arranged to meet Chelsea Steve at The Town and Country Club; he'd decided that he was going to check out Shane's new band too. I did offer Teresa the chance to go to this one – she was 'conveniently' working, but would see us back at the flat after our night out. Martin had a really smart car, for a young chap. It was a silver Citroen (not a dolly). There was plenty of space inside, so Keith and I settled into the back and organised a little bar with our various refreshments for our drive from Surrey to North London. We had gin, tonic water, whisky, lemonade, ice and even slices of lemon, and a few cold bottles of beer, just to wash it all down! We were travelling to the concert in style; it was a wonderful treat for us both to be driven to our night's entertainment. We arrived and Martin parked. Keith and I were very merry by this time, and well up to see Mr MacGowan and his Popes. We met Steve, and we had a clash of tickets again; this time he was scheduled to be upstairs and us down in the stalls. So we reversed the process we had carried out at Brixton, and Steve joined us downstairs; the ticket mission was both accomplished and smooth.

We headed for the bar. Keith and I were getting seriously rubbered by now, so much so that Keith thought the music the venue was playing before the support band came on was the support band itself. "They are fuckin' brilliant!" he cried. After explaining that the stage was empty, he told the company that he was going up on the stage itself, when Shane sang 'Nancy Whiskey', one of his favourite numbers that Shane and the Popes had played at Clapham. He was clearly getting the on stage/backstage bug then! When the 'In the flesh' support band did appear, it proved to be a very eventful opening set. Fronting the band was none other than Terry Woods, The Pogues mandolin player, joined by various other band members unknown to us. He did a very enjoyable short set of mainly Pogues material that he had written himself, or had sung the vocals on originally, such as 'Young Ned of the Hill' and 'South Australia'.

I was thrilled by his performance; I thought it was fantastic to hear these songs live again, being sung by the original vocalist. Sadly though, I appeared to be in the minority with my opinion. At gigs, with an element of Punk present, there's always a few beers slung on to the stage at some point. First of all, why, oh why, would you want to throw your beer away? Secondly, you would assume that you were there because you actually like who's performing, so why pelt them with ale? Poor Terry Woods. He was bombarded with plastic beer glasses during his set; he must have been soaking. He didn't flinch once though; he manfully sang his songs, and sung them really well. You'd have thought the audience would have appreciated a support band of this nature, considering who they were there to see. Let's face it, most support acts are pretty crap. I can't help thinking that Terry got such a hard time of it with the beer throwing because of what had happened to Shane, regarding his exit from The Pogues. The treatment Terry Woods was receiving sobered me up somewhat. We were right down at the front (Keith preparing to assault the stage), and I felt so sorry for him. Maybe in hindsight it was not such a good idea to support Shane's new band. The beer was thrown at him with plenty of aggression and Terry did not deserve that. I'm quite sure he wasn't a singular aggressor in Shane's exit from The Pogues – he was just a very easy target on the night.

He finished his most excellent, enjoyable set, and went backstage to dry off, poor bugger. After the usual interval between band and a shuffle of the stage by the road crew, on came Shane and his Popes. We knew all the songs now, as we had the album, and so knew what to expect to a certain extent after Clapham. Shane looked rough, a bit more out of it than usual, and pretty uninterested in what he was doing. The band were rough round the edges too, their set settled down to a disappointing standard. And what about 'Nancy Whiskey'? Well, it was played very early days, and we were geeing up Keith to do his thing. Blocking the way between him and instant glory was a burly bouncer not to be messed with – he sensed something was up, and Keith, after a wee sober moment, and a wee think, made the correct decision to abort his plan.

The gig wasn't terrible, it just could've been better. The downside of Shane MacGowan's shows is when he can't be arsed then everybody seems to suffer. Punters pay a lot of money for tickets, make elaborate travel arrangements (with chauffeurs etc!) and look forward with great excitement to see their hero perform. All the shenanigans that go on when attending the gig, to me, are great, but secondary, compared to the actual performance of the band or artist. It's true to say that Shane appears to get away with a shit performance, more than most would – maybe it's because he's expected to be out of it, maybe it's because we just love him. The Popes however, did not paper over the cracks like The Pogues could during a dodgy Shane performance. Yes, it's a good night out, but it's also a missed opportunity, to see a truly great artist perform his songs to his fans, to a decent standard at least. And tonight, at The Town and Country Club, it was exactly that: a missed opportunity. At least Shane was able to stand on his two feet. Keith was having problems staying upright on his, which sobered me up even more. Between Steve, Martin and me, we managed to see the concert out, keeping him alive; every now and again, he'd be down, but we soon got him back up. Even with a sub standard performance, there was no let up down at the front with the audience, it was mad and wild.

We said our goodbyes to Steve, and Martin drove through the now quieter London streets, and on our way home. Getting a lift straight from the venue was indeed luxurious, it would've been a thought negotiating tube, train and taxi with a rubbered Keith. The car was a lot quieter now too, compared to the high jinx on the way there, apart from Keith snoring his head off. Martin didn't have much to say about the gig. I had a feeling that he wouldn't be rushing back to see Shane MacGowan and The Popes though.

When we reached the flat, I was already thinking ahead to our Everest stairs, and how we were going to get up them, when the welcome sight of Teresa met us. The look on her face was priceless, when she saw the two of us in the light, a right fucking mess. Keith was black from head to toe, and I wasn't far behind him. "What on earth have you been doing?" she enquired, totally puzzled. She hauled us up the stairs. I did try to help, but I got a fit of the giggles and this proved to be a bloody hindrance against the task of getting us into the flat. But we made it, and I sloped gratefully into bed, no gymnastics tonight! In the morning, I think Keith was still half pissed. There was a full, cold cup of tea, right in the middle of his floor. He kept asking Teresa why she had put it there. Teresa explained that she did no such thing but he wasn't having it. He was still black, especially round the face, from his falls at the concert; he wasn't a pretty sight, but he was a funny one. Eventually, he stopped going on about the cup of tea scandal – once he gets something into his head, he's like a dog with a bone.

Shane MacGowan and The Popes released another single from their album called 'That woman's got me drinking'. Again it had a rocky theme to it. They plugged it on Top of the Pops with the actor Johnny Depp, Shane's newest, new best mate playing guitar. The single didn't trouble the higher end of the charts. Again, it was ok, but not amongst Shane's finest work. Shane though was quite funny, when he appeared on Top of the Pops. His performance years earlier with The Pogues for the Christmas classic 'Fairytale of New York' is amazing. He just doesn't do the miming thing very well at all, his timing is atrocious, it's so bad; it's like he's sticking two fingers up to the whole Top of the Pops scene which, let's face it, is hardly a live gig, it's a teenage-girls-and-a-Keith programme. Apparently, the Beeb received letters of complaint regarding his miming performance, dear oh dear! That may sound contradictory after my views when he fucks up his live shows, but hey, TOTP is not to be taken too seriously. How could miming music ever be taken seriously? Good on you Shane, you always knew that Jimmy Saville was a cunt!

Teresa was, by now, a permanent fixture in the flat. When she first started staying over, she used to put her gear on the single chair I had in my room. Through choice, I didn't have a lot of stuff in my room, my Sony separates stereo probably being my most important possession. So now Teresa was starting to put her mark on my living quarters, I ended up using the chair for my gear! My room was just too small for us to live like this, so Keith, who had a much bigger room, agreed to swap rooms with me, to give us a bit more space. I'll never forget that kind gesture from Keith. Somehow, he managed to get his more numerous possessions crammed into the little room, and he actually made the room very homely and practical. It was a big sacrifice he had made for me; I did give him a few bob as a thank you, but that paled into insignificance compared to what he had given up for me. He didn't complain about his now smaller space once – what a lovely man. Teresa was not, obviously, employed by the Hotel, so officially she shouldn't have been living there. Luckily for me, my boss turned a blind eye to this, as did the personnel manageress at the time, who actually left the Hotel soon after. No need to alert the new personnel wifie though, she was a different proposition, but we were to sort her out in the near future.

It was time for our staff party at the hotel. Usually we held the event in the actual building, but this one was to be different. We were playing away from home, and going to The Bramley Grange hotel in Guildford, a hotel that belonged to the same group as ours. In return, at a later date, the Bramley Grange staff would come to us, in the second leg of the deal. This was a welcome change for the staff. We travelled in two coaches and arrived in Guildford anticipating a good night. Teresa was present, as my guest. She was dolled up to the nines – I was a lucky man. The new personnel manageress was not dolled up to the nines, she was somewhat beyond any of that, and she approached me and Keith with a task. We were not enthusiastic, but listened to what she had to say nevertheless. She wanted us to organise the raffle. The prizes were already in place, and we had to sell the tickets, do our bit for the staff. Aye, ok then. We were then given five other raffle tickets – these were vouchers for free drinks at the bar. Once your vouchers were finished, then you paid for your drinks thereafter.

An opportunity was just biting our arses was it not? The raffle tickets we had to sell and the tickets for the drinks were similar enough, game on! We were treated to a three course meal, but as usual, at these type of events, the bar was the focus of people's attention. It really didn't take long to use up the raffle tickets for the gratis drinks. Then, suddenly, as if by magic even, more drink vouchers appeared!

The drink vouchers were light blue in colour, so the strips of tickets in the light blue book we had at our disposal were handed out to the more popular members of staff, the ones that were popular with me and Mr Keith Clifford Williams. The bar was busy, and the hotel bar staff didn't appear to notice, or mind too much. Of course with the new found bar currency being used very steadily, the sharpness of the raffle ticket sellers' senses were being severely blunted. Senses like counting and collecting money were getting blunter by the glass. Lots of raffle tickets were 'sold', a deal was to be had, negotiating with the sellers was easy. When it was time for the raffle to be drawn by our personnel manageress, Keith and I did reasonably well, winning a few prizes. We didn't hit the 'jackpot' better ones, but we were out of the door with rubbish like sweeties, cuddly toys and the odd bottle of shite wine.

The music for our disco was pretty awful – no Pogues, pah! But that apart, what a great night, not a penny spent at the bar, everyone suitably and enjoyably marinated, and a load of crap raffle prizes. It was a fun night all right, but life was about to get a wee bit more serious, when thinking of the future.

FORK AND KNIFE... AND RIBENA!

My new position at The Anugraha Hotel and conference centre as Philip Borthwick's senior sous chef was, I felt, going well, I was enjoying the new responsibilities I had, deputising directly for him in his absence. Philip was in the process of going through a divorce at the time. I know that he had a few dark days, but he's a strong willed man, and he got through it. Our regular visits to the golf and the odd drink in the pub at night certainly provided plenty of laughs, and I hoped these times would help Philip see the brighter side of life, for part of his day anyway. The three of us were quite close.

I was approaching the big 3-0, and maybe, just maybe, was starting to become a bit more mature about things. It took a while, but perhaps my promotion in the kitchen helped the much needed speed- up of this maturing process gig. How far would this new maturity thing go? Well, I asked Teresa to go to dinner with me one night at the hotel, I got down on one knee, and asked her to marry me. After my previous antics, this question was not a formality, or even a penalty kick against a nervous keeper. However, luckily for me, she agreed with the man from Del Monte and said "YES!" I ordered a bottle of champagne. I wasn't familiar with drinking champagne, but it would appear that the bubbles did absolute wonders for the celebratory gymnastics later that evening. As us boys all know, it can be a fine line with the amount one has had to drink, but the champagne certainly kept me well above the equator of failure!

All of a sudden there was lots to organise. We decided to get married in the South, as opposed to Scotland, so we booked the registry office in Weybridge. The date was set: Saturday 30th September 1995.

At the hotel, I got on really well with the general manager in office at the time, Mr James Higgins. He was a Leicester City fan as I recall, and spoke with impeccable clarity. He would have been good for the hotel, if he was allowed the time to stay around for a while, but unfortunately he wasn't. The group that owned the hotel had changed hands, and, as is usually the case in these circumstances, the manager's position was sacrificed after transition, for a fresh start at the top. Before Mr Higgins had left, I knocked on his door one day, and told him that I would like to hold my wedding reception at the hotel. I had an outline of the plans we had made, and asked him if it would be at all possible, with a stiff sharpening of the pencil when it came to cost. "No problem," he said, and duly added his signature to the bits of paper I had prepared. "Take these plans to the sales office, and get them put in the hotel diary." Result! Good man, Mr Higgins. We would never have been able to look at the normal tariff for what we had proposed, at somewhere as grand as The Anugraha Hotel, but now, with his blessing, we would have a brilliant day to look forward to.

Early indications were that a good number of my family and close friends were going to travel south and be in attendance on the big day. I felt really grateful for this. Everyone who was intending to come down was known to be up for a good time, socially. The manager had agreed a really good rate for them to stay at the hotel for a couple of nights, which made things easier for everyone, and I couldn't have wished for more.

I asked Davo, my childhood chum and the dude who had introduced me to the pleasures of The Pogues, to be Best Man. Teresa had her big sister, Michelle, as Matron of Honour. During a visit home to Perth, Davo and I arranged, in advance, for kilt hire, with all the trimmings, for us to wear on the day. Would be good to get married in England in our national dress. Teresa's mother was actually making the bride's dress by hand – she was a skilled dressmaker, and there was to be a hint of green trim present in her outfit, which I was really pleased about. There really was a lot to organise, but we both enjoyed the task, to help make our wedding day as smooth as possible, and one that folk could have a right good time at.

The day before the wedding, on the Friday, our guests started to arrive from the North. I made numerous trips to the thankfully nearby Heathrow Airport, picking folk up and taking them to the hotel, including my parents. We got word round that everyone was going down to The Sun pub in the evening for a bit of a get-together. The Sun was just a very short walk down the lane from the hotel, the place had an annexe building at the back, and it's here that we settled, family and close friends, a right cross section in terms of age groups, but it worked – what an absolutely fantastic night we had. The beer was flowing, as were the gin and oranges that Teresa's mum was heartily partaking in; she was lit up all right, she clearly wasn't used to drinking, but was having a whale of a time. We had a right good sing-song, mostly Hibs songs; the parts that had swear words were edited out for the benefit of our more mature members of the company. Lots of Scottish songs, and The Pogues were also represented. We did our best, the bar till must have been bursting, the landlord had a big cheesy smile on his red coupon that night.

Two of the company, two of the biggest characters, were already making their mark as the main men in the bar for the weekend. Davo's Father, Bob, and my Uncle Iain, my mum's brother, were a couple of chancers when it came to the bevvy, and the crack. They got along, as I expected they would, like a house on fire, and kept me and Davo highly entertained throughout the duration of their trip to the South. There was always a story to be told, always another drink to be had, they just fed off each other, with more to come from them, later, during the speeches.

As our night in The Sun drew to a close, our guests started making their way back up to the hotel, the short walk seeming a bit longer now – strange that! Everyone had a great time, real comfortable enjoyable company for everyone, that's what it's all about I thought to myself. My mother and my Auntie Ruby (Iain's wife) were just getting warmed up. When they arrived back at the hotel, they discovered the legendary singer, Frankie Vaughan, was performing at a posh dinner dance in the great hall, so without further ado, they invited themselves in, and even had a wee dance among the beautiful people who were already up on the dance floor. They were pretty soon to be rumbled however, and invited, politely but firmly, to leave. On their way up to their rooms, they embarked on a game of 'chap the door and run away' in the corridors, giggling like excited hyenas all the way. God only knows what my father was doing at the time, but eventually fatigue set in and they settled down for the night... which was just as well, as I've a feeling the fire alarm may have been next!

On to the day itself. Davo and I enjoyed a can or two of McEwan's Export as we wrestled with our kilt outfits. The two of us didn't have a clue, but we got there, and we all made our way to Weybridge for the formalities, photos then back to the hotel for our wedding breakfast in the intimate setting of the Library. The decorations on the tables etc were heavily green and white influenced, lovely!

Chef did us proud with a superb meal. Keith also had to work, as we were one of three weddings taking place in the hotel on the day, and of course, the senior sous chef was off duty! On to the speeches then. Firstly, Teresa's brother in law spoke, as her father just didn't fancy it; I'm not quite sure why, but there we are. Pete's speech, it has to be said, was long drawn out and a bit toothless regarding humour. Uncle Iain showed his dislike of the speech by almost falling asleep, of course in his own way, making sure everyone was aware of this. Things got a bit more tasty when Pete started taking the piss about the lads in kilts. Enter Davo's old man, Bob. Bob was, quite rightly heckling Pete for his comments; Pete responded by offering to 'see' Bob later, to which Bob replied: "No problem pal, pick the windae that you're leaving through!" Now, if there's one thing that you just don't do, it's insult Scotsmen, in their kilts, especially south of the border. Not a good idea. After Pete's speech, there was a little break, and a lot of the lads went for a piss. I was one of them, and there was a definite undercurrent of bad feeling towards Pete. I'd like to think I saved him from an unsavoury incident. Davo was mighty pissed off with him too, when Pete was mocking the fact that Davo had his speech written down, and Pete himself didn't need to do that, to send my uncles to sleep!

My speech next, I kept it shortish, then Davo entered the speech arena, and blew us all away with a sterling performance, doing his best to make an arse of the groom, reading out all the cards and recalling some of the many adventures we had been through together with lots of humour. Brilliant. All my close Hibs mates were there, with the exception of Jimmy (British Rail nightmare) and Geoff 'the flyer' Ford. Jimmy had booked a holiday abroad, and Geoff's wife Carol was heavily pregnant at the time. He was leaving nothing to chance, they didn't want their bairn born in England... Geoff was the man that came up with his own rhyming slang for 'Trouble and strife' in the South, obviously meaning 'the wife'. I preferred his version, 'Fork and knife' – and I had one of those now!

After the speeches, another of my pals, Postie Paul, stood up on his chair and did an a cappella version of a song that means a lot to the Hibs boys. Aztec Camera's 'Somewhere in my heart' is Postie's party piece, has been for years – I'll explain later on how this came about. He sings it for us at both weddings and funerals, and any other time that we may get together. At Alan's wedding, there was a full band for the evening, and Postie replaced the vocalist for the song and put in the performance of a lifetime. He received a standing ovation from around 100 punters. I actually felt sorry for the band's singer getting back on the mic after Postie.

We had our evening do in the Indoor Garden of the hotel, a large conservatory function suite, again decked out in lots of green and white. We hired a local DJ – what a good man he was, he played anything I wanted him to! There was plenty of Pogues, we were all up burling each other round. The Pogues never, ever fail to cause a stir at a function, and I saw plenty of people clapping away in their chairs, if they weren't already up having a jig. Our DJ also played a bit of the old punk stuff, X-Ray Spex in particular tickled me; I'm a big fan, and I doubt very much if Poly Styrene's unique vocals were ever heard before in The Anugraha, but they were on this night, wonderful!

The chef really pulled out all the stops for me and Teresa during the evening. He produced a buffet of the highest quality, with ice carvings and fat carvings decorating the room, with lots of extras on the actual buffet platters; we really were very lucky to be looked after so well.

Davo and I went for a wander, into the great hall, where the Bootleg Beatles, nowadays quite famous (I hate tribute bands!), were playing for the wedding guests in there. It was quite a plush affair, and it was a free bar. We decided to chance our luck. They had their own barmen in for the event, so it wasn't a case of hotel staff recognising me. "Two pints of bitter please, mate." The barman looked at us in our kilts – perhaps we stuck out a bit in this company. "Who invited you two?" he asked. "John," I said. After a wee moment, he shrugged his shoulders and poured two pints, for me and Davo, thank you very much. I didn't like The Bootleg Beatles, so back, with our pints, to the wedding in the indoor garden. "Get the Pogues on!"

Of course, the day has to end, even your wedding day; it was a day everyone enjoyed, but a lot of our friends and family said that they enjoyed the night in The Sun pub just as much. Teresa and I travelled northbound the next day in the afternoon; we were having our honeymoon in Scotland, but we didn't make it. On the M6 my car broke down, it was an AA job and we were towed to a hotel somewhere in Staffordshire, followed by a long tow next morning, all the way to Perth. Fucking hell, my first gig as a husband (well, maybe my second) and I fail to transport my lovely wife to our honeymoon destination, in my shit Peugeot 205 car. Worst car I've ever had, the geezer (and he was a geezer) that sold me it, definitely saw me coming!

First night at home in Perth, in Mum and Dad's house, we were given the absolute honour of the double bed in my parents' room – my Mum's idea, which I just know would be killing her inside, but we were married now, so she was trying to do the right thing I guess. Dad always went to bed early; Teresa and I said our goodnights to Mum, a real night bird, so not her bedtime yet. We turned the light out and celebrated being married again. Just as I was getting to that tickly bit, the bedroom door burst open, the light went on, and Mum was standing there with a stern look on her face. "Just wondered if you'd like some Ribena?" she said.

A GAVIN BLACK NIGHT

Teresa and I managed to stay in the flat, in the room that Keith had sacrificed for us, for a year. This was really handy, and most welcome. If we'd tried to buy a house, it would have taken everything we had financially, there wouldn't be much left for living, and that just wasn't for us. I was grateful that the hotel management, especially Philip, turned a blind eye to our situation.

It wasn't long until we were attending another wedding; one of Teresa's pals was getting spliced. There must have been something in the water, as everybody was getting hitched. The evening do for this wedding was in the grounds of a very large house, a short walk from the flat. The set up was fantastic, they had a free bar, an amazing display of food; they even had a very entertaining steel band playing during the early part of the evening, just to set the mood. The mood. I've never seen a group of such miserable bastards in one place at one time. Nobody was hardly talking to each other, never mind a dance and a laugh. We left, discreetly, in time to make last orders in The Holly Tree. As we walked down the road, they had started lighting the fireworks at the wedding, they started cracking above our heads, lighting up the dark sky. Somehow I doubt that they would have done the trick, in lighting up the company! All this made me realise how lucky we were to have the wedding that we did, with the most important ingredient of all, our people. People are everything in life, that's what really matters. What doesn't matter is how many trinkets you may have – look after your family, and be good to your friends, and life will be sweeter, fireworks or not.

Keith meanwhile was to meet his own lady. She was from Norway, her name was Berrit, and smoothy Keith had wooed her over several nights out, and they became an item. I often wonder, looking back on one particular incident, if the night that he produced his penis on the street, to attempt to urinate, without much discretion, finally sealed the deal for him, as Berrit witnessed the whole 'show' in person.

All was quiet on The Pogues front; if there were any Shane and The Popes concerts going on, well I didn't hear about them, so there was a definite barren spell going on regarding live shows etc.

Our situation in the staff flat couldn't go on forever, so, after many a late night discussion, we decided to try our luck back in Scotland, where we had a realistic chance of getting a decent house as property was much cheaper, and there would be the added bonus of being near my Mum and Dad, Hibs and the boys. Teresa would have to sacrifice being near her parents and leave her job at the nursing home, which she loved. It was a big move for her all right. I arranged to see The Chef over a pint and explained to him what we had planned. As usual, he saw it coming, and gave me his blessing and offer of help regarding fining a job up North – he was very well connected in the catering industry. I gave him two months' notice as opposed to the one I was required to, for which he thanked me.

There was just time, however, before we ventured north of the border, to see Shane MacGowan and his Popes once again – nice of Shane to give me a partin' glass concert. This one was open air again (oh no, Finsbury Park farce?) in Guildford which wasn't that far away, on a Sunday, and a fine day weather-wise it was too. The dynamic duo of me and Mr Keith Clifford Williams were up for this one. I decided to be a martyr again, and took the car. Of the other bands on the bill that day, the only one that interested me, apart from Shane who was headlining, was The Men They Couldn't Hang. I was a fan of their first album, 'Night of a thousand candles.' Shane's ex-girlfriend, and co founding member of the Nips, Shanne Bradley, had played bass on that album. She was no longer with the band, and their performance that day was non-spectacular for me. I'd lost interest after that first album, so I didn't know a lot of their material. What *was* good though, was their last number, the excellent 'Ironmasters'.

They were playing on a different stage to the headlining act, so Keith and I moved to where Shane was to be playing; it was already busy, the crowd anticipating Mr MacGowan's presence. We met a young lad down at the crash barrier in front of the stage, right in the middle. He was on his own, and had a crutch to help with his disability. We started talking, and both took an instant liking to him. He asked if we could help him out a bit, when things got rowdy, and hold him up. No problem at all pal – Keith was in better condition than he had been at Kentish Town, and I was sober, so yes, we would be happy to help. The young chap was a big fan of Shane's and The Pogues, he knew his stuff, and his spirit enabled him to survive at the front, during Shane's set. We gave him a wee hand now and again, but he was strong, and was determined to keep his place, his disability not holding him back in the slightest.

Shane himself looked as if he'd been dabbling in something much more potent than drink, something really naughty in fact. He actually appeared to be angry almost, when he looked at the audience. But fuck me, what a show he put on, it was by far, the best performance I'd seen from him with the Popes up until then; the band were shit hot as well. The set was heavy with Pogues songs, which were executed superbly, and it was great to see Shane on top of his game on the stage, despite the suspicion that he was perhaps abusing himself with something dangerous, but that was his business. Shane MacGowan and the Popes put on a performance that just proved the point that it was worth sticking with the legend that a few thousand people at Guildford that afternoon believed in. When he got it right, no one could touch him – he was the man! The set ended, and the large festival crowd went home happy, like their team had just won the cup.

I really enjoyed everything about working at The Anugraha, but I couldn't live in staff accommodation forever. I was getting older and maturing (remember) so the move was the correct one. On my last day at work, The Chef, Philip, was due to travel into central London to a meeting, staying overnight. My leaving do was later that same night.

He was going in on the train, and as work was really quiet, I offered to drive him to the station, down the road in Egham, leaving a junior member of kitchen staff holding the fort for a short while. This was goodbye then. When we arrived at the station, I got out of the car with Chef. I didn't have time to utter a single word to him, when he shook my hand and said, "Thanks Calum, I couldn't have done it without you." Then he was gone. I still hadn't managed to say anything. During my drive back to the hotel I started weeping like a bairn; I honestly couldn't remember the last time I had cried. It was really upsetting to see him go, knowing that this time, that would probably be it – I wouldn't be back as part of his kitchen brigade again. I'd worked for him for a period of almost 15 years. I was lucky: he'd taught me so much at work and also valuable snippets about life itself. Philip Borthwick is like the Alex Ferguson of chefs. He's so well organised and cares passionately about the hotel he works in; he's been through lots of changes in the catering industry. He acclimatises and deals with them all. I do wonder how he'll fill his time, when eventually he does hang his apron up.

I managed to compose myself back at work, and had a really good night in the bars of Staines later that evening for my leaving do. Teresa was doing the same in a bar/restaurant near Virginia Water for her leaving night. Of course, Keith and I ended up rat arsed; Berrit was staying in the flat that night, so the relatively sober Teresa looked after me and Berrit looked after Keith. Just before we all retired to sleep, Keith did a party trick that I will never forget. One of his drawers in his room was open, where he kept his smalls. Keith obviously saw this as some sort of target, as he spewed a huge cascading fountain of yellow vomit straight into the open drawer. Shot! He was working early in the morning, and we were driving north, so I believe the drawer was just closed – it could be sorted later... nice!

By this time, I had already crashed the Peugeot car – best thing for that pile of shite – and now had a more modest, but reliable white Ford Fiesta. Since I had got married, the possessions I had in the flat had multiplied greatly. Indeed, when I went to town with Teresa we ended up buying curtains and furniture and allsorts, all very foreign to me. It actually used to freak me out. "We're going to buy curtains today!"

Joy! Most of our stuff had been taken up already by a haulage firm, but we still had quite a bit of gear to fit in the Fiesta. Keith had made his work ok – Berrit would have seen to that – and we loaded up the car to bursting point. Some items were going to have to be sacrificed; they were increasing by the minute. Of all the things we left behind, I remember I had a copy of The Proclaimers' first album, thinking they were ok when I first heard them – that was an easy item to leave behind; it felt good.

We said our goodbyes to Berrit – she was getting ready to move, with Keith, back into his own room – and we started the long road up to Scotland, and our future. Our reliable Fiesta did the business with ease, and we spent the first couple of nights at my parents' house. It felt a bit weird to be back in Scotland again, this time with my wife – a new chapter right enough. We stayed in what could only be described as a bedsit first of all; the house was owned by an old lady, but it was a start. I found employment at the local Lovat Hotel, as sous chef. I was interviewed by the assistant manager, Andrew Seal. I hit it off with him straight away; he was very genuine and loyal to the hotel. I found working under another Chef very strange though. I was set in the ways of Philip Borthwick, good ways, and this chef was very different, most of the time in it for himself. I struggled a bit with this, but I kept my head down. Teresa started working at Argos and was making friends; we were starting to settle down, and eventually moved to our own rented flat – it was modest, but cosy, and it was our own space, the first we'd had.

Davo had arranged a gig. Happy days. It wasn't Shane MacGowan and his Popes though, it was to see X-Ray Spex, in Edinburgh, at a venue called The Venue. Gavin 'useless C' Black was putting us up in his flat. He lived in the Hearts end of the city, but nobody's perfect, especially Gavin. I drove us through in the trusty Fiesta and we parked up outside Gavin's flat, deep in Jamboland. An early afternoon drink in The Tynecastle Arms, a real staunch Hearts pub, was a show of defiance, so it was, from the three Hibees going to see X-Ray Spex later that evening. Much later. "By five o'clock in the evening, every bastard there was pisky" right enough – couldn't have put it better myself, Shane! We did try to stem the flow of alcohol slightly when we visited the chippie – nae luck for Davo though, as Gavin obnoxiously booted his pizza supper out of his hands and onto the dirty pavement.

We headed for a pub near the Grassmarket area of the city, and were served by a chatty barman, who saw spirits were high and asked us where we were going that night. We proudly told him we were going to see Punk legends X-Ray Spex, when he delivered, in his next breath, a fucking huge hammer blow! "Oh aye, X-Ray Spex, pity Poly Styrene is not with them!" I couldn't take it in, the feeling of disappointment was huge – it would be like seeing The Pogues without MacGowan... So, there was to be a replacement vocalist filling in for Poly Styrene. What can you do but get on with it?

I'd liked X-Ray Spex since they came on the scene in the punk days, but I'd never seen them live. Davo was a big fan too and Gavin was just there for the crack. Aye, Gavin. When we got to The Venue, the place was full of some heavyweight punk geezers, the three of us were very much worse for wear... enter Gavin's party piece. He would go up to the side of the scariest looking fucker he could find, and very gently place a condom, freshly unwrapped from its packet, on to the meat head's shoulder. Of course, this was hilarious, watching Gavin's victim for a while, a quizzical expression appearing on his face, every time someone clocked the condom on his shoulder and started sniggering. I can't begin to imagine what would have happened, if the huge geezer had caught Gavin in the act.

X-Ray Spex came on stage, Davo and I sobered up and were right down the front. The band played a great set. The vocalist was a young blonde girl, she was good looking, but she wasn't Poly Styrene, complete with her teeth braces and unique, almost screaming voice. I'm always wary of good looking music artists – somehow the ones that are not so easy on the eye seem to have the most talent. What made X-Ray Spex that wee bit different in their day was the presence of a saxophone in their music. The original sax player, Laura Logic, was on the brass that night in Edinburgh. Davo was convinced that she fancied him. X-Ray Spex's career was a short one. Back in the day, they only released one studio album called 'Germfree adolescents' – it's a fucking monster of a record, very original, clever and I just can't praise it highly enough, but this meant they had a limited amount of material to play at a gig, so they ended up playing some of their better songs twice in the same concert. I've never come across that before!

The band finished their set, and Davo and I followed them, through the back, down the stairs and into their dressing room. Gavin had fucked off earlier, bored with the band no doubt, and away up the town to deposit more condoms – probably the only use he had for them! No one challenged our presence in the dressing room, and the band were happy enough talking away to us, so we hung around for a bit and had a beer with them. Of course, as predictable as I am, I kept asking about Poly Styrene; the replies I received were non committal and lukewarm – I never learn! Davo was even more convinced that Laura Logic was fancying a bit of him, although there was no concrete evidence of this, not even circumstantial. We eventually left The Venue, but not before the band said they would put us both on the guest list at their next gig in Dundee the very next day. Of course, we said we'd be there, without fail! We failed.

The night was over for us, we'd seen a very decent gig, and had been on the go with the peeve since lunchtime, so we hailed a black taxi (steady!) and let ourselves into Gavin's flat with the key he had given us earlier. No sign of the host though. We did the very responsible thing of putting the snib down on the lock, just for extra security. Davo reminded me, much more than once, that Laura Logic was absolutely gagging for some activity with him! A wee while later, we heard the unmistakable sound of yet another black cab, pulling up outside the tenement that Gavin's flat was in. We actually heard him say to the driver "I'll be back in a minute mate, just going to get some cash". Problem was, when he got to the front door, he couldn't get his key to work, the snib saw to that, and we were pissing ourselves listening to poor Gavin's colourful frustrations. The key clicked and clicked, but wouldn't turn; meanwhile, the diesel engine outside purred and purred. Eventually, the engine changed its pitch, and the black cab drove off into the night. We let Gavin in, mystified at his initial anger, until we pointed out that he'd got away with the taxi fare (and even avoided broken limbs), and this seemed to lighten his mood somewhat.

The three of us fell asleep soon after, all of us on top of Gavin's double bed. By the morning, we were all under the covers, only to be rudely awoken at some stupid early hour by a Sky TV engineer. Gavin had arranged for Sky TV to be installed into his pad, and had forgotten about the appointment. After he let the bloke in, he got back into the bed –Davo and I were still there – and the TV engineer couldn't believe his eyes, he was genuinely shocked, seeing three blokes in the bed, but we were not giving a fuck. We all had serious industrial hangovers, matey could think what he liked! The rest of the morning was pretty subdued to say the least. There were frequent visits to Gavin's toilet though, which had been turned into a temporary vomitorium. Somehow I summoned the energy and concentration to drive me and Davo back to Perth, my passenger sleeping for the whole duration of the journey. When I woke him and told him we were back, he was genuinely amazed. He said to me, "How the fuck did you manage that?"

Seeing X-Ray Spex, and having a blast with my pals in Scotland, was great, but I was still missing The Pogues. The band were still going, and indeed had recorded a second album, obviously without Shane, called somewhat ironically, 'Pogue Mahone'. This was the original name of the group, before it was understandably shortened to The Pogues. Pogue Mahone translates as "Kiss my arse" in Gaelic – The Beeb wouldn't have liked that! The original Pogues line up was being decimated however. Philip Chevron, Terry Woods and, more alarmingly, James Fearnley, had left the band. There were a couple of replacements put in, but this was of no interest to me whatsoever. I mean no disrespect to Mr Chevron or Mr Woods, but James Fearnley's exit from the band must have been a large nail in the coffin, him being a founder member, and unique in my opinion to the band's chemistry. I took no interest in the latest album they had out either. This album was to turn out to be their last.

Teresa was settling in well, but we both missed different things about the south, so we secured a bit of time off, and went down for a visit. One afternoon, we went up to Camden Town with Keith and had a mooch around. It was on this day I decided to start up my record collection again. There were lots of different record shops in Camden still, and I secured a copy of the Nips & Nipple Erectors' 'Bops, babes, booze and bovver'. It was in great condition; the artwork on the sleeve of a very young Mr MacGowan and pre-Pogues pals got my vinyl juices flowing once again. On our return home, my mother had recorded a

TV programme for me on the video. It was called 'The Great Hunger' and it was a documentary about yer man, Shane MacGowan. I sat glued to the television, demanding silence to watch it. My parents wanted to talk about our trip south, but I was rudely engrossed by the programme on the box. The documentary was good, albeit you didn't learn an awful lot from it – the history part was all stuff that was already known – but there was some great footage of Shane back in his original Irish home, a modest farmhouse in Tipperary which he was clearly passionate about. Mind you, the interviewer must have thought he'd struck gold, as Shane was just about hanging together by a thin thread, he was so out of it – that may sound daft, but this is what the media always wanted from Shane. There were some famous guests on the programme, such as Bono from U2, Sinead O'Connor, Ronnie Drew from The Dubliners and Christy Moore of Finsbury Park familiarity. Maybe Christy wasn't such a bad lad after all, the way he talked about the great Shane MacGowan, as they all did, with huge admiration.

Shane was still plugging away with The Popes, and they had released a single called 'Lonesome Highway'. It was a slow number, the lyrics were good, but, it has to be said, sparse and repetitive. I honestly thought, with another verse or so, and a wee change of the last part of the song, then we were mighty close to a MacGowan blockbuster classic. He appeared to be getting a bit lazy with the songwriting; it really wasn't that far away from his earlier work. This new single was very listenable and likeable, it still roused that emotion he was so famous for, but I just felt it was a shame – it could have been so much better, lyric wise, with a full-fat functioning Shane, not a diet one.

There was to be yet another change – are you keeping up? One day, I bumped into a guy called Tellos, who was the assistant head waiter at The Station Hotel, when I was a boy. After all this time, he still worked there; he was the head waiter now. He told me the head chef's position was currently up for grabs, so I wasted no time in throwing my chef's hat into the ring. I really wanted this; it had been an ambition of mine to go back there one day, and become head chef – this was an obvious opportunity. My work at The Lovat was not stimulating enough for me; I needed to get my teeth into something bigger. I was impatient, hoping to hear from the manager, after my application went in.

A 'FAST' CAR TO
THE GARAGE

I did indeed hear from the manager of the Station Hotel. Back in the hotel's heyday, in the area it was surpassed only by the world famous Gleneagles Hotel, a short drive south. When Gleneagles was full, they sent the punters to the Station Hotel in Perth. Originally run by British Transport Hotels, they, like the railway itself, were losing huge amounts of money. Even if the BTH hotels were right up there in terms of grandeur, the haemorrhaging of money couldn't go on, so major changes had to take place. Philip Borthwick was the first chef at the Station Hotel Perth to implement those changes and make money for the powers that be. That was the first proper kitchen environment I came across early in my career. Luckily for me though, the place was still grand, and a lot of the practices had remained from the BTH days. Back then, a lot of really talented chefs went through their training at The Station Hotel; Andrew Fairlie springs to mind – he has his own famous restaurant at the aforementioned Gleneagles Hotel today, and a nicer fella you couldn't meet. The Station Hotel has a fond place in the hearts of many a successful chef on these shores; the hotel was like a grand old lady.

My interview was quite strange. I got suited and booted, and when I entered the hotel, the distinctive smells took me right back to the times I had spent there when I was younger; usually they were the smells of fear a lot of the time, wondering if I would survive the shift I was about to start. The assistant manager, John Armstrong, a friendly giant of a chap hailing from Paisley, made me comfortable straight away. He took me to the bar, and asked if I would like a pint! He wasn't joking. I made do with an Irn Bru, whilst he had a pint, and we waited for the general manager. When the manager appeared, I was glad I wasn't sitting with a dirty pint – maybe Mr Armstrong was testing me, to see if I was a boozer. I'm sure you realise by now that I am nothing of the kind! The manager, Colin, was straight to the point in what he expected – the place was struggling a bit food wise, and it couldn't go on. Was I up for the job to raise the bar? I told him that I was. We started talking money. We had a wee joust for a few minutes, before we shook hands. That was it then, I was back at The Station Hotel. I felt amazing. Very naively so.

I put my notice in at The Lovat. I was sad to tell Andrew Seal, the assistant manager I got on so well with, that I was going, but not so much The Chef. He showed his class, by immediately embarking on an extended holiday, meaning I would not have a single day off between my notice going in and the day I eventually finished – almost three weeks. That was just the kind of him. But I got my head down, got on with it, and left on good terms. I was never totally comfortable or happy in The Lovat's kitchen environment. Philip Borthwick was a hard act to follow, right enough. If, however, I thought The Lovat was a struggle, fuck me, I was in for a right shock back at The Station.

The staff in the kitchen of the hotel had no rudder whatsoever; there was no organisation at all. A professional kitchen is run by a system of 'corners' where each chef has a specific area to cover – for example, the sauce corner, the vegetable corner or the larder, producing cold items. Well this lot were almost falling over each other, because they didn't know what to do next. One minute this geezer is making desserts, the next he's putting the soup on! No, No, No, No, No! The place was also filthy. Philip had sent me a card, saying good luck, and that he was proud of me, which meant a lot. I phoned him, and started harping on about this, that and the next thing, moan, wail, complain I went! He said to me, "What the fuck did you expect?" Naïve, right enough!

The health inspector paid me a visit, about the third day after I'd started. He quite rightly slaughtered the place. I tried to explain that

I had very recently inherited this situation I'd found myself in, so I thought I was off the hook. The bloke was from the West coast, he pushed me into the office, and told me in no uncertain terms, with some choice language, that he'd be back soon, and if the kitchen wasn't up to standard cleanliness wise, then I would be for the guillotine. If I was lucky. That was me telt then! I cracked the whip, and we scrubbed the kitchen from top to bottom, until it sparkled. One thing that did not sparkle was the way that they catered for functions – what a fucking disaster! The service of the vegetables in particular was so bad, it was imaginatively amazing – whoever thought of this was an absolute genius, in getting it wrong! It was a mixed variety of vegetables that were served with the main course: carrots, broccoli, cauliflower, courgettes, green beans, mange tout and baby corn cobs. They all take different times to cook – apparently not though, in this kitchen. A massive pot of water was put on to boil, with a block of butter, salt and white ground pepper added to it. Lovely. All the prepared vegetables were crammed into this pan, altogether; a wee while later, they were all fished out with a large spider utensil and the vegetables were 'put' into serving dishes, for our lucky guests. There was water everywhere, most of the veg was still raw, the only thing missing was Laurel and Hardy to take them to the function room. The General Manager, Colin, to my amazement, saw nothing wrong with this. I had a feeling that this was his system – he was hanging about the kitchen a bit too much for my liking.

We started doing the veg the way I was taught. We steamed the different types individually, refreshing them in cold water when they were done, so not overcooking them. Once all cooked, mix them together, and tray them up cold in the serving dishes, season and butter, cover with greaseproof paper and tin foil, and then back in the steamer, ready for the function. The next time we catered for a large dinner party, we did exactly this. The waiting staff in particular gave us lots of feedback about how good the vegetables were, but the manager wasn't best pleased. I thought I was going to have trouble with him. But I was lucky. He announced that he was moving on – what a relief – and his replacement was a man called Kevin Ramsay. I had a meeting with him when he got settled, and asked, politely, if he would just leave me alone in the kitchen. He promised he would, as long as I was reaching my financial targets, and keeping the punters happy. We shook hands. I was in with a shout of holding this job down. I really wanted to do well in this hotel; I actually cared about the place. Kevin was true to his word, and I like to think that I kept my end of the bargain.

Only one of the chefs I inherited stayed in my kitchen; the rest either left when they didn't fancy the way I was doing things or they were persuaded to leave. Gary Carle was the survivor, he was a real workhorse, and was adapting well to the changes taking place. It was all starting to work, I was lucky to assemble a fantastic kitchen brigade and the hotel benefited from this. One day, one of the waitresses approached me. Donna was a 'gobby' teenage girl, and she wanted a job in the kitchen. I did have a vacancy, and very much against my better judgement, I gave her a chance. She simply amazed me; she was a natural, but she needed putting in her place, oh, about once a month, not quite losing her 'gobby' tag!

Also needing a mention would be Angus, from The Isle of Skye. I used to play a wee trick on Angus, when he worked on the cold food, in the larder. If a salad or starter was ordered, he would take it up to a side table where the waiting staff could collect it, just away from the hotplate. I would, naturally, cast an eye on the cold dish he had created, then I would scream "ANGUS, C'MERE!" He would come up to where I was standing, right next to the salad, and I would pause for a while before saying, "That salad is just superb, well done!" He would just look at me with a mixture of relief and anger, all good fun!

Colin Menzies was my sous chef and young Chris, the commis chef, a massive Nick Cave fan, with some dark moods to suit! The breakfast chef was an older Italian lady called Lina. Anyone who worked at The Station Hotel knew Lina. She was a diamond, with a filthy tongue language wise, but she got through her work really well, and was a vital member of the team. She actually worked in the hotel back when I had first started as a boy; she used to do a funny trick, involving a mouthful of 'hidden' milk and a 'dirty' movement of her hand! She also had a reputation for distributing unwanted laxatives. What a character!

Things were going along all right, Christmas was approaching, we had lots of bookings, big functions (hopefully with nice vegetables) – it was going to be a very hectic festive period in the hotel.

Shane MacGowan was to rear his head once again, with a brand new album recorded with The Popes, and a tour to follow – very welcome news. The album was called, 'The Crock of Gold' and, in many respects, it's a difficult one to judge. It's an album that I feel divided his fans and the critics. I'll give you my take on The Crock of Gold in a wee while. The tour dates were announced; the Scottish leg of the tour was taking place in Glasgow, at a city centre venue called The Garage. Davo and I secured two briefs for the show, but I just knew I would be faced with a big conflict of interests between the show and the growing amount of Christmas bookings at work. And sure enough, Shane's concert couldn't have been on a worse night, one of the busiest in the hotel that December, with one of the functions being a really important one. It was business that the hotel had lost previously, but they were coming back for another try. If it went wrong, then my throat was for cutting, no two ways about it.

So, I had to hatch a compromising plan. I told Davo to go through to Glasgow on the train as usual, and that I would meet him at The Garage, in time for Mr MacGowan walking on stage, ready to perform. We were to meet at the right hand side of the stage as you looked at it, as near the front as possible. I stayed at work. Earlier that afternoon I hired a car, for a very fast journey to Glasgow from Perth. My Fiesta was getting old, and I just had this vision of the bloody thing breaking down if I were to start whipping it like a desperate jockey. The function at work was running late, inconsiderate bastards! I was pacing about the kitchen like a hyperactive idiot; it must have been a nightmare for the kitchen staff. Eventually, we got started. I warned the head waiter that if they were doing speeches, or any other likewise shite, then it had to be after dessert – I was going to see Shane sing his songs, and that was final! The function went well enough, albeit not quick enough for me obviously, I got out of my whites, into my clothes and out to find my hired car, a Fiat Punto I think it was. It was absolutely lashing with rain, making 'desperate jockey' driving even more difficult, and in truth, the Fiat motor was not any better, performance wise, than my Fiesta.

Perth to Glasgow is about a fifty odd mile drive. I got through that bit ok, but once I got to the centre of Scotland's biggest city, surprise, surprise, their inhabitants were busy stuffing themselves with turkey as well – there wasn't a fucking parking space to be found anywhere. Shane has a reputation for being late, but I had a feeling if he was ready, then he wouldn't be waiting for me somehow. I did, at last, find a somewhat dubious place to park. I made a very dubious assumption,that the fact I was in a hired car made me immune from a ticket, but fuck all that, where was this Garage place? Not too far away it turned out. I got in, went to the right of the stage, bustling my way as near to the front as a small chappie can, and hey presto! There was Davo, the lights went down in an instant, and on came Shane MacGowan and his Popes – the timing was just fucking pinpoint! This was actually going to be the very first time I had witnessed Shane perform in Scotland, so I didn't want to be missing anything. Davo even had a cold pint in his hand, just for me; the adrenaline I had experienced on the night, made me feel the effect of that one pint a lot more than should have been the case, but it didn't matter: mission was accomplished!

Shane's first task was to thank his fans, for sticking with "the cause" as he put it, no problem there Shane! The Popes line up seemed to be forever changing; they had recruited a young accordion player, Kieran Kiely. He was very talented for sure, and was at the centre of things musically, holding it all together. The songs that they played from the new album had a more welcoming Irish feel to them compared to the first album, and Shane's latter work with The Pogues. Some of the numbers sounded amazing, some others a bit rougher around the edges, but the concert was a huge success to a sell out, appreciative, receptive crowd. I thoroughly enjoyed the gig from start to finish, as did Davo, so it was worth all the planning and stresses of earlier in the Kitchen, trying to get finished, and then driving far too fast in the stoating rain. The balance of the set was perfect. Shane and his Popes had a considerable repertoire of their own songs now but they still included a good dose of Pogues numbers too, keeping his live audience more than happy. Most of the attendees appeared to be familiar with the new album as well as the old stuff, singing along with approval. When the encores were done, Shane was led from the stage by a strange 'ramp' that appeared from nowhere at the side. The crowd rushed to where this was happening, and a shaky Shane, with some steadying help, seemed to negotiate his way off the stage, a huge smile on his face, and right out of the building, into a waiting car.

Joey Cashman was in the foyer of the venue, sorting out the T shirt sales, and I managed to catch a word or two with him. As I had the car for me and Davo, there was no real rush to leave, for a train or whatever, so I asked Joey where Shane would be having a drink in Glasgow, and would it be ok to see him for a short while. To his eternal credit, he did say that would be all right, as long as I didn't stay around too long, as Shane hadn't slept for two days and was knackered! He told me where to go to find him, but, incredibly, I just couldn't understand the name of the place he was telling me, through his thick Irish accent. I must have asked him to repeat what he said about four times, but I still wasn't getting it, and by the third time I asked him, my embarrassment was reaching fever pitch, so I had to accept defeat, and leave Shane in peace, from me anyway. Davo was never one for hanging about after concerts, so I think he was quietly pleased at the prospect of getting in the car, and heading back to Perth; we both had work the next day.

Thankfully, there was no parking ticket or clamp on the car, so we headed north, weaving our way through the drunken Christmas party revellers in Glasgow's main streets first, before the relative calm of the dual carriageway that would take us home. Davo gave me a real surprise in the car that night, when he produced a 10 pack of fags and a lighter. A surprise because he just didn't smoke. "Just fancied it," he said, passing me one of his Benson and Hedges. It was weird having a fag with him as we drove home and spoke about the concert we'd just been to. It turned out Davo's smoking had been an isolated event; he didn't partake again – when I was with him anyway.

Thankfully, the next day at the hotel, all was normal, and the function the night before seemed happy enough with the fare we had dished up to them, before they all went and got pissed, and got off with people they weren't supposed to. The organisation that I had put in to get to the gig was minimal, compared to what lay in store in future

Decembers. And what about this album, The Crock of Gold? We'd better discuss this one some more. Methinks.

CROCK OF GOLD, FOR SURE!

The Crock of Gold. It's an uncomplicated album, with lots of humorous lyrics, and a big sound is to be had as the music comes through the speakers, with a crisp, fresh result production wise. There's a big slant of Irishness present, something that was unfortunately phasing out somewhat, in latter Pogues material. There weren't quite any Shane MacGowan life changing classics in the track listing though, his lyrics didn't run as smoothly and as fluently as before, his actual voice fluctuates somewhat in terms of quality. Some of the lyrics, throughout the album, are glued together with some ugly joints. He's clearly borrowed more than a good few bits and pieces from elsewhere. However, if those are the negatives, then here's the case for the defence. The songs are accessible, toe tapping fare, there's a good cross section of different stuff, in true MacGowan style – the fast and furious, the ballad, even a bit of reggae.

As usual, he doesn't fuck about in the stories he's telling, the way it should be, Shane. It's what we expect from you. In the track 'Back in the County Hell' he tells us: "With me in charge, I'd execute the artistic queers, and all the fuckin' bastards that drink trendy Irish beers." You have been warned! The first three tracks all have the word 'Paddy' in the title, the second, 'Rock 'n' roll Paddy' was released as a single, a follow up to 'Lonesome Highway'. Shane mentions a few old time music stars in this track, such as Elvis and Roy Orbison, and the song has a sing-along quality to it, with a funny introduction: "And they let me out the hole, just to crush me on the dole, I'm the lowest of the low, a rockin', boppin', lunatic!"

There's a large volume of traditional stuff in the album, with Shane putting, as usual, his own brilliant take on things. "Come to the bower" is one of those, and one of my favourite tracks on the album, full of references to his beloved Ireland. 'Ceilidh Cowboy' has our man showing off, with his lyrics referring to his sexual prowess, clearly a man with a major horn; he even treats us to a bit of yodelling! A lot of the songs are short and sweet, but one that isn't short is 'St John of Gods' – a tale of a crushed up man, compared to an empty fag packet, standing up in court, telling anyone that will listen "F yez all!". There isn't a lot of variation in the tune of this one, and there's not a great amount of lyrics, but the song ploughs along merrily for seven minutes or so. It concludes by 'recording' a busy atmosphere where there's a few conversations going on, over a few jars; you can hear Shane say "I wanna drink!" followed by another geezer saying "Anyone fancy going town Filthy's after?" The reply to this is "After what?" This track is certainly a bit different; despite its long running time and constantly repeated melody, it's very easy on the ear, and a definite highlight on the album. Shane and his crew were more than regular visitors to Filthy MacNasty's Whiskey Café in Islington, North London at the time, and so it's no great surprise that the place is mentioned in the album's musical content, and features in the artwork. Talking of Shane's crew, The Popes, their playing of the instruments, as a band, comes across really well on the record.

The album is a winner in my eyes; the biggest tribute I can pay to it, is that it's still a very regular visitor to my music machine these days; for me it's a vital cog in the wheel of Shane's career. I love the album, as do my wife and father. I play it a lot more than I do the likes of 'Peace and Love' and prefer it to Shane's first album with The Popes. The aforementioned artwork on the sleeve also appeals to me, the pictures of Shane in Filthy's with the group, their various refreshments across a table, another picture of yer man sucking the dear life out of a recently lit cigarette, and the cover itself, a painting by Shane himself, of leprechauns around a blazing fire. It's a definite favourite of mine, and an important part of the music in my playlist. It's perhaps not to be taken too seriously, but it rolls along just fine.

This album, 'The Crock of Gold' was actually to be, the last full studio album of new material that Shane was to complete (to date), Shane can be contradictory about his work at times – sometimes he'll say an album is brilliant, sometimes he'll say it's shit. This album was to be one of those for him. He was quoted, after the album performed miserably in the charts, as saying "It's the crock of shit!" Apart from a few instances, such as 'Fairytale of New York' and 'The Irish Rover' in the singles charts, and the massive success of the album 'If I Should Fall from Grace with God', The Pogues, and the Popes have never really set the screaming teenage girls' (and Keith's) charts on fire. I would imagine that over the years the album sales, in particular, would be steady, after the obviously busy initial release period is past, certainly in The Pogues' case anyway. But none of this, in my opinion, makes them good records or bad. The group's fans are by far the best judges of the music released; it's very simple: they'll know what the crack is, if it's vintage material they are putting out, or not, as the case may be. The album received mixed reviews, the differing opinions of some of these reviews couldn't have been wider at times. Even when the music press write about it nowadays, the same applies. I concede that the material is not nearly as original as Shane's earlier work, the lyrics could certainly have done with their raw edges filed smoother, but, accepted for what it is, it plays well, and is there to be enjoyed. If you're looking for more than that, ie the life changing stuff, then you'll be disappointed. It's a winner for me though, through and through.

There were a few bits and pieces on the box in conjunction with Shane's new album. He appeared on The Jack Docherty show, for an interview, which was a bit predictable, the host focussing on Shane's recreational pleasures a bit too much. Poor Shane must have been sick of those types of questions coming his way, but he got through it, looking pretty uninterested in the whole episode – fitting, I think, for a very uninteresting chat show host.

In the meantime, things continued to go well at The Station Hotel. Business was good, and on the increase, we had some competent staff and team spirit generally was upbeat, a key ingredient for success. The manager, Kevin, very kindly put me forward for a company award, for best newcomer of the year. Friendly Hotels, which we were part of, had establishments the length and breadth of the country, and overseas. Lina, our lovely Italian, milk spitting, laxative providing, breakfast chef was also put forward as a nomination for an award. A few of us travelled down to Hull, for a quite lavish dinner and awards presentation; the company were clearly spending serious sovereign on this awards gig. It was nice just to get a night out on the company, but it was clear that the actual awards, much to my surprise, were quite competitive among the staff from all the different hotels – indeed some of the staff were taking it just a bit too seriously. This geezer, from Bristol or somewhere, asked what award I was up for, so I told him. He was in my face almost, when he told me that I had no chance, as he was in the same category, and the award was his for the taking, it was a given, after the successful year he had had. Much to his surprise, and mine, it was my name that was called, and I had to go up to the stage, receive a cheque (nice) and a ridiculous large bunch of flowers (unnecessary) from the big cheeses in the company. I had had to buy a suit for the occasion in a hurry, my old suit was finished, so I just got a cheap one out of a charity shop, got the legs of the breeks altered in a hurry (not easy being a short arse ye know) but I'd forgotten to take the price label off from the inside pocket. When I went to my hotel room that night, and took my jacket off, I couldn't help wondering how many people had seen the tag with 'British Heart Foundation' all over it, in big red fuck off letters, £6.95! Still, it didn't matter, at least overconfident Bristolian was eating humble pie all night, after grudgingly congratulating me. Kevin was delighted, and even more so, when Lina won her award as well. Lina and I were lucky to work with such good staff, and for a first class management team of Kevin Ramsay, and big Johnnie Armstrong, the one who offered me a pint at my interview.

My mother had pulled more than a few strings to acquire a house for me and Teresa to settle in, in a lovely area of Perth, called Gannochy. The house, which you could only rent, was used for the workers of Bell's Whisky years ago. They were stunning bungalows, with massive gardens, probably enough for a full tennis court, and that was just at the back of the house. Teresa had just landed herself a really good job at Next, the High Street clothes peddlers, and for someone who kept telling me that she wasn't interested in a career, progressed to the position of assistant manager. So things were really looking up for us; we even replaced our rusty but trusty Fiesta with a newer Ford, an Escort this time.

In professional kitchens, it's a general rule that unless you're dressed in 'whites' then you just keep out – it's both dangerous and unhygienic to enter the kitchen in civvies. My mother came down to the hotel one afternoon, after a busy lunch service. I was taking her somewhere, but I hadn't quite finished my shift. She came marching in, right through the kitchen, towards my office. I tried to stop her, saying that she shouldn't be in the kitchen – she responded by giving me a clip round the ear, much to the delight of the staff! I had an account I could use at the hotel bar and restaurant, within reason. Mum and Teresa came down one night to attend a murder mystery night, and by the time I was finished, the two of them were slightly tipsy. I joined them in the bar. Mum asked me very politely, if I would get them a bottle of wine "on my account thingy" which of course I did. Mum could be a bit of a character, with a drink in her, more of which later. The bottle of wine was consumed, another one was required, this time though it was, "I need another bottle of wine, NOW!" That was Mum, she had the place in uproar, some presence for just a wee wifie!

Hibs had been relegated from The Scottish Premier League, and were now playing in the first division, a real come down for a club of our stature, playing in Scotland's capital city. They had actually been in severe financial trouble a good few years earlier, when local business tycoon, Sir Tom Farmer, of Kwik Fit fame, stepped in and helped the club with some stability. Sir Tom was attending a big dinner being held at the hotel, he had been invited by a chap from the local Rotary club that I knew, and he was doing an after dinner speech, in front of 300 guests. I was going to nip round to the function room after the food was served to listen to his speech and catch a glimpse of the man who had arguably saved our club from severe financial trouble and possible extinction. No need. I looked up towards the service area of the kitchen, aware of some presence or other, and there was Sir Tom, along with Alastair, my friend from the Rotary and also a Hibby. Tom was a wee chap, Alastair introduced us, but Tom was more interested in the goings on in the kitchen. I almost got him a tall chef's hat, and he could have helped with the starters. We did eventually start talking about all things Hibs. It was interesting that he almost wanted to distance himself from the club in a way, and let others run things, hopefully better than they had before. And then he was off. He didn't help us with the starters after all, he settled down to his dinner, and on my way out of the hotel that night, I did indeed catch a bit of his speech, all about business, things that were way over my little napper.

A few weeks later, Alastair came in to see me, with a grin as wide as the River Forth – he was clearly pleased about something. Sir Tom had invited him, me and two others, to attend hospitality at Easter Road, at his table on the Saturday, in our mouth watering fixture against the footballing might of Clydebank! Caught short again, time to look out the Heart Foundation suit, label removed! Alastair kindly told me I could take two of my Hibby mates, so I asked Davo and Mike Simpson. Alastair, who was quite considerably older than the three of us, was driving us through to Edinburgh. There was to be peeve a plenty at these hospitality things I was led to believe, but Alastair told us early in the journey that he didn't mind driving as he was a recovering alcoholic. None of us knew what to say, but I felt for him; it was almost as if telling us was a help to him.

We had a great day at the football. Sir Tom was not present at his table, but a fellow called Lawrie Reilly was, much to our delight. Mr Reilly is a Hibs legend, in every sense of the word, one of our most famous players in the club's long history. He was a member of The Famous Five, the legendary Hibs forward line of the 1950s, during our most successful period in regards to silverware, when we were winning league titles. Lawrie played for Scotland 38 times, scoring 22 goals; a few of those goals were scored at Wembley for The Pogues, sorry, against England I mean. He inherited a nickname of 'Last minute Reilly' due to his knack of scoring crucial goals in the very last minute of matches. Sometimes my wife had called me 'First minute Bruce'!

We were hanging on Lawrie's every word as he told us story after wonderful story of life with Hibs in the old days, and his take on things in today's very different football world. The only negative was a very annoying compère geezer, who was supposed to be keeping things ticking along during the afternoon's hospitality. He had a very unfortunate nasal whine as he was talking, and he spoke far, far too much. He kept coming up to our table with useless information about this that and the next thing, whilst we were desperate for more stories from Mr Reilly. At one point, when he was telling us about a transfer rumour involving Hibs, that we all knew about, I asked him to leave us alone. He wasn't happy and nasal whined away from our table, but it appeared to do the trick. Hibs went on to win the match, I backed the first goal scorer at the in house bookies, and we ate and drank like lords. A great day, thanks to Mr Farmer. Sir Tom Farmer gets a lot of stick from the Hibs support at times, for lack of ambition at our great club. One thing that I'll always think of though, is that when we were in big trouble, and about to go to the wall, there didn't appear to be anyone else around to sort out the mess we were in. People have short memories. And how can I criticise him, after treating us four chaps to a day out, and lunch with Mr Lawrie Reilly?

The millennium was fast approaching. It was obviously going to be a big night in the hotel, so I arranged for Teresa and my folks to be part of the hotel's celebrations, joining 200 other guests at a lavish dinner dance. The chefs carved Aberdeen Angus beef in the room, and everyone drank and danced their way into the wee small hours of a new century. As the fireworks went off at the end of the night, I was wondering to myself, more than I normally would, what the future would hold for us all.

An old colleague and friend, David Mundell, had recently bought The Bein Inn, at Glenfarg, around ten miles from Perth. The place had a great reputation for food a few years back, but had slipped dramatically in more recent years. I had worked with David at The Station Hotel when I was younger, at Ilkley and at The Anugraha in Surrey, him being assistant manager, and general manager itself for a while down South. David was also close friends with Philip Borthwick and 'Sumo' Keith. David used to come into the Station Hotel for a drink just as I was finishing my shift in the kitchen. We used to joke, that I would come and work for him, at his recently acquired new place in

Glenfarg.

One day, things changed dramatically at the hotel. I was really disappointed to receive a fax late one night at work. It would appear that the company we were part of were turning out to be very large seagulls with huge slicking arses, and were just about to drop a tonne of shit on our heads. An outside firm was brought in to oversee how things were run. They were involved in everything – it was put upon us literally overnight, they told us where to buy our supplies, what prices to charge and had control over all our everyday tasks. There was no warning, nothing; the next day, people were coming into the hotel to replace our stock there and then, suppliers came in and told us that we would be buying their wares if we liked it or not, at their unattractive prices, and even the General Manager was ignorant to what was going on. I had my doubts that I would be able to handle this change – I worked better if left alone. The senior management and heads of departments in the hotel felt the same; the worst thing of all was the hurtful, insensitive way it was done. Fucking seagulls!

I can't help but compare what happened to The Pogues, and to Shane, after they split from one another. I've never heard, or read a comment from either party regarding the other's work; indeed Jem Finer and Spider Stacy assisted Shane on occasions during his time with The Popes, both in a recording capacity and a live one.

I didn't buy the two Pogues albums released after Shane's departure, partly as a personal (pathetic) protest to myself, and partly because I just knew that even if I put my bias to one side, the albums would just not float my boat the way that they should. Shane should still be singing the songs. I relented from my stance on this a few years ago, and bought the damned things. The two albums are ok, but you can't help thinking what could have been, with Shane present. There's a couple of tracks that held my interest, but only Spider's 'Tuesday Morning' is worthy, to be a standout nowadays. Perhaps that opinion would anger the band members, but, my view is probably backed up directly by the band themselves, as it's the only regular, ever present song from these two albums, in a Pogues setlist today. Of course the split at the time was probably inevitable; the band were sick of working with an unco-operative Shane, and Shane himself wanted out, so what can you do? The Pogues, or what was left of them, split in 1996, playing their last gig in a pub at Tufnell Park in London. Their last line up was missing Messrs MacGowan, Fearnley, Chevron and Woods. Shane though, was actually at the gig, and was heard to say "Thank God that's all fucking over!" Terry Woods was fearful that The Pogues would go out with a whimper, and his fears were indeed well founded. Terry thought The Pogues were far too big to finish the way they did – hear, hear, Terry! I couldn't have agreed more with him. But for then, for The Pogues, that was that, the flickering light went out. Game over.

Meanwhile, Shane and The Popes did the decent thing, and soldiered on, like a merry ploughboy, and visited Scotland quite regularly. There's a music festival, Celtic Connections, held in Glasgow, every January/February. Word was that the organiser was a big Shane/Pogues fan, and so booked the band to appear at a smart city centre venue called The Old Fruitmarket. As the name suggests, it was once an actual fruitmarket for traders, and had been made into a concert venue, still keeping much of its old features, like cast iron columns and signage from various greengrocers that had traded years before; the place was a charming setting for a gig. Davo and I, once again, were through for Shane's first appearance at the venue, a one off gig rather than part of a tour. His timekeeping that night was appalling, the 1200 capacity crowd waiting around for what seemed ages, for yer man to appear. Our last train home to Perth was at a quarter to midnight, and things were not looking good. Shane did grace us with his presence, eventually, and played a steady but unremarkable set with The Popes. He was just getting to the tastier Pogues numbers, when Davo and I had to bale out. We had a jig together to 'Sally MacLennane' at the exit of the venue, before we ran like fuck, to catch that train, leaving Shane to finish his set without us. We did catch the train, with literally seconds to spare. Episodes like this just underlined how unfit I was, as I heaved my way back to taking normal breaths, in a heap, on the train seat!

One night, when David Mundell came in to The Station Hotel for a pint, I told him that I wasn't joking any more and that if he still wanted me, then I would come and work for him.

THE BOYS ARE
BACK IN TOWN

Things were moving along very quickly at The Station Hotel; the move by the company to get these 'outsiders' in had unsettled everyone. As much as I tried to get my head round what was going on, I knew deep down that I wouldn't be able to run the kitchen within the methods that were being put in place. It's perhaps a fault of mine at times, but I had to work in a way that I was comfortable with, and use my own judgements – if things went wrong, then I would take up the slack. This new regime wanted us to use sauces for the dishes straight from plastic sachets. Nice! These sachets really were expensive shite. The chefs wanted to make their own sauces, better quality all round and more economical. The pressure on me to make the required profit margins was reviewed on a weekly basis – if it was slightly out, then I heard about it, no mistake! I took pride in my work, and tried to pass this on to the kitchen staff in my brigade. I was lucky to be trained under Philip Borthwick, and I took many of his ways forward with me, and passed them on. The greatest satisfaction to be had is to see some young boy or girl making something of themselves in their chosen career, knowing you've managed to help them a bit. As the writing was definitely on the wall, I arranged for Donna (the gobby but talented one) to go down to The Anugraha, and Philip's kitchen, for a week's work experience. It worked out well for her, she enjoyed her week, and showed enough of her skills to secure a job down there. I was delighted. Angus could have made the Bosman transfer there too, and went for an interview; however he decided to stay closer to home, which was fair enough.

So I decided to work for David at The Bein Inn. We had a talk about a salary, and we reached an agreement quickly. The Bein Inn was a much smaller operation than I had been used to, but I didn't want to work for this new regime at The Station, and I also felt that I couldn't achieve anything more there. I was first to resign, but one by one, and in not too long a time, all the management went elsewhere to other employment.

I was lucky to receive some nice gifts from the staff when I left, and had a very memorable leaving party, actually held in another hotel just up the road. It was a surprise to me, and Kevin the manager actually hosted a 'This is your life' type event and compiled a large book of stories and photographs from my time at the hotel. I was genuinely moved and humbled. After this, a few of us continued the evening in a local nightclub. At one point I was in the middle of a group of the staff (boys and girls), I was trapped and they started removing my clothes. Once my trousers were loosened, I thought – hoped – that would be it, but before I knew it, my boxers were down, JESUS! Humbled again! Teresa wasn't happy, trying to seek out the culprit that exposed my chap. I think she knew who the guilty party was, but couldn't prove it.

So that was it, another era over. I'm very proud to have worked at The Station Hotel Perth on two occasions, one of them, realising a boyhood ambition of being head chef there. It's three years of my career that I look back on with great fondness.

The only negative about me moving from one job to another, was the timing. Keith had popped the question to his Norwegian girlfriend Berrit, she had said "Ja" and Keith in turn asked me to be his best man at their wedding in Norway. Because this clashed with me starting work at The Bein Inn, I felt I couldn't start a new job by asking for time off, so I had to tell Keith that I couldn't do the best man bit. If I had organised things a bit better, I could have sorted something out, but David was waiting for me at the Inn, his old chef had been punted, and I felt that I had to start as soon as possible, and get going. I don't have many regrets in my life, but the fact that I didn't do the right thing by Keith, and be his best man is one of my biggest. I've regretted that decision ever since, I made a massive mistake, a job is one thing, but you don't get married every day. Keith, being the way he is, never held it against me.

I was not prepared for my baptism at the Bein Inn. I was the only chef on the books, and I really was like a fish out of water. I'd never really worked in a place as small as this before, and any misconception I had of the smaller place being easier, disappeared very quickly. My earliest memory of working there was on my first night, after service, mopping the fucking floor and putting the fucking rubbish out into the bin. The bin was on the roadside outside the hotel. I hoped nobody would see me. I felt like I had fallen from grace right enough: head chef one minute, putting the rubbish out the next. I must have had an arseholing opinion of myself for a while! I had to do the bloody washing up as well. All in all, I think I had my bottom lip well and truly out for about a month or so, while I got my head round my very new working environment. I did manage to settle down to it all, I incorporated my own menus, and as we got busier, some new staff arrived to give me a hand.

David Mundell was a big music fan. It had been him many years ago who took me to see Bob Dylan, in the front row of Wembley Arena. We had also seen Neil Young, Toto, Tom Petty and Bryan Adams whilst in London – those were the sort of groups that David leaned towards. His big ambition at The Bein Inn was to host live music there, and he achieved this, the live music becoming a regular feature, held in the small restaurant that was transformed into a 'living room' environment, holding about 55 punters. The type of acts that played at the hotel were not really my cup of tea. To be fair, they just came from a different era from mine, mostly artists that I'd never heard of, but now and again he did book some 'bigger' names, the first of which was probably Curtis Stiegers. The first artist that 'blew me away' at The Bein Inn though was Ian McNabb, of The Icicle Works fame. I was working away in the kitchen, which was right next door to the gig room, listening to him warming up, and I thought he was amazing. It was a pleasure to cook the geezer a steak, and once I finished my shift, I hung around to hear his set. He was just brilliant, I loved his songs and lyrics. He was a good guy to talk to, not a billy big time, quite a humble man he was. Glenn Tilbrook from Squeeze was also a regular; his set was also very good. I compiled a specials menu on the first night he played the Inn, with 'hidden' Squeeze titles within – I think he liked it.

All this is well and good, but I still needed a real fix of gear, so right on cue, Shane and The Popes came back to the Fruitmarket in Glasgow. Once again, predictably, Davo and I were to the fore (we were loyal, Shane,) – we were not going to give up on you, that's for sure! And thank God we didn't. I drove through to this one, mindful of Shane's late appearance last time. Sure enough, history, timekeeping wise, repeated itself. Davo and I were right down the front for this one, the lights dimmed and on came The Popes. The personnel had changed AGAIN, the bass player was different, and they had a new man on the accordion. Both of these boys, whoever they were, turned out to be musical stallions! And yer man? Well! He graced us with his presence, looking rather dapper in a powder blue sports jacket and an ironmongers' store worth of jewellery. He was calm, relaxed, happy and fucking outstanding actually! He had the audience in the palm of his tan, smoke stained hand; he gave a quite simply awesome performance. At one point, he made eye contact with me and Davo, giving us a playful middle finger salute to be going on with, with a big cheesy grin on his coupon, fucking magic! The songs he recorded with The Popes, especially on 'The Crock of Gold' came over really well, they were played with a real tightness. The gig was just classic. Worth sticking with you Shane? You fucking bet! He was passionate about his performance, he was enjoying himself. I've always had the feeling that if Shane was enjoying himself, then the company would too, whether it be a company of 1200 or a company of 12000 at Wembley, palm of the hand I said! What a brilliant concert and we got to stay right until the end, courtesy of the car. We would have been gutted to have left this one early – in fact, I just wouldn't have, simple as that. This gig was to prove to be the best one I would witness with him and The Popes. I remember the weekend after the gig, opening up The Sunday Mail newspaper, at the gig review page, baying for blood if Shane's concert didn't get five stars. The reviewer could indeed relax to his Sunday roast that day: five stars were awarded to Shane, with an unusually accurate report of the man's fabulous concert.

A bloke called Matthew Gilmour came to work at The Bein Inn with me in the kitchen. He was a young lad, and had no kitchen experience; he was also a big fella, but his first taste of proper work saw the pounds flying off him – he worked hard and picked things up really well. We had a radio/CD player in the kitchen – you would never have such a thing in one of Philip Borthwick's kitchens, but I needed to know the Hibs score on a Saturday, or better still, if they were featured in the live commentary game being covered. I wasn't too fussed about playing CDs in the kitchen, but Matthew did. I brought in a copy of 'If I Should Fall From Grace With God' for him to have a listen. Matthew liked his music, but was not prepared for this. Predictably, he looked at me as if to say, "What the hell is THAT?" (Hmmmm, we've been here before, eh?) but predictably he was curious, and predictably, a very short while later, he was hooked, in a big way. He played the CD solidly for about a month, whilst he was working. Bearing in mind that's it's my favourite album of all time, you might think that even this was overdoing it for me, but it wasn't – you can never get too much of a good thing. Other members of The Bein Inn staff were listening to the album with interest too, and I know a few of them went off and bought an album or two. The band really are infectious, they have a real unique quality to draw you in to their musical world, their appeal is just so strong, once you get your head round it. The minute you do this, I think that the excitement in their music, be it the fast or the slower numbers, is actually a rare gift that the band possess; it's just pure chemistry, with MacGowan at the fore with his Bunsen burner and white lab coat (Christ, what a thought!).

I was out with my boss David one day in Perth, we were in his car doing an errand to do with the hotel, and he had Radio 2 on in the background. After a tune had reached its conclusion, and the usual DJ chat started, the subject focussed on, of all things, The Pogues. I COULDN'T BELIEVE MY FUCKING EARS! Nothing unusual for radio presenters to be talking about the best band in the world, no, but did they actually say THAT? "The Pogues have re-formed, with the original line-up, and are doing a series of Christmas shows throughout the UK."

I simply howled with delight, giving David a bit of a fright, but I'm sure he understood my unexpected state of high emotion. I was grateful that Shane had continued to play live with The Popes, but this was fucking exciting, and I certainly hadn't seen it coming. There's always a wee doubt though, isn't there? That wee doubt can still be in force to a certain extent, to this day. This wee doubt was instantly dissolved however, when the radio presenter went on to say: "Shane MacGowan, will be appearing with the band." Halli fuckin' looya! Shane's girlfriend, Victoria Clarke, had recently published a book called 'A drink with Shane MacGowan'. It's based on taped conversations that she had with Shane, and it's fair to say, in the book's content, that he was less than complimentary towards his former band mates. I assumed that, thankfully, they must have kissed and made up, before this reunion tour was announced. Talking of Victoria's book, I didn't particularly enjoy it at the time of release, but, having read it again (recently), I actually enjoyed it, very much so – did I mention that I was a bit slow on the uptake! I'm not saying that I enjoyed Shane having a pop at his pals, not at all, but the way the book was written is actually very clever and original, it just, ahem, took me a wee while to get my head round it!

It turned out that The Scottish leg of the one-off Christmas tour would be in Glasgow, at the SECC. Still, up to this point, I had never seen The Pogues live in Scotland, and I'd never been to the SECC. I quickly secured tickets for a mini crew of us, all good Hibs boys from Perth: me, Davo, Ed the Gazelle, Postie and Mike.

There was still a good while to wait for the most eagerly awaited concert to arrive, plenty of time to look forward to it, and plenty of time to think...fuck it, I'm going to the London show as well! So I booked a couple of tickets, for mysen and Keith, for the Brixton Academy gig, scheduled to happen about a week after Glasgow. Little did I know at the time, but this scenario of a Pogues gig in Glasgow, followed by another (or two) in the Big Smoke, in December, when I'm busy with turkey and stuffing, set the scene for years to come. Marvellous! So I booked a train ticket and arranged to stay at Keith's gaff in Englefield Green, my old stomping ground, which I'm still very fond of to this day.

As the date neared for the first gig at Glasgow, I was

understandably getting really excited. There were lots of articles appearing in newspapers and magazines about the band once again, which was really brilliant after the barren years when they weren't doing anything. General opinion was The Pogues' comeback tour was a really welcome one for the music industry in general – I couldn't agree more. It's always nice to have something to look forward to, be it a holiday or whatever, but this? A Pogues gig, after all them years, bring it on pa-lease! I never thought I'd see the band live again, Christ, what a thought that is, even now.

So, at last, the big day arrived. I woke up in the morning, a bit like a kid on Christmas Day, thinking to myself initially, whilst still dozy, "What's happening today then? Work? No, oh yes, tonight, I'M GOING TO SEE THE POGUES." I went out for a late lunch with my folks that day, my mother in particular kept commenting that my mind was elsewhere, and the meal was a bit of a non event, which was both rude and selfish of me.

The five Hibs boys met at the train station, with the usual refreshments to hand. Well that's not strictly true. Around this time, those awful Bacardi Breezers were on the go, and were the popular drink. We all ended up with them that night, primarily because there was a green variety, fucking awful, sickly things, but we drank them anyway, lots of them. On the way through, Davo and I were speculating what song The Pogues would open their show with. I guessed the 4/9 shot 'Streams of Whiskey' would be the one to propel the band into their musical activities for that evening.

The SECC is a huge barn of a place, and I took an instant dislike to it. It was sterile and clinically modern, soulless. I still couldn't get my head round the fact that we were GOING TO SEE THE POGUES, and it was going to happen really quite soon. The venue, however, did nothing to dampen my enthusiasm. We stocked up on sickly, sweet, fluorescent green Bacardi Breezers, at vastly inflated prices, and settled into our positions in the arena. Mike headed for a pre-concert toilet visit, and announced to all and sundry on his return, "My shite has turned fucking green!" These green Breezer things had taken their toll on Mike's digestive and waste system – nice of him to share that with us. I also needed a toilet, but just for a number one. I really didn't want to miss anything, so I found myself an empty plastic pint pot, which I used as my very own portaloo. I just couldn't handle going to the toilet and then hearing that roar of anticipation, that roar of acknowledgement, that the band were on. This is always a very special moment at a gig, and I wasn't missing it, being shut away in a smelly, white tiled capsule of a room, with my dick in my hand – no, I don't think so! With this most delicate of number one operations out of the way, I calmly placed my 'portaloo' out of harm's way, and waited eagerly for the lights to dim, for that roar, and for The Pogues to appear, before my very eyes, and now comfortably relieved bladder.

Suddenly, it happened. Those lights did go down and that roar, from a very healthy in numbers audience went up, and on came that band. A visual difference from the start was that James Fearnley and Terry Woods had dispensed with their hair. Most of the others looked much the same as they did years before, though I thought Philip Chevron looked thinner. And what about yer man? Well it was business as usual from him; he looked like he'd been partaking in more than a few Bacardi Breezers himself (green I hope) and he looked scruffy and unwashed, but that's ok. I was hoping he could still sing and remember the lyrics to the wonderful songs, most of which he wrote himself.

The band steadied themselves, as did we, five Hibs supporters in amongst thousands of Celtic supporters. Glasgow Pogues gigs are something of a Celtic supporters' night out, I can live with that – we had a few Hibs songs up our sleeves, that fell on mainly deaf ears, but they made us feel we were representing our club at this very 'green' occasion. To be fair to the mainly Celtic throng, they never fail to give the band a lively audience, and I've read many times how much they appreciate this, especially Spider. Off we go then! 'Streams of whiskey' being first past the post, and a high five from Davo! I have to say, the sound was simply fucking awful; it was far too quiet. Shane kept pointing at the various crew chappies with a finger pointing to the sky, as if to say, "turn it up!"

I think that the excitement and build up to seeing the band live after all those years, coupled with the shit, shit venue, the insufficient volume level and quality of the sound in general, and, it has to be said, a shaky Shane MacGowan led to one almighty anticlimax. The gig did get better as the night went on; the set list was really solid with all the songs that you were expecting and wanting to hear. Postie in particular seemed to be really getting into it – he had joined Mr Woods and Mr Fearnley's club of the hairless and his dome was bobbing about, up and down with the best of them. The gig concluded, the lights went up, and we had a long walk back to Glasgow Queen Street station, via the chip shop. Once settled on the train, Eddie the Gazelle said, "Well, what did you all think of that?" His question was met with an unfortunate silence – that kind of said it all. I felt disappointed, but at the same time, felt grateful for the whole occasion, and the excited anticipation leading up to the gig. The actual concert didn't match up to the quality and emotion of years gone by – maybe I was expecting too much, a bit like asking a mercurial footballer to play an outstanding first match, after a long lay-off through injury.

At least I had Brixton to look forward to, and I just had a strong feeling that things would improve, and it would be much better. I just knew it would.

So, a week or so passed, and I was heading down to London. I arrived the night before the gig, catching up with Keith, had lunch the next day with Philip, my old gaffer, then Keith and I set off into town for a night with the Pogues, round two. We went to Sticky Fingers in Kensington for a few ales and a scoff, then down to Brixton with its lovely boulevards, to see the boys who were back in town, right enough. Further shows had been added at Brixton, and all sold out with ease, but I had to make do with just the one. Unfortunately, I had booked my time off at work and train ticket in advance – another night in London would've been swell, but not to be. I was to get the hang of this too in years to come, but for the present, I really did think, along with everyone else, that this would be the last chance saloon to see the mighty Pogues strutting their stuff live, in front of our very eyes.

The gig was a cracker, MacGowan had certainly got his act together compared to Glasgow, and the band seemed to be enjoying themselves. The sound was superb, the venue, well, one of my favourites. Keith and I 'sat' upstairs – you're not supposed to stand, however the security boys gave up on this one pretty early, such was the enthusiasm and love, on show, for this simply amazing band. What got me more than anything about the audience was there really was a large cross section of punters, those who had seen the band back in the day, like me with extra chins, thinning hair and much bigger tits, but also a lot of younger fans, some of whom wouldn't even have been barely alive when the Pogues first came on the scene. But there they were, having it large, singing along with Shane, probably more word perfect than him – well, ok, most definitely more word perfect than him, but that's all right, Shane, you were at the races tonight, son! The show was a real success, but alas, inevitably, it came to an end, the band walking to the sides and rear of the stage, having taken their rightful applause, away to the comfort of their dressing rooms, to reflect, I hoped, on what had been a fantastic night for everyone. Have I ever told you that the Pogues is the best night out in town? Bar none?

Time for those lights to go up again, for the tube back to Waterloo, for the last train to Egham, and on to Keith's gaff in Englefield Green for a kip, before my journey back to Perth on the train next day. What a shite thought it was that The Pogues were in Brixton again tonight, as the train shuddered into life, and out of King's Cross, going in the opposite direction, away from Brixton, and its Academy and The Pogues show.

At this point, one couldn't help thinking that the band had obviously made a few bob, and good on them, but would they be doing it again? Even the wording on the T shirts said 'For one week only' – maybe that was it then, but it was only natural to want more.

KEITH'S MAGIC ROUNDABOUT

The reviews for The Pogues' reunion tour were very favourable – the whole thing sold out with ease, Shane had appeared to play the game, and by all accounts, all band members had enjoyed themselves, and had been paid accordingly. This was apparently a problem in days gone by for The Pogues. Mr Frank Murray, their longest serving manager, always seemed to do very well financially, and during tours had his own hotel rooms, whilst the band members shared. They had a new guy in tow, and he made sure that they all did ok this time, financially, the way it should be. There were no plans for the future though, and definitely no plans to record any new material. That was that then, but the fact that the tickets all sold, in major venues, and the concerts were so well received, made you just hope that there may be a future for the band – if that's what was in their thoughts though then they were giving nothing away. They never bloody do!

At the Bein Inn, David Mundell took me and his book keeper, Cathleen, on a trip to Ireland – this was the first time I had set foot in The Emerald Isle. Ireland's economy was booming at the time, and David wanted to market the hotel over there. Cathleen had family in Dungloe, to the West of Donegal, and that's where we were to be eventually headed. I was quite excited to be visiting Ireland for obvious reasons. We left Perth early morning, and in David's Suzuki jeep I drove us to Stranraer, in the south-west of Scotland, to catch the ferry to Belfast. We left it a bit tight time-wise; the pressure was on re my driving, but I made it with a few minutes to spare, despite a few concerned sounds from Cathleen, a very gentle soul, in the back of the jeep. The ferry was ok, nought flash, and before we knew it we were docking in Belfast. David, to my great relief, took over driving duties, and as he drove on our way out of Belfast, we saw some of the gable ends of the houses, with the national or republican artwork, depending of course on that street's particular persuasion. We were stopped at the border, and a security bloke had a wee chat with us, before waving us on, through to the Republic.

We settled in Donegal on the first night, at a hotel on the main drag. Later on that evening we ventured out into a boozer, where I tasted my first proper pint of Guinness – it was delicious! Various musicians started to arrive at different times; they all started to play their instruments – a banjo, an accordion, a guitar, a bodhran – it was all very natural, and sounded amazing. Next day we travelled to Dungloe, Cathleen caught up with her family, and showed us where Daniel O'Donnell stayed, when he wasn't wooing the blue rinse brigade, causing them to fiddle under the tartan rugs on their laps! We talked to loads of friendly people and thrust leaflets about The Bein Inn into their palms, before heading back over the border to spend the last night of our stay in Londonderry. Different ball game here: we were in the busy hotel bar and I got chatting to the barman. He asked me what we were doing later on that evening so I told him we were just going for a stroll up the town. He told me in no uncertain terms to be back in the hotel by 9pm. Later on I saw what he meant, as the town was almost deserted, apart from the armoured vehicles patrolling – scary to an ignorant Jock and his two workmates. Good advice from the barman.

John Hume, the Irish politician, was in attendance, having a drink in this very bar. I actually really had no idea who he was, but I was over to him in a flash, telling him all about The Bein Inn, back in sleepy Perthshire, and he left with a crisp, colourful leaflet in his hand, and a vivid description of the chef's 'wonderful' food that could be had there. I think David was pleased. I kept on at him that I wanted to go to Tipperary, and to see the River Shannon that Shane had sung so fondly about; it didn't happen though, and instead we ended up back in Belfast, to kill a few hours before the ferry home. He took me and Cathleen to The Hard Rock Café for a scoff, and amongst the displayed memorabilia was a framed silver disc of "If I Should Fall From Grace With God" presented to Shane MacGowan. I looked at the very desirable piece, and couldn't help thinking that it would have looked much better on the wall of my living room, back home in Perth. My first taste of Ireland was good, but I still wanted to pay a visit to Dublin, and the aforementioned Tipperary and the River Shannon. Maybe one day.

It was back to Shane and The Popes again, when he returned to Glasgow, to its wonderful Fruitmarket venue. When Shane appeared on stage, he settled himself onto a stool. There were hardly any band members with him: a guitarist, a bass player and a drummer – that was it! Shane announced, "There's not many of us tonight" and it was almost an apology. Surprisingly, the sound that the shrunken band achieved wasn't as bad as expected; it was far from terrific, but it was passable.

The bass player, who we first saw with Shane last time at the Fruitmarket, had changed a bit in appearance. On the first night he had looked fresh and healthy – it took him a while that night to warm up musically, but once he did, he turned out to be quite a magician on his bass, very good indeed. This time, he had clearly been partaking in whatever recreational activity that was on the go at the time backstage, and he was totally out of it, fucked out of his brains, but, surprisingly, his fingers were still nimble enough to navigate their way competently over the neck of his bass guitar. The ever-present Popes guitarist, Paul 'mad dog' McGuinness, was playing out of his skin. Keith used to call him 'Scissor Kick' due to the fact that every now and again, that's what he would do whilst on stage, give out to a kung fu kind of kick, before he got serious with his axe.

Some of the numbers that Shane was introducing that night made me and Davo wonder how on earth they were going to manage it, without a banjo and an accordion, but they kind of got away with it. Then Shane said: "We're gonna do Fairytale of New York!" Fucking Hell! Tragically, the original female vocalist for Fairytale, Kirsty

MacColl, had been killed in 2000, in a really horrendous incident involving a speedboat as she was swimming with her children in Mexico. The culprit that killed Kirsty that day amazingly escaped punishment, a real hellish scenario all round. The roadies had got hold of a girl from the audience, to duet with Shane; the man himself looked thoroughly disgusted with his temporary singing partner, looking at her with utter contempt. Perhaps he was thinking of Kirsty. Scissor Kick kicked things off, plinking his guitar to the opening bars of Fairytale, the opening bars that are usually done by James Fearnley, so richly, on the piano, but Scissor Kick was keeping it all together. Davo and I called him the new Michael Schenker, his axe was just so versatile – I'm sure he could have used it to fit double glazing! Shane and the bint got through The Pogues' most famous song without incident, both word perfect, but Shane was still giving her dirty looks aplenty. One thing about Shane and the Popes gigs: it was never, ever, same old, same old, that's for sure.

Matthew, my assistant chef at The Bein Inn, was starting to resemble Twiggy; he had lost so much weight, he brought his old belt in for me to see, and how it was now too big for him – he'd used up all the holes to tighten it further and further. We had a menu that we hoped would suit everyone, a good cross section with steaks, pasta , salads, and a few local specialities involving venison and smoked duck, but one item on the menu was to become the stuff of legend. If you were paying attention earlier, I told you about my mother's stovies... well, I invented a dish based on her wonderful recipe, but before you slaughter me for nicking her take on Stovies, let me finish the fucking story, thanks!

Back at the Station Hotel, there was a food festival going on in Perth. The manager wanted me to create something unique, so the hotel was doing its bit for the time the food festival was on. This was all well and good, but the thing I was to create was to be given away as a freebie, to our customers in the restaurant, who were having dinner. This always sets alarm bells ringing amongst chefs, as the fat controllers who do the finances are always there, with their stinking breath, first thing on a Monday morning, wondering why the profits are down. Doh! I made a batch of stovies, Mrs Bruce-style, and let them cool. I then moulded the stovies into small patties and dressed them in a mix of breadcrumbs and oatmeal, then lightly fried them in butter. These delicacies were then presented with a Drambuie sauce, Drambuie being a sweet whisky-based liqueur, originating from the Isle of Skye. I served each diner in the restaurant that week a wee taste of this, in-between their starter and main course. They were christened 'Ma Bruce's World Famous Stovie Cakes'. And they went down well. Ma Bruce was delighted!

We had a bit to go with the world famous bit, but we'd get there one day, and that day came at The Bein Inn, when they went on our menu as a starter, people having to pay good currency this time, all the while helping Ma Bruce conquer the world! I'm glad to say they were an absolute winner, though one of the Kitchen Porters at the Inn didn't think so when she promptly threw out my cooling stovies one day, in the bin, thinking they were literally rubbish. Once I got over this tragedy with some choice language, it dawned on me that stovies in her house were clearly of the corned beef and baked bean variety – yeuch!

Shane was continuing to play live dates with The Popes. They were doing a St Patrick's night bash at the Shepherd's Bush Empire, in London. Sounded a good excuse to pay Keith and Philip a visit. I arranged to spend a few days in the South, and Keith very kindly agreed to put me up in his new house, in Bracknell. I liked his house, he made me very comfortable. There was a wee bit park at the side of the street he lived in, and on the park was a small set of goalposts. We would go down there, usually when we were pissed (and in the dark) and display our shockingly bad football skills, coming back to the house both muckit and knackered.

The day of the concert was a really long one, but also one full of incident. Philip picked me up at Keith's house at 4 in the morning, and we went to France for the day, travelling through the Channel Tunnel. It was a weird sensation, him driving his car onto the train, and then disappearing under the English Channel, the two of us reading our newspapers as the train did all the hard work. Philip did his shopping over in France; the supermarket there sold fucking everything, even a bloody cement mixer, if you fancied one! Philip stocked up on wine and cement mixers then, and we went for something to eat, on the seafront, and a look at the shops in Calais. It was an enjoyable experience, and nice to spend some time with my old boss. When we arrived back in England, Philip dropped me at a tube station, and I met up with Keith in Shepherd's Bush, settling down in an Irish themed pub, next to The Empire. Keith had driven into London after his shift at work. I was quite surprised; I'd thought that he would have came in by train. He told me we would get the train back to Bracknell after Shane's show, then go back into London the next day, him to get his motor, and me to catch the train back to Perth. Ok then. We started getting in the beers in the Irish boozer – seemed only right to partake in a Guinness or two… it was fucking rotten though, compared to the stuff I had been quaffing in Ireland.

The Shepherd's Bush Empire was a smart venue, well situated bars made getting a drink easy, which was handy as the place was heaving. We got talking to a group of lads, a bit younger than us, but big Pogues/Shane fans, talking about gigs we'd been to in years gone by, the demise of our favourite band, and what we thought about what Shane was doing nowadays. The stories and the beer were flowing. The little group Keith and I found ourselves in, was situated downstairs, quite near the back (but with a remarkably good view of the stage), just in front of the stairs that took you up a few feet to the level where the bogs were.

The Popes arrived on the stage, but no Shane. They started playing some instrumentals, and thankfully had their big, hairy banjo player in tow this evening, big Tom 'The Beast' McManamon. Big hairy Tom couldn't half play that banjo; he was a true banjo axeman! They played some more instrumentals, no sign of yer man, and then a few more. The crowd was becoming slightly restless, nothing major, but you could certainly feel it, as you started to wonder if he was going to show at all. He did. Without warning, he almost glided on from the side of the stage, to take up position at his mic, with the huge, ever present, blowing fan in front of where he performed. He didn't appear to be happy, almost sneering at his audience. The sound was good though, and Shane was up to the job in hand. Soon enough the crowd were bobbing up and down, everyone getting into the swing of things, and

Shane was thawing out, looking as if he was enjoying himself. He kept asking the punters, "Do you want another one?" Of course we fucking did!

Keith and I and our new pals were being obnoxious. We'd formed a human chain, right along that staircase that led you to the toilets and we decided that we were not going to break it. Fuck knows where this plan came from, but everytime a poor punter made his way toward us, to visit the conveniences, we just didn't move, or break our chain of linked arms, thus making the poor bastards take a detour round the long way by the sides of the venue. Hellish. We stood our ground to a man, getting involved with the music, pretending to be oblivious to the people that wanted to pass us by and onto a relieving piss, shit, or both. We upset a few folk, we really did, but met our marker, when one extremely large angry geezer, literally broke his way through our chain, and thus brought to an end our pathetic, but funny stance. Time was getting on, and the curfew time for the venue was rapidly approaching. Shane however, looked like he would be happy to play all night. He was buzzing now, his grumpy opening very much a thing of the past. The roadies almost had to remove him from the stage, bless him! A particular highlight for me of the night's entertainment was when he sang a faultless 'Auld Triangle' – it almost had me in tears. The crowd chanted, "There's only one Shane MacGowan!" I couldn't agree more.

We said farewell to our comrades in the 'chain' and then, well, what? Keith and I had had a bucketful to drink; I was absolutely fucked by now, after my early kick-off with Philip. As we made our way to the tube, Keith said that he wanted to drive home. I'm ashamed to say that I didn't try very hard to put him off this crazy idea – the prospect of a comfy seat in his car, compared to a slog through London on the tube and the train at Waterloo was a no brainer, but a dangerous, stupid one. Before we knew it, we were on our way, and I, being no help to Keith whatsoever, fell akip almost instantly. I woke up when we were on the M4; Keith had kept his nerve, and had broken the back of the journey – we were almost there. Almost. We came off the M4 and as we were approaching a roundabout, Keith saw in his mirror that a police car was up his arse. Fucking hell, surely not, he'd done all right up till now. The car was clearly on Keith's case, and understandably this panicked him; he ended up going round the roundabout twice, his nerves cut to shreds now. The blue lights went on, we were fucked. I felt absolutely fucking awful, thinking ahead to the terrible consequences of this mad journey I should have talked him out of making.

Now, to tell you something about Keith, over the years that I've known him, he's either desperately unlucky going through life, or, very lucky indeed – there's not much in between on the luck score. I've known him to put two lines on the lottery, and mistakenly put on two identical lines of numbers, then winning, obviously, twice. He's been at the greyhounds, went up to the bookie, fucking up his bet by backing a dog he wasn't intending to, for more money that he wanted to put on (you don't fuck about with these boys, stuttering, changing your mind at the last moment) only for the hound to win at big odds, with Keith's enhanced stake! He's actually, generally, very lucky at the bookies. Then there's the other end of the luck scale – for example, when he got his money stolen at my previous leaving party, as he lay innocently sleeping. Well, his luck was in tonight, more than it's ever been in his whole life, when the cops must have got a call, an urgent one, as they exited Keith's magic roundabout, and sped off, into the blackness of night. JESUS! The relief was ridiculous; it wasn't me driving, but I was just as responsible for the pickle we found ourselves in. Keith might have lost his job if the fuzz had stopped us, and I just couldn't have lived with that. We very gratefully made it back to his place, as I hit the bed, I reflected on what might have been, and couldn't quite take in the fact that we'd got away with it. Whatever incident made Old Bill speed away from us, I was grateful for it. Maybe plod were just late for their tea.

A LITTLE GEM

My mother, Roselle Wilkie Bruce, was a character in her own right. The thing she enjoyed most in life was people. She didn't care too much for material possessions as such – the most valuable thing she had was probably the phone, so she could keep in touch with her cronies.

She was born and raised in Aberdeen, she never knew her real father, and had a pretty tough upbringing with her mother and brother Iain. She gave birth to me in Stirling, and had a really hard time of it again, bringing me into the world. I didn't actually know this until I was 19 years old. One night when we were having dinner at home, my mum and dad casually brought up the subject of me being born into the conversation, as you do... it really freaked me out. Apparently, my dad ended up walking the streets overnight as he thought the two of us were not going to make it. Obviously, all was well in the end, but that was that, as far as family was concerned, so the three of us it was, no brothers or sisters to be added to this branch of the Bruce clan. I had a loving and caring upbringing, was closest to Mum, but Dad kept my feet well and truly grounded if I was getting wide. He didn't say much. He didn't have to.

Dad worked for Radio Rentals for 25 plus years, starting as a TV engineer, then to a shop manager and eventually to head office. He hated his work, and so when Mum found her ideal way to make a living, he retired early, to help her. She started working in an antique shop and fell in love with the whole scene. Eventually she started up on her own with a shop in Perth. She really did have a natural flair for the antiques game, specialising in decorative china and porcelain. I think her people skills definitely helped her as she was a brilliant salesperson, and was very popular within the trade with her fellow dealers. My parents would have liked me to get involved in the antiques game, but I just didn't take to it. I often accompanied them to fairs and auctions etc, and I pretty much hated it.

When it was almost time for me to leave school, I didn't really know what I wanted to do, and felt a wee bit under pressure to make a decision regarding how I was going to earn a crust. One day when I was off school with the cold, I watched a programme for schools and colleges (do you remember them?). It was about careers, this one being a chef; the geezer with the white hat was making a prawn cocktail. I really like prawn cocktail, and I got it into my head that old whitehat was going to eat the precious starter after the cameraman had fucked off. So there it was, a chef I was going to be – that prawn cocktail was responsible for the next 30 years of my working life.

I don't think maw and paw Bruce were too enthralled about my calculated, fishy decision; however, they respected it and gave me all the backing and encouragement I needed to make a go of it.

The day I left school, I felt for the first time a strange emotion of loss, not because of the school as such, but the loss of the company of my comrades, wondering if I would ever see them again. Walking home that day, on my own, was really weird and I can remember the emotion I felt very clearly. It was an unexpectedly sad one.

Next day, I got the shock of my life, when I started work in a small seasonal hotel in Pitlochry, which was about 20 odd miles from home, therefore I had to live-in, albeit just for the summer as I was due to start college later that year. First proper job as general dogsbody assisting the 'chef' proprietor of the little hotel. He was an absolute nutter, and ultimately gave me a wee taster of what life in a kitchen could be like – you'll recall, I told you a wee bit about this earlier on. When we started breakfast service, at a ridiculously early time, he made me pick up the sausages by hand; they were still bloody sizzling, and the bastard wasn't impressed by my "oooh, aaah, it's burning me aaah!" dancing about trying to handle the molten hot parcels of dodgy ingredients, so now and again he would just plunge my hands onto the tray of bangers to toughen me up. And no doubt relieve his frustration at my lack of experience. During my three months or so working there, as you can imagine, I really felt like twatting him, but I kept the heid, and kept my lip buttoned. Part of the reason for this was probably because he said to me at the start that he would pay me a bonus if I saw out the summer with him. The bastard did though give me a really hard time when I had two weeks to go; he really went for it, but I didn't break, and I got my bonus. It wasn't a fortune but getting it gave me obvious satisfaction.

I found being away from home very difficult and missed my mother in particular, but she would come up to see me once a week on the train, timed to be there to coincide with my afternoon break between lunch and dinner service. She always brought me a bag of goodies for my room: sweets, crisps, and of course, clean pants! I used to live for those visits and hated it when she had to go back, but she never failed to turn up, which was a brilliant effort on her part as she was pretty busy with her shop at the time.

We were always close, but also had our fair share of ups and downs – they never lasted too long though. When it came to the time that I started seeing girls she would make things, shall I say, difficult! It's true to say that Mum and my wife Teresa often didn't see eye to eye; however, they did find a level with each other and all was good between them in the end, to the extent that they actually enjoyed each other's company.

Mum didn't lead the healthiest of lifestyles really, but it seemed to work for her. She was a very poor eater, as in she didn't eat nearly enough. She lived on sherry and cigarettes mostly and partook heartily in both. It was a bottle of sherry every night. She had this ritual, almost, of opening a second bottle, just before she called it a night (or very early morning) and just had a very small amount out of this new bottle – maybe it was a thing about her brew breathing or something. We were always naturally concerned for her health and I suppose we got on at her about it, but as time went on, I actually stopped moaning at her, but my father didn't. He meant well though. I got to thinking that she wasn't going to change at her age, and if it was a fag and a 'veek' that she liked then so be it. The strange thing was though, the fact she hardly ate anything, you would think she didn't care for cooking, but that couldn't be further from the truth. She was a brilliant cook; she really could do it all, be it plain and homely or she could up her game and do things a bit more 'flowery' if we had friends or relatives round. Hardly anyone who set foot in the family home was not treated to some kind of top notch hospitality, Mum didn't do cheap ingredients, it was always the best quality she could buy, and the lucky recipients of her kitchen produce never failed to show their approval of what she served up to them. Obviously my father and I were very lucky indeed to be fed by her for all those years. I really couldn't imagine what it would be like to have a mother that was a rubbish cook. This was also reflected whenever I went to a pal's place for tea when I was a kid. I'd like to think that I was never too rude about the shortcomings of the fare dished up!

My job involved working split shifts, which usually meant a few hours off in the afternoon. One thing that most chefs are not good at is cooking for themselves, especially if still at work. A lot of people find this hard to believe. I think the problem is, they just don't know what to have, even though they have just about everything at their disposal. Every chef I have worked with over the years has been the same. I had Ma Bruce to help me with this though. During my break in the afternoon, I would go up to her house, and she would be good enough to cook me a meal. Nothing was discussed, she just plonked a plate down in front of me, and I devoured the delicious food that she served up. Afterwards, I would take her to look at antiques, or whatever else she had on the agenda; there was always something on the go. My belly was well impressed with its lot.

Mum's homemade tomato soup was simply out of this world. It wasn't even a recipe she kept secret; she just had a knack of making tomato soup. It was her favourite soup, and mine. It tasted absolutely divine. She really enjoyed teasing me, after I'd been a chef for a while, that my tomato soup didn't even come close to the quality of hers. She was right, and would happily tell anyone that would listen – fair play! When she'd made it, she used to ask me, mockingly, to taste the finished soup for seasoning, then give me a smug, knowing look, when I told her "It needs nothing, it's perfect!"

ROSELLE BRUCE'S TOMATO SOUP

- 1 kg of large, fresh vine tomatoes. 8 rashers of lean, unsmoked back bacon.
- Knob of butter. 1 heaped teaspoon of brown sugar. 1 chicken stock cube. 1 ham stock cube. 150 grams tomato puree. 1 small clove garlic. Salt and Pepper.

1. Chop the tomatoes roughly, removing the stems. Also, roughly dice the bacon, keeping the fat on, and crush the clove of garlic. In a saucepan, melt the knob of butter, add the tomatoes, bacon, garlic, sugar and a little salt and pepper, and cook on a moderate heat, with a lid on the pan, stirring periodically, for about ten minutes. Remove from the heat and add the tomato puree, stir in well. Add the chicken/ham stock (about 3.5 pints of liquid) and return to the heat, lid off the pan now. Bring to the boil and then simmer for 35 minutes.

2. Liquidise with a hand blender, then pass the soup through a sieve, forcing as much of the pulp through as possible. Season to taste, and adjust consistency if necessary.

3. Depending on the acidity of the tomatoes you used, if an extra "tang" is needed, place a small amount of vinegar in a pan with some brown sugar, heat and reduce these together for a few minutes. Then add to the soup. Fucking delicious.

4. If you want to really show off, add a touch of double cream to the served soup and a sprinkling of freshly chopped parsley. Wiggle your arse, whilst adding the garnish of cream and parsley. You've done well!

When Teresa and I decided to settle back in Perth, we ended up buying a house in the same street as Mum and Dad, the very same street that witnessed, all those years earlier, the magical roars and wails of Shane and finger picking good accordion playing of Mr James Fearnley on that warm summer afternoon. Mum was always a fan of The Pogues; from that very day she used to ask me what antics "The boy" (MacGowan) was getting up to. Her favourite band member however was Jem Finer; she called him "The banjo mannie" and she loved the instrumental bit in the middle of the track "If I should fall from grace with god" when I think Jem's banjo playing gave her a 'hairs on the back of the neck' moment.

I regret not taking her to a gig to see the band. I actually think that she just about might have handled it ok, if we were sitting upstairs. I guess that's just another example of my selfishness towards seeing the band live, the fact that I would've had to look after her, rather than doing my usual get as many pints down my neck as possible. I used to call her on my mobile phone when the band played 'Dirty old town' so she could sample a bit of the atmosphere, but that's obviously a very poor second to being there and getting caught up in the whole thing.

There was another side to my mother, a more mischievous side if you like. She could be a bit of a 'chancer' as I often called her. When she got a little worse for wear with her 'grape juice' she could be quite nasty to her loved ones and try and sort out everyone's problems without compassion or compromise. Come the next morning, she would just carry on as if nothing had ever happened, and fully expect everybody to be A-ok. She didn't have hangovers either; I wish I could say the same!

I used to do her shopping for her when Dad gave up driving his car. I really didn't mind this at all, but when she forgot something, and I had to go back to the supermarket, she had an uncanny knack of picking the worst possible time, when I was busy with work or whatever. I did however try to be the dutiful son and 99% of the time I was able to oblige. One such time really sticks out in the memory though, and it was a brilliant example of my mother's chancer side. I was having a nightmare of a day, when there is simply not enough hours to achieve your agenda. She calls me on my mobile phone and the conversation went something like this. "Calum, can you go back to Tesco's for me, I've forgotten something in the shopping, that's really important." "Ok, will go when I can, but I'm really busy. What is it that you need so desperately?" "Can you get me a little gem lettuce please?" I said: "Is that it? A little gem lettuce?" "Yes," she replied. "And while you're there you'd better get six bottles of sherry and 200 Berkley red fags!

THE STRANGLED ACCORDIONIST

Life is never dull in the world of catering. It's not the easiest of places to earn a crust; if you're a lazy bugger, then you'll be found out rather quickly. One of the big advantages of this industry, for me anyway, was the fact that two days are never the same. There's always something different going on, and some of the situations can be unique, with lots of humour thrown in. David had started hiring staff from Poland and Hungary. We also had an addition to the kitchen staff in the shape of Satya, from Mumbai in India. One fella though, Conrad from Poland, used to crack me up. He was a tall, thin lad, with short dark hair and wasn't the best at keeping on top of shaving duties. He looked quite scary, until you got to know him. I used to call him the undertaker. One thing that always impressed me about these overseas geezers was their adaptability in speaking English. Most of them got over this barrier really well. Conrad was struggling a bit though. He worked as a waiter, so this would have been a problem for him, especially this one day. We had a daily specials board, and the first item was always the soup of the day. This particular day, the soup was Cullen Skink, a traditional Scottish soup, principally made from leeks, potatoes and smoked haddock (don't worry, no recipe this time!). An old couple came through the door of the Inn, contemplating whether they were going to eat or not; they weren't sure. Conrad really helped them make up their mind though! The bloke asked: "What's the soup of the day?" Conrad, after a wee thought to himself, proudly announced that the soup was indeed, "Cream of Skunk!" That was two diners we were going to miss out on then. I wonder if they went home and told their friends of the wonderful soup that could be had at The Bein Inn.

After I had been away with Teresa for a holiday, first day back at work I got a very pleasant surprise, masterminded by David Mundell. Glenn Tilbrook from Squeeze had been back to play a couple of gigs at the Inn, and was staying on for a few days' rest. After I got changed into my whites, there appeared to be a welcoming committee, waiting for me in the kitchen. It was a small kitchen, and every member of staff seemed to be there. I wanted to get on, there was a lot of giggling so naturally I was becoming paranoid, and agitated. No one was answering my question of "What the fuck are you all doing here?" when all of a sudden Mr Tilbrook burst through the kitchen door, armed with his acoustic guitar, asking me if I'd had a nice holiday, while at the same time cursing me for missing his shows. "No matter," he said. "These two are for you!" I had to tell him two songs that I wanted him to play, in the kitchen, in front of the staff, for a very private, mini gig. Fantastic. I thought he was joking. I requested 'Up the Junction', a big Squeeze hit in its day. I had this 7 inch single in a rather fetching lilac vinyl.

Glenn wasted no time and was into the song in an instant, putting in 100% effort to his voice and guitar playing. It was simply brilliant, and so off the cuff, I couldn't believe it was happening. After he finished the song, we clapped and hooted, then it was time for song two. I chose 'Electric Trains', another Squeeze favourite of mine, and off he went again. As soon as he was finished, he was off in a flash, just as quickly as he had initially appeared. What a welcome back to work. David could certainly manipulate a situation at times, and turn it into something quite brilliant – what a treat for the staff, especially the older members, who had memories of Squeeze when they were in their prime.

Mike Peters from The Alarm was another who played a show at the Inn. He told the story of his career with a slideshow punctuated by him bursting into song, playing snippets from The Alarm's catalogue. It was almost surreal the next morning, when I had to make him a packed lunch for his onward journey – that's not very Rock 'n' Roll is it? Who did he think I was – his mother?

Yet again, Shane was coming to Glasgow with The Popes, but not the Fruitmarket this time. They were still part of Cetic Connections, but were booked to appear at The Barrowlands, which is probably The Pogues' spiritual Scottish home, even if I had never seen them play there. The Barrowland Ballroom was a larger venue than the Fruitmarket, so everyone would be benefiting financially with a larger attendance expected, as Shane could always sell out a venue.

As usual, it was me and Davo at this gig. There was a pub across the road from the Barrowlands called The Saracen's Head (The Sarry Heid!). There was always a character or two in this hostelry. The night of the gig, we found ourselves in there for a grease of the throat, when this bloke came up to us and said, "Hoi! Yous! Duz yez want tae buy a jumper?" Davo asked him, "What jumper?" He pointed to his chest and replied: "This fuckin' jumper!" – the one he was wearing. It was freezing outside. I think we gave him a couple of bob for his brilliant patter, and let him keep his jumper.

Next door to Barrowlands, there's a pub called Baird's. The pub is a Celtic FC stronghold, full of pictures and memorabilia. Someone told us a wonderful story about how Baird's was famous for something different to the Celtic thing. Apparently, many moons ago, there was a very healthy trade in female clothing going on in the ladies toilets; the goods could be 'ordered', and all the big brands were available. The best bit though, was about Saturdays – well, that was 'exchange' day, where you could organise a size bigger or whatever to be provided in the near future. You didn't need a receipt at this shop though, what a service! I really don't know if this tale was true or not, but the geezer telling us was quite convincing, and it is a great story!

So, no jumper, and no ladies' clothing, but a concert, yes, so we went up the stairs into The Barrowland Ballroom, to see what Shane was going to provide his punters with this time. The place was full, so the change of venue had worked, but we wondered if the band and their singer were going to be able to work – each and every one of them were fucked, oot o' their trees, especially the drummer who seemed to be playing a totally different song from everyone else. At least they had their usual hairy banjo man present tonight, but no accordion. Or so we thought. The gig was somehow rolling along, quality was obviously not a great concern of the performers bearing in mind the state they were in, but they were getting by. About three quarters of the way through the set, an accordionist did appear, from nowhere, and one of the roadies was hooking his squeezebox up for amplification of some sort. This was causing a small delay, which nobody seemed to mind. Shane went over to the accordion mannie, and grabbed some of the cables the roadie was trying to arrange and promptly wrapped them round the new musician's neck! He started pulling them tighter. Then tighter. The poor bloke was laughing, but the longer this went on, his face was changing to one of concern. Shane was not for stopping, things were getting serious now, when the roadie man had to wrestle Shane away from the cable and the neck he was strangling the very life out of. I'm telling you, it must have been close. The audience had been looking on with humour at first, then with sheer horror. The assault victim recovered, and played his accordion very well, to the likes of 'The Broad Majestic Shannon' amongst some other Pogues favourites; in fact his accordion playing made all the difference, it's a pity he wasn't up on the stage earlier in the evening. I've got a feeling the guy was just a punter that offered his services for the band totally unplanned – I could be wrong, but that's the impression I got. I bet he didn't bargain for Shane throttling him though!

There was no new material released by Shane and his band, but at least he gave us regular live shows to go to, which I was really grateful for. What were released however, were all the Pogues' studio albums, re-mastered, with extra 'rare' tracks, new sleeve-notes and artwork. Basically the B sides from the singles appeared towards the end of the album that corresponded with them time-wise; this was a great move, to have these songs on CD. As I mentioned before, the Pogues don't do 'bad' B sides, and there was some brilliant Pogues stuff added here, such as 'Muirshin Durkin', 'The Curse of Love', 'Wild Rover' and 'Bastard Landlord' to name just a few.

I really wasn't expecting, however, the next announcement, of Shane's next musical adventure, pending. The Pogues were doing a Christmas tour, similar to the schedule of dates they had played in

2001. Fucking superb! Thank you Lord! Even better, they were giving the awful SECC in Glasgow a swerve, and instead, playing two nights at The Carling Academy, a venue that ticks all my boxes. The Pogues had done a couple of one off festival type gigs since the reunion, but there was no indication that they were going to do a tour again. The dates being, as usual, in the run up to the festive period, I had to get my organiser's head on sharpish, and try and balance a busy time at turkey infested work with a gig or two with the mercurial Pogues. Or three. I booked tickets for one night at Glasgow's Academy, and two more at Brixton's. Davo and Postie were accompanying me in Glasgow, and for the southern branch, Keith was attending one of the London shows, the other I would be on my own. But that is just not a problem at a Pogues gig, the audience are all in each other's company, well that's how I feel anyway. The train was booked for London as well as a cheap hotel room in Victoria for two nights. Great to have something to look forward to, that's what makes life sweet.

Shane had appeared on the Frank Skinner show, on the box. I wasn't really a fan of Mr Skinner, but he was clearly a fan of Shane's. The interview was a cracker, with plenty of humour throughout. Shane was rattling off the places that The Pogues were going to be taking in, on their upcoming tour, fondly referring to the cities mentioned as "Basically every shit hole in the country!" There was another hilarious bit, where first Frank, then Shane, try out a set of false teeth, the results being quite amazing. Shane certainly didn't look right – waste of time, mate. I loved it when previously someone had asked Shane if he was going to get new teeth, he'd replied with a "No, getting rid of the first lot was hell!"

David being involved in the live music scene certainly threw up some interesting perks. As well as getting mini gigs in the kitchen, he took me to see Steve Earle in the Usher Hall in Edinburgh. Steve Earle had a connection with The Pogues, when they guested with him, making a brilliant song together, called 'Johnny Come Lately'. The track combines Steve's voice with a song about a soldier coming home from Vietnam, with the unmistakable Pogues musicianship backing up the vocals. It featured on his 'Copperhead Road' album. He had guested as that 'extra' Pogue at their concerts on occasions, joining the list of fellow extras such as Joe Strummer, Lynval Golding and of course, Kirsty MacColl. David had managed to get backstage passes for his gig in Edinburgh – we were on the guest list, how about that? The Pogues had brought Steve Earle to my music attention, and I liked him, having a couple of his albums in my CD racks, so I was looking forward to seeing him live. The show was quality, just what I'd been expecting; he had a very talented band behind him, and a female vocalist, Allison Moorer, joined him for a few numbers. The audience were surprisingly quiet though; they applauded, almost politely between songs, but there was absolutely no bouncing about, or anything like it, and I think this was getting on Steve Earle's tits. He looked grumpy throughout, and eventually said, "What's wrong with you 'Eddies' tonight?" David and I looked at each other – nothing needed to be said. As we were going to say "Hello" to Steve after the show, he'd probably kick oor heids in! But I had a plan to keep oor heids intact.

After the show, we were escorted to Steve Earle's dressing room by his brother, Jack. He was a nice guy, very chatty. We asked him what humour his brother was in now, and he just laughed. Yer man's dressing room wasn't full of beer, whisky, scantily clad vixens or anything else that could've been dodgy, but he did have a hamper of shortbread, very nice. David spoke to him first, telling him about the Bein Inn (angling for a gig, David? Well, you've got to try). He did a couple of autographs for David onto guitar scratchplates which he collected, then it was my turn. I had bought a copy of 'The Big Issue' magazine earlier in the night, and was desperately trying to keep it neat, as on the cover was Mr Shane MacGowan. The magazine was NOT suggesting Shane was homeless; instead it was concentrating on their forthcoming Christmas tour, with an interview and some pictures. I showed the article to Mr Earle, and suggested he get himself down to the Carling Academy in Glasgow in time for their first night's show, the one I was attending. Seeing the pictures and the article brought a big smile to his face, probably the first cheesy grin he had managed all night, and he started asking me more about where else they were playing etc. It was great to see his face like that when reminded of The Pogues; he clearly held them in high regard, and in his affections. With that, David and I were off, not outstaying our welcome. I hope the stirring of The Pogues in his memory chilled him out accordingly for his next gig.

The article in the magazine was a really good one; the pictures were of Shane, Spider and a certain Cait O'Riordan. She had split from being Elvis Costello's fork and knife, and was appearing with The Pogues during the Christmas tour, fucking marvellous! Davo had always taunted me that I'd never seen her play live with the band (he had!) but that was about to be sorted, and I was elated at the prospect of hearing "I'm a man you don't meet every day" from the Rum, Sodomy and the Lash album, sung live by Cait. The photograph in the magazine probably did the three of them no favours – they looked quite wrinkly and aged, but who was I kidding? Compared to the fresh faced, slim, full head of hair bloke on The Pogues video all those years ago, I was fatter, thinning on top, had a chin to spare and had grown a pair of tits so big, I was wondering when I was going to start menstruating!

As the date for The Pogues' Glasgow gig got nearer, there was inevitably more coverage in both the music and mainstream press, which just kept excitement levels bubbling away nicely. The three of us got the train through and settled in a pub near to the bridge that would take us over the River Clyde, for a short walk to The Carling Academy. In the pub, I had a moment to myself. I announced to Davo and Postie, from nowhere, totally disregarding whatever we were talking about, that "I just can't believe, that we are going to see The Pogues!" It just doesn't get any better does it? A night out, I mean, a Pogues gig, I was past myself with excited anticipation of what lay ahead. I just had a feeling that tonight was going to be a fucking belter!

The Academy is on two main levels, the usual balcony, but the stalls were really smart, with a raised part at the back, so if you did find yourself a bit away from the stage, at least you had a slight advantage, height-wise, to those in front. Very important for a short arse. There's also plenty of bars, very important to three pissheads. We settled at a great vantage point, at the front of the raised bit in the stalls, and found ourselves next to two guys through from Edinburgh, both Hibees, so we were five strong, in amongst two and a half thousand Celtic! At last, the lights dimmed and on came the greatest band in the history of music, stick your Beatles up yer arse! Tonight it was different from their previous gig in weegieland at the SECC – the sound was spot on, and as for Shane and the band, well, they made my 'moment' in the pub across the water very justified... they were fucking amazing!

I ended up on the shoulders of one of the Edinburgh lads; he was a tall fellow, so for a while, I had the best view in the house. The band were looking at me, probably thinking "look at that prick!" The set list was also terrific; one monster song ran into the next. Then on she came. The now divorced Miss O'Riordan entered proceedings to a heroine's welcome, and she did sing "I'm a man you don't meet every day". She had an angelic voice, and it sounded just as good as it did on the record. She did a few other numbers with the band. Shane wasn't complaining. He made a comment on the size of her breasts – they were probably just a bit bigger than mine! She obviously was present for 'Fairytale of New York' – this was also a big moment, I thought, as the song was originally written with her in mind, to do a duet with Shane, but by the time the song was ready, she had fucked off with Elvis. She sang her part perfectly, it was a real joy to see and hear all this, it really was. 'Fairytale' is an emotional Christmas song in its own right, but even more so since Kirsty MacColl's death. There were to be a lot of different female vocalists over the years since Kirsty was killed, and for me they have all been truly awful, apart from Cait, and Jem Finer's daughter, Ella.

Postie's favourite Pogues song 'Fiesta' closed proceedings, and that was it, they were gone; the message, as always from Shane, "Goodnight, good luck, and happy Christmas!" This gig had been, by far, the best I had seen them play since their first reunion, they were on at least a par, on what they sounded like back before Shane had left. The dynamics of the band in both appearance and sound were, for me, breathtaking. And here, present in Glasgow, tonight, were ALL The Pogues, original members, and the later additions, just wonderful. For those of you out there wanting to split hairs, John Hassler, the drummer for five minutes, doesn't count! Andrew Ranken is the man!

Our longish walk back to the train station was euphoric; we were buzzing after the magnificent gig we'd just witnessed, and what a feeling, I tell you, that I had two more, in the big smoke to look forward to. When we settled on the train with our greasy chip shop scoff, we got talking to three whippersnappers who had been at the gig; they were just teenagers, and it was really interesting to hear what they made of it all. It turned out that they had got 'into' The Pogues through their parents playing the songs at home, and, surprise, surprise, they had gotten themselves hooked! That just says it all, it really does. They were enthusing about James Fearnley's bit during 'The repeal of the licensing laws' when he dives onto the stage from the speaker cabinets at the back, and then runs up and down the length of the same stage, whipping up the audience into a frenzy – a show off right enough, but the young Pogues fans loved it! They were extremely knowledgeable about the history of the band, and it was a brilliant end to our evening, listening to their stories and views; they couldn't wait to tell their pals all about The Pogues at school the next day! Just fucking superb, apprentice Pogues no less, the band's longevity is not in doubt; the future is, indeed, fantastically bright!

With Mum and Dad. Happy days

Me and the man himself, Shane MacGowan © Paul McCluskey

A late 80s vintage shot of the Perth Hibs boys. L-R. Geoff, Les, Cousin Scott, Ed The Gazelle, Gavin, Davo (just) and me. Lots of hair present on all!

At Hampden Park, supporting The Hibees. (L-R) Ed The Gazelle, Charley, Geoff, Davo and me

The kitchen brigade, with a sprinkling of management, Anugraha Hotel, Surrey, early 90s. Front row, L-R, Me, Kyran Bradley, Steve Dowell, Philip Borthwick, David Mundell, Roger Halford, Keith, Sue Palmer

In the kitchen at The Aviator, trying to look as if I know what I'm doing, as well as busy

In Dublin, before Philip Chevron's Testimonial concert. Captain Paul McCluskey (centre) and David Lally. Earlier in the day, we had turned down an approach to join One Direction, even though I had clearly forgotten to put on my bra and corset

With Teresa at The Boogaloo, Highgate, North London. Shane's lyrics on the wall

Teresa, looking rather delicious, St Andrews beach

Teresa with a rather dapper looking Spider Stacy, Glasgow Academy

Teresa with Victoria Clarke and big Tom Creagh from Tipperary. Speaking Suppers, Dublin

"Never gonna give you up!" Me and Keith with some tasty South London geezers, singing Rick Astley songs. I'm on the vinegar! Greenwich, summer 2011.

Keith asks me for sex in the bar at Sticky Fingers, London. I had to say "No!"

*The glamorous 'security' at The Royal Naval College,
Greenwich. I didn't spill a drop of my black gold!*

Me, Philip Borthwick and Keith 'Sumo, Mick Mcmanus, The Hat' Williams, at Sticky Fingers, Kensington

One of my favourite sights in this world of ours. The best night out in town, comes to Brixton Academy, with its wonderful neon lit dome

The Pogues © Josie Montserrat

Discussing Masterchef with Shane. Dublin

And his reaction...

Scary Jem Finer – he didn't even speak! Glasgow Academy

With "Minister" James Fearnley, Congregational church, Laugharne, Wales

I need an 'at!' James 'Maestro' Fearnley, clearly enjoying himself, but not sure about Mr Spock at the back! Glasgow Academy

The Pogues take you to some fantastic
venues. A lampost in Greenwich telling the
locals all about the best night out in town

Shane and Victoria, Mean Fiddler,
Harlesden, North London, mid 80s
© Carmel Armstrong

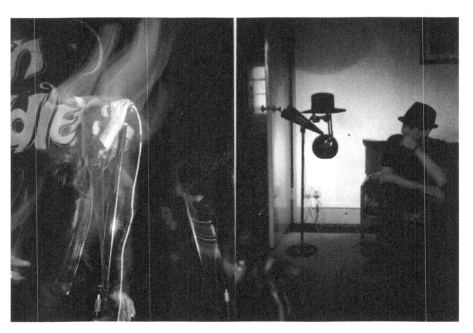

Shane 'on fire' at the Mean Fiddler, Harlesden, North London. And admiring his
lampshade sculpture in Carmel's flat, Camden Town © Carmel Armstrong

POSTER THIEF!

The poor staff at The Bein Inn, Teresa and my folks had to listen to me going on and on and on about the Pogues concert I'd just been to at Glasgow. I had to work the second night they played there, and during my evening shift, whilst churning out the turkey, my mind kept wandering to what was going on at The Carling Academy. Surely, it couldn't be as good tonight, compared with what Davo, Postie and I had witnessed last night? There was lots to sort out and organise before I disappeared a week or so later down to London on the train. Christmas is obviously such a busy time in the catering world, the slightest thing going wrong can screw things up severely, so I had to leave the staff very well prepared before my selfish, but very necessary adventure. Everything boxed then at work, Mum stocked up with Berkleys and sherry, and then off to the railway station, to catch the 9:56 am direct service to London King's Cross.

I love the train to London. Lots of people are always telling me that the plane is the way to go. Absolute shite. The train takes me from Perth, where I live, right into central London. The journey takes just short of six hours, but it's a very relaxing six hours, watching the world go by. Comparing this to travelling to Edinburgh or Glasgow airports, both of them not directly accessible from Perth, checking in an hour before the flight leaves, through security for a good frisking from an ugly bird, then every cunt acting like spoiled kids, whilst queuing to get themselves on the aircraft. Even being a short arse, there's hardly enough room for me on the glider. God only knows how really tall people, or folk that visit 'All you can eat' buffets and get more than their money's worth, get on. Then there's getting off the fucking thing. You stand up from your tiny seat, then some bastard twats you on the head with their bag, that's dubiously close to the limit of measurements that are accepted as 'hand luggage' and certainly heavier than it should be. You know this from the lump throbbing on yer napper! Then we commence the scrum and spoilt kid syndrome reappears, to physically get out and get your feet back on the ground. Once you've walked, for eight miles in the terminal, you've to wait for your fucking bag. And hope that it appears. Oh, and the airports. Whether it be Heathrow, Luton or Gatwick, they are all actually in another continent, in proximity to Central London. The only one that's decently located is London City airport, but you need to pay £3,199 to go there. And that's a single ticket! Apart from these things, the plane is just fine!

So back to the train... I can stretch my legs out, read a book, have a bite to eat, a few beers, a little bit of dozing, and I can do all this without the person next to me thinking that I'm trying to shag them or nick their wallet. You're just too close to each other on the plane. One minor, but rather funny drawback on the train is the toilets. Inevitably, you'll find that you're bursting for a piss just as the train is rolling into a station. Pissing whilst in the station is not allowed – nobody on the platform wants to see your steaming, golden liquid passing onto the track. Or worse. I think that would be quite a laugh actually, especially if you were a person on the platform, and tried to pick out the pissing culprit going back to their seat! So the train is in motion when you're urinating, and swings violently to say, the left, going over the points, as your piss goes all over the floor, never mind the toilet seat. This always makes me laugh out loud. If anyone's waiting outside, then they really must be wondering what on earth I am doing in there! A more violent swing from the train can mean a disaster, your trousers bearing the brunt of the mishap!

Very early in this journey, Satya, my assistant chef at The Bein Inn, calls me on my mobile phone, explaining to me that the bastard fishmonger has screwed up these best laid plans that I mentioned: he has failed to deliver the monkfish I ordered with him, giving him a week's notice, so he would be sure to arrange delivery. They would have to change the fish dish on the menu, what a nightmare. Menus would have to be reprinted, and we had to hope the diners would be happy with salmon. "Good luck, Satya, hope it works out!"

If that was the worst bit of this journey, then the best was the fact that I managed not to piss all over my strides, and then…. when I opened the train door after it had arrived in King's Cross. What a feeling. Smelling that cold London air at Christmas time, stepping on to the unforgiving grey station platform, walking to the exit (not eight miles away) and just thinking to myself, "The Pogues are in town!" Now what a buzz that was, everything in front of me, absolutely fucking tremendous, dynamite! Grab an Evening Standard, then on to the tube, Victoria my destination this time. There's always an article about The Pogues in the Standard, and usually a review the day after a gig; they are still big news, and especially in London, where they were born, as a band.

I had booked a cheap hotel in Victoria, not too far away from Brixton, just a few stops away on the Victoria Line tube. The room was really small, but still managed to contain two twin beds. Keith would be occupying one on the next night. He was too busy doing sumo with turkeys and chipolatas at work, and so had to sacrifice the Pogues' first night at the Academy. Ticket sales were so good, once again, that they'd added a third night in London, but I couldn't be greedy: two London gigs, on consecutive nights, wasn't too bad I suppose, I could just about live with it.

I managed to shoe horn a trip to Notting Hill, just after I'd checked into the hotel, to have a browse in the exchange record shops there; they certainly were not cheap, but often had some brilliant stock, especially up on the first floor, in the rarities department. The staff in these shops were just oozing with personality though, so helpful and just on another planet when it came to good customer service. NOT! But the gear they had was definitely worth a look, and I always had a rake in the ELO bit for Keithy – he was an anorak at the collecting bit as well. After Notting Hill, down to Leicester Square for a beer and a quality scran in Chinatown, a sad table for one, just me and my Evening Standard, lovely.

I got to Brixton early, and had a ticket for the balcony. I was starting to feel my age at concerts, and I really didn't want to miss anything, so I officially retired myself from the rough and tumble of the front of the stalls, the wild nights that I used to love, before my tits, belly and chin chiminey chin duplicated itself! A couple of beers purchased at the bar, and a prime seat, right at the front of the balcony, beside two very interesting Pogues fans. After the train journey home from Glasgow, with the apprentice Pogues, this was the other end of the Pogues scale, and yet another measure of how diversely popular the name of The Pogues can be. My two comrades for tonight turned out to be two elderly ladies, very grand ones at that; they both had fur coats on (no jokes about knickers please!) and were very, very well spoken. We had a lovely conversation. They loved the fact that I had travelled from Scotland to be at the shows, and they themselves were big fans, and had been regulars back in the day; they certainly knew their stuff, and were asking me all about how Cait was at Glasgow, saying they were excited when they heard she was appearing. The two grand ladies were attending the three Brixton shows, no fucking about then, just brilliant, loyal fans, who were about to witness their favourite night out in town!

I finished my two beers a bit too quickly, so I enquired if the ladies fancied a snifter for the show; they giggled but declined, said they wanted to keep their wits about them and enjoy the evening. I asked the ladies to watch my seat, as I headed back to the now crazy, busy bar, to get supplies in line for the start of The Pogues' set. This took a while, and when I got back, my new mates said they had had a battle royal to keep the seat, but they had defended my territory, with honour!

The noise in Brixton Academy was at fever pitch, when the lights dimmed, and on came the band. James Fearnley was always keen, usually first out, and Shane, well, forever the showman, he was last out, very last, he knew the crack, that's for sure! The Brixton crowd were in song: "One Shane MacGowan! There's only one Shane MacGowan!" And then The Pogues kicked things off with their own songs. The gig was not on a par with the Glasgow one the week before; it seemed to take the band and their sound engineers a while to get into gear, but it did all fall into place. Cait entered the stage again, and did her vocals, as she did in Glasgow, also dueting with Shane on 'A pair of brown eyes'. The two fur coated punters to my side showed their delight by frantically clapping, huge smiles never off their excited faces.

I kept looking down at the crowd in the stalls – it was mental down there, brought back lots of memories of a balancing act (enjoying the gig and pure survival) when The Pogues played here first time around. Tonight, I was more than happy, sipping my beer and taking it all in, missing nothing. A toilet break was always when Spider sang 'Tuesday Morning'. Sorry Spider. 'Fiesta' closed the show, and then, alas, it's time to leave, with five and a bit thousand other souls. All appeared happy with their lot, and a lovely thought in the back of my mind that I was coming back tomorrow!

At Brixton, as you exit the venue, there's almost a pavement supermarket going on, of T shirts being sold by South London geezers; they were making a packet, their powers of persuasion proving to be fruitful. The tube train, after a Pogues gig at Brixton, always gives me a problem. Brixton being the end of the Victoria Line (South) means that the train is standing there for a good while, waiting for the carriages to be bursting, just like in the busiest rush hour, before it starts its journey. Just when you think to yourself that surely no one else will fit in, they do, and then some! I'm a bit claustrophobic – not good! What is good though is there's usually a sing-song, Pogues numbers of course, as the train rattles along, back towards the centre of town. This sing-song keeps me going, and it's not too far to Victoria, where I get my head down after a long day, and realise just how lucky I am to be able to see my favourite band, with all their original members, play live.

Next day, Keith arrives on the scene, and we head up to Kensington, and, inevitably, to Sticky Fingers. A few beers and a meal, the place full of Christmas revellers, the waitress asks if we are going on to something after we pay our bill. So I tell her. "That's fantastic!" she says. I had a feeling she was just being polite, so I asked her if she knew who The Pogues were. She didn't, and I instantly regretted putting her in an embarrassing spot, but I also felt sorry for her not yet having been able to sample the charms of The Pogues. She said it was now on her 'to do' list! Keith and I embarked on a slightly boozy journey from Kensington High Street to Brixton, via Victoria. We were not in a hurry – we would settle for a place further back in the Academy balcony tonight – so, upon arrival at Victoria tube station, we arranged to take the 'long way' to Brixton. We got out of the tube, up to the main line station, to catch an overhead train to our destination. The reason for this is quite simple: just a 'thing' of mine, but when you get the overhead train to Brixton, soon after you cross the Thames, you actually see the most majestic dome of the Academy, all lit up in bright green neon stripes, just before you get to the station. I love the atmosphere outside the Academy, the queue to get in, folk looking for last minute tickets. And it's a real welcome sight, to see the bright, lit entrance, with tonight's artist's name, proudly displayed along the front. THE POGUES. Just doesn't get better than that, does it? This little part of the world is hosting the best night out in town tonight! Gives you a monumental reason to be there, for fuck's sake!

However, wits about you time, yes, Brixton is not the scary place it was years ago, but you still have to, well, just be careful, and treat the location with the respect it deserves, especially in the dark and almost deserted station. The ticket touts were out in force at the entrance to the tube station. "Tickets for the Pogues, buy or sell, tickets for the Pogues!" Once we were in the venue, anticipating another show, Keith and I were given a very gentle, but poignant reminder that life itself did not always go to plan. In the foyer of the Academy, we would usually go and have a peep at the merchandise stall. If they had anything I fancied, then I would buy it at the end of the gig – much more convenient than hanging on to anything during a Pogues jamboree. I spotted a t shirt that I was going to buy for Teresa, for Christmas – how thoughtful of me! As we prepared to make our way upstairs, and take our chances in the mêlée at the bar, we bumped into Jean MacColl, Kirsty's mother, and the three of us had a chat. She was raising awareness about her daughter's tragic accident in Mexico, and how the person ultimately responsible for her death appeared to be immune to prosecution, as he was a powerful figure in the country. Jean was a gently spoken, charming lady – you could sense a mix of great pride, tarnished with deep hurt, when she spoke to us about Kirsty. She told us she felt comforted, when she heard her voice through her songs.

She loved hearing her on 'Fairytale of New York', which receives lots of airplay throughout the festive season; one can only imagine how emotional that song would be for Jean. It was a real pleasure to talk to her for those few minutes, and we both made a contribution to the Justice For Kirsty campaign. She smiled and told us to enjoy our evening. Better do what we were told then.

We were about three quarters of the way back on the balcony; the people round about us were definitely up for a bit of rough and tumble – Keith was delighted! Up there, the rule of the house is simply: no standing. Fat chance of that happening when The Pogues are in town – the band were out of the blocks quicker tonight, and the stewards were pissing against the wind, trying to get the balcony punters to sit down. The gig was swinging along splendidly, everyone was on their feet, and it was rowdy enough for me and Keith. Still, the unfortunate people right in front of Keith got their earlobes tickled and pulled, and as usual, they looked around, and stared at me! Keith also has a 'thing' about Jem Finer. It's definitely not sexual though, he just feels that Jem never looks interested, and is just going through the motions whilst on stage. I've tried to tell him many times that Jem is just like that, he's never going to do a scissor kick thing like the axeman in The Popes. A measure of how 'cool' Jem is, at the conclusion of the most wonderful 'The body of an American' when the instrumental finale kicks in, Jem is needed to assist Andrew Ranken on his drums. Jem, very calmly, removes his banjo strap from round his neck, and walks, steadily, round the stage, and comes into the side of Andrew's drumkit, then commences his extra drumming duties. There's no hurry, or urgency for him to get there, although, in theory, I think he's needed at the drums a bit earlier, but he is totally unfazed, and will arrive when he's good and ready. That should tell Keith all he wants to know about Jem!

Shane also has drumming duties at the end of this one; he stands in front of the drums, with a single stick, battering it, in time to the beat, when required. Three drummers then? Actually four! When Andrew Ranken comes up to Shane's microphone to sing 'Star of the County Down', Darryl Hunt leaves his bass guitar, and drums for the duration of this song, with Shane on backing vocals. Usually when Shane isn't involved in a song, he goes off, backstage, to partake in something positive, like weightlifting or squat thrusts or something, then reappears when it's his turn to sing again. I like the fact that he hangs around for 'Star' – it's better to have him on stage, makes the whole thing much more complete.

There's a pub, practically next door to Brixton Academy. Needless to say, on concert nights, the place is packed out, but not so packed that I didn't notice a massive, green advertising poster for the Pogues' tour, with the band members' names featured along with the various dates when they were performing, and where. I liked the poster; it had played on my mind at the gig. Keith had no inkling at all, at what was about to happen, as we were passing the pub, just before we turned onto the High Street in big bad Brixton, on our way to the claustrophobic tube train. I entered the pub; it was starting to fill up again, but was far from full. I grabbed a chair and stood on it to elevate me to a level where I could safely remove the object of my desire from the pub wall. I was surprisingly slick, and had the poster down in a flash. I was aware of the eyes that were on me, especially that of the burly barman and a shocked, less burly barmaid, but no words were spoken, just looks of disbelief. And with that, I was on my way – thank you, I thought to myself, but still no actual conversation. Keith just looked at me and said, "You've got a thing about posters!" Well I did about this one; I still have it to this day. The way I saw it, the pub probably didn't need the poster anymore, the Pogues gigs were sold out, there was only one night to go at The Academy, so I was actually doing them a favour, making the wall space available for the next poster, for another band, and thus saving greatly on the South London refuse collection – what a considerate guy I can be at times, really!

In the morning, in the hotel room, we woke up early. It's a chef thing, but Keith is always ok in the hangover stakes, whereas I most definitely am not. In our tiny room, he lit up a fag (this was all before the smoking ban) and his cigarette had me wretching, and away to the toilet, to spew my stomach contents into the big white china bowl.

Breakfast was harder work than it should have been, for me anyway, and it was time to say our goodbyes. I still love London. When I lived in Surrey it was great to go into Central London on my days off etc, but equally good to go back into 'the sticks' later in the day. Like so many times before, as the train headed north, I was mixed up about where I wanted to be: Teresa, Mum and Dad were in Perth, so were our reasonably good jobs, Hibs and the lads – quite a lot going for heading north then. The train carriages were full of people travelling to be with their families, get round the fire, maybe sing 'Fairytale of New York', arguments on who is going to be Kirsty, and who's going to be Shane, who's going to carve the turkey, who likes breast, who likes leg. I like both. Family is everything? Well, that's the way it should be, but more often than not it isn't. Christmas can be a real shit time of year for some folk. I was lucky: I had people to travel home to, after a self indulgent trip, to the best social occasion there is to be had – a Pogues gig (or two) in the big smoke!

THERE'S ONLY FOUR SHANE MACGOWANS!

Peter, a regular punter at the Bein Inn, was a Jambo. If you don't know what a Jambo is, then let me tell you: it's a (dirty) Hearts fan, Hearts being Hibernian's fiercest rivals, peddling in the west of the city of Edinburgh. Peter was forever present at David's music nights, and we could talk about the football, despite our differences, with a bit of common sense and honesty. Peter asked me one night if I fancied tagging along with him to the Edinburgh derby, being played at the Hearts ground, Tynecastle. "You what?" "It'll be all right," said Peter. "I've got a spare ticket – would you like to go to the game?" I asked him how that was going to work – his spare ticket was in a Hearts part of the ground, and I, obviously, was a Hibby. These games are pretty highly charged to say the least – how on earth could I watch a game like this in THEIR end? It would be as dodgy as walking about feeling horny in Africa, with a raging hard on, and no condom!

Peter was sincere – sitting next to a Hibby, at the Edinburgh derby, was not a problem to him – so I thought it would be just rude, to refuse. Peter lived in the village of Glenfarg, a short distance from the Bein Inn, so I drove to his house, and he was going to organise the rest, for my night in enemy territory! We made a small detour to the journey, when we picked up his son in Bo'ness, on the way to Tynedump that night; I think he was a bit surprised that his old man had invited a Hibs fan to sit and watch this game with them. We parked up about a 20 minute walk from the ground, but there was no beer for us before the match. That felt a bit weird, but probably the right thing, considering that I was going to have to control my emotions. Our viewing position was actually quite close to the Hibs end, opposite the main stand. The first thing I noticed about Tynedump was how the concourse, when you went through the turnstile, was 'open', you could see in folks' back gardens, and see if the vanish liquid had worked, in the gussets of the knickers that were hanging on the washing lines. No chance, in this end of town!

As we settled into our seats, the atmosphere started hotting up. I found myself in amongst lots of people that were calling my team for everything. If there was a bad tackle, near to where we were sitting, everything was upside down – I'd be raging if a Hibs player was the victim of the tackle, THEY would be delighted, but I was managing, just about, to keep my emotions in check. Peter's son kept saying, "Hibs bastards!" and I did wonder, once or twice, if he would follow through with a pointed finger, "And he's one of them!"

The first half of the match passed without major incident, and then, right on 45 minutes, the Hibs keeper, Simon Brown, misjudged a tame shot, that he thought was going safely passed his goalpost. He watched, as the ball ended up in the back of the net – what a cheap goal to lose. The bastard should have gone to Specsavers! Every cunt round about me erupted; this horrible woman, with a thatched moustache, grabbed my shoulders as she celebrated the Hearts goal. I could have cut her throat without even thinking about it. But I did nothing, I just stood there, as the Spambo fans whooped it up. The Hibs keeper just didn't realise what he had done to me and the Hibbies behind the opposite goal. At least they could have a moan and whinge about it, unlike me. It's a wonder no one clocked my torn faced coupon! Half time was a long one; I just hoped that the floodgates were not about to open, and for Hibs to get a doing, whilst I was sitting in amongst this lot.

The second half started brightly though. Hibs were dominating, and a soft equaliser came the way of the boys in green, when Hibs striker Garry O'Connor rolled the ball into the Hearts net, right in front of the Hibs support. I was remarkably calm, the Hibs end was anything but; Peter was cool, but his son was raging, howling at the Hearts players to get their fingers out. I was given a few sideways glances from him, but my cover was still intact. The game was one way traffic now; Hibs had really come onto their game, and were having a right good go at trying to get a winner. I sat on my hands, just in case. This proved to be a good move, as Dean Shiels smacked the ball, high into the Hearts goal; the roar that came from the Hibs end was both awesome and deafening. I was fit to burst. I had this almost uncontrollable urge to run onto the pitch, just to show the whole stadium that I wasn't one of them; I was a hibby, and a fuckin' delighted one at that. It was all quiet around me now, I daren't even look at Peter's son; meanwhile the Hibs end was going bouncy, bouncy. The result thereafter never looked in danger, and the referee blew his whistle, 2-1 to Hibs then. I kept my head down and left along with the disgruntled Hearts fans; inside I was laughing, buzzing, it felt surreal, but brilliant!

I had told a few of my pals that I was going to the match, in the Hearts end, and as we walked back to the car, my mobile phone was on fire with text messages, all of them asking if I was still alive, and also celebrating our victory. You can imagine what the son thought of all this! It was brilliant walking with all the sick Jambos after the game; they were taking it bad, just as we do when they beat us. Peter dropped his laddie off, and we shook hands. He grudgingly said "well done" but told his Dad not to take me to the football again. Fair dos. It was one of my most memorable experiences following Hibs, and I'm grateful to Peter for making it happen. If any Jambos are reading this, and are upset by my comments, well go and get over yourself! You wouldn't want a Hibs fan writing nice things about your club now, would you? And if the roles were reversed, you'd feel exactly the same about my lot!

As things were getting steadily busier at The Bein Inn, we hired another chef. Dave was from Hungary, amazingly he came from Szekesfehervar, the very place where we had witnessed the mighty Hibees triumph in a European tie, followed by a drunken rampage through the town with the players. Dave was a clever bloke – once he got his head round the fact that our punters would not want to eat goulash all the time, he turned out to be a great asset to the Inn. There was no language barrier for Dave whatsoever; in fact he wanted to learn slang. One of his favourite slang sayings that he picked up (not from me, I may add) was he would look at an attractive female then say, "I wonder if she takes it up the cooncil gritter?!"

We had a very strong kitchen team, with the Scotsman, Hungarian and an Indian. Both Satya and Dave were very strong chefs, who worked fast and well when under pressure, and between the three of us we successfully got through a serious number of diners, in a single dinner service, regularly. The two of them also had big personalities, and they just didn't get on – they couldn't stand each other. I've never come across this in a kitchen before, especially in one as small as this, where two big characters practically hated each other, yet worked so well together, in a really confined space. I didn't have a problem with either of them, and tried to act as peacemaker more than once, but they were just not having it. They were both smokers (I had packed it in by then) and just before service started, I would tell them both to go for a fag. There was a wee room downstairs, where they went for a smoke, and they would sit there, right next to each other, in total silence. They kept this up for months. I keep saying that I'm a wee shite; well I'm glad to say that this never held me back in the kitchen, when the shit hits the fan. I never found it a problem to 'encourage' the staff, if they needed it, and it was no different with Dave and Satya – they were loyal lads, and their loathing of one another, amazingly, just did not affect the quality of their work. Having said that, if one of them fancied taking the head chef outside for a physical showdown, then I would have probably lasted oh, about 15 seconds! I would have paid good money to see them have a showdown with each other, I'm sure it would have been a box office Sky job, and I would struggle to predict a winner with those two. Probably good then, that we never found out.

We added a kitchen porter to the team, someone to wash the dishes and pots, and to generally assist the chefs when they needed it. I've met so many kitchen porters over the years, there's never a dull moment with them. This one, a lad called Tim, told us a story that had us all in stitches. He was so sincere when telling his tale, and that just added to the drama. He'd been babysitting, looking after his nephew. After his brother and his wife had taken off to their social event, Tim had got the kid settled in his kip really quickly, result! He then went hunting (matter of factly) for some porn, that he was sure his brother would have, as "He was a dirty bastard!". After searching, fruitlessly, for ages, he looked under a bed, and right in the corner was a VHS video tape. Bingo! Tim was a big chap, and he had to strain and grunt (steady, to get the video) and eventually he reached it, and prised it out, from under the bed. He fed the video machine, got himself settled, trousers and pants down, and by now, throbbing manhood ready. All was in hand! His excitement level was going through the roof, what could the tape be – perhaps 'Shaved Nuns on the rampage for a thick, stiff porking!'? The fuzzy screen cleared, and the video started: 'Phil Collins live in concert'. Tim was furious, but, somewhat amazingly, told us: "I just got on with it anyway!"

Surprisingly, Shane and The Popes were coming back to Glasgow. Bloody hell, he was keeping busy, it wasn't that long ago that he'd finished the tour with The Pogues – I had this snazzy green and white poster, that had all the dates of that tour on it... Shane was due to appear at The Garage again, the venue where he appeared for The Crock Of Gold tour. This was happening on a Friday night; Davo secured a couple of briefs – we would be going along to support yer man. The date of the gig was a busy one at work, I started really early that day, and got through loads of prep for the two chums to get through service at night, when I'd be at the gig. Then they could have a cuddle. Maybe not.

Davo and I decided to get the train – always a bit dodgy when it was Shane and The Popes, due to their timekeeping. It would be hellish if we had to leave before the end of the gig again. We needn't have worried. As we settled in a pub, directly across the road from The Garage, a punter in the pub must have heard our conversation, talking about the gig we were going to see. "The gig's aff!" he said. "Been fuckin' cancelled, there's a note on the door!" Sure enough, it did seem to be really quiet across the road, and there was a piece of paper flapping about on the door of the venue. Davo was now a master of all things internet, and he told me there was no message or anything from the site he had bought the tickets from, nothing at all. We finished our drinks and crossed the road to read the bit of paper. It was a note, like you would leave for the milkman, it really was that professional.

But, quality notice, note or whatever, the gig was indeed cancelled, no other explanation was forthcoming. Nothing we could do about it, very disappointing though. We decided to just have a few drinks in the centre of Glasgow, and get the last train home – what else could we do? The pub we chose was a bad move, full of youngsters out to start their weekend. The bar was packed, and it took ages for us to get served, you couldn't hear yourself think, never mind have a crack. This was a 'moment'. I felt, all of a sudden, old. I don't think Davo was far behind me, so we bailed out, and got an earlier than scheduled train home. That was to be the last of Shane and The Popes for me; he didn't do anything with them in Scotland after that. To be fair though, the two albums, and the numerous shows I had been to had been enjoyable enough, especially that second album, 'The Crock of gold'. It kept things going for Pogues/Shane fans for a few years, and I for one was very grateful for that. Of course, The Pogues appeared to be back, they even ventured over to Japan, the very scene of Shane and the band's previous parting, to play a handful of very successful, sold out concerts.

And they were doing ANOTHER Christmas tour! They were on a roll now, and I was in Pogues heaven with this news. Again, later, through Carol Clerk's book, 'Pogue Mahone', we learned why Cait O'Riordan was not going to be appearing with the band this time. In the early days of the Pogues, Cait's relationship with some of the band, Andrew Ranken in particular, was not a very harmonious one. It would appear that years later, during the Christmas 2004 tour, that not much had changed, as far as the feeling towards Cait was concerned. Shane may have admired her jugs, but maybe that wasn't enough to keep her in the fold. There's a photograph in the book – a group photo, featuring Cait – and the look that James Fearnley is shooting her way speaks volumes regarding how he's feeling about her presence. Not good. He looks disappointed, to say the least! But let's not dwell on the Cait thing, arrangements had to be made, same again methinks, a night at Glasgow, and perhaps another two more in big bad, fuck off Brixton? Davo wasn't playing this time, he didn't fancy The Pogues in Glasgow. Maybe Shane's no-show at the Garage had helped make his mind up?

I now had a bit of experience to call upon, regarding getting organised for the Christmas gigs – for example, the quicker you booked the train to London (oh yes, was it ever in doubt, I was going again!) the cheaper the fare. So I got my arse into gear, and booked the train for another two shows at Brixton, could worry about the hotel at a later date. But what about Glasgow? Well, again, I thought I'd better settle for one night at The Carling Academy, work would be busy again. No Davo, and no Postie – he too was obviously busy at Christmas, as his nickname suggests. Getting back from The Pogues at 2 am, then up for work at 4.30, was too big an ask for him, so I was on my Jack Jones. Not quite! Teresa, my missus, had been 'getting' the Pogues bug, they were making their mark on her, and she threw her hat into the ring, telling me that she would be delighted to accompany me, to the best night out in town.

And so, it was Teresa who got on the train with me at a cold and wet Perth station, We'd been in the railway buffet beforehand, for a couple of beers. Teresa told me she didn't want to get too drunk, as she wanted to enjoy the occasion. I said nothing, but thought to myself that her desire to stay sober would prove to be somewhat difficult, when going to see The Pogues. Hey ho! We had another couple of beers on the train, well on the way now, Teresa! When we got off the train in Glasgow, we were straight into Sammy Dow's, opposite the station, for a drink on arrival. Time to make our way to the Academy.

Just before we got on the underground, we spotted an outdoor ice rink in George Square. My wife loves Christmas time, and the ice rink was like a frozen Christmas grotto. We had a look, but I was getting impatient, and told her that we'd do the ice thing another day. We had a date, and so onto the local underground network it was, which takes you out, very close to our function venue for the night. I was enjoying being with Teresa, she was nicely excited about the night that lay ahead of her, the beer was really kicking in, and, she wanted more. Who was I to refuse, if she was thirsty. We had tickets for the balcony, and there was a slightly different rule in Glasgow, compared to the balcony in Brixton. In the first three rows in Glasgow, you were required to remain seated, but, in rows four and beyond, you were free to stand, dance, laugh, cry, blow your nose, scratch your knob, whatever. So we settled in row four. We were sat next to a young lad on his own. I felt a bit sorry for him, so I bought him a drink, a brandy, no less. Teresa and I were getting seriously pickled. I tried to tell her that it was ok to feel like we did at The Pogues, it kind of goes hand in glove, and not to worry, she'd have a great time.

Just as we were anticipating the band coming on, I went and got another round in, and another brandy for matey. The band appeared and, as usual, Shane was to be last out. Teresa was desperately trying to locate him, but I told her not to worry, she'd know all right, when he decided to grace us with his company. When he did, Teresa went mad. "Shane!" she roared, and turned to me saying, "I can see him, I can see him, all four of him!" Teresa was drunk, she was at The Pogues, and she was pissed, how fabulous! As 'Streams of Whiskey' kicked in, Teresa became part of The Pogues family, it was brilliant to see her so into it and happy. There were two or three punters in the third row, up on their feet, getting hassled from the security blokes, and the more stiff members of the audience next to them, telling them to sit down. Well we weren't having that, the fourth row punters, hauled them up, up to our row, the standing, scratching bit, and they danced to the music – and they danced! The boys put on a brilliant show, they always do in Glasgow, where they never fail to get a Premier League reaction from their fans. I had to give matey with the brandy a nudge, and tell him it was his round – once he got the hint, he was happy to oblige.

Teresa took herself off to the ladies. I told her not to be too long, but whilst she was away, she heard the first notes to 'Fairytale' being played, and a huge roar of anticipation from the audience. Teresa tried as best she could to get out of the ladies quickly, but by the time she got back to her place, the song was half way through, with the magnificent Ella Finer back on vocal duties with Mr MacGowan. It was the only negative of the night, but it made her more determined to go to another Pogues show, and see the classic song performed in its entirety. She loved the subtle charms of Shane, when he was squinting down at the set list taped to the stage floor, realising that he could take a break at the next song, then THUD! He just threw his microphone on the floor, before shuffling off to the back, and out of sight for a while – what a diva! As Fiesta came to a close, and Shane wished us all a happy Christmas, the Pogues, once again, were gone.

Teresa hit the cold Glasgow air, ready for the long hike back to Queen Street station, and was by now, well and truly rubbered. Sensible head kicked in with me, and I had to help her negotiate one foot in front of the other. I suggested a taxi, but she wasn't having it. Once she's made her mind up, then that's it! We just made it in time for a dubious carry out chippy, and on to the train, along with many others who'd had a few shandies, after their night out. Not all of them though had been at the best night in town, but a good lot of them had – there were Pogues t shirts everywhere. We both had work the next morning, Teresa was fragile to say the least, but she'd caught the bug now, she loved the experience, she wanted more, and I informed her that over the course of the evening, she had actually drunk TWELVE pints of beer. Not quite the fifteen Shane sang about in 'Streams of Whiskey', but still disgusting nonetheless. "Just wait till I tell your pals," I teased.

Hungarian Dave, from Szekesfehervar, had by now left The Bein Inn for pastures new. I was sorry to see him go, and even sorrier to have met his replacement, a big German geezer; I can't even remember his name, so we'll call him Hans. This bag of wind had apparently worked in big hotels and good quality restaurants back in his home country. This is another little issue, that is rife in the catering industry: plenty of 'talking' about how an individual will tell you that they're the dog's bollocks to all things kitchen, then when it comes down to actually doing it, well, you can guess the rest. Hans was a prime candidate in this category – if we had more than one order on, then he was fucked. On a Saturday night we could have fifteen orders on at once, and the quality of food he was producing was not up to scratch. Still, he maintained he could do it all. He was really tall – as my mother would say: "A long drink of water!" This is where you are caught in a classic Catch 22. Do we send him back to Germany? Well, better not, because Christmas is almost upon us, we'd better put up with it then, especially as I was going down the road to see The Pogues. Satya would need a hand when I was away, no matter how limited it was. But the German cunt beat us to it! When I was on the train with Teresa, going to the Glasgow show, I got a call, telling me that Hans was calling it a day; he wanted to be home for Christmas, and the food we were preparing was not his cup of Sauerkraut. Fuck knows what kind of food he dished up at home – really, the boy would struggle to boil an egg. Anyway, this gave me a massive headache for my trip south; it was in the balance unless I could sort something out. This certainly didn't spoil my night in Glasgow with alkie Teresa, definitely not. But as I drove to work next day, my mind was working overtime. I had to get to these shows at Brixton. I was thinking what I always thought: make the most of this, these shows may be their last!

LEARNING TO DRIBBLE

I did manage to sort cover at work; Hitler, sorry, Hans, fucked off back to Germany, and a lad at the Inn, who didn't have much kitchen experience, proved to be a more capable replacement for our departed friend, and Alison, Satya's new girlfriend, could also do a turn with the carrots and sprouts. Alison was also a whiz-kid on this internet thing that was slowly taking over, and she very kindly booked me a cheap hotel in Notting Hill for my Pogues trip. The day before I was due to travel, I started to feel unwell; my chest was tight, and I knew, from previous experience, what was going on. I had a touch of bronchitis; it was going to get worse, before I got better. Nothing was getting in the way of my adventure though, so I settled on the usual train. The plan was to get my head down, and hopefully feel a bit perkier when I arrived at King's Cross. As the train sped down the country, as I had feared I went downhill, and felt like shite when we arrived. It wasn't bad enough to spoil the bit when the train door opens, however – the best night out in town is happening just down the road in Brixton. It was freezing cold, and London was buzzing, as usual, on the run up to Christmas.

I caught the tube to Westbourne Park, and followed my computer print out directions to the hotel that Alison had booked for me. The description of the location as Notting Hill, was a wee bit misleading! Despite it being so cold, I was sweating like a prostitute's chuff by the time I got to the dubious establishment. Now, this was all my own fault – I had told Alison that I wanted cheap, but the place was a rat hole – you get what you pay for. I remember thinking to myself that I wasn't exactly on the breadline money-wise, so why the fuck was I booking a hotel like this? The geezer on reception showed me to the room; there were three beds in it, all squashed together, the place was musty and cold... perfect for my bronchitis then! I had to go back to reception, and ask the receptionist for a bit of scrap paper and to borrow a pen; a small request I thought. I'd had a phone call from work, and had to compile a menu for an enquiry they'd received. The person that was making the potential booking was needing the menu today, so I decided to write it down, before reading it out on the phone. The receptionist assumed that I was down to complain about my room (fancy that?) and before I could open my mouth, he was spouting on that he couldn't change my room, as they were all much the same, and what did I expect for the few shillings I had paid, blah, blah, blah! I managed to get a word or two in, asked him for a pen and paper, and he just looked at me, totally bamboozled. He wasn't happy about my request in the end – it was as if I'd asked him for one of his kidneys – before he produced a biro, and a piece of paper. Hard work, but I managed to splutter a menu to Satya, back at The Bein Inn. Normally, I would have walked to where Notting Hill really was, and have a look at the record shops, but decided just to get something to eat, and take my time getting to Brixton. Same as last year, Keith couldn't make it tonight, but was scheduled to arrive in all his glory tomorrow, and hopefully, I'd be in better form for him.

It did feel a bit weird to settle into my seat at The Academy, having had no beer whatsoever, and I was still feeling really rough. We got through the support band, and on they came, fucking brilliant. I started, slowly, to feel much better, the brilliant music taking my mind off being ill; the sound was just superb, Shane was on fine form, and they just blew me away. There were a couple of times that the band and singer lost their way with one another, Shane missing his timing a bit, like he did occasionally. Much to my amazement, they just stopped, during 'The Sick Bed of Cuchulainn' and started again. Nailed it this time, Shane! Same again, during 'The Irish Rover'. I thought it was fantastic that they did this, they were playing so well on the night, that they thought they should get it right for their audience. There was to be a real personal highlight for me tonight though. My favourite all time Pogues track, 'Lullaby of London' was played, just like it sounded on the record. I'd always been disappointed by the band performing this one in the past, I just felt they didn't do it justice, live. Not tonight though; they played it, and Shane sung it beautifully. It brought a tear or two to my eyes; there's absolutely nowhere else in this whole world I would rather have been, but in Brixton, witnessing The Pogues playing Lullaby. It's moments like this, that makes all the hassle worthwhile, the juggling things at home and at work, the journey, the shitty hotel room, the expense of it all. I bought a couple of old style posters from the merchandise stall at the end, good enough for framing they were, and left the Academy, totally at ease with myself, having been entertained to the very highest standard. What a boost, the feel good factor must have helped me get over my symptoms – maybe I had man flu right enough!

I passed the Brixton pub, next to the academy, the scene of last year's poster crime, and hung around for a while in the tube station, until the bursting, busy trains had left. I certainly couldn't have handled that tonight. When I got to Westbourne Park, I started walking towards my luxury hotel, and walked down one of the dodgiest roads I've ever seen in my life. I was lucky. All the 'youths' that were hanging about were looking at me all right – apart from me and them, the long road was deserted; I was easy pickings, that's for sure. My heart was in my mouth as I passed one group, then another, and then a final one. I was lucky, and I didn't look back, as I scuttled towards safety. It's a good job they didn't clock my posters, or I would have been dead meat – they were so good, they were worth killing for. The same receptionist was still on duty; he must have been confused, because I was really pleased to see him. He could keep his kidney! I collapsed into a welcome, exhausted sleep, still having that great feeling about the show I had seen earlier on.

I met Keith in a Notting Hill pub the next afternoon; he too was looking a bit worse for wear, he had been working long hours, the hotel had been experiencing one of their busiest Christmas periods on record, and he was actually lucky to be getting to this one show. After he dumped his bag in our less than salubrious lodgings (he didn't mind) we did our usual, and made the short trip to Kensington and Sticky Fingers. The beer was kicking into Keith really quickly tonight, and I was much the same. When we left Sticky Fingers and got on the tube at Kensington High Street, the doors closed, with me on the train, and Keith still on the platform. Our mobile phones wouldn't work underground, so I hoped he would follow me on the next tube, to Victoria, which he did. A wee phonecall later, we were reunited, and onto the overhead train again to Brixton, taking in that view of the neoned dome, with the green lights – magic!

We were about halfway back in the balcony, the band were playing away fine, but despite being full, the audience up there were unusually subdued. We were sitting next to the aisle, and were in the mood, so we tried to get things going, by standing and having a bit of a boogie. This security chappie walked up to Keith, who was nearest the aisle, and told him to sit down, which he did. But I didn't. The bloke went away, seemingly oblivious to the fact that I was still up on my feet. Keith was raging, so he got back up; the bloke came back, and again told him, and him only, to sit down. Keith, reluctantly, sat on his arse, with me still standing, and the boy fucked off back down the stairs. When Keith got up again, matey again paid him a visit, and told him firmly that if he didn't sit down, then he was being ejected from the venue. Well that was it. Keith was in the boy's face, telling him that if he didn't fuck off and leave him alone, then he would be bringing the matter up with the Government, first thing in the morning! Of course, the whole episode had been watched and enjoyed by the people around us, and brilliantly they helped the 'Government grass' of Brixton out, when, during the next 'fast' Pogues number, a lot of them too were on their feet, and eventually just about everyone was.

I often wondered what it's like in the balcony there with other bands, because every time The Pogues are there, the balcony is bouncing, like tonight – it may take a while, but it gets there all the same. At the bar for the balcony, this big coloured girl said that she remembered me and Keith from previous years. She told us that the Academy bars' busiest nights on the calendar were the ones when The

Pogues were in residence. No surprise there then; the boys even boost the economy – is there just no end to their talents? I once heard a story that the comedian Roy Chubby Brown, when he was at his popularity peak, used to get a percentage of the bar takings in the places he performed. Perhaps Mr Addis, the band's accountant, could look into that for his clients...

Keith has a habit during the show of going for a round of beers, and taking a longer time than is expected, before his return. I'm sure he has a few fly nips at the bar, and tonight, after his trip to see our new coloured friend, it was obvious that he had reached the end of the line. He was absolutely finished, so much so he could hardly stand. He kept singing 'Sally MacLennane' even though that one had been done by Mr MacGowan and co, but nobody seemed to mind. I knew I was in for a hard time, getting us back to the hotel; it was quite a thought, I can tell you. At the end, the crowd kept us both on a pretty tight straight and narrow as it were, but once we were outside, there was only one option: it would have to be a taxi, if a cabbie would accept the fare. Keith was roaring out at him, "Shrewsbury! Shrewsbury! Shrewsbury!" sharing the love he has for his favourite football team with the residents of Brixton. "Just shut the fuck up, until we get in a taxi!" I pleaded. He did manage this, for about 20 seconds, before he was off again, adding his own words to a Pogues classic, "If I should fall from the kitchen sink!" Amazingly, we did manage to get a black cab. I knew the fare was not going to be good, but we got on with it; £30 later, we arrived at the hotel, and thankfully, Keith kept his spewing until we were out of the cab, and before we entered the hotel. Old kidney bean was still on duty (did he never get a bit of time off?) and he certainly did not look pleased when he saw the state of my comrade in his hour of need, but thankfully, he said nothing.

Keith snored his way through the night, and I slept less well, but as usual we were up with the larks, and on our way into Notting Hill for our breakfast. The only place that was open was McDonald's. It was 5 30am, and the place was busy. It became apparent that the vast majority of people in McDonald's that morning were actually homeless people, who must have been waiting for the place to open. I felt bad, whingeing about a sub-standard hotel, whereas these poor souls were up against the elements, in freezing December. Keith and I went back to collect our gear, and bid farewell to Steak and Kidney at reception. I wished him a Happy Christmas, and I got the usual, blank stare in return!

Most years, a chef has to work on Christmas Day; this was no different at The Bein Inn. Teresa used to come to work with me and very kindly help us out with the starters and wash the dishes. She had her own hard shift on Boxing Day, when Next held a massive sale, usually commencing at a very early time. On one occasion Teresa started work at 4.30 am. Back to Christmas Day itself, we'd have a meal with Mum and Dad Bruce, and we always, always, raised a glass to Shane MacGowan – well, it was his birthday, cheers Shane! New Year was much the same. It used to be such a big thing in Scotland, but it's been on the decline for a long time now. After the festive season (The Pogues bit apart) I just like things to get back to normal. Whatever that is.

The New Year, in some respects, can refresh your mind, and mine was working overtime: I felt I needed a change. I knew what I ultimately wanted to happen, but there was to be a very different gig to be hosted, in-between. I'd been talking, at length, with Davo about my future. Davo worked for a large insurance firm in Perth, and I was always envious of the sociable hours he worked, even if earlier in my career, the 9 to 5 thing didn't suit me too well, when I was at Dewar's Whisky. Anyway, Davo reckoned I could get employment somewhere within the massive building where he worked, in a department where one of his friends was the chief. So I went for it; the interview I had was interesting, I answered all the questions thrown at me in with 'chef' answers, but somehow I got through it, and secured a job. I'd enjoyed The Bein Inn, with lots of good memories, but I put my notice in; it was time to turn another page, and try something very different.

The large office that I worked in was populated mainly by women, and I can honestly say that I have never came across an environment so rife with insecurity, bitchiness and incompetence in my whole working life, within the confines of one area. I was used to professional kitchens, often run similar to the military: if things went wrong, it was 'discussed' and then sorted, pronto. Not so in this fucking place –the office and I were not a marriage made in heaven, more like a packet of pork itchings at a Muslim party. One thing that being there taught me though, is that when you phone up one of these places, the vast majority of the time, you end up talking to a dribbling idiot, who either isn't up to the job (that'll be moi then!) or is so busy trying to sell you something else, that they fuck up the thing you phoned them about in the first place. You've all been there, haven't you?

I often wonder how the people that run these places manage to dress themselves in the morning. The training was practically non-existent. I started at the same time as a young girl and an older lady. No one could be arsed showing us anything, and as things went on, that suited me just fine. We were all told to go 'live' on the phones (you what?) – the older lady and I refused, but the young girl did what she was told. I was sitting next to her, and will never forget the first time her phone rang. Through no fault of her own, she was dribbling within seconds, and I could hear the raised tone of the geezer shouting at her on the end of the line; she couldn't help this man with anything, and kept asking him to hold as she asked her so called superior, tart, who wasn't helping her at all. Fucking amazing, but real – as I say, we've all been there! The poor young girl was in tears, and spent the rest of the morning bubbling in the toilets. Yes, the catering industry is hard, but I had never seen anything like this.

One of the bosses came to my desk one day and started having a go about some work I had 'managed' to do, under instruction. It turned out that my instructions were wrong (I only did what I was shown to do) – I had processed some cheques to punters getting refunds, and the amounts were, apparently, too high. I wasn't having any of this, and to be honest, I wasn't used to people talking to me like he did at work, so he was told, in no uncertain terms, to back off, and start sorting the real problem, ie the tart who had instructed me to do the cheques and their amount. Maybe you got a nice unexpectedly large cheque, from a large insurance firm at some point – well if you did, good on ye, and mine's a pint!

I used to meet Davo at lunchtimes; we'd eat our sandwiches, then go for a walk round the grounds, usually with me moaning like fuck about the morning I'd just had. Poor Davo must have dreaded lunchtimes. His post within the firm was quite high up; Davo is no fool, he is a clever chap, with a sharp brain. I must state here and now, that if you got him on the phone, his mouth would be bone dry, no dribbling! He did well to get me a job there, and I actually have no regrets whatsoever about the wee while I 'worked' there – it was an experience, as they say. I resigned from my post quite sharpish though, and I told the wifie who was supposed to be in charge that day, that I was actually doing her a big favour, as I would have been unable to add anything positive at all to her little bunch of treasures. On the last shift, on the last day, it was customary for the departee to be escorted from the premises. I assumed this was in case I was thinking of stealing the pencil sharpener. So out the door I went, wiped my mouth, and left the dribblers behind me, to dribble some more. We shall return to dribbling idiots, a little later on. Joy.

So, what to do? Back to what I really wanted to happen. I'd been pretty lucky in my career thus far; I'd achieved two ambitions I had in being Philip Borthwick's senior sous chef at the Anugraha, and returning to The Station Hotel in Perth as head chef. I did have another ambition though: I wanted to run my own restaurant, and be ultimately responsible for everything, establishing a new business, success or failure. My stint at the insurance place confirmed that I just wasn't cut out for anything like that; it actually made me realise how grateful I was to choose the career path I did. Sometimes chefs worked long hours, under constant pressure, but the job could be very rewarding in financial terms as well as job satisfaction. I would never have settled working in an office – horses for courses and all that.

I came across a bar and restaurant, a brand new one, that was looking for a tenant. It was situated about five miles outside Perth, at the airport in Scone. The airport was a small affair, used mainly for flying tuition and private planes. There were a number of businesses on the airport grounds, and an antique centre next door to the restaurant. Plenty of potential then to make a go of it, get bums on seats, wallets and purses open! The size of the restaurant was a lot bigger than I actually had in mind, and at first it put me off a bit, but when I thought about it, the bigger the better – if I was going into this, there was no point fucking about with a wee café or something similar. The whole thing gathered pace like a tsunami, and before I knew it I had shaken hands with the landlord. SPLASH! Straight into the deepest of deep ends, but I was lucky that Teresa was going to save me from the sharks and the menacing electric eels! She resigned from her job at Next. She had done really well for herself there; it was a big decision for her to change her career, and go into something she had hardly any experience in. We called the new place 'The Aviator', and if I thought that I had worked long hours before, nothing had prepared me for this latest project. Everything that had gone before was a walk in the park, compared to this gig.

LEARNING TO FLY, THE AVIATOR

The initial set up of The Aviator Bar and Restaurant, regarding the amount of work and organisation involved, was staggering. I can honestly say that if we knew how much had to be done, not to mention the expense, just to get up and running and the front door open, we may have thought twice about having our own business. But we got there. We held an 'open' weekend to launch the place in September 2006, where friends, family and potential customers were invited to come and give The Aviator the once over. We provided tea, coffee and a smoked salmon sandwich or two, all complimentary of course. We also opened the bar, towards the evening. The drinkers arrived, but the bar was NOT complimentary. I sold the Aviator's very first drink – it was a vodka and coke, and I sold it to a bloke called Aldo, who was to become a regular. I actually felt guilty asking him for the money for his drink, but that feeling didn't last long... in the early days, every penny was a prisoner.

We kept our food menu simple, honest and, I'd like to think, value for money. I've never been a fan of five chefs round a single massive plate, containing one seared scallop, a drizzle of this and that, and the punters paying £45 for the privilege. We tried to give the customers good helpings, so a visit to the chip shop was not required on their way home. I actually detest fashions and trends in the food industry; my philosophy is very simple: give your paying customers something to eat, not something to look at and poke with a fork. If they're not happy, then they'll either tell you, or, they won't come back. But if they do, there's a good chance they may want what they had last time, so make sure that you can do this for them. Not complicated.

I had been in touch with Dave from Hungary; he was returning to the UK and I persuaded him to come and work with me at The Aviator. He brought a friend with him, and to start off, Dave was going to look after the day-to-day running of the kitchen, as I was still too busy setting other things up with Teresa. Stuff that no one really gives a thought to, like alarms, fire drill, health and safety manuals, contracts, accountants, suppliers. I could go on, but you get the picture.

On the night that we opened the doors for business proper, it was me who was in the kitchen though, and I really struggled with the vast sum of 16 punters. Right at the start of service, someone ordered the smoked haddock and parsley omelette. To do this I needed to heat up my omelette pan until the oil in it was smoking. Unfortunately, the fire alarms in the kitchen were too sensitive, and all hell broke loose, as we had to evacuate the joint, with everybody looking at the chef, who must have burnt something... my face was the only thing on fire!

Just about every day, we made small, or sometimes big, mistakes, but we learned from them, and managed to streamline things slowly into place. At The Bein Inn David was a big fan of advertising, and spent a lot of money on promoting the Inn. Our landlords were mad about advertising as well, but we kept it simple. We did a four week advert in the local paper, to tell people we were open, and another advert in a regional newspaper, then left it, firmly, at that. Our hopes were with word of mouth – the best kind of advertising there is, and it costs nothing, except getting it right for your customers. That's why we were there. I'm not saying for a minute here that I was right, and they were wrong about the advertising thing, but I do know that your own judgement is usually best, and that was how I felt about advertising. It's just so expensive, and easily forgotten when next day's papers or magazines arrive. We were hard on the staff, some would put their arms on our long bar, and rest their heads down, as they were tired – well not in here you're not. The girls would start playing with their hair... very professional when you're serving food!

We had a slow start; one Saturday night we were particularly quiet, and I started to think that it was over, before it had begun. But things all of a sudden picked up, we had people booking small functions with us, the word of mouth thing was working, and we started gathering regular customers, who were really positive about the food and what we were trying to achieve with the service our punters received. We tried to instil into the waiting staff that everyone who came in the building were VIPs and to treat them as such. Not all the staff could do this of course, and believe me, we had a few crackers, but slowly we got round to weeding out the driftwood. We got busier, and word was spreading.

Our first proper function was actually for a Harley-Davidson motorbike club. Our bar and restaurant was suddenly full with about 150 hairy bikers one Friday afternoon. I took charge of the music that we played on our in-house system that day, and I kicked things off with a Motorhead greatest hits album, and I played it really loud. Everyone was happy with this, except for the staff (myself excluded) – remember, give the punters what they want. It was brilliant watching them sup their beer, with Lemmy giving it big licks to 'The Ace of Spades' at a head-frying volume, just wonderful! The bikers hung around all weekend, and we took in some serious money for the first time.

Somebody had told me when we opened that we would need a thick skin to survive in business; they weren't joking. The amount of unwanted advice we received from people that hadn't worked a single day in the catering business was just off the scale. Some of the 'helpful suggestions' we had put upon us were just ridiculous. One person said to me, "Your food and drink is too cheap." A few weeks later, the same person said to me, "Your stuff is too expensive!" Also, a real streak of jealousy was never far away, sometimes, surprisingly, from people that you might have thought were on your side. As far as we were concerned, nobody had anything to be jealous about – there was absolutely nothing glamorous about what we were doing, we were working stupidly long hours, and taking very little home, in the way of a reward of cash. One bloke that came into the bar of an evening, a solicitor, said to me one night "I'll give you six months, and you'll be finished, closed!" This comment really came out of nowhere. I am far from being an angel, but I would never have said something like that to anybody about their business. I thought to myself "Fuck you pal" and stored his comment away in the back of my mind. I heard later that his own business was not doing so hot, and we didn't see him again for a good while...

Once Teresa found her feet, she settled into pushing the Aviator forward, in a way that I never could have. She was always trying new products out with the bar, and talking endlessly to reps, getting the best deals. She did particularly well with our beer suppliers, getting them to sharpen their money pencils until they were lethal weapons! By now we had some regular drinkers in the bar most nights, and their business was essential on a daily basis. There were two lads from The Czech Republic that came in daily, and another lad, Iain, who was also a daily regular. Their business was very welcome. Teresa recruited a member of staff that she had worked with at Next, Janice. This was just the tonic Teresa needed to push things on even further; Janice was a real asset to our pool of staff, treating the business as if it were her own and totally trustworthy.

Teresa and I actually worked really well together, probably because we looked after totally different things to do with the business. One role that I took on was that of 'sales' when it came to enquiries for functions and bookings. We created our menus for functions on an individual basis, rather than having menu packages – back to giving the punters what they wanted. I would discuss their requirements over a cup of coffee at the restaurant, and see if I could secure their business. Sometimes it was impossible – some folk wanted the world for nothing – but I think, in general, our customers liked that personal touch. We were lucky that the building was very flexible; we could host almost any kind of function. The restaurant was separated from the bar area and could sit 75 covers, for seated dining. We could also do functions like buffets in the bar area, and we had a separate games room, in the bar side, with a pool table and a dart board.

Christmas was looming, and as we had only been open for a few months, our bookings were on the sparse side, which was just as well for me, as, yes, The Pogues were doing Christmas yet again! Luckily, there was nothing booked on The Pogues' first night at

Glasgow Academy, so me and the wife went through to the West, to be entertained. Teresa told me, in no uncertain terms, that The Pogues in Glasgow was 'our' gig now, and she wasn't for missing it. As an added bonus, the date for the concert was December 11th, Teresa's birthday! We didn't drink quite as much at this one – I think it might have been eleven beers. We sat on the fourth row of the balcony, where we could stand, and I sensed trouble right away, as there were three very large ladies directly behind us, who might have not fancied standing. There was nowhere to move, the place was packed as usual, so I had a word with one of the ladies, telling her that we would be standing up when the headlining band appeared on stage. She wasn't happy. I explained to her that any other night I would be happy to sit on my arse, but not tonight, not at The Pogues. Selfish, yes, but I did say, when it comes to The Pogues, that's what I am. Their gigs are just so precious to me, that very little gets in the way. I'm not a heartless person, maybe the wibble wobblers at the back of us would have benefited from wobbling a bit, to the sound of a most excellent live band anyway.

On they came. The smoking ban had kicked in, and as expected, Shane was still smoking his tab, after tab, right on stage. He 'cupped' his hand round his smouldering dog end, trying to hide it from view, but he got fed up with this very quickly and just smoked his fags openly. I wonder if anyone told him to stop. He had a long black coat on, and he was on form; when he is, the whole thing falls into place, and the band go to the top of the Premier league, as far as a live show goes. Of course, like everyone else on our row, Teresa and I were on our feet, much to the annoyance of the wobbling sisters. They called over the security mannie to get us to sit down, but they were told that there was nothing that could be done. At 'Fairytale', not only was Teresa present to witness the whole song (not in the toilet), but the sisters behind us were suddenly on their feet, giving it big sways, this way and that. I turned round and told them all, in no uncertain terms, to "Bloody sit down!" They were all happy now, so I gave them all a wee cuddle. More amazingly though, at Fiesta, the next and final song, they were bopping about, going mental like the rest of the audience. At the end, when the lights went up, they were all smiles, and we were exchanging "Happy Christmases". My goodness me, a Pogues gig can even extinguish the threat of a small chap getting squashed from people that I had previously made unhappy. Thanks boys! I hope that the three ladies went to The Pogues again, and got 'into it' a wee bit earlier next time.

I was getting a bit better at this internet lark, and had managed to book a couple of nights in the King's Cross Travelodge, for my stay, to cover the two nights at dear old Brixton, and Keith this year was going to both nights. I couldn't believe my luck, the Travelodge was only £15 per night, and that was for a family room that could accommodate both of us.

Before all this was going to happen though, we were holding our first Christmas party night at The Aviator. Teresa had managed to secure the Next Christmas bash, the usual sort of thing, with a meal, drinks, dancing and more drinks. The restaurant had a wooden floor, so after their meal it was easy to turn the room into a disco environment. We thought we would do the DJ duties ourselves, using the excellent in-house music system we had, and we bought some disco lights; they were cheap and nasty, but they did the job well enough.

The evening was going well, the 'Next' girls were in high spirits, they'd got the meal out of the way (?) and the cocktails were kicking in, so naturally they wanted to dance. Myself and this other chap sat ourselves in front of the stereo (which was out of sight to the dance floor) and started playing some tunes. The first wee while was easy enough, but then we started struggling, badly. "What the fuck will we put on next?" The suggestions coming from my assistant would've got our throats cut: "How about The Birdie Song, or So Macho?" All I can say is I was very grateful to a certain Kylie Minogue that night – her song, "La la la, la, la la la la, Can't get you out of my head" saved our bacon many times; the girls loved it, so I played it to plug the gaps when we were struggling to find the next song. I think they saw it as a bit of a joke, but every time I played it they were all up, shaking their toots!

The night was a great success, but we made a decision that if we were to do party nights for the public next year, then we'd be hiring a proper DJ with all the gear. The DJ thing was a lot more stressful than

I had anticipated. If I'd had my way, the girls could've had a tear up all night to the likes of X-Ray Spex, The Pistols, Siouxsie and the Banshees and for the smoochers, perhaps Sham 69. I might have even treated them to a wee bit of The Pogues, if they were lucky – which in fact I did. A tradition started that night with the 'Next' party: the last song of the night was 'Fairytale of New York' and that was the case for every single Christmas party night we held at The Aviator, in the future.

The first Pogues show in London was on a Sunday. The train leaves for London at 12 noon on the Sabbath, so I had time to go to work for a bit in the morning. All I can say is that Teresa was brilliant, covering things at work for me, whilst I went away for my next adventure south, to see my heroes play live. I was still collecting anything to do with The Pogues, and Keith was doing the same with ELO and Jeff Lynne. I'd managed to get hold of an electric guitar, signed by Jeff Lynne, and was taking it down on the train for Keith. I wrapped it up very carefully with sellotape and bubblewrap, and then protected all this with a stiff cardboard case; it took me ages, but thank God I did! When I got to the station, I dropped the fucking thing, straight on to the railway track. I didn't hesitate, I was down there in a flash, despite a member of the station staff screaming at me to get off the track. Leaving his guitar there was not an option! I apologised to the angry station man; he really wasn't happy with me at all, but at least the packaging to the guitar was intact. When I was negotiating getting onto the track, and back up to the platform, I wasn't exactly athletic and nimble, and as a result, I was black with oil and grime, my hands were filthy, I was in a right fucking mess. I managed to wash and change on the train, what a carry on.

With being so busy at work etc, I hadn't written my Christmas cards as yet, so I took them with me and did them on the train. When the conductor came round to check the tickets, she commented on what a good idea she thought it was to do the cards whilst travelling, and for the last bit of the journey, she sat down with me, and produced her own Christmas cards and started writing her own messages of festive joy. We had a good laugh about this. "We must get together soon", "It's been too long since we saw you all"... I smell shite more like!

On arrival at King's Cross, it was the now familiar feeling of opening the train door to that London air I keep harping on about, and that feeling, you know the one by now... I did, however, keep a firm grip on Keith's Jeff Lynne-autographed guitar. I popped my Christmas cards in the post box, and the ones that were sent to the "We must get together soon" brigade actually caused mass confusion – they had assumed with the London postmark that we had moved back down south. I just love a bit of speculative mystery!

There wasn't much time to play with tonight – the train didn't get in until 6 – but the Travelodge was just across the road, and I arranged to meet Keith, who was driving in, at the entrance to King's Cross Station. I checked into the hotel first and was very impressed; it was plain, but very clean and fresh, with two beds, a TV, a kettle and a shitehouse – what more could you want, and all for fifteen snips! Back to the station, and there was the welcome sight of Keith in his white Toyota, sooking away on a fag. He opened the passenger door for me, and revealed that he had The Pogues, playing loudly on the stereo, just getting himself into the groove. He parked up, and we were on our way to Brixton. Lovely!

We changed the habit of a lifetime, and entered a big boozer on Brixton High Street, something we just didn't do back in the day, but now we were getting brave, even nicking posters... The pub was packed, and we shared a table with some students, who were about to do The Pogues thing, live, for the first time. They were hassling me and Keith for stories about The Pogues; they were past themselves with excitement about tonight's imminent show. There appeared to be something in the air that night in South London, as we settled ourselves into good seats near the front of the balcony, and the time got closer for the band to grace the stage, the crowd downstairs had whipped themselves up into an absolute frenzy. It was much rowdier than usual, and the band were not even on yet! The Brixton stalls audience could be a bit unpredictable at Pogues shows, sometimes full throttle, sometimes more subdued, whereas at Glasgow, it was always the same: mental! But tonight, it was off the Richter scale, maybe the gig being on a Sunday, folk had more time to partake in the odd Vermouth before entering the Academy, and were now in the mood for a party, whereas on a week day, they may be coming right after their work, or dinner at home of faggots, gravy, mash and marrowfat peas. Well, I don't know?

Time was getting on, something wasn't right, and the natives were indeed getting restless. There was an announcement. Someone had tipped their beer onto the mixing desk, and 'they' were doing everything they could to sort things out, but it may take some time. The crowd downstairs were still going mental. At Brixton, when the Pogues played, they had this rather strange DJ chap, on the actual stage, trying to look very busy, while playing his tunes. His name was DJ Scratchy; perhaps he should have got some ointment. Now just recently, I told you all about my little experience of DJing, and I was far from being the next Fatboy Slim, but Scratchy fella really did make a meal of things. He actually made an art of making himself look 'busy' on the stage, his tunes were generally good, but he was totally trying to justify his existence, overdoing all his movements, like loading a new CD, ooh, the drama, a pen would come out, his glasses would be put on, all very dramatically, he would make a note in a book, a large folded piece of paper would appear – it reminded me of an architect's building plans. Then he would twiddle away at some knobs on his 'stereo'. I think I might have scratched my own knob once or twice right enough, during my one night of being DJ at the Aviator; 'DJ Scratch knob' I should have called mesen. Keith, in particular started roaring at him, which obviously fell on deaf ears due to the distance and the rowdiness of downstairs. At least DJ Itchy kept us entertained, to a certain extent, and in hindsight, perhaps I shouldn't be too hard on him. I repeat, my effort at being an organised DJ was dismal.

The lights went down, DJ Scratchplate was lost in the darkness, and The Pogues intro track pounded through the Academy, the most excellent 'Straight to Hell' by The Clash. The intro was the ultimate feelgood tonic, its significance indicating that you were about to have a most fucking marvellous time, right now!

Jem Finer was out of the traps quickly tonight, and fuck me, he was straight to the microphone. What on earth was going on? He angrily condemned 'The wanker' that couped his beer onto the mixing desk, saying that he should have put his money into The Justice for Kirsty Fund. Nice to see you too, Jem. I turned to Keith and said, "Well? Is that passionate enough for ya?" Mr Finer is clearly a man not to be messed with; there's plenty of bits and pieces in James Fearnley's book that would back that statement up. You have been warned!

When the band got round to start playing, the sound, as expected, was just awful. Jem's banjo in particular was far too loud, and the general mix was way off the mark. This didn't put off the hardcore fans in the stalls though – it was as rowdy a Pogues audience as I had ever seen, and that's really saying something. The sound did improve, but it was far from a memorable gig, probably because of mixing desk gate.

In the morning, Keith and I were looking for a place to have breakfast. We were both starving, as we had skipped dinner the night before. Keith was out of the hotel before me to sook on another fag – hellish, morning fags after a night on the beer! We made our way across Gray's Inn Road, and came across a truly wonderful discovery, that I will share with you all, right now. Café Plaka. It would be totally wrong to call it a greasy spoon; it's much better than that. The sitting area is through the back. We ordered the biggest breakfast they had; it was called 'The Oz Special'. The waitress said, "Are you sure?" "Of course, bring it on!" we told her. The café was quite busy, there was a real cross section of people in there: couples, a family, road workers, a guy that looked like a journalist, and two Pogues fans. All of a sudden, this bloke with an apron put his head round the corner. "Who's having the Oz Specials?" "That'll be us," I said, putting my hand up like a swot would at the school. The bloke just gave us the biggest smile, before cracking into laughter, and then he was away again. We hadn't read the menu properly; the Oz Special arrived, on large ashets for plates. The ashets had every breakfast item you could imagine on it, served with CHIPS! There was also a stack of buttered thick toast, orange juice, and two mugs of tea. It was the ultimate heart attack breakfast, and we ate the lot; the bloke with the infectious smile was delighted. Turned out he was Oz, the proprietor of Café Plaka, and that day started an institution for us. A breakfast in Oz's café is just a sign of good times. Oz is a lovely bloke, we had a brilliant chat (while he was working); he is such a positive man, and a real go getter when it comes to his business. The breakfast gig was just the tip of the iceberg – he had a production kitchen downstairs, providing buffets and such like, for meetings across the road, at King's Cross station.

We struck up a brilliant rapport with Oz, and promised we would return the next morning. He was so impressed that we'd polished off The Oz Special – just a couple of fat twats then! As much as I love London, the folk can be a bit reserved at times, so it was a nice change to come across someone who had a bit of personality about him, and willing to pass the time of day with you, even if he was up to his neck in bacon, egg and sausage (and chips!). Londoners usually just seem too busy; I just reckon that sometimes, they should never forget what life is all about, it's about people... just my opinion. Oz is from Cyprus originally, but had lived in and had been establishing his business in London for years. He is a real breath of fresh air; I'm so glad that we stumbled into his café that morning.

Inevitably, we ended up in Sticky Fingers later that afternoon (eating again!) and inevitably the tube to Victoria, inevitably the overhead train to Brixton, and our big black girl was behind the bar again in The Academy. We got a distant wave – she was busy pouring gallons of the black stuff. The show was a big improvement after last night; they'd nailed the sound and it made all the difference. The Pogues' setlist for their live shows, was by and large, the same most of the time, apart from the odd welcome tweak here and there. An average Pogues setlist would be:

STREAMS OF WHISKEY, IF I SHOULD FALL FROM GRACE WITH GOD, THE BROAD MAJESTIC SHANNON, TURKISH SONG OF THE DAMNED, YOUNG NED OF THE HILL, A PAIR OF BROWN EYES, WHITE CITY, TUESDAY MORNING, THE OLD MAIN DRAG, REPEAL OF THE LICENSING LAWS, SUNNY SIDE OF THE STREET, THE BODY OF AN AMERICAN, LULLABY OF LONDON, THOUSANDS ARE SAILING, DIRTY OLD TOWN, BOTTLE OF SMOKE, SICK BED OF CUCHULAINN, SALLY MACLENNANE, A RAINY NIGHT IN SOHO, THE IRISH ROVER, STAR OF THE COUNTY DOWN, FAIRYTALE OF NEW YORK, FIESTA.

All the 'big boys' are there in the Pogues' back catalogue; now and again, a 'POOR PADDY' OR 'GREENLAND WHALE FISHERIES' would be thrown in, just to keep the punters on their toes, brilliant.

We went back to see Oz in the morning, had a mild stroke of a breakfast, rather than a heart attack this time, and said our farewells. The Pogues had given us a reason to meet before Christmas, to clink a glass or ten, and to discover a gem of a café, with a gem of an owner.

Back to The Aviator then. We closed on Christmas Day and Boxing Day. Because we could. It was the first Christmas Day that I had had off work for about 16 years, and we really enjoyed being at home, relaxing and having Christmas dinner before 8 o'clock at night. The staff at The Aviator appreciated us being closed over Christmas; most of them went out on Christmas Eve, and had a good drink, in the knowledge that they would have a day off to follow. Not so at New Year though. We decided to do a Hogmanay dinner, and keep the bar open until the wee small hours. I had a set menu on, a five courser, which featured Ma Bruce's world Famous Stovie Cakes, this time served with a rusty nail (whisky and Drambuie) sauce. Ma and Pa Bruce were both present, Mum was holding court, as she usually does, and kept lighting fags up in the bar. Something very much in common with Mr MacGowan then! I had to keep telling her to put them out, so she thought she'd be 'fly' and took herself off to the ladies to finish her tab! She said to me, "What bloody good is it your son having a restaurant, if you can't have a smoke?!" The smoking ban, clearly, meant bugger all – to her, or to Shane. Some of the regulars at the bar were telling her that she should be getting a commission, for the stovie cake gig. I told her that we'd call it quits, regarding her drinks bill and the food that she and Dad had eaten. I just about got away with it!

LAURA SUNDAE

Our first festive season at The Aviator over, albeit a quiet one, then January bites, and things get really sparse, business-wise. We were lucky to get a shooting party of plus-foured 'gentlemen' in for lunch over a few days, then we got a real welcome boost, from unfortunate circumstances. A distressed family came in to see me one day; the father had just passed away unexpectedly. He was a local minister, and they wanted to hold the wake at The Aviator, having been there previously for dinner, and enjoyed their experience. No bother at all then, we can do that, a few sausage rolls, a bit of quiche and a scone, drinks at the bar for those who wished to partake. "How many people would you like us to cater for madam?" "Oh, about 200," was the reply. I must have gone a whiter shade of pale (that wasn't The Pogues, was it?) and worked my Adam's apple up and down a few times, before assuring the grieving lady with a "No problem at all, madam. Leave it with me." When I told Teresa and Janice of the booking I had just taken, they looked at me as if to say, "What the fuck have you done?" "C'mon girls, with a bit of forward planning, we'll get everyone in, and there's no one better at forward planning than you two. I'll get the quiche organised, and leave the rest with you!"

And they did plan, and we did get everyone in, and I did have enough quiche (pressure!). In some parts of the building, the people were very familiar with one another; it actually reminded me of the tube train, after the Pogues at Brixton. The family were so happy with the way the girls organised things, they put a 'Thank you' notice in a national newspaper, thanking CALUM BRUCE. Nice one, recognition for the art of delegation! How I laughed about that one; the girls were secure enough about themselves however to just be grateful that we managed to put a few sovereigns in the till.

Our clientele were generally well behaved; our location, away from the centre of town, had a lot to do with that. However, one Saturday evening, we got our first taste of what a bar can be like, when problems start. A large group of people descended upon the bar mid-afternoon, and pretty much stayed there, having a right good scoop, a real session. A lot of the people appeared to be family, and then, as par for the course at these types of gatherings, when the ale kicks in, somebody obviously said something they shouldn't have. Very quickly, a full scale riot erupted. I'm not exaggerating here: there were fists flying, one woman had grabbed another by her long hair, had her down and was actually kicking her head in. A body flew past me, the bloke was almost horizontal as he crashed awkwardly into one of the comfy couches we had in the bar, but he wasn't very comfy. Fucking hell.

Working in the bar that night were me (Mike Tyson didn't you know?), Janice's husband Paul (who IS a big lad) and another chap, even more useless at the physical thing than me. By now the mêlée was in a group, it was like a hornet's nest, it was moving sideways with legs, fists and heads everywhere; there was also a good bit of claret flying around. At one point, the hornet's nest was heading towards the door, so the three of us, very gently, helped direct them on their way, and thankfully we got them out into the car park, and firmly locked the door. What a relief!

The really bad thing was we were just starting to get busy with diners, for what was shaping up to be a prosperous Saturday night. I went round all the tables of diners, and drinkers in the bar, explaining that this was an isolated incident, and it certainly was not what The Aviator was all about. One table of three walked out, disgusted with what they had witnessed – the brawl had been really bad at one point, and I didn't try to persuade them to stay, but all the other customers were fine, apart from this one table, who were right in the middle of the bar, where the action had taken place. It was a table of four, an old couple and what looked like son and daughter. They were a well to do family, and I sensed they were going to walk out too. I needn't have worried. When I apologised, the old lady told me that the battle was the best thing she had seen in ages, better than anything she would see on Eastenders and that she thoroughly enjoyed every minute of it! Not what I was expecting to hear, but hey, more satisfied customers, music to my ears. The police arrived a little later on, but we had seen nothing, absolutely not officer! We didn't want our own heads kicked in at a later date, thank you very much.

As things were getting busier, we put the word out locally for some more staff, including a new kitchen assistant. A couple of young lassies came up from the nearby village of Scone. Laura wanted to be a chef; her pal Rachael was applying to be a waitress. We gave them both a chance, and they arrived 'live' ready for a shift, about a week later. Rachael did all right in the restaurant, and then there was Laura! She started her chef career as many chefs do, washing the dishes. She turned up for work dressed in a shell suit, and with an attitude that did her no favours at all. Her face was a picture – ask her to do something, and it was a BIG problem. This went on all night. I overheard her talking to her pal Rachael, referring to me as "The bastirt has made me sweep the flair!" Quite what she was expecting to get paid for was a bit of a mystery, so at the end of the night, I thanked her very much for her industrious efforts, but not to get in touch; if I needed her, then I would do the phoning.

But about a week later, she did phone me, she asked for another chance, and very reluctantly, I agreed to give her another shift. One of my better decisions at The Aviator then – I was more than capable of making bad ones. One bank holiday, I was the only chef in the kitchen, and I got hammered; we were so busy, and I was in the shit, big time. I howled for Laura to leave the pots and the dishes, get her arse over to the big table, and start making salads, quickly! And that's what she did. During the few shifts she had worked up until now, where thankfully she had left her previous attitude behind, she'd been watching what the chefs had been preparing, and taking it all in. The salads she made for me that day were just superb, just the way I wanted them. It was a trademark of The Aviator, our salads were a mosaic of fresh exotic ingredients with a heavy influence of fruit present, and they were an important part of our menu; Laura's salads that day were certainly up to the standard I was looking for.

Hungarian Dave and his pal were on the way out, I was grateful to him for helping us get going, but it was never a long term thing for either of us, and so, he departed, heading down to Leeds to pursue the next part of his career. I took up a more permanent role in the kitchen now; we had to push things on and increase our business, and Laura gradually started to realise her ambition of becoming a chef. It was probably more difficult than it normally would be for staff to work with me in the kitchen – naturally, there is a different mindset, if it's your own money on the line. We had to really limit wasting money, our overheads were high, and there was a different pressure on now – not just getting the food out and getting it right, but the pressure of taking enough money to pay the wages and the bills. A lot of our staff over the course were youngsters; we always paid them for the correct hours that they worked. This simple fact is something that is really badly abused in the catering industry. Fair enough, if you were on a nice salary, work hours that are required, but the kids working a few hours a week should get the correct pay. I was always lucky in the past with Mr Borthwick on this score: if you did a bit extra, then when things got quieter, you got more time off, but I had seen, in other places, how staff can be exploited really badly, and expected to work their balls off for little reward, just because, "That's what catering is like". Absolute shite! Treat people fairly and you'll get a good day's work from them. Hell, they may even smile at the customers! The other side of all this though is when the staff come in with hangovers. This happened a few times at The Aviator. I used to have a line that went something like "Oh, you're not well today, shame. Since you are working so slow, how about I pay you the hangover rate – that's about a third of what you normally get?" This usually did the trick. If I were to say to Mr Borthwick that I had a hangover, well, I dread to think...

Laura was a real geezeress – she smoked, drank like a fish and loved a late night visit to kebab shops. She would often partake in a large Doner then, a little later on, partake in the dark skinned bloke that put his meat and sauce into her pitta bread wrap! In the kitchen, she's one of the best natural talents I've ever worked with – everything I threw at her she mastered; she thrived on pressure, and she saw off a lot of pretenders, who thought they were better chefs than they really were, in the Aviator kitchen (some of them literally couldn't hard boil an egg) to make a permanent position her own.

She was head and shoulders more competent than me, when I was at her stage of career. When we changed the menu, she would often come up with brilliant, practical ideas. One that stood out was a summer ice cream coupe. It was made from Pavlova ice cream, with fresh strawberries and raspberries, mini meringues, strawberry sauce and whipped cream, garnished with a wafer, a sprig of fresh mint and redcurrants. We called it 'The Laura Sundae' and it was a winner; soon, the punters were asking to meet Laura – one young chap even asked for her autograph. I felt like telling him, that when he got older, if he chose a career in kebabs, then he would get more than an autograph!

Hibs were in the League Cup final again, on bloody Mother's Day, and we were fully booked, or as Janice used to say 'Bully Fooked!'. I managed to carve out a day off for the match at Hampden, Teresa did a stint in the kitchen with Laura and a hired help, and coped admirably without me – maybe I wasn't all that in the kitchen after all! Hibs did the business though, thumping Kilmarnock by 5 goals to 1. Every time Hibs scored, big Les 'Reg'Rennie and I would perform a dodgy dance movement. Les loved dance music, not my cup of beer, but I did my best with the moves! The triumphant green and white heroes lifted the cup in front of their green and white army, around 30,000 of them. The Hampden PA system was playing The Proclaimers' song 'Sunshine on Leith' and the Hibs fans, to a man and woman, sang along in perfect time. It was a really emotional moment. I wonder how the two Proclaimer blokes felt that day; it must have been mind blowing for them.

Having Laura, and some other members of quality staff, certainly helped when it came to Christmas time. Bookings were really good this year, and of course, by now, I was actually almost expecting The Pogues to announce a tour in December. It was indeed their 25th anniversary tour. I can't ever say it was becoming a way of life as such, but I was always hopeful, and they did indeed do the decent thing – the concert dates were revealed, they were doing it all over again, yip ay aye! Once again, the Glasgow show was bang on Teresa's birthday, and she was looking forward to the now annual coincidental date immensely. To surprise her, I wrote a letter to Philip Chevron, the Pogues guitarist, and addressed it to The Pogues' dressing room at the Glasgow Academy. I asked if he would be so kind, to wish Teresa a happy birthday, just before 'Thousands are sailing'. I posted the letter a few days before the gig, and kept my fingers crossed for her.

On the day of the concert, we finished lunch service and drove quickly home for a shower, then we were on our way, as usual, on the train, with a beverage to hand. When we arrived in Glasgow it was pissing down with rain, a real dreich night, so we decided to get a taxi to The Academy. Glaswegians are the salt of the earth generally, but our cabbie that night was a prime prick, a right 'know it all'. It was a relief to get to our destination, and I've a feeling this cab driver didn't do too well with tips – he got fuck all from me. We got into the venue, out of the rain, and settled down for the rest of the evening. When the Pogues came on, Philip Chevron was missing, his replacement, a youngish looking lad, recruited to play rhythm guitar. It turned out that poor Philip was unwell, a form of throat cancer, that certainly did not sound good, and put in prospective the mild disappointment that Teresa would not be getting a "Happy birthday" after all.

I was expecting 'Streams of whiskey' as usual, to kick things off, but wait, what was going on here? James Fearnley had positioned himself a lot more central on the stage, and was starting things off with his accordion, Jem Finer followed suit with his banjo, what the fuck is this all about? It was only the opening to a monumental Pogues classic, that I had not heard for years, in the shape of 'Transmetropolitan'. I got instantly emotional, and I actually started to weep. Unfortunately, Shane couldn't live with performing the song; he had a sheet of paper in his hand, presumably with the lyrics, and was totally left behind, confused and agitated. Spider made up for Shane's vocal absence, but just hearing the superb instrumental part of the song was absolutely fantastic. However, on the whole, the start of the show, because of this blip, had perhaps lost two early wickets, but it was far too soon to be showing signs of alarm. 'Transmetropolitan' is the first track on The Pogues' first album, 'Red Roses For Me' and it's in my top five Pogues tunes; even though Shane had not come up trumps, hearing the music to the song, for me, was worth the ticket money alone.

I mentioned that I had a wee cry to myself, when it was being played. Well, the crying thing was actually happening quite a lot for me at the gigs I had been lucky enough to attend over the past few years. And I was not alone. I witnessed quite a few people crying at the gigs, mostly blokes; the slower numbers just got you right in the gut, especially if Shane and the boys nailed it, performance wise. 'Rainy Night in Soho' was always a candidate for a greet, 'Kitty' was another, and 'A Pair of Brown Eyes' wasn't that far behind. Tonight though, the start of The Pogues show, with the very unorthadox 'Transmetropolitan' left me really not knowing what to expect from Shane – if he wasn't up to it, then the whole thing was usually no good, so I was wondering just how things were going to pan out tonight. Shane *was* up to it, and of course, the band followed suit. I can honestly say that this was one of the best shows I'd witnessed since the first reunion, in terms of quality – yes, they were getting better and better.

I went for a piss. There's a Gents at the side of the balcony at the Glasgow Academy, and walking to this sweet smelling haven takes you right to the side of the stage, albeit high up. There's a couple of 'bays' here for members of the audience – they can stand in here, there are no seats – and I squeezed myself into one of the bays to get a close up of The Pogues. The natives in the bay were not happy with my presence, and really, was I giving a fuck? That'll be a 'No' then, but let's relax, I wasn't staying, I was just having a wee peek, on my way for a piss, and I was glad I did. Shane was very clearly enjoying himself, he was smiling, he was happy, he was having the banter with Spider, and I think, I just might have seen Jem Finer's mouth curl up a little, into a small, conservative grin. The sound was spot on, and then, my God, what a treat, 'Streams of Whiskey' played later in the set, as opposed to when things were somewhat rawer at the start. It's quite simply the best time I've heard the song live, it was perfect; this Pogues gem deserves to be delivered this way – man, I was in heaven!

It was a gig that you wished would never end, but, of course it did. This gig was huge though, it really was one of the best, a gig that showed its attendees how massive the mighty Pogues could be, when they put their minds, and their smiles to it!

Par for the course, I was all booked up for London again. I was 'gushing' to Keith on the phone about how good the group were at Glasgow, and that we were in for a real treat, in Brixton, with its lovely boulevards. Keith didn't manage the first night; I had bought him a ticket, and I was lucky, as I hung out beside the touts at Brixton tube station, just watching what was going on. One bloke approached one of the entrepreneurs selling the briefs, and baulked at the price (which I didn't hear) quoted. I followed the bloke down the High Street, a bit away from the businessmen, and told him that I had a spare that he could have for what I paid for it. He was dubious at first, but I managed to convince him that I was a chicken and steak peddler to trade, and not a ticket tout. He was delighted to be sorted for tonight's show. I'm not quite sure what he would be thinking later on though. Shane, to my great surprise, put in a shocker of a performance; he had another big dark coat on, and looked as enthusiastic as a pig on its way to the abattoir. Back to 'Streams of Whiskey' for an opener, they'd obviously given up totally with 'Transmetropolitan', and he slurred his way through the opening song, a good beat and a bit behind the band – what a contrast from hearing it later in the set at Glasgow.

As for the rest of the gig, Shane did OK in parts, usually with the slower numbers, but the night, on the whole, was a big disappointment. He certainly kept you on your toes; I actually think that speculating to yourself what Shane is going to be like adds a bit of excitement and intrigue to the whole thing. But it was still a feeling of deflation I felt, as I made my way back to The Travelodge, in King's Cross, knowingly thinking how good their shows could be, and then seeing a crap one like tonight. Just before I did depart the Academy, I purchased a limited edition print that had caught my eye on the merchandise stall. It was an abstract picture, done in black, white and gold, depicting a New York scene, with the dates of the Christmas tour displayed. When I settled back into my room at the hotel, I unfurled the print to marvel and appreciate my purchase. Some bright spark had the dates for Belfast down as the 22th of December, and Dublin as the 23th! Maybe I have a 'specia' print, the only copy with 'ths' on the dates that should have an 'nd' and a 'rd' but I don't think so somehow. No matter, I was totally convinced that Shane would be up for the cup tomorrow night, that's usually how it worked, if he was sub standard – I was thinking of the old days, Finsbury Park farce, followed by his majestic performance a few weeks later with The Chieftains.

Over to see Oz, in his wonderful café in the morning, treated like royalty, what a fuss he made of me. I could get used to this. I wasn't even ordering my breakfast now – he just brought me what he thought I would like. It was always spot on, and plenty of it. Keith arrived in the afternoon, yes, up to Sticky Fingers again. The place had been slipping badly over the years, the draught Budweiser had been replaced, the new beer they had was pish. The food also had taken a dive, but Sticky Fingers itself was like a spiritual home to us in London, it was just where we went to relax and enjoy ourselves. As we sat in the bar that night, trying to get enthusiastic about the pints we were drinking, we looked at the very unappealing menu and, deciding to find somewhere else to eat, we almost felt like traitors.

We settled for a place on the High Street; it was busy, we sat next to an old couple, and they asked what we were up to that night. They both knew about The Pogues, and were amazed to learn that Shane was still alive. I'm actually not sure they were convinced though, even when I told them that I had seen him in the flesh on the previous evening. I don't know what they'd have thought if they had gone to Brixton Academy a little later on. Shane was even worse than the previous evening, he was fucked, and the evening came to a climax for him, when trying to read the setlist on the stage floor, he collapsed in a heap, right on top of the monitors. Spider and Darryl helped him up onto his feet. At another point, Shane slurred, "This is called Dirty Old Town!" Spider hit back with "No it aint, it's Sunny side of the street!" "All right then," said Shane, "it's Sunny side of the Street." Sounded like he was sulking a bit.

The gig petered out; there were still some good moments, but fewer than last night. As we walked back to the tube, I thought to myself, well that's it, another Christmas tour over, the two shows in London this year, a massive anti-climax. On the tube, once the carriages emptied out a bit at Victoria, we were sat next to an old bloke and his daughter, who had been at Brixton. As I ear wigged into their conversation, I found it fascinating. They were enthusing about the show they had just witnessed, talking about the songs on the setlist, the ones they were hoping to hear but didn't, and inevitably, things moved on to the state of the vocalist. The lady was more than sympathetic: "He did his best, bless him." I didn't intrude into their conversation, but actually love, he didn't do his best, he did his worst. But. On reflection, I still felt eternally grateful that we had shows to go to at all, I was grateful for the hours of absolute pleasure this man, Shane MacGowan, had given to me personally, through his songs. With these thoughts, maybe this year at Brixton wasn't quite so bad, and Shane MacGowan was still alive after all, and would live to fight another day.

New Year's Eve at The Aviator was a huge success this time, we were really busy, and the atmosphere in the place was fantastic. After the latest late stragglers went home, we locked the doors, but kept the lights on and the beer flowed; we had a very spur of the moment, unofficial staff party, and we didn't fuck about... I think we left the building about 9am.

So, we were now into 2008, we had to be pleased with the way things were going. If I've built up an illusion that everything went our way all the time, then that would be wrong; we did fuck up from time to time, and then some. In fact some of the complaints we had could actually be quite amusing – I'll get to that soon. But we were well established now, and had the confidence to try even harder to increase our business further, and push the boundaries just a little bit more; there was no choice, with Teresa on the premises. 2008 though. This was the year that something was to go very, very wrong.

DOCTOR LES REG RENNIE AND POLY STYRENE

The in-house music system at The Aviator was never far away from everyday conversation. Basically, if there were any punters in, the music went on. We had a 5 CD changer, so now and again, it was easy to slip in the odd disc, and educate the nation. One Saturday night, I put 'Rum, Sodomy and the Lash' in for good measure. Right in the middle of service, Teresa came tearing into the kitchen, and angrily said to me, "I've just been serving a couple of pensioners on Table 4, and all I can hear is Shane MacGowan going on about blacks and packs and jocks!" Bloody Hell, what about the bits that go "lazy drunken bastards" and "Fuckin' blackshirt"? Teresa was obviously thinking about the very politically correct world that we live in today; well Shane did not offend me with the 'Jocks' bit. Through playing music in the bar and restaurant, we had to pay our yearly dues to the PPL (Phonographic Performance Ltd). I said phonographic! They tell us that somewhere down the line, the artists get some of this cash as royalties. Well I hope the boys in The Pogues got some of our dosh; not too worried however about the likes of Michael Bubbles, The Sugar Sluts or even Miley's Clitoris!

Now one table of punters that would not have minded one bit, to hear Shane singing, would be the 'Reggies'. Early in the year, big

Les, his wife Lorraine and their two boys came up to Perth from
Hornchurch for a visit, and came to The Aviator for lunch. I managed
to get out of the scullery for a while, and have a wee half pint with Les.
Les Rennie was the main man in our group of Hibs supporting friends;
he'd been South for a good few years now, but he was a frequent
enough visitor back home. We gave him numerous nicknames, 'Reg'
after Reg Kray, the East-end gangster, and 'The Doctor' as he would
sort you out in a flash, but more likely to give you a hiding, rather than
a cure. During our chat at the restaurant that afternoon, he told me
that he had bought tickets to see X-Ray Spex in London, but the gig
wasn't until September, a good nine months away. I didn't say a word,
but my brain was working overtime by now. I love X-Ray Spex, but had
only seen them once in Edinburgh a few years back with Gavin 'Frank
Spencer' Black and Davo, without their legendary singer, Poly Styrene,
so I felt that I had some unfinished business with the group. Poly
Styrene was indeed guaranteed to be performing this time Les told me.
I replied with "Well I hope you enjoy it, when the gig comes around",
and left it at that.

Meanwhile, talking of Gavin/Frank Black, he had never been to The
Aviator, but he kept teasing me, calling me names. His favourite line
was "You think you're a restaurant magnet now – well you're certainly
no' a babe magnet, are ye?" Well Gav, I beg to differ! Every now and
again, we got a booking for around ten old ladies, probably in their
seventies, for a late lunch. Obviously not short of a few bob, they didn't
muck about: it was sherries all round, before they sat down to lunch,
which was three courses with wine and Irish coffees to finish. They
would be in the restaurant all afternoon, swapping stories, with lots of
laughter; it was lovely that these ladies had kept in touch and enjoyed
each other socially. They asked to see the chef, so I was happy to go
out and face the music, word was that they were happy with their lot
today, but you never know, maybe I had got something wrong, and was
about to be reprimanded. The ladies were singing my praises, phew!
Nothing to worry about then, and I chatted to them for a wee while,
being careful not to outstay my welcome. One lady said to me, "I could
do with taking you home with me" and the company broke into a fit of
tipsy old lady cackling laughter. The poor love that had delivered the

line was waving her hands saying, "No, no, just to cook my food, not for sex or anything!" I couldn't believe what I was hearing, and yet another round of cackling. When this died down, one of her friends said, "Oh no, I would definitely want the sex as well!" So there we have it Gavin Black, a babe magnet after all; it was the first time I had been chatted up for an absolute age!

I'm well aware that I am definitely no oil painting, but Teresa, in particular, kept me right if I was wearing the 'wrong' uncoordinated clothes or whatever, so much so that when I got it wrong one day, she refused to walk down the High Street with me! We were on holiday one year, in Spain. I had gone to the shop to get a few bits and pieces for the room, and on my return got into the lift to take me to the high floor, where we were staying. There was a mirror all the way round the inside of the lift. To my utter fucking horror, I discovered that I had a big baldie bit on the back of my heid! I couldn't believe it. I started tugging at my hair to cover it, but it was well beyond any of that – there was no quick fix, that was it! I tore into the room and asked Teresa what the fuck was going on with the back of my head. She very calmly informed me, "Oh, it's been like that for ages!" I couldn't take this in. "Why didn't you tell me?" "Didn't seem like any point," was her cool reply. I was a fuckin' baldie! I didn't expect that. I had the whole shooting match now: big tits, bloated belly, a chin to spare if you need one, and now a penalty spot on the back of my nut. Fucking marvellous. One major consolation though, unless I'm in a mirrored lift, I can't see it. I'm grateful for small mercies; maybe I should get myself a piece!

We held our first wedding reception at The Aviator. A lovely couple, Gary and Joanne, booked their big day celebrations with us, and I'm pleased to say that they were very happy with their lot. It was a young crowd, the bar was into overdrive, everyone happy. I still see the couple nowadays, and they always cherish their reception at The Aviator. That's when you feel that you've actually achieved something, when you see nice people, happy and appreciative – makes all those long hours well worthwhile. The functions were so diverse. We had a boys' football team, from the Highlands, arriving for a pre match lunch. The kids sat down to buttered pasta, while the parents were ordering burgers, pints and nips – good to set an example right enough! We hosted a yachting club's annual bash, and they showed slides of various sailing vessels, on the wall of the games room. The games room!

This thing of Teresa's, to push things forward, reached a new level when she announced that she was going to convert the games room, with the pool table, into a classy, private dining room. We were all speechless, but I knew that she wouldn't rest until she achieved her goal. She painted the room, almost single-handedly, she was both determined and sore, but she got there; the result was amazingly professional. She added a couple of tasteful prints, one was of a scooter parked up at a lampost on the seaside. Some lamps were added, and furniture to sit 36 covers, natural wood and leather backed chairs. The investment of Teresa's time and efforts, coupled with the finance involved, was an absolute, stonewall winner. We even had an extra stereo in there – even more opportunity then, to educate the public about the charms of Shane MacGowan! The 'Dining room' was to prove both popular and lucrative.

It was time for a staff function. Monday nights generally were quiet, so we closed the restaurant for the night and booked a table at The Jade Garden, the main Chinese eatery in the town. They had an added facility of a small function room upstairs with a karaoke machine. Perfect. We treated the entire staff to their drinks and food, then headed upstairs to the wee function room. We played a game, where we all did impressions of each other, little things and habits that people had when at work; it was a scream, all good natured and we had a grand night. The waiter, keeping the drinks flowing for us, had the very oriental name of 'Eddie'; we wiped the place out of Tiger beer, and gave Eddie a song to recognise his efforts. "Eddie! Eddie! Eddie!" was the extent of the song's lyrics. At the end of the evening, Laura, Rachel and I got into a bit of a mess on the stairway on the way down, and we ended up going down on our arses. Mine was extremely sore in the morning. It was great to give something back to the staff though; we received lots of praise for what we were doing at the restaurant, but we were nothing, without the staff, and we appreciated them.

If I'm painting a rosy picture of The Aviator, then I must balance the books here. That indeed was it, in a nutshell: balance the books.

On a cold Monday night for example, deep in winter, we had to keep the place heated, lighted and staffed, and you could have just two customers darken your door all night. There were many nights like this, it could be soul destroying, and you would start to doubt what you were doing – were you really giving the people what they wanted? Sometimes even the weekends would be quiet, which was an absolute disaster, or a function would cancel. That was one of the worst things, as you would have to turn business away, as the place was booked for the function, then it would cancel and you'd end up with nothing. Big companies take deposits for functions, but most of our potential clients were not prepared to put down a deposit, and you had to be careful if insisting they did, as they might not book. It was a real Catch 22. Again, some so called locals couldn't understand this part of our business, and were always quick with downright ignorant, unwanted comments; oh yes, we had plenty of providers of this sort of shit. Thick skin required, but now and again, we would bite back. During busy times like Christmas party nights, I could be in the Cash and Carry at 7 30am, and away to work. We might lock the door at 3am the next morning, and do exactly the same the next day, so the last thing you needed was some arse hole, who knew fuck all about fuck all, trying to tell you what you were doing wrong! Teresa's trump card, her private dining room, enabled us to cater for both function and restaurant bookings at the same time. She knew about more than fuck all!

The TV show 'Bargain Hunt' were doing a show in connection with the antique centre next door, and we received an enquiry to cater for the TV crew and the maverick, adjective flowing presenter, Tim Wonnacott. Pound signs must have come to my eyes; I assumed that because it was the TV, money would be no object, but I couldn't have been more wrong. Their budget was pathetically small, I couldn't believe they wanted us to feed and water them for the amount quoted, but we did indeed accommodate them in the end, with something quite unexciting and sparse. I got the impression that the crew were used to this, but not so Mr Wonnacott. He dined by himself, and ordered up a fresh salmon salad. He thought the salad was wonderful, and he enthused about it in his own remarkable TV style, "Fresh, Scottish Salmon, with an early morning country garden salad and an orchard of ripe, perfumed fruit!" He could have come back and written my menus for me with descriptions like that! He was a good bloke, very enthusiastic about the restaurant; it was a pleasure to meet him.

Davo and I had arranged to go to London and see the X-Ray Spex gig, but we didn't tell big Les – we wanted to surprise him, just turn up on the night. The gig was at The Roundhouse, a venue we'd never been to before, on a Saturday night, so we travelled down on the train on the Friday morning. Predictably, we had a bucket to drink on the way down; we were sat next to a couple of well to do charity workers, they were wary at first, but we were mates by the time we got to the big smoke. We had a quiet night, but arranged to meet Keith on Saturday lunchtime, and we were going to see a Millwall match that afternoon. I had been to Millwall once before, at their old Cold Blow Lane ground, The Den, watching my beloved Hibs in a pre-season 'friendly'. I don't think Millwall do friendly, and the Hibs 'boys' were down in force that night, looking for a bit of a row, and they got a right result as it goes. Millwall, as a club and their fans, hold a fascination for me and Davo, we're not supporters as such, not at all, but they intrigue us. We were going to their New Den that afternoon, and wanted to go behind the goal, in the end named in memory of the old ground, in amongst the 'geezers'. We had to buy tickets at the office, so I volunteered to do that, and up I went to the box. In my best East London accent, I said "Free foh fe col' blo' pleez guvnur!" (three tickets for The Cold Blow Lane end please). The bloke smiled at me asking if I wanted upper or lower. That was me fucked, "Ehh, ehrm." He said: "That'll be upper then" and produced the tickets. I'm sure they were used to bloody tourists at Millwall. We enjoyed the match, the natives were superb. At half time, we went for a beer (very civilised) and Keith went for a piss. When he came out of the Gents, his eyes were watering, telling us that all the punters in there were having a fag. He asked a steward if it was ok to smoke in the toilets, and naturally, the bloke said that it wasn't. There was a pause, then he said to Keith, "Would you go in there, and tell them to put their smokes out?" He had a point, and Keith went back in for some more watery eyes. Millwall won their match, beating Hartlepool United by two goals to nil, the Millwall geezers were happy enough, taunting the Hartlepool support, "Two nil, an' a long way 'ome!"

We made our way up to Camden town at night, eagerly anticipating seeing Poly Styrene and X-Ray Spex. We had a few beers in The World's End boozer, then walked the short distance to Chalk Farm, to The Roundhouse. I was praying to myself that the gig would be good; we'd been looking forward to it for months. The venue was fantastic, we were downstairs, in the mix for this one, and I sent Les a text, generally asking how he was doing, and what was he up to tonight? I got a quick reply from him saying that he was at X-Ray Spex, fancy that! I fired another text back saying "Yes, but where exactly are you, right now?" Once we had the desired information from big Reg, we descended on him and Lorraine. He knew that we were going to literally jump on him, so he held back a bit, fervently trying to tell us to go easy, as he was recovering from a hernia operation. So, a respectable man hug or three later, we settled with fresh drinks, and waited to see Poly. Keith had been working earlier in the day, and by now was getting well juiced; he'd started the ear lobe thing early tonight, taking a healthy interest in Davo's, and, hellishly, there was a bloke near us with a blue dyed goatee beard. He didn't escape Keith's attentions either. The bloke was ok at first, but Keith wasn't for letting go; as Beardie's patience was snapping, we made Keith's apologies for him, and basically got him out of a hole.

We didn't have a very good vantage point for the gig, we were at the side, and viewing the stage was difficult. We had to stay away from the 'mosh pit' as such, as Les was tender after his operation. On came X-Ray Spex, consisting of Poly Styrene, the original bass player of the group Paul Dean, and three others, on drums, lead guitar and saxophone. Poly roared her introduction to the opener: "Some people say little girls should be seen and not heard, but I say, OH BONDAGE, UP YOURS, 1, 2, 3, 4 !" and they were off, it was just fucking awesome! If you take The Pogues out of the equation, the gig was the best one, for me, that I have ever witnessed, by a proverbial mile. Poly Styrene was a heroine of mine, and I felt genuinely privileged to be there, and hear the old X-Ray Spex numbers being played brilliantly to a sold out ecstatic audience.

I looked at big Les, at the guitar intro to "The day the world turned day glo" and he was just gone, caught up in the moment. I can't emphasise enough how great the gig was. The sound was incredible, the lucky people at The Roundhouse that Saturday night were seeing and hearing something very special. A personal highlight for me was during 'Warrior in Woolworths'; Davo and I had a wee 'jam' together singing the lyrics, "Youths meet at Stockwell Tube, weapons rule their li-ives". The worst thing ever happened, worse than the biggest natural disaster, when the end of the set was nigh. Couldn't believe it was nearly finished. They played 'Oh Bondage' again right at the end, and Davo and I got right down the front for a pogo. I had this incredibly strong urge to get a hold of Poly and tell her to do the show all over again, right now! And then she was gone. Phew! What a gig, a fucking monster.

I've not gone into too much detail about other bands and artists I've seen over the years, and I've seen lots, but I could not omit this concert; X-Ray Spex and Poly Styrene richly deserve their place in punk history, and I was lucky enough to witness their last hurrah with people that I love. The concert really was a one off, as Poly Styrene passed away a few years later, losing her battle with breast cancer. I was gutted when I heard the news, but grateful that I'd seen the great lady strutt her stuff live. Rest in peace Poly, you'll never know how happy you made a lot of people that night at The Roundhouse.

We retired, over the road, to a brilliant boozer; it was a warm September night, and we all felt brilliant. Les was elated that we'd surprised him – you can't beat quality, comfortable company, and it didn't get much better than this. Keith by now was severely rubbered. I had to take him to the toilet, and whilst we were there, Poly Styrene and her daughter had walked by, over the road from the pub. Davo, Lorraine and Les had spotted her, walking casually with her handbag in tow, looking quite pleased with herself apparently. I really wished I'd been there, I would have been over the road in a shot, to win or lose, but I would have loved to have told her how much I admired her music, and how much I had enjoyed her very latest delivery to London.

Keith meanwhile was keeping us all busy. Somehow, he'd fallen, and managed to push the hard plastic things that held his glasses in place on his nose, right into his skin, causing him to bleed. When I pointed this out to him, asking him what had happened, he took his glasses off, saw the blood, and promptly squared up to the nearest available male! There must have been 200 people in the pub, inside and out, so that's long odds, but Keith was convinced that this poor bloke was indeed the culprit for his bloodshed. A lot of delicate negotiating was needed to get out of this particular round of Keith's night; indeed, Keith reminded me of the old time wrestler Mick McManus, the way he was twirling his clenched fists in front of him, all he needed was a black one piece wrestling suit.

Earlier in the evening, Lorraine had driven herself and Les to Chalk Farm, and at closing time she very kindly offered to drive us to our hotel, near Tower Bridge. Keith was residing with me and Davo tonight, as a non paying, or arranged guest. Les sat in front, me, Davo and Mick McManus in the back. Les produced some liquid refreshment from the glove compartment that helped keep our throats oiled, and put some sounds on the car stereo, that suited the mood to perfection. It was a 'Faithless' CD. Les was a big fan; I was ignorant, and the standout track was a song called 'Don't leave' – a slow number, it was unexpectedly awesome, and also ironic. It was time for us to depart, we said goodbye to the big man, kissed Lorraine, and watched them, as they sped off, onto the now quieter connecting roads of London Town.

We still had a short walk to negotiate to the hotel, and we had to keep a suicidal Keith on his feet. "Leave me here, getting old now, just leave me here to die." No, I don't think so, Keith, so we marched on, defiantlyuntil we came across a parked police car, that was occupied. The window slowly came down, and plod was having a butchers, he wasn't impressed, but equally, looked as if he couldn't be arsed either, so we got on our way, as sharpish as Mick would let us. We managed to get up to the room and we pushed the twin beds together, and duly collapsed on top, in single file, like three Arbroath Smokies, laying out to dry.

Keith was away very early on the Sunday morning; he said he had to look in at work. He had driven into London the previous day, and was going to collect his car. I walked with him out of the hotel (the fags were on the go again); it was pissing down rain, so I suggested he get a taxi to the car park. On the nearest main road, I hailed a black cab, which stopped and Keith got in. "Where to?" said the cabbie. No reply. "Where are ya goin' mate?" Keith spoke up this time saying meekly, "Ehrm, I'm not sure." He'd momentarily forgotten where he'd parked the car. My head was thumping, I had a sandpaper mouth, with a helping of dried flies, and I shut the cab door, waved and fucked off back to the hotel. After a wee kip, I phoned Keith; he'd made it back, he always does, and sounded remarkably fresh – he always does this too, after a heavy day on the beer.

Les had been wondering the night before what we were planning for the Sunday. I sussed out a small gig that I thought might suit me and Davo. It was in a pub, The George VI, in Chiswick, the band were an up and coming one, called Mumford and Sons. We were in touch with Les on the Sunday lunchtime, he was reluctantly going to give tonight's gig a swerve, but he was raving about the night we'd had at X-Ray Spex and how pleased he was to discover we were there – you just can't beat surprises. He really did go on about how good it was to see us, making a real point that it was one of the best nights he'd had for a long time.

Davo was wanting to go to the sauna in the hotel, and I wasn't sure about this, purely as I'd never been in one. We were reading the papers in the room and I thought that if I didn't say anything, the sauna gig would just go away, he would just forget about it. He didn't. So we ended up going into the sweatshop with our towels and it was actually quite refreshing; it certainly cured my hangover, and we were ready for the off again. We caught the tube to Turnham Green, and found the pub on a main road, in a classy, leafy area of London. I ordered the beer, and asked the barmaid about the gig. She told me that the gig room was in the back, it was to be a special night they had on, with many bands and artists performing; Mumford and Sons were headlining. I asked for a couple of tickets, to be told that wasn't really how it worked. You just headed through, to the back of the pub and got your tickets at the door; it was going to be a busy one though, so don't leave it too late. Me and Davo ordered our dinner and had a conflab, Ding! I'd had a brainwave! I explained to the barmaid that we had just motored all the way down from Scotland, especially to see Mumford and Sons, and didn't want to leave anything to chance, so could she give us a shout when it was time to go through. No problem.

We'd just finished our meal, when the young lady came to our table, and asked us to follow her through to the gig room. She'd been talking to the Mumford boys, and they were really chuffed that two 'fan'" had made the long, long journey, just to see their show. The Mumfords were in the infancy of their career still, they were virtually unheard of as yet. The gig room was quite intimate, with a few candle-lit tables and a good bit of standing room behind them; we were escorted to the most prominent table, right in front of the stage, and there were two foaming mugs of ale on the table, just begging to be caressed by two Jocks. The band had insisted that we were made comfortable and had bought us a drink, how very splendiferous! So with the best seat in the house, we were treated to a very entertaining night featuring many good artists. A standout for me was Jamie T, he was certainly worth further investigation; he played two really good songs, just him and his bass guitar. Davo was quite clued up about the majority of acts on that night, and he particularly enjoyed us being there; the place was mobbed, but we were comfortable, a right couple of fascists, with the best seats in the gaff.

And what of Mumford and Sons? Well, they played a fuller set than the rest of the acts, and I personally thought they were ok, they had a good full on sound, at times their instrumentation threatened to be similar to The Pogues with a fast banjo beat here and there, but I couldn't take to the main man, the singer, Marcus Mumford. I found him a bit too self indulgent, and just didn't like his voice. Time was getting on, and we had to leave before the end; we were a long way from our hotel and had to watch our time with the tube. Maybe just as well, in case any of The Mumford lot wanted to speak to the Scottish diehard fans afterwards – that conversation might have been awkward as we really didn't know much about them at all. Of course, Mumford and Sons are now massive, they've come a long way, very quickly, and are international superstars, selling out huge Arenas with their live shows, and have album sales that can't be argued with. They're just not 'dirty' enough for me, but they gave me and Davo a night to remember, and I know for a fact that he bores his teenage daughters to death, with the story, of the night that he and 'Uncle Calum' were guests of the Mumfords.

We were on a massive high, after our trip to London. Never a dull moment with Keith 'Mick McManus' Williams, but providing we get home unscathed, I love him for his antics; he's certainly not a nasty guy, he's just, well, playful. The train journey down, the Millwall match, the X-Ray Spex gig, seeing Les and Lorraine, the fearful sauna, being Mumford's guests – it was just a magic weekend, one of the best.

My house phone rang one evening, a couple of weeks later. I recognised the number on the display panel, not like this number to call on landline. It was Lorraine. I don't know how, but I just knew what she was going to say. Big Les was dead.

SUNSHINE ON LEITH

Lorraine's phonecall was devastating. Les being taken from us was a
brand new experience for me personally. She briefly told me that Les
had suffered a heart attack, and just didn't make it. He left behind
two lovely boys, Craig and Leith, as well as two older daughters from
a previous marriage, Angela and Karen. I felt almost physically sick
for them all, and for poor Lorraine, who was doing all the necessary
phonecalls. I in turn, gave Davo, Mike and Keith the hellish news.
Lorraine told me, again that Les had been over the moon to see us
a few weeks previously at X-Ray Spex; she was very kind when she
told me that he was particularly pleased to have seen me, maybe he
said that because, out of the company that night, he'd known me the
longest. Looking back on our night at X-Ray Spex, the fact he was
delighted to see us, and the way he was when we said goodbye on
the roadside, I can't help feeling big Reg knew he was on the way out.
Little did we know that night, as Lorraine and he drove away, that it
would be the last time we saw him alive. It was an emotional goodbye,
without a reason really, apart from the fact that we'd had a brilliant
time. Even the Faithless track in the car gave you cause for thought,
'Don't leave'. I contacted Geoff Ford, a Perth Hibee, who actually kept
in touch with Les more than any of us, and we arranged to meet for
a drink that night; we found a little comfort, by being in each other's
company.

I had experienced my grandparents dying, three of them when I
was quite young, my Dad's mother when I was 18 – nothing remarkable

in that. Poor Geoff and his wife Carole tragically lost their daughter Jackie when she was just three years old. Davo had recently lost his father. Death affects us all in different ways; this was one of my close friends – as Morrissey sang "The first of the gang to die"... that summed things up perfectly I thought, and I couldn't come to terms with his death, I just couldn't.

Les Rennie was actually a legend. Les was tall, he had a shock of blonde hair, and he didn't half fancy himself! He was very much the main man in the Perth Hibs supporters, and had a reputation for handing out the odd slap at the football. If we were at an away game for example, we might pass a pub that was obviously a home team stronghold. That was a big green light for big Les; he'd have us all going into their pub, showing our colours until someone told us otherwise. Most of the time I would be shitting myself, but I think the barefaced front of us doing something like this saved us from many a hiding. Les would be charm itself, as he asked the confused and amazed bar staff for a round of drinks for the troops. Mostly, the punters would just stare at us in disbelief; rarely anything would actually happen.

Les enjoyed life to the full, always up for a party and to socialise. He was a very popular chap; if you'd had a row with him, chances were you'd be having a beer with him a week later. He was still on good terms with his ex-wife, Angela and Karen's Mum. We had another name for him, yes there were many: Doctor, Reggie and 'The Windmill'. If he was part of a tear up at the Hibs matches, you would just see his long arms going like the clappers, handing out punches, smacks and slaps, his arms were like a windmill's arms, like they would be when a hurricane was blowing. Just about everyone who went to watch Hibs knew big Les, and had crossed his path at some point, whether it be in a bar, on a train or on the terraces. I first met him when I was 14, on a train, and straight away, I felt that I wanted to impress him, I wanted him to like me; he had an infectious personality.

We had catered for many different functions at The Aviator, but when Lorraine decided that Les's funeral was to be in Perth, the Monday page in our diary was the most important function to date. Les was taken to a funeral rest house, and the Hibs boys were invited to say their goodbyes to Les for the very last time. Again, this was a new experience for me. I hadn't seen a dead person before, let alone a very close pal. Davo, Geoff and I met Les's immediate family at the funeral home; I felt sick for his wife and children. They went into the room where Les was resting first, then it was our turn. Geoff was in first and freaked out a bit, bursting into tears. I went in last, like the brave coward I am. Les had died a good while ago by now and his body seemed bloated, I just couldn't believe it. Lorraine had thoughtfully arranged for Les to be dressed as if he were going to a music festival, that was his bag; he had his Hibs scarf on, he had a bit more than a smile on his face. We left the funeral home, and hugged each other. I had arranged to meet Teresa and Janice in town. I needed a drink. I was really frightened that I would remember Les as I had seen him in the funeral home, it was bothering me. But my fears were on the minimal scale when I thought of his two young laddies in particular – Leith was only 11 years old.

Monday came round, I was up at the crack of dawn, Teresa and I went into work early to prepare the cold food and get The Aviator ready for folk wishing to toast Les Rennie's life. We'd been given some photos by the family, and we got them blown up, and placed them throughout the building.

Les's funeral was at the crematorium. For someone who had lived down South for years, the attendance was amazing, standing room only at the back. I had contacted Paul Kane, the ex Hibs player, and the President of our Perth supporters club. We hadn't seen him for a while, but he showed his class, like the man he is, when he turned up at the crematorium to the delight of Les's sons. They had Hibs shirts on; the Perth Hibbies wore Hibs ties, as opposed to black ones. Ed the Gazelle had posted a message on a Hibs fans' website about Les's death – the messages that followed on from that, from Hibs fans upset at the big man's passing just went on and on.

The service was carried out by a humanist, Les's coffin was decorated with green and white colours, the song they played when the family arrived and the service was to start was 'Sunshine on Leith'. Les was represented from Hornchurch, as well as Perth, by a group of friends that had made the long journey up north, to say farewell to their comrade. Rob, in particular, was at the fore, doing a speech at the funeral. He told the assembled mourners how much Les had enjoyed X-Ray Spex. So did Les's brother Ally, during his speech. Our very own Jimmy Duthie, of British Rail male model, fare dodging fame completed the speeches. It was a beautiful, fulfilling service, the humanist element meant that Les was the main topic of whoever was conversing – there's definitely something to be said for that. Lorraine had got everything spot on; I admired how well she had coped, under the worst circumstances. A Faithless tune was played on our departure, as we said our very final farewell to Dr Les Reg Windmill Rennie.

A large number of people came back to The Aviator and pretty much stayed there, in the bar area, all afternoon, and well into the evening. Leith said a few words at the gathering, and was extremely mature and clinical for one so young. He walked through to the empty restaurant, and sat at the same table where he and his family had sat all those months ago, and said to me "This is where we were – why can't Dad be here?"

Our music system was playing a mix of dance, punk, Pogues and The Proclaimers; 'Sunshine on Leith' came on randomly, we turned the volume up, and Les's Hibs mates put their arms round each other and formed a line. If the song was emotional before, well it was off the scale now, and always will be – everyone at The Aviator, there must have been 100 or so, felt the emotion, and the sense of loss. One fella who was present, Big Fergie, a Rangers man through and through, but one of Les's good friends, burst unashamedly into tears during Sunshine on Leith. Fergie is a real hard man, hailing originally from Inverness, but the occasion coupled with the song got the better of him; it was a lovely, tender moment, for a bear of a man to show his soft side.

I got involved with Rob from Hornchurch at the bar; we were necking straight whisky, one after the other, and I was in big trouble. I can't handle whisky; I like the taste and the burning bit when it's going down, but I was plastered very early in proceedings, down to my indulgence of Scotland's liquid gold. Another attendee who was worse for wear was my dear mother; the fags were being lit again, right in the bar, and Teresa had to keep taking her out, under protest, to finish her snout. The Hibs songs crept into proceedings, and basically, everyone had a good time – that sounds pretty awful, but it's exactly what the big man would've wanted; the only thing missing was him. My mother had to be carried home, Dad was raging, I wasn't far behind her. Teresa told me in the morning that she had to put my suit in the bin; it was well past cleaning or repair, whoops! When I phoned Mum, we had a giggle with each other, that we were the 'troublemakers' of the day – nothing wrong with that. Mum had a great relationship with Les over the years, he was certainly going to be missed. He died when he was 52 years old. He was the youngest 52 year old that ever lived.

Pogues greatest hits albums were being released periodically, but there was no talk of new material being recorded by the band. A lot of press stories and interviews begged the question, why wasn't this on the Pogues' agenda. For me, I wasn't too bothered about new material, although I sometimes wished that they would play more of their most wonderful back catalogue at their live shows, such as the aforementioned 'Transmetropolitan'. On one greatest hits release, there was a bonus CD, 'Live at the Brixton Academy', recorded in the 2001 first reunion tour. I think that the live disc fails to capture the atmosphere of a Pogues show; there are moments though, especially right at the beginning. James Fearnley's up to the microphone first, in his unmistakeable Mancunian accent, "Sorry we're late, the traffic was bad!" It's a line that Teresa and I use now, for everything, when we're running late. Shane's next, teasing the crowd, saying "Here's a brand new one!" just before the band launch themselves into 'Streams of Whiskey' as per normal, from the band's first album.

If we were harking after a brand new one, earlier in 2008, us Pogues enthusiasts received a gift so good, it just must have come from heaven itself. "Just look them straight in the eye and say...Pogue Mahone!!" was the title of The Pogues box set, 5 CDs of rare tracks, outtakes, cover versions, live tracks, demos and recordings by the band that had never previously seen the light of day. I was into my local HMV store on the Friday, before the Monday it was being released. Matey got onto his computer and said, "Yes, we're getting a few of those in" and I told him in no uncertain terms that one of them had my name on it. Come the Monday morning, when back in the shop, there was a bit of confusion, as they couldn't find the damned thing in their stock. I wanted it there and then – this is what new releases should be all about. I'd been waiting for this for ages and now they couldn't fucking find it. Try harder. They did try harder, and pulled a plum from the pie, with the little brown, antique looking boxset; in front of my eyes, a little picture of Shane and Spider in the corner, looking menacing, just for a change!

I handed over some folding vouchers with Lizzie's napper on them, and off I went, with my purchase, straight to work. Janice was in before me, typing away on the computer in the office, no doubt doing something vitally important to Aviator business; she was very rudely interrupted, when I demanded her attention, saying, "You'll never guess just exactly what I've got in this bag". Her body language was heavily sighing, as she turned to humour me, and I very carefully, very slowly, revealed the contents of the bag, as if it were a really rare, fragile piece of precious, period porcelain, and produced something much more valuable than that, in front of Janice's eyes. No, it wasn't my penis (tut, tut, shame on you!) but The Pogues box set, crammed with sounds and artwork and words that were going to keep me entertained for quite some time, for ever actually. Janice just looked at me, didn't say anything. I think she may actually have felt sorry for me, pitying me, perhaps thinking I was ill!

Each disc on the box set has 20 odd tracks on it, what an absolute treat. Ewan MacColl, Kirsty's father, was a songwriter and a half in his day. He of course wrote the Pogues favourite 'Dirty old town' and there's a fucking belter of a track written by him on disc 1, 'The travelling people', one of my favourites from the box. He also wrote 'North Sea Holes', with Terry Woods singing the excellent lyrics, all about hardy fishermen. There's actually quite a few cover versions present, 'Maggie May' is another, the band released this live earlier in their career as a B side; the one on the box set is a studio version and it's very accomplished.

There's also a lot of material that amazingly never managed to get on to a Pogues album, but appeared a little later, when Shane was with The Popes; one of those is a track called 'NW3', appearing later as 'Mother Mo Chroi' – an absolute MacGowan classic, what on earth were they thinking about, to omit this from a Pogues album? I guess only the band themselves, or perhaps Mr Frank 'The Cash' Murray can answer that. Indeed, there's easily another album of the highest quality material here that could've been released by the band; it would have been an album to rate alongside their first three album releases; I truly believe it would have been as good as that. I'm thinking of 'Aisling' and 'Victoria' as two really obvious tracks, that again came later with Shane and The Popes.

Another gem is a track called 'Rake at the gates of Hell'. This MacGowan masterpiece featured on a soundtrack album for a film the band appeared in called Straight to Hell. The song deserved much more exposure than the film or its soundtrack offered; it's a brilliant Pogues composition. Shane's writing really was something else in his heyday. The songs on the box set are just so diverse. James Fearnley once said that they couldn't do harmonies – well, just about everything else is here. There's a couple of punky tracks where Spider is singing, and it really does sound like he wants to kick your fucking head in!

All in all the box set is a 100% winner, a real tonic for the fans who, I'm positive, welcomed its release with open, grateful arms. Box sets can be filled with absolute drivel at times, just to fill space up – I have a few of those – and whilst every track on The Pogues one may not be as strong as others, there's no 'filla' present here. The Pogues were never a weak B side or album kind of band. Not a new album though, five new albums instead, wonderful.

Have you ever had a perfect, and I mean perfect, day? After the hurt of losing Les, it was really welcome to experience that perfect day.

A PERFECT DAY

Christmas 2008. There was just so much going on, the party nights at The Aviator were at bursting point, bookings wise, with the extra spaces created by the dining room. Nights like this really kept us going, and financially saw us through the lean times, where there was next to nothing doing. During the summer, one of those nights that kept things right was another wedding, again with a young crowd of very serious drinkers. After my stint was finished in the kitchen, I had to make numerous trips to the off licence, to keep us stocked up with vodka, WKD blues and bottled Budweiser – not that I was complaining. I think we locked the door at 4am that morning, and were back at 8am to sort the place out, ready for Sunday lunches, knackered, but happy that you could pay the bills for a wee while. We all got stuck in; before I got changed into my whites, I was in cleaning the toilets, not very glamorous, but necessary after the wedding, as you would imagine – a bit of spew here and there to negotiate, as well as stocking up on the shite roll. I can be really slow at times, to catch on to things, so much so that Teresa, who is not slow, said to me once, "The only thing quick about you, is your sperm!" Charming! This one morning though, I was indeed slow to realise that the reason the toilet cisterns were all powdery, was not because someone had failed to rinse the Vim off, when cleaning before. It was pointed out to me that it would be the cocaine, that had been consumed by our punters at the wedding, and I was told that this was indeed perfectly normal these days. OK then, I stand educated. As you know by now, I like a drink, but the toilet cistern stuff, happy tablets and the like actually scares the shit out of me. I know what I'm doing with a bottle of beer, and I know what the likes of a load of whisky is going to do to me too!

I was also probably a bit on the slow side when it came to getting to grips with the internet, however I did manage to log on to the official Pogues website, 'The wake of the Medusa', named after the painting on the album cover of 'Rum, Sodomy and the Lash'. The website was essential for up to date information, especially the Christmas tours, where I could get my arse into gear and get booked up with tickets, trains and hotels. The forums were good to, where you could read what the punters were saying about gigs etc. Back in the day, it would be a music paper to tell you of upcoming gigs, or to see a billboard poster, pasted onto where the window of the Chinese takeaway used to be. Philip Chevron was heavily involved on the Medusa, you could even ask him a question, but you had to be careful – if you asked a stupid one, he'd tell you so!

Jimmy's 50th birthday party was on Saturday, 6th December. The Pogues were in Glasgow the next night, and work was really busy. After a long shift at The Aviator, I got home for a shower, and made an appearance at Jimmy's bash. I didn't want to miss it. Lorraine, Craig and Leith were up from the South; everything was still a bit raw, regarding Les. By the time I got to the party, everyone had a good shine on them with the drink. I was both knackered and sober, sometimes not easy to get into the swing of things, but I got there. Teresa had to stay at work, but she had arranged a treat for the next night, with an overnight stay in Glasgow for The Pogues gig. The idea was we could get a good kip, before travelling back in the morning, and into work, fighting fit, ready for more chipolatas. The late train home from Glasgow can be soul destroying, it seems to stop everywhere, and takes an age to get to Perth.

We had a few hours at work on the Sunday morning, then caught the train through to Glasgow Queen Street. There's a pub called Sammy Dow's, right outside the station, and we timed it perfectly for me to get comfortable and watch the televised Hibs v Celtic game, while enjoying a beer. I looked after our overnight bags, and Teresa went up the street, to brave the manic shops as they are at Christmas time. The pub was really busy, mainly blokes, and it was obvious very quickly that they were all Celtic fans – well, we were in Glasgow right enough. A lot of them were railway workers, and I assumed that they were off duty, otherwise they were drinking on the job! Hibs were doing all right in the match against Celtic, the punters in the pub were visually disgruntled; I kept quiet. They had even more reason to be pissed off, when Hibs player John Rankin hit a shot from way out, the ball seemed to swerve as it bounced in front of the Celtic keeper, and foxed him totally, ending in the back of the net. Ya fuckin' beauty! What a goal! I managed to keep my calm, a bit like at Swinecastle, the Hearts ground, previously. The bloke next to me had his suspicions that I may have been a quietly gloating Rangers fan (fuck me, perish the thought!) but I remained silent, as he was muttering to himself.

Towards the end of the match, Hibs scored again, just as Teresa was coming in the door of the boozer. She looked at the TV, saw the Hibs players celebrating, and quickly realised (see, I telt you she was quick) that I must have been in singular minority as the pub's customers were not happy! The bloke next to me was cursing by now, he was staring at me, but I still remained calm and emotionless. Two pints or so later, it might have been a different matter. I did feel elated but it was still controlled. The match ended, and the pub's population was instantly depleted, what a result, 2-0 to the Hibees! A fantastic way to kick off our visit to Glasgow. The suspicious bloke next to me drained his lager and gave me a wink before he left; I just smiled a bit in response. I thought that was a nice touch on his behalf. Teresa showed me her purchases, and then we walked, with a Hibee-aided spring in my step, to our budget hotel; it was nought flash, but nice and central.

Once we were checked in, we were out again sharp, and had a casual walk over the river, to the area where the Academy stood. We were a bit early, so we dropped into a hostelry on the main road, called The Glaswegian. I ordered a couple of drinks at the bar, and as I looked around, realised the place was a Rangers stronghold. The memorabilia displayed on the walls of the bar confirmed this. The clientele was very interesting to say the least; the place was full of people that looked as if they lived off their very wits. Unfortunately, one of the punters fell foul of the burly, bald barman; he was taken outside, and I kid you not, the whole bar could hear him howl, as he was reprimanded for whatever sin he might have committed. Teresa's face was a picture of concern. I told her to sook her drink, and keep her head down. We racked up a game of pool – the table was squint: when the white ball was hit softly, it sloped alarmingly to the right. We were certainly not going to complain though, didn't fancy one bit a howling session with baldie blue nose. In fact as we left, we dutifully took our empty tumblers to the bar, and wished him goodnight. I wondered what he would have thought of The Pogues concert and the hordes of Celtic fans lapping up their Irish flavoured magical music had he wished to walk up the road a bit and partake.

Upstairs in the Academy as standard, and yet another fantastic Glasgow show unfolded before our eyes and ears. I loved the venue that the band decided to call 'home' in Glasgow these days, and it was a nice feeling to know that we were not getting the train from Hades home tonight. The show was a vast improvement, Shane-wise, compared to Brixton last year. He always seemed to be up for it at Glasgow, and we were buzzing, having witnessed the best night out in town, yet again! Indeed, the feel-good factor of a sparkling Pogues concert led to a spur of the moment idea at the end of the night. We decided that we were going to stick around, and try to see the band members as they left the Academy – quite what for, well, we were not really sure to be honest, it just felt like the right thing to do though, fuck the train!

It's not a long distance from the front of the venue to the back, and we positioned ourselves close to the only conceivable place where the artists would leave the venue. Before we knew it, Spider appeared, and we were soon engaged in conversation. Spider loves the Glasgow audience. I asked him if he wanted me to call him Peter (his first name) or Spider; he replied that I could call him whatever I wanted. Somehow, I very, very much doubted that! He had a light coloured top hat on and a big pair of trendy spectacles. I took a picture of him and Teresa on my phone; it's here for all to see. Spider wasn't giving much away regarding my questions about how long they were going to do Christmas tours for. I was petrified of the idea that they would suddenly stop them, I was just fishing a bit. James Fearnley came out, and just as he did, I unfortunately felt the effects of the day's ale intake.

James compiled a blog, on the official Pogues website, of life on the road, since the first reunion in 2001. There's a bit about him going to the Bradford tearooms in Glasgow for breakfast, which I found quite fascinating. James goes into the experience in much detail, talking of the crisp linen and various other descriptive notes, before eventually settling down to sardines on toast. For some fucking ridiculous unknown crazy reason, I had it in my head that James enjoyed croissants at Bradfords, so I was right in there when he appeared from the exit to the venue, "Hi James, are ye looking forward tae yer croissants in the morning?" James didn't answer, a look of confusion enveloping his face; he looked as if he wanted to understand, but he just, very understandably didn't. SHIT! I really like James Fearnley, he's a big part of The Pogues for me personally, and here I was speaking to him, but speaking absolute drunken drivel. I told him I had really enjoyed the brief appearance of 'Transmetropolitan' last year and at least James could identify with this saying, "When Shane forgot the words!" He made his way to the waiting car, and just before he closed the door behind him, I shouted: "How's America, James?" to which he replied "'Ot!" And he was gone.

And then there HE was. Shane MacGowan appeared; there was a young bloke looking after him, and the guy was not keen for the people assembled to talk to the lead singer. Shane was more than pleased to talk though, posing for photos and gladly signing autographs; he had a green and white bar scarf round his neck, and he was more than comfortable with meeting the punters; I would go as far to say that he was enjoying the attention. When it was our turn, I told him of the Hibees' exploits earlier in the day, defeating Celtic by two goals to nil, and went on about how the green colours were ours first, before Celtic; it was actually a Hibs scarf he was really wearing. "Hibernian," I said to Shane, belonging to Ireland. He liked that, "That's good!" he said. Teresa said it was almost her birthday, could she get a kiss? You fucking bet, Teresa. Shane attempted to put his tongue down her throat, a situation which she diplomatically diffused, and what was I supposed to do, watch, rub, and get myself excited, oh I don't know?

Shane was brilliant to talk to, his voice was a bit hoarse after his vocal exploits in the building he had just left, but he signed a piece of paper for Teresa "Happy birthday, love Shane xx" and told us Teresa was his mother's name. We got a girl to take a photo of the three of us, we shook hands and he was gone, away in his car. He couldn't have been more pleasant and friendly – very, in Teresa's case!

So there you have it, a perfect day, The Hibees doing Celtic, a vintage Pogues show, more than a few beers, a crack with Spider, James and Shane, and no train at night, just a comfy bed in the centre of town. We were just positively elated walking back to the hotel, it felt like a sweetener in amongst a busy time at work and after the trauma of losing Les. Lou Reed had (re)released a single for charity called 'Perfect day' featuring lots of different artists contributing vocals on the song. Shane makes a very brief appearance, and sings the line "It's such fun!". That's exactly what today was, Mr MacGowan, I couldn't have put it any better. If there were any negatives, there was one, but as far as we were concerned, it wasn't major. The photo with us and Shane wasn't the best, it was a bit too dark, but hey, we would just have to try and get another one, sometime in the future. It was just really good to have a wee chat to the great man, and for Teresa to receive a Christmas cracker of a birthday kiss!

After breakfast the next morning, we caught an earlyish train home, and I bought a newspaper to read on the journey. The paper is great, the day after a big Hibs win, they were calling John Rankin's goal against Celtic 'The Squiggler' Apparently he was practising long range shots like this in training. John Rankin under achieved during his time at Easter Road in my opinion, and I had my doubts about his intention, or ability to create a squiggler to score a goal, but still, the feeling of content from all yesterday's happenings were still warm, Squiggler and all, so maybe we'll give him the benefit of the doubt – although I don't think he's ever scored a goal like that again.

As if this wasn't enough, Teresa had treated me to first class ticket on the train, for my jaunt to Brixton; I was travelling down on the Thursday. The Saturday before, we had our busiest day in history, during our time at The Aviator. We did 110 Christmas lunches, a party night for 115, and in-between did an outside catering function for 60 people, at the local aeroclub. We wondered if we would manage to get through the day, and keep up with everything, and I'm pleased to say we did, every member of staff played their part and we made it with a bit to spare, pure adrenaline kept us going, and the till went 'ker-ching'. I'd be able to pay the fishmonger's bill in January, happy days!

The dates of The Pogues gigs at Brixton were actually quite conveniently placed, date wise – I could travel back on the Saturday, due to arrive at Perth station at 6pm, just perfect for getting to work, for another busy Christmas party night. The first class lark was, well, just first class. I had a seat with a table to my absolute self, with loads of room, tea and coffee on tap, and a bloke that brought me a nice toastie for my lunch. Being on my own, for six hours on the train, gave me time to have a good think about things, where we were at at The Aviator, and what I wanted for the future. Of course, never far from my thoughts, was the fact that the group spawned from the dear old streets of King's Cross were playing a bit further south in Brixton tonight, and I was going to be there; so was Mr Keith Sumo Mick McManus Williams, who was available for the two nights. We were staying at the Travelodge again, so a breakfast or two at Oz's was on the cards.

Things were getting routine now, in a good way, with the Brixton shows; we were usually quite sensible with the ale on the first night, and I liked to get to the venue nice and sharp, to get a good seat, and just take it all in. Again, the band were on top form. I remember telling Keith to "Pay attention" when James Fearnley took up position at the piano for 'Rainy Night in Soho'. Keith liked the faster Pogues numbers, but it was time he was experiencing the emotion, that hit you in the gut, on the slower, ballady songs. I'm not sure if it worked, but 'Rainy Night' was outstanding, as was everything else the band played. At 'Fairytale', once Shane and Ella Finer's vocals were over, they have a 'waltz', usually with Ella holding yer man up, and a shower of fake snowflakes cascade down onto the stage, giving The Pogues' most famous song a realistic festive feel; the audience go into raptures, as the classic track reaches its climax. 'Fiesta' finishes a Pogues set, the stage is an absolute mess, with streamers, spray string stuff and beer trays that have been bashed off Spider's and Shane's nuts during the song, joining the fake snow on the stage. It must be murder for whoever cleans up after the band depart to the sanctuary of their dressing rooms.

Next day, after reacquainting with, and being nourished by Oz, we were straight up to Kensington High Street. We did a bit of Christmas shopping, then, as usual, ended up in the boozer – on this occasion, The Goat, a pub we were familiar with, usually having one or two in there before a visit to Sticky Fingers. We'd decided that we would not abandon Sticky Fingers today, but got a few good quality peeves in at The Goat first, just in case the beer up the road was to the poor standard it had been lately. The Goat is almost opposite a very smart hotel, The Royal Garden. It just so happens, that during their London Christmas shows, The Pogues actually reside here. It's a small world! How exactly was I privy to this information? I have my sources! Anyway, after a good few scoops in The Goat, Keith and I decided we would go to The Royal Garden for a nosy, and maybe a beer (it was Keith's round!). We moseyed our way across the busy road, and made for the revolving door at the entrance to the hotel, where we were met by the stare of the elaborately dressed doorman, complete with tall hat. Our doorman's body language was turbulent, to say the least, when he clocked the two of us headed in his direction. As we got nearer that turbulence was getting more intense. I wouldn't say we were that badly dressed, but we had a shine on us, and the doorman was experienced enough to know that we were not attending a seminar regarding stocks and shares of any kind in his hotel. It was in his best interests to swat away these particular two insects before they got too close. I picked up on all of this, probably just in time, as I grabbed Keith's arm and diverted us away, and up the High Street. He wasn't happy; he wanted a pint or two with Shane. Sorry Mick, some other time perhaps.

Sticky Fingers was ok; we accepted that nothing stays the same forever, and it was still good just to be there. The beer wasn't so bad when you'd had a few already, and as for the grub, well, we just get on with it. We arrived at the Academy, with not too much time to spare before The Pogues were due on. There was an almighty scramble at the balcony's bar, this girl in particular was trying her very best to get to the front before it was her turn, and she was getting away with it, upsetting everyone. Keith and I formed a two-man human barrier when she was behind us, that's as far as she got with her queue hopping, and she knew it. Surprisingly, she started chatting to us, quite pleasantly, informing us that she actually used to be Shane MacGowan's girlfriend. It wasn't Victoria Clarke, and it wasn't Shanne Bradley, although she did have similarities to the latter. I had no reason to disbelieve her; however, as Keith and I each got a round in, she looked disappointed – maybe she was expecting us to include her in the rounds we bought, maybe the "I'm Shane's ex girlfriend" gig managed to get her drinks at Christmas time. We did wish her a merry Christmas, but the response was lukewarm at best.

The audience was rowdy in the balcony tonight, no chance of anyone remaining seated; that was the case pretty much from the word go. We were positioned directly in front of the walkway that divides the balcony in two, where folk can get to the central stairway exit. We were in the company of some young folk, both boys and girls who were well up for the cup, on their arses as much as they were on their feet. Of course Keith was loving this, and I, to be fair, wasn't far behind him, the band's brilliant performance definitely adding fuel to the fire. Unbeknown to me though, yer man had been at the earlobes thing again. This time, he had to physically position himself to reach over a small barrier, to the seats in front of the walkway, where his victim was bopping away with whom I assumed to be his girlfriend. When I did eventually cotton field on to the earlobe episode, and saw the size of the geezer, I instantly knew we were in trouble – the disgruntled look on his face was indeed confirmation. Trouble was, he was looking at me! He hopped over the barrier like an Olympic high jumper, and was in my face in an instant; the comparison of our physiques was ridiculous, David and Goliath, didn't even come close to this mismatch. He was shoving me a bit, and clearly wanted to do more aggressive, nasty things to me. Remarkably I kept very calm, and roared at him, over the music, "I haven't done anything, so fuck off!" The shoving became more aggressive, and the security chappies were now on the scene. One of the blokes got a hold of me, and I was spluttering my way through my case for the defence, he told me to shut up, walk down to the exit at the side, then come back in after five minutes. At least I wasn't getting dispatched onto a freezing Stockwell Road outside!

That sounded fair enough, but I wasn't missing any more of the show, so I settled for a minute and a half, then I was back in, made my way to a guilty-looking, unreprimanded Keith, and we were enjoying live Pogues music again, without Olympic earlobing this time.

So that was it again for another year, routine kicks in again, I hoped that the shows we had seen were not to be the last, fingers crossed for next year. We got back to King's Cross, with an apologetic earlober, and went into the all night McDonald's, for yet more grub. Keith got a seat, as I ordered our late, late supper. There was a girl sitting on the table next to Keith, and she was seriously giving him the eye. Keith's face was a combination of surprise and flattery. The girl smiled – her teeth would have given Shane MacGowan's a run for their money. She was looking for business. I took our scran back to the table, highly amused at Keith's situation with Colgate Daisy. Before I settled into my Big Mac, I went for a piss, still smiling to myself. This was short-lived when a huge black fella in a full length leather jacket appeared for a chat as I was pissing. You know what they say about black fellas, well I hope he didn't look at my chap, transferring my waste water onto the china. He was straight to the point. "That gorgeous girl looking at your mate would be very happy to suck both yer cocks all night, if I ask her to! Why don't you have a word with him, and get back to me, we'll talk about it, I even have a place for you all to go." Suddenly, I might have needed a shite as well, but that would have to wait. I thanked the nice business man, and confess to not washing my hands, then went back out to a very relaxed Keith and told him to grab his burger, we were leaving. As you would expect, he looked at me with confusion. I told him once more, very forcibly, that we were fucking going right now! "For fuck's sake, blah, blah, blah!" came the muttered response. As soon as we were out the door, I was on my toes, tugging at Keith to keep up with me; I'd explain in a minute; there were chips everywhere! As we turned into Gray's Inn Road, and caught our breath, I explained, with intervals for panting, exactly what was going on in McDonald's. Keith just looked at me, somewhat amazed, then he said, "How much was it?!"

We had a less eventful breakfast at Oz's in the morning; he really knew how to look after us and the pleasant waitress that worked in his café had herself a fine set of teeth. Oz kept asking what brought us back to London every Christmas; I kept telling him the reason and he kept saying the same thing back to me, "Man, they must be some group." Yes Oz, they were that all right.

I arrived back in Perth after my first class return journey, which I could definitely get used to, and into work, ready for a busy Christmas party night, the last one of 2008, telling all the staff that could be bothered to listen of my tales from another Pogues expedition down south. They really were just fantastic times, and somehow, I appreciated them even more, when looking back and reflecting on the trip I'd just completed. As was now standard, Shane, Kirsty, Spider, Darryl, James, Andrew, Philip, Jem and Terry brought Christmas to a close at The Aviator with 'Fairytale of New York' for the now amorous couples on the dance floor, probably already thinking of what might be happening next.

THERE'S A FLY
IN MY SOUP!

When we received complaints from customers in the restaurant, they tended to be like unreliable buses, and come all at once. We always tried to sort out grievances quickly and with a bit of common sense if at all possible, but sometimes it would have been easier to climb Kilimanjaro with a garden shed tied to your back. Throughout this chapter, I will 'treat' you to some of the more colourful complaints we received, as well as some of the strange requests that were put upon us. Here's your starter for ten. "My pork spare ribs have been cooked with a plastic carrier bag still underneath them." Really.

We had one particular hard day at The Aviator, when just nothing was going right; it really was the proverbial day from hell. Come 5pm, we made an executive decision to close for the evening (we had no bookings) and we took the staff out, again, for a drink and a cheap and cheerful carvery meal. I think we all needed to let our hair down a bit. It was a pleasant evening, we all sat outside and the beer was coming thick and fast. Of course, as we'd had a difficult day, the adrenaline was pumping and emotions were running high, so a few of us were juiced rather quickly; I was right in there as one of them. Our behaviour in the carvery place was shocking: we were loud, obnoxious and funny – or at least we thought we were. The carvery staff were laughing along with us, but the good folk out for a nice meal that night were not laughing. As the night went on, we went steadily downhill, so did our language and topic of conversation. Our behaviour was not clever, and when it was time to go, I think the whole building released a huge sigh of relief. Nothing to be proud of, but hey, shit happens, it gives folk something to talk about. At least it wasn't a brawl, like we had experienced at The Aviator, on that Saturday afternoon previously.

Next day at the restaurant, there was a phonecall. From the carvery place. Teresa took the call, and to be fair to her, as usual, she was not one of the culprits in carvery gate, Teresa would always try to restore order. The manager from the carvery was not at all happy, and demanded that the Aviator management, reprimanded their rowdy, uncontrollable staff. Teresa had a right pop at me, I was embarrassed, and I promised her that I would sort it all out, and restore The Aviator's relatively good name. I made the phonecall in the empty dining room, and when I got through to the disgruntled manager, I listened to all the grievances he had, in regards to our rowdy staff. The main culprit was a little fella, with black hair and a white Fred Perry T shirt on. I assured the manager that I knew EXACTLY who he was talking about and he could count on me to punish the little bastard accordingly! He then went on to say that he had some of the 'action' on CCTV, and the worst offenders were now banned from his establishment. I thought I would ask him if that included the little chap with the Fred Perry. "Most definitely, I don't understand how you can employ someone as bad as him," he said. With that, I apologised to the bloke, on our terrible staff's behalf, little shit and all, and reconfirmed that I would be dealing with them without leniency. For those of you still not sure, yes, short arse Fred was indeed ME! Arf Arf! I had chosen to forego the path of revelation, and was looking forward to reprimanding myself with a right good thrashing! Teresa was calmer once I told her of the conversation, but it took me a wee while to get back into her good books, although I do think she found the thought of me punishing myself, as the main criminal, just a tiny bit funny, perhaps. A few weeks later, we heard through the catering grapevine, that the manager from the carvery had been dismissed; he was helping himself to the contents of the till apparently. We've all been back many times, and behaved impeccably, especially the little runt who would take his folks there from time to time!

One day, a single lady diner at The Aviator complained quite forcibly, that the plate her Hawaiian ham and chicken salad was served on, was cold. I kid you not! Another diner complained that their omelette was actually "Too eggy!".

A few of the Perth Hibs boys organised a fundraising day, in honour of big Les's immediate family. A Sunday in May was chosen for a sponsored walk of about 15 miles, followed by a night at The Aviator with a buffet, a disco and a karaoke. The response from our fellow Hibs boys, friends and family was nothing short of superb. A good Hibs mate, Craig from Glasgow, came through to Perth with his family and completed the walk with us. It was a beautiful day, Geoff and Ed the Gazelle had worked out the route, and it alerted a few of us to the natural beauty of the countryside that virtually lay on our doorstep, taking in some lovely views by the River Tay as well as the River Almond. There were a couple of well thought out stops on the way, at local hostelries; it was a really enjoyable, if somewhat sore afternoon. Teresa's feet were swollen, and giving her serious gyp, but she completed the walk, as did everyone present. We were all wearing our Hibs tops, and one fella, Graham Hay, proudly wore his Hearts top. Graham actually raised the most money in sponsorship for the walk by a long way; it was a brilliant effort on his part. A few of us have had run-ins with Graham over the years, we're all good now, but he was always a mate of big Les's, and he was certainly not letting him down today. The Aviator was busy, busy in the evening; we had a wonderful night, with a quiz, a raffle, kids' drawing competitions and a right good night, going into the wee small hours. 'Sunshine on Leith' at the end of the night proved just too much for a lot of us, myself included, but the whole day was a fabulous success.

Lorraine's wishes were that a good portion of the monies raised would go towards a day of match hospitality at Easter Road, to see a Hibs v Celtic match; Les's boys were keen on this, so Geoff organised it all, with him, myself and Ed the Gazelle joining the family on the day, but of course, paying for our places ourselves. I wrote to the Hibs Chairman, Rod Petrie, asking if he would make an appearance at our table and say hello to the family, Lorraine, Leith, Craig, Angela and Karen. I received a lovely letter back from him, saying he would do just that, and that he was really pleased at the family's choice, regarding the treat from the raised monies. It's always weird going to the match with a suit, shirt and tie, but we had a good day, the young lads got to meet a few of the players, and were happy enough, despite Hibs losing the match by a goal to nil. Hibs have never been that reliable on the big occasion to produce the goods, and today was no exception.

A bloke came into The Aviator one lunchtime and asked for a cheese and pickle sandwich, but with no bread! You think I'm making this up, don't you? Another punter ordered a fillet steak, rare, but with no blood whatsoever! A lady complained that her monkfish was not indeed real monkfish, "It's that pretend monkfish that you're using instead!"

Summer was upon us and The Pogues didn't half give me and Teresa something to look forward to, with a very unexpected announcement that they were playing a gig in Liverpool, in the middle of July. The venue was The Echo Arena, it looked huge, and when enquiring about the tickets, I came across a situation that had never before surfaced when booking briefs for a Pogues gig. The ticket agencies were pushing 'Gold' tickets for VIP packages. Fuck me, didn't they know anything about a Pogues audience? I couldn't forsee many partaking in this VIP lark – apart from anything else, the price of the gold tickets were ridiculously high; if a free bar was included, then maybe, but there was no free bar, so we bought tickets for an area at the side of the stage, about half way back. The gig was part of a music week called Pop Tarts or something, and included the likes of Squeeze and The Pretenders. The Liverpool angle was certainly something a bit different for us, so we booked at a Premier Inn, virtually next door to The Echo Arena, overlooking the Albert Dock. The Pogues, in summer, in Liverpool, down near the water, oh yes, sounded great, we were really digging having that to look forward to.

A customer at The Aviator ate every last scrap of their wild mushroom risotto. On clearing the scraped clean bowl, the waiter was told that the risotto was rubbish, the worst they had ever eaten. "What was wrong with it, sir?" The reply? "I actually don't know, but I just ate it anyway!" One Saturday night, a bloke was so incensed that his steakburger was actually a very low budget supermarket type burger,

THE POGUES - THE BEST NIGHT OUT IN TOWN

that he asked the waitress for me to come out of the kitchen so he could give me a kicking. I was, er, busy, and didn't have time to receive my hiding, but I told the waitress to inform the kindly gentleman that when I finished my shift, I would lock myself in the office and whip myself accordingly. This appeared to do the trick, and he was happy to leave, without us meeting, much to everyone's relief, including the 50 or so diners tuning into the scenario.

I went to see The Pretenders in Glasgow with Davo and Postie, the night before we were going to Liverpool and its Albert Bridge, sorry, Dock. Chrissie Hynde's band were superb, they rocked the ABC on Glasgow's Sauchiehall Street, a real tidy venue, apart from the height of the urinals in the bogs – I could've done with a box to stand on rather than trying to bend my hose over the top of the cold metal! I volunteered to take the car, and had myself a quiet night, with my mind on the long drive to Liverpool in the morning.

We had a great journey down, in glorious sunshine, and as we weaved our way through the city of Liverpool, we passed the famous Aintree racecourse, which held The Grand National, and Liverpool FC's ground, Anfield. The Albert Dock itself was very impressive, everything that we needed was so close to each other, and The Echo Arena did indeed look massive. The hotel was a building converted from an old factory that had served the dock; there were a lot of fixtures from those days still present throughout, it was very cleverly done. We were out in the sunshine in no time, sitting outside, with a cold bottle of beer in our hands, looking out over the dock, and into the Mersey. This part of Liverpool was stunning – I just hoped the Liver birds didn't fancy flying over us and opening their bowels! We relaxed into the evening a bit too much, we hadn't eaten and the beer went straight to our heads, and by the time we were ready to get ourselves into the massive Arena we were both a bit more than wobbly. The Dock was surprisingly quiet, but there was a crowd outside the bar at the nearby Jury's Inn, they looked like Poguey people, but apart from this, it was quietish all round. We decided to have another beer at The Jury's Inn, and got talking to some of the scouse Pogues fans. Word was that the show had not sold well, ticket-wise; the locals were blaming high ticket prices, and a lack of publicity in the city itself for the gig. They were not exactly enthusiastic about the Echo Arena as a venue either. Sure enough, it looked like the attendance was going to be a sparse one, the VIP area to the left/front of the stage as you looked at it was, well, fucking surprise, empty. Still, no matter, the best night out in town was in Liverpool, and just because the place wasn't full would surely not spoil the night.

I've worked with a good few Scousers over the years, both boys and girls, and have always found them to be warm and friendly. Characters, with something to say. There was a family sitting in the row in front of me and Teresa; we were having a great chat, and a right good laugh – one lady in particular was laughing so hard she had tears in her eyes. Suddenly the mood changed, when whom I assumed to be her husband appeared, he'd probably been at the toilet or the bar, and he wasn't happy, taking exception to something I had said. The mood up until then was a very bubbly, good humoured one, but yer man changed all of that. His missus was trying to get him to lighten up, but he was still agitated. Fucking hell, after the carvery gig, I was getting good at upsetting folk. This situation was a strange one though, everyone was in good spirits apart from grumps. Everyone was quiet now, and as 'Straight to hell' came over the speakers, the angry bloke turned round to me, and offered to shake my hand, saying "Enjoy the show". I reluctantly took him up on his handshake, but I was fucking raging – in my view, I hadn't caused any trouble. Still, it was time to enjoy The Pogues – no one would stand in the way of that particular process! But I couldn't get yer man out of my mind.

The band were solid, and despite the pitifully low attendance, they more than did their bit and performed superbly. Shane was sporting a pirate's eye patch – I wasn't sure if it was patter or someone had poked him, but he looked the part with his ear rings. Maybe after the gig, he was planning on raising the skull and crossbones, sailing across the water, on the raft of the Medusa, to his beloved Ireland. Hell, even looking to gather treasure (gin, tonic and cigarettes) from another vessel on the way...OK, Ok, I'd had a bit to drink remember. And that was the problem with the demon I was currently facing. I'm ashamed to say I had this almost uncontrollable urge to rugby tackle the grumpy bloke, who was right in front of me, round the waist, and take my chances as we tumbled down the rows of seats. Thank fuck I didn't, but I tell you it was close. The consequences of that just do not bear thinking about for a million reasons; I'm really not a fighter, and this bloke would have not had a problem sorting me out, but I was angry. It was a relief when eventually the feeling subsided.

The Pogues' performance gathered even more momentum. I wondered how they would feel, with the place not being full, but that wasn't putting them off; it was a brilliant show, with a predictable but solid set list. There was no further incident as we left The Echo Arena quietly, everyone had enjoyed The Pogues. I guess that's all that really mattered. It's very rare for there to be trouble at a Pogues gig, so I'm really glad that I managed not to do my 'All Blacks' bit. It was a relief that the hotel was such a short walk away, literally two minutes, but once in the room, the night ended with yet another incident, when I accidentally tattooed the towel rail in the bathroom, and as it fell, it cut my foot open. It was time to go to bed. Night night!

A Christmas reveller at a party night in The Aviator asked for a cheese and biscuits platter, with no cheese. This request was checked with the customer, twice. She then complained that there was no cheese with her biscuits, celery and grapes!

Teresa and I had a night in Manchester after The Pogues show in Liverpool – we went to the dog racing at Belle Vue, and I managed not to upset anyone, honest.

Some parasite prick managed to upset me though, when we got home. A no doubt dodgy moustachioed, power hungry person, pointed their hairdryer at me on the motorway as I was driving to Liverpool and was now writing, telling me that they wanted 60 snips off me, generously giving me 3 bonus points for my driving licence and thus giving my insurers a Brucey bonus come renewal time! I had been doing 81 mph – didn't the moustache fucking realise that I was excited? I was going to see The Pogues, for fuck's sake, I didn't rape anyone!

My mother was in a busy mood. She asked me to help her, being busy, when I next had a day off work. "Yes, of course," I said. I wasn't expecting what she had in mind though. I drove Mum and Dad downtown, to visit a funeral firm. Mum was sorting out hers and Dad's funeral arrangements. As we sat in the small, tastefully decorated office, and Mum was sorting everything out, my father and I sat there, motionless, voiceless, like a couple of plums. I thought Mum was crazy – surely better waiting until something happened, no? Dad, when he did talk, told the lady at the funeral company, quite clearly, with a straight face that he wasn't dead yet! It was a weird experience, but Mum agreed a price with the lady, Jackie, and she said she felt good that things were sorted. This did nothing to kick-start enthusiasm from the two plums!

Teresa and I would usually go on a holiday abroad in the summer; however, things were changing at The Aviator, and we felt that we really couldn't disappear for two weeks at a time any more. The economic state of the country was affecting us, as it was everyone else, things were tight, and we decided that if we were going to take a break, then it would have to be a short one; we really had to keep on top of things to keep our business afloat, and in turn, keep us all in jobs. The natural option was a few days in London, so I booked up a trip on the fly, to give Teresa a wee surprise. The day before we were due to travel, I told her to go home from work early, and pack a bag for me and her. We were going away for three nights, and told her, "There are no more details at this point!" It took a while to convince her I was serious, and eventually off she went.

Next morning, I ordered a taxi, and had a word with the driver, before Teresa came out of the house. He dropped us at the bus station, and I told my puzzled wife that we were "roughing it" and were getting the bus, to our mystery destination. Teresa hates the bus. Her face merely confirmed this, but the taxi driver, after driving round the block reappeared and told us to get in; he took us the very short distance to the train station. We were booked in first class (told you, nothing else would do any more) and as we arrived in Edinburgh Waverley Station, I told Teresa that we were getting off. Once on the platform, I told her that we should get back on, or we'd miss our train! "What the fuck is going on?" was her subtle question. We went back to our original seats, and I revealed that we were actually going to Newcastle. Maybe. When we reached Geordie land, I didn't move, and told her just to relax, we were really going to York. Really. As the train left Newcastle station, some passengers who had just got on, occupied the seats opposite us; one of the geezers looked familiar, but I couldn't put a name to him. Never mind. The bloke was looking at us, or more to the point, was looking at the bottles of beer we were quaffing. "Where did you get them?" he said. I told him that we had brought them onto the train ourselves, but we had a few in reserve – "Did he want one?" That'll be a "Yes", and one of his mates too would like to partake, if you don't mind. The penny dropped, it was Anton Ferdinand, the Sunderland (at the time) footballer. We were soon engaged in conversation, he seemed pleased that I eventually recognised who he was, and a session was developing, as the train sped south. Bottles of wine and more beer was purchased from the buffet car. It wasn't our intention to get blootered on the train, but we would never say no to a party.

As we approached York station Teresa told me I could get off here if I wanted, but she was going to London, the same destination as Anton and his mates. Mr Ferdinand was actually delighted that Teresa had no idea who his brother was, Rio, who of course plays for Manchester United. She got a high five for her blissful ignorance. Anton told me lots of football related stories about Roy Keane and various other characters that had crossed his path, which I thoroughly enjoyed. We were all a mess with the drink when we got to King's Cross. Anton asked what we were doing later, and I told him we were planning to go to the greyhounds at Romford later that evening; I was so drunk though, I wondered if we would make it. He took Teresa's mobile number (?) and said he'd see us later at the dogs, as you do, after a drink or twelve.

We checked into the hotel. As the receptionist asked my name, I had the feeling I was squeaking rather than talking and I'm sure there were bubbles coming out of my lungs, I was plastered. We did get checked in though, and somehow negotiated a trip by tube and taxi to the Romford greyhound stadium, where I had booked a table in the restaurant for us. After a while, Teresa's mobile rang, Anton and crew were in the bar. "Where are you?" he was asking. We finished our meal, accidentally left without paying our drinks tab, honest, and sure enough, there was yer man and some pals of his in the bar. Another session unfolded, amongst betting on the canine athletes strutting their stuff. We had a great night. Anton was a top bloke; he was really good with the folk that approached him for pictures and autographs. He told me that the minute people stopped doing that, then he would feel shit, so he was grateful that people came up to him. I thought that was a really refreshing attitude. As we slurred our goodbyes, he assured us he would be visiting The Aviator in the future. Just before we left, a frantic looking fella had come up to me; I wondered what on earth was going on. It was the restaurant manager, waving our bar bill in front of my face. We had genuinely never given it a thought, and thankfully frantic mannie saw the funny side of the story as we squared him up, with a tip on top for his troubles.

Next night, another surprise was awaiting Teresa, I had got tickets for 'Fithy, Mucket, Disgusting Dancing', the West End show. I think every girl is a fan of the film, or rather Petrick Sweezie's pelvic region! I wasn't looking forward to it, but was pleasantly surprised to find myself enjoying the show; the people acting it all out were just so professional, and one young lad who sang had a voice that blew me away – he reached the high notes effortlessly... I'm sure his 'Primarks' were too tight! Teresa loved it, everyone happy then.

On our last night, it was my turn, but still a surprise or two for the missus. We went to – where else? – Sticky Fingers for our tea, and who were waiting for us in the bar, but Philip and Keith? Teresa was delighted. Philip told Teresa that we were going to a Karaoke bar after we'd eaten, and he had arranged for a car to take us there. Philip wouldn't be seen dead near any karaoke gig, so Teresa was suspicious, but went along with it anyway. A bloke that the lads worked with picked us up, and we were on our way, to karaoke heaven. As the car negotiated its way through the busy London streets, the journey was perhaps taking longer than Teresa anticipated. She needed to go to the loo. "No worries, we'll be there in two minutes," said Philip. Ten minutes later we were still in transit. "Just another five minutes," Teresa was told. We all got a fit of the giggles, which did her no favours whatsoever. We arrived at 'The Karaoke pub' which was actually Wembley Arena, and in we went sharpish, so Teresa could go to the ladies, still having no idea why we were there. A relieved Teresa returned, to be informed that we were about to see ZZ Top. I'm not sure what she thought of the prospect, but two guys with beards hogged the damned Karaoke machine all night! I'd seen ZZ Top at Brixton Academy, a good few years back when I was working in the South, and they were awesome – what a racket they made for a three piece band. Tonight was a bit disappointing, they just didn't sound as good, but the mystery game with Teresa kept us going. I'd actually booked seats in roughly the same area as we had seen The Pogues twice previously, all those years ago in the Arena. Positioned here again brought back many great memories, The Wembley shows really were out of this world, if only....!

At the end of the gig, it was my turn to be bursting for the bog. There was a massive queue at the gents and I couldn't wait any longer, so I went out an exit door, found what I thought was a quiet spot and relieved myself on the Arena wall, the pain just washed out of me. A female security worker had spotted me though, she wasn't happy, and as I shook the drips off my chap, she started running towards me, so maybe with a drip or two still left, I zipped up (steady) and was on my toes, back into the Arena to meet the others. She was actually chasing me, it was like something out of The Benny Hill Show, so I stopped, and asked the girl, "Can I help you?" She said that I was disgusting. "Yes, ok," I agreed. I asked her what she was planning to do regarding my disgusting behaviour. "Well, nothing," came the reply. "Goodnight then!" I said. I *was* going to be smart and say something about her ogling my chap, but I thought I'd better quit while I was ahead, or I'd be on a register or something. Philip's driver picked us up outside Wembley Arena and dropped me and Teresa at Hanger Lane tube station, to catch a train back into the centre of London, whilst the boys sped off towards Bracknell. The tube station was deserted, and our tickets were being rejected by the barrier, we were too far out of town, and in a zone we hadn't paid enough to be in, so with no one about, only one thing for it – a hoof over the barrier it was. I reassured Teresa by telling her not to worry, we'd be on Crimewatch next week. She was a lot more nimble than me getting over the damned thing; the giggles kicked in again.

A ZZ Top gig is obviously not The Pogues. Nothing like it. Christmas wasn't too far away though!

4 AM TURKEY!

Teresa was approaching the beginning of life itself: 40. Her birthday being right in the middle of December meant that this Christmas period was going to be more hectic than ever. The night before her actual birthday we were in Glasgow, at the Academy, to see some music concert or something like that. I'd written to Philip Chevron again, telling him playfully that this year was the big one, so c'mon, a happy birthday to Teresa was essential, at least. The Pogues were at the races again, big style, the gig was fantastic, Shane was immense, he really was lyric perfect, fuck, we really were so lucky to still be able to see this band live and on fire! Glasgow and The Pogues are like hands in good fitting gloves. The Academy is actually quite intimate, it's compressed in a good way, honestly, I'm boring I know, best night out...

Shane fucked off to the side of the stage, and a very dapper Mr Philip Chevron approached the central microphone. This was it then: shit or bust. Fucking Hell, he did not disappoint, howling into the mic, "This is for TERESA!" Obviously, the punters didn't know who Teresa was, but they roared back anyway; what a magical expression came over her face, a true memory to cherish, thanks to Philip Chevron. 'Thousands are sailing' never sounded so good, even though (whisper it) I still preferred it when Shane sang the song. We waited outside again, after the show; time was no object as we were in a hotel again – it was fucking freezing though. Word was that Shane was ahead of the game, and he'd gone already, sped away to the hotel. Philip Chevron came out of the stage door, I introduced him to "TERESA" and he laughed. Erm, the beer had kicked in, again, and as a hired help tried to take a photo on my phone, of me, Teresa and Philip, something was amiss. The bloody phone was on video mode rather than photos. The three of us were standing there like lemons, waiting for the click, but what we actually got was a funny video of three posers saying "cheese" for far too long. Philip's man assistant was adamant that he get out of the cold quick, so after a "Merry Christmas" he was off, into his waiting automobile, and on this occasion we were photo-less. James Fearnley was out next, he was in a hurry, but he did say to me, "I remember you from last year!" and then he was also gone. Andrew Ranken was out next, heading somewhere in a hurry, not the solace of the waiting cars though; Andrew was heading for the bushes, presumably for a leak! How I wished that I had a convenient bush outside Wembley Arena at the ZZ Top concert – a bush might have saved me the Benny Hill chase from cock snooping Annie!

Back at our hotel, the fucking fire alarm went off about 3 in the morning. The noise really was deafening in our room; it certainly did the job of getting you out of there, no matter how tired or boozy you were. We found ourselves heading down the stairs and onto the street; it was so cold, some folk were out there in flimsy pyjamas and nightwear, it was definitely tiny cock weather. We were out for a good while, before we were let back in to thaw out, fucking freezing I tell ya! After breakfast in the morning, we went to check out, there was a queue, and as I got nearer the desk, it became apparent that everyone checking out were getting their money back because of the fire alarm. I have to confess that the thought never entered my head, but I was onto it now, and I got our payment refunded also. I felt a bit sorry for the girl on reception, but I suppose it was no skin off her nose. The Premier Inn group would indeed survive. Nice to get the snips back though.

Back to work, a party night on the Saturday, and Teresa's 40th birthday party, also at The Aviator, on the Sunday night, where we closed the doors to the public. She got a tremendous response, numbers-wise, and we had ourselves a brilliant night celebrating her birthday. I've often thought that a good social night, right in the middle of a busy period is a wonderful tonic for everyone involved, to help get through it. Highlight of the night for me was a mass game of pass the parcel. I loved the excitement of that game as a kid; I think the party goers enjoyed it too. We stopped short of jelly and ice cream though. The party finished around 5 in the morning; we were keeping some hellish hours, and they were starting to take their toll.

We were busy for the rest of the week. I was all booked up as usual for Brixton, but I was struggling big time this year. The first show was on Friday 18th December. Two days before, I thought to myself that there was just no way that I was going to make it. We had a core of staff, every one of them a superstar in their own right – they had to be good, as during the tight times, they were asked to heighten the bar performance-wise, in order for the restaurant to survive. In the kitchen, it was now myself, Laura and Teresa when she could. We hired an Indian lad to do the dishes over the Christmas period, Chris was a likeable fellow, and a relative hard worker, but he was just fucking mad. He had no sense of time in regards to when he was supposed to start a shift – he would either turn up three hours early or, tragically, two hours late. It didn't matter how many times you went over his shifts with him, write it down or whatever, he just appeared when he appeared. We needed him though, so we went with along with it, and put up with his very suspect timekeeping.

Thursday came, the day before The Pogues in London, we were busy as fuck all day. We started work at 8am; I drove Laura and Teresa home at 11pm, then returned to the restaurant to do more preparation, to see them through the two days I was scheduled to be away, enjoying myself, at The Pogues. The last of Thursday's party goers left, as did the remaining staff, which left me in the kitchen, making soup, sauces, cooking salmon and carving turkey – this went on until 4.30 am. It was a really weird sensation being in The Aviator on my own at this time of day, night, what was it? Word was that the building itself was supposed to be haunted, some deceased pilot no doubt, but I was too tired tonight. If Mr Ghosty was going to make an appearance with his leather hat and goggles, then he could get on with it and do whatever he wanted, joy stick and all, I was passed caring. I got home at 5am, and started to get a bag together for London. I felt I had left the girls prepared enough, and I had told our Indian friend, Chris, that if he wasn't on time the next two days, then I would simply cut his bollocks off!

Teresa was sleeping when I got in, but she was full of the cold. I felt such a cunt, that I was pissing off to London, leaving her and the team to soldier on bravely, whilst I was whooping it up to 'The body of an American'. I had one more thing to do. When the Cash and Carry opened at 7, I was there as the shutters went up, to buy some more supplies, out to The Aviator again, then back home, a shower, a shave and some fresh clothes. Teresa was up and about, we talked, and she insisted I went to London. I felt awful, but before you knew it, I was on the platform at Perth railway station, waiting for The Highland Chieftain service, the very train that was going to take me down to The Smoke. I was desperate to sleep, but, of course, I couldn't. Teresa showed her class when she phoned me when the train was going through Peterborough. It was snowing heavily outside the train window. Teresa told me that lunch had gone well, and they were bang on track for the party night commencing in a few hours' time. Laura had stepped up to the plate yet again;, she and Teresa worked well together. Graham, a staff member who occasionally worked in the kitchen had helped out too, and Chris, well his bollocks were safe, for now. Teresa's phone call gave me a green light to enjoy myself. What can I say? It was not an understatement when I said I was selfish, when it comes to The Pogues.

Yet again, the train door swings open, the freezing London air, I could almost smell it, I really could; The Pogues are in town, time to wander the dark streets of London then, was it not? I'd booked the Premier Inn at King's Cross this time, Keith was not going to make the first night, so I just had a little bit of dinner in the hotel and made my way over to Brixton. As knackered as I was, I was always going to muster the energy to go and see The Pogues. I got myself a good seat and let the band's performance wash over me like a comfort blanket, and it felt great. The Pogues had added an instrumental to their set list this year in the shape of 'Metropolis' from their third album – it sounded brilliant live, with a big, loud sound incorporating the brass section, Philip Chevron treating us to some unorthadox dance movements mid song. Some of the band's instrumentals from their early albums would have been good to hear now and again, to mix things up a bit; word was that Shane didn't show up at rehearsals much, so I can understand why they had to stick to the faithful favourites with lyrics. But the band wouldn't have needed him for a 'Dingle Regatta' or a 'Wild Cats of Kilkenny'. Of course, Spider's 'Repeal of the licensing laws' was an ever present, and a very popular one, especially with the punters who loved James Fearnley's antics of jumping off the speaker cabinet on to the stage, then darting along the front, hoofing his accordion like a man possessed. By the time the Brixton shows came about, usually at or towards the end of the tour, you could sometimes see the knees of his trousers hanging down, like two pieces of material on hinges, no doubt a result of his frolicking to 'Repeal...'

As much as I enjoyed the show tonight, and I really did, I was looking forward to going to bed, for a different kind of comfort blanket: sleep. As I settled down, I was struggling to nod off; the room appeared to be freezing, I checked the heater and it had packed in. For fuck's sake. It was late now so I got some clothes on and went down to reception to see what they could do, if anything. The night manager was sympathetic, but couldn't do anything until morning – the hotel had full occupancy, so I couldn't be moved. I did my best to remain calm; I hadn't been sleeping since about 6.30 Thursday morning, and it was now 1.30 Saturday morning. I had a rotten night, the room was like an ice box, I caught a few dozes here and there, but as you'll know, if you're a poor sleeper like me, the harder you try, the worse it gets, trying to nod off. I wasn't happy in the morning. The night manager said he would move me to another room ASAP, which he did, although it took a while, and I didn't need to ask this time – he refunded the room tariff for the first night of my stay. I had breakfast and a hot bath when I changed rooms and actually felt remarkably fresh. As I waited for Keith, I just read the paper and watched some crap TV, dozing off here and there, but not for too long at a time.

I arranged to meet Keith in a Ladbrokes bookies in King's Cross; I was early and had a few bets whilst I was waiting. I'm glad to say, that I don't have a problem with betting any more – sure I still enjoy a bet now and again, but that's what it is, an enjoyment, I never let it take over, it's all about discipline. I am aware, however, that it would be really easy to fall into that trap again. If I'm having a bet and it's not going my way, I can now leave it alone, very quickly – that's the difference – rather than trying to chase my losses. In the bookies were a bunch of well dressed young lads, who were heading up to the nearby Emirates Stadium, Arsenal's football ground. They were going for some corporate match hospitality, and were clearly excited by the prospect. I got talking to one of the lads, and he told me that one of their party had failed to turn up at their meeting point, and the feeling was that he was definitely going to be a no show. He said to me, "Do you fancy goin' to see The Arsenal?" I most certainly would have sir, but I had a date with Mick McManus, and I didn't have suitable threads to hand to mix in with this group. It was a genuine offer, the bloke couldn't believe it when I turned him down – maybe his mate would turn up after all though, at the last minute.

Keithy did indeed turn up as expected, and we did our usual up in Kensington then onto Brixton for yet another wonderful Pogues show without too much incident of any note, for a change. Back at the hotel, the room had a double bed; Keith was looking at it and wondering how this was going to work. I said to him that I was past knackered and past caring. "Just get in." He was also tired from his Christmas shifts at the hotel. "Let's just skip the foreplay tonight," I told him. "Fuck off" was the reply. Of course the minute he got in I started clawing at him, lots more "Fuck offs!" were delivered my way! I slept like a fat royal king, after a feast; it was truly blissful to at last get some shut eye.

I was awoken though about 4 30am; the TV had a clock on it. Keith was up and about, probably going for a piss. What I didn't tell him though, was that the light for the bathroom was in the most unobvious place imaginable, half way down the wall, outside the actual bathroom itself – you had to actually bend down to reach it. If I had spoke and told him, that would have been us awake for the day; Keith would've talked and talked and that would've been it. I certainly wasn't ready for that yet, so I let him try and find the light. Listening to his frustrations and grumpy bellowing was funny as fuck; it took me all my time not to burst out laughing. He eventually disappeared into 'Lavatory noir' and negotiated whatever he was doing best he could. He was in the black hole for a good while, before appearing as a shadow, cursing as on the way back to his pillow he accidentally kicked the side of the bed, hurting his toe. He settled down eventually, and I made a note to be mindful if I was next in to the loo, just in case Keith had missed, then it was gratefully back into the land of nod.

We breakfasted in the hotel (Oz was never at his café at weekends, so what was the point?). Keith was grateful that the only sausage he had come across in The Premier Inn was the pork one on his plate! We had a few games of pool in the bar before we parted. I never let on about the light switch thing, but kept having a laugh to myself; I hope he didn't notice.

Back in Perth, when opening the mail and going through the Christmas cards, I came across a very unexpected, most fantastic surprise. Philip Chevron had sent me and Teresa a Christmas card, with a little note inside, thanking me for the letter regarding Teresa's birthday request at the Glasgow gig. Nice one Philip, very thoughtful of you sir, we cherished that card and showed it to everyone that darkened our door between Christmas and New Year, as you would.

We hosted a buffet on New Year's Eve, at a cheap price. Our thinking was, if we filled the place then obviously the bar would do well. And it worked. A young crowd was attracted, and indeed hammered the bar. We'd had a successful festive period again – absolutely essential to get through January and February, when business was desperate. Laura was doing great things in the kitchen; she was set for a big career in this catering lark if she kept her head down, and didn't get too involved with Abdul's meat at the kebab shop! Indeed the core staff I mentioned earlier had all been with us for a good while now, a settled team made all the difference; all the driftwood, staff-wise, was well down the river, a long time ago. Janice, Paul, Gary, Amy, Suzannah, Sammy, Graham, Jordan, Tony, Laura, Stevie, Stuart – you can all take a bow!

My old friend the solicitor paid an unexpected visit to The Aviator – you know, the one that said to me that we wouldn't last six months. It was really braw to see him. I gave him a very over the top friendly welcome, that went right over his little soliciting head. It had been three and a half years since we'd seen him last. Bless!

SLIPPING AWAY

Your parents. Some are better than others I guess. I was lucky. I
was cared for and looked out for when I was a child. Parents have a
massive influence on a young person's whole life, how they turn out
to be adults. They are not responsible, however, for their offspring
doing runners from taxis! I really was naïve enough to assume that
most families were much the same, and that all parents cared deeply
for their children. One day, whilst I was working in the South, a work
colleague and myself were engaged in conversation about a trip to
Perth I was about to embark on. I was enthusing about the prospect of
seeing my mates, a Hibs match and of course, spending a bit of quality
time with Mum and Dad (and eating PROPER stovies!). I asked my
mate, who was from the North of England, when he was going home
next, and he almost chewed my head off. He didn't do going home, as
he actually didn't like his parents, he'd always been better off without
the home/parents thing. He told me there had been no contact with
his family for years; he was a little older than me, and I just couldn't
understand this scenario he was presenting. How could your own flesh
and blood not know if you were doing well, shit, alive or dead? It was
not something I could understand at the time – just how naïve can you
be?

A good while later, I was on a train one day, and had bought a copy
of 'The Big Issue' magazine, not one of my regular purchases, but the
boy selling it had some quality patter about him, which he used to
maximum effect to increase sales. As I was flicking through the pages,

there was a section in the middle, which had details of four separate missing persons, and their families were looking to get in touch. My eyes about popped out of their sockets, when here was a photo of yer man, the one I had been talking to at work about not so happy families – his family were looking for him, and the message from the written script was one of concern. I handed the magazine to Philip, my boss; this was way over my head, I'd already upset this chap when 'blowing' about how good my trip home was going to be, so I handed this over to Philip, who always knew what to do. And I didn't mention the Big Issue gig again. Maybe I was starting to mature just a wee bit, keeping my big mooth shut, just for once. There were actually a lot of staff in the catering industry, who lived away from 'home' who were very much on their own; they just, understandably, tended not to talk about their family situations a lot. I really was lucky to have parents to go home to, especially if things were to go wrong...damned taxis again!

Into Summer 2010 – my mother in particular appeared to be struggling a bit with the everyday chores. Trouble was that Dad was becoming more withdrawn; he wasn't helping her with much around the house, things were changing from their normal routine. The first thing that was to give us a hint to where the problem may have lay, was actually the washing up of all things. This had been Dad's 'job' in the house for as long as I could remember, and he had introduced a new trick of washing the dishes and pots in cold water. Eventually he blocked the sink. Mum had a regular plumber that she used, but he was busy and Mum would have to wait a few days before he could sort the sink out. I'd never seen my Mum so stressed, and just over a blocked sink. Even when the plumber did his bit and the sink was in working order again, Dad would still use cold water, no matter how many bollockings he got from his wife. Looking back on it now, it was the first clue he was revealing of his dementia; none of us, Mum included, really knew what was going on with him.

When they went away for a wee holiday, usually still to Southport, they would go on a 'Blue rinser' tour, but even that was becoming difficult for Mum, as Dad would leave just about everything for her to sort out; the packing and all the other things you've to organise around a holiday, was just too much pressure for her now. So I arranged to take them away for a few days, they could get a change of scenery, and I could do the organising bit for them. I hired a fancy car and off we set, for hopefully Sunny Southport. We stayed in their usual hotel, The Scarisbrick, on Southport's main street, they'd been staying here for years now, having upgraded themselves from the holiday flat on the seafront. We stayed just the one night, but had a lovely time; Southport will always be a special place for our family.

Next day, we were on the move again, further down country, destination Bracknell, to stay a couple of nights with Keith, and catch up with him and Philip. Both Keith and Philip knew my folks quite well; over the years Philip has spoiled my mother rotten, with flowers, lobsters and of course, whatever her favourite sherry might be at the time. Well there were no lobsters around, as we stopped at a service station somewhere on the M6, to grab some overpriced, shite food, as you do. Mum and I ordered up our well suspect nourishment (she would probably be thinking more of the fag to be lit afterwards no doubt) but Dad wouldn't say what he wanted. This continued to the point where we were almost falling out, he just wouldn't say. I really didn't know what had got into him. In actual fact, he wouldn't tell me, because he couldn't – he didn't know how to choose something from the menu. Mum had gone off to find a seat, she would normally say what he would have, like she had done in the restaurant on the previous night, but without that, Dad was snookered. Of course, I didn't understand this, to be honest. I thought he was taking the piss.

As our short trip continued, more and more strange events involving my father unfolded. He appeared to have little concept of time; he would rise from bed in Keith's house at 3.30 or 4 am. On one of those mornings I heard my mother roaring at him, "Get back in here, you bloody idiot!" He was rolling about on the carpet, trying to get both his legs into one leg of his trousers. Yes, there's lots of funny incidents, but Mum and I still didn't really know what was going on. When we got home, he got back into synch and settled down a bit, familiar territory and routine obviously got him through his day, and of course we thought he was relatively OK again. He did though, start to get worse; it was a slow process. I felt really sorry for him one day when I took him to the Post Office to get his pension. He'd totally forgotten his PIN for his card; he was devastated, and it didn't matter one bit me telling him that I forgot my PIN numbers all the time, it was as if the Post Office event had confirmed to him personally, that he was in trouble. As you can imagine, Mum had a terrible time with this, but it was another thing for her to accept help, which she clearly needed – trying to convince her of this was very difficult. Teresa and I upped our game a bit, and helped as much as we could, in between running the restaurant, where we had to increase our own working hours, due to the general economic decline that was affecting the whole country.

I went up to their house one afternoon. Mum was in her bed; she wasn't feeling too good. She was a tough old bird, she wasn't guilty of hogging the waiting room of the local doctor's surgery – her way of getting better, if she wasn't in the pink, was to sleep; it always did the trick, just total rest. Whilst she was in her bed, Dad just sat in the living room; apart from making a cup of tea now and again, he wasn't really any use at looking after her, and certainly couldn't make dinner or whatever. As it was getting near to the time they would have their evening meal, I cooked him some dinner, made Mum comfortable and left them to it. She'd have to let him wash up with the cold water tonight!

Next day, Mum was still in bed, and Dad was sat in the living room. I knew, from the look on my mother's face, that sleep wasn't going to be enough this time. I'll never forget that look, I still think of it often. Dad told me he was hungry, he hadn't had his lunch, unheard of before in this house – this merely confirmed that something was seriously wrong in the Bruce household. I went against her wishes, and was called everything, as I arranged for the family doctor to pay her a visit. She had high levels of calcium in her blood, this had floored her and she had to go for a week's stay in hospital, to sort this out. Her bottom lip was protruding as the ambulance came to pick her up; she was more worried about the neighbours twitching at their curtains to look at her, than anything else. As she was admitted to hospital, the weather took a dramatic change for the worse, we had snow like we hadn't seen for years, and it actually did us a big favour, as the roads that led to the restaurant were undrivable, so we closed up for a while, giving us time to see to Mum, and look after Dad. I couldn't drive my car, the snow was just so deep, so Teresa and I, and a very physically fit father, had regular hiking trips, through the snow to the hospital.

It was on the second day of her admission, with just me by her bedside, when a very insensitive lady doctor came to see her, and told us that Mum "May have cancer". She said that a specialist would be round in a short while, to talk to us some more. We didn't talk for a while, God knows how she felt. I was just numb, but, let's see what the specialist was going to say, and we'll take it from there, I was trying to think myself positive. We were given this news at 10 am. I sat there all day with her, it was an extremely long day, but, by 9 that night, there was still no sign of any damned specialist. I lost the plot, and asked the head nurse what was going on, regarding the cancer, she apologised for the insensitivity shown by the doctor earlier and was honest enough to tell me that the specialist was not on duty today. She did though, confirm to me and Teresa, who was now present, that Mum did have cancer, it was well advanced, it wasn't looking good for her. Deep down I knew it would be bad news, but neither Mum nor I appreciated waiting all day for a specialist that wasn't even in the building. Indeed, I was actually quite shocked, at how much of a shambles the hospital was in. None of us, thankfully had been to hospital for a while, things had changed, all the fuss they make about hospitals under performing on the TV news was actually pretty accurate. I'm not politically inclined at all, but I think it's a crying shame, the mess our health service is in now. It was perhaps the one good thing left on these islands that was worth keeping right. No fucking chance, with the self funding, egotistic, greedy individuals that are running our country into the ground these days. Cunts, the lot of them!

Mum was in a ward of six and it wasn't long until she was holding court again with her five new comrades. As she started to feel better, she formed a bond with her fellow patients, sharing out the chocolates and magazines that we brought in for her. When the food came round, I had to tell her to be polite when refusing certain things; her face told another story. I was just grateful that the hospital version of stovies did not make an appearance. We didn't tell Dad about the cancer, he didn't understand too much about the hospital – that was apparent during a visit, when he announced that he was away for a wander, "To see if there was anything exciting happening!" On our way out that night, he duly got his 'Excitement'! We passed a room that had a single male patient who was howling in pain; before you knew it, Dad was in his room, singing along to the bloke's painful wails, waving his hands like an orchestra's conductor, or as Shane himself would during the instrumental part of 'The Broad Majestic Shannon'! Fucking Hell. I had to grab him and get us out of there and as quickly as possible, before there was a hospital stewards' enquiry. God only knows what the poor bloke that was ill thought; I'm quite convinced that my father did not make his day! Mum's negotiating skills were responsible, I think, for an earlier discharge from hospital than expected. We got her back home and she was remarkably perky, once she settled down; she was delighted to be back in her own domain. Her timing was perfect, as it was Pogues time again, with Christmas approaching.

This one though was different. When the tour was announced, after the euphoria had passed in regards to them doing it again, a grim realisation hit home, with the words that accompanied the various dates, 'Farewell Christmas tour'! Fuck, was this 'IT' then, the end. What a thought. Spider posted on The Pogues' website something about the band members dragging their bones around a frozen island in December, Philip Chevron contrastingly hinted that it could be the first of their farewell Christmas tours. Isn't that what a load of premier artists have done in the past, farewell after farewell – a little bit of hope from Philip Chevron then, thank God! Better make the most of this one though, just in case.

Mum was doing all right. She had a conversation with me, telling me with no uncertainty that she did not want radiotherapy or chemotherapy. This would have meant a jaunt through to Dundee, and for no doubt endless hanging around the hospital there. She couldn't face all that and I respected her wishes. Nothing was going to save her from the inevitable, she wanted to be at home, and I think she made the correct decision. It was still difficult for her to accept help, but she got on really well with her downstairs neighbour, Ann, and reluctantly agreed for Ann to keep an eye on her, when I was busy at work, or off on Pogues duty.

We booked a smart hotel in Glasgow, quite near The Academy.

There was no let up in the weather, there was plenty of snow still around and the temperatures were always away in the minuses. The gig was fantastic – how could this be the end? Farewell tour – it was just wrong. A massive highlight of the show was a very unexpected 'Waltzing Matilda'. Of course, I was weeping in no time, after I'd given way very quickly to the lump in my throat. This band, Shane in particular, really knew how to do emotional. I wasn't the only one moistening the atmosphere with tears – I saw more than a few blokes unsuccessfully fighting back their emotions. Shane's recollection of the lyrics was a bit shaky in parts, but it took nothing away from the song, the reaction the band received at its conclusion merely confirmed that their decision to include it was a masterstroke, a real treat for both the hardcore Pogues fans and the newer ones too, who had probably never heard it live before. Awesome.

I phoned Mum during 'Dirty Old Town' so she could hear it at home, the audience singing along word perfect with Shane, 'The boy' as she called him. I got emotional again at the end of the show, as Shane was addressing the crowd, as he always did, "Thanks a lot, goodnight, good luck, Happy Christmas!" Surely this wasn't to be the last time I would see The Pogues in Scotland?

Another thing that was becoming routine was me and Teresa going round the back, to try and get a crack with our heroes of the night. It was absolutely Siberian fucking freezing by now; coming out of the hot, sweaty venue, it was a sure fire way of getting pneumonia. James Fearnley was out first, but when he realised just how cold it was, he immediately retreated back inside. I heard him say to someone, "I need an 'at!" He appeared again with some nifty headgear; he wasn't hanging around though, but I did manage to grab him for an express photo. I told him to try and look as if he was enjoying himself, and he duly obliged. That was three times I'd seen James, and I still hadn't managed a decent conversation with him, through my sherry intake and now the weather – yes, I know, perhaps he was trying to tell me something! Teresa and I had a great chat to a bloke called Eddy, who was one of the band's drivers. He spoke very fondly of Shane in particular, and told us that behind all the hellraising that people seemed to focus on, he was just a great guy, with his feet firmly on the ground when it came to the fame thing. Eddy wore glasses, but when Teresa wanted her picture taken with him, the gregorys were off, the hair was sorted, then Eddy was ready to pose. He was a nice man, there was a flurry of activity at the stage door, some folk got into his car, and he was off. Jem Finer came out, and I got a photo with him. I felt honoured. Jem didn't talk at all, it was as if he really didn't need to – what a presence, I was grateful for his pose.

We hung around a wee while longer, hoping to see Shane but we had to surrender to the Glasgow chill. I honestly couldn't ever remember being this cold in my whole life, it was Baltic – it's a wonder my cock didn't freeze, and fall off! We wearily negotiated the relatively short walk to the hotel, my cock survived, and we tried to get warm. The morning arrived a bit too quickly. During breakfast, discussing the night before, we both agreed that what we had witnessed was simply the best – nothing to do with Glasgow Rangers whatsoever, simply the best – well, that would be The Pogues then, wouldn't it! Their concerts in Glasgow really were the dog's bollocks, and there was still Brixton to look forward to, providing my mother was OK. The way business panned out at the Aviator meant, that for once, Teresa was going to London, to see the Pogues, in big bad, scary Brixton.

What wasn't lovely, still, was the climate, the one that Spider was talking about. The train service was in serious doubt, and it was touch and go, due to the snow and freezing conditions, whether the Highland chieftain service would run between Inverness (via Perth) to London. Thankfully we got there, an hour and a half late, to find Keith already waiting for us outside WH Smiths on the King's Cross concourse. He wasn't expecting Teresa to be there, I hadn't told him. His opening line to her was "What the fuck are you doing here?" Swiftly followed by, "Since we're in King's Cross, how much is it?" Teresa told him it would be £75, "for a smile"! Keithy must have been thinking of the Colgate wifie again, that he had a very brief flirtation with last year. Into Chateau Travelodge, Keith with a room and bed to himself this time, and a quick tube train to Brixton. Teresa loved the neon lit dome outside, all the things that I had been telling her about, she was experiencing for herself now, and she marvelled at how vast The Academy in South London was compared to its Glasgow cousin. I've seen The Pogues so many times at Brixton Academy, and I have a real soft spot for the place. Philip Chevron describes the venue as 'Home' when he has a chat to the audience before 'Thousands'. I kind of know what he means. I don't know the exact statistics, but I wonder if The Pogues have played any other venue in the world, as many times as they have played Brixton's Academy.

The beer was flowing; it was a relief that we'd made it to the gig after all the usual planning and expense, the bar was doing its usual trade when The Pogues are around – terrible influence this band has, on some of us trying to embrace a modern, healthy lifestyle. It's just not the same without a wee snifter. The gig was terrific again, at a sold out Academy. Teresa loved the atmosphere; we were in the first row of the balcony, and we remained seated, taking it all in, sometimes that was cool, especially when Shane and the boys were on the same wavelength, and everything clicked. Shane was getting to grips with 'Waltzing Matilda', practice makes perfect I guess, it's a long song time-wise, and they had adapted it a bit to make it slightly shorter. I just didn't want it to end though, fucking marvellous stuff, let the tears just flow – as usual, I wasn't the only one. I seriously wonder how many other bands make their punters cry with emotional happiness through their live music? Hello? Hello?

Teresa loved the tube journey back to King's Cross; there was a big sing-song tonight, 'Streams Of Whiskey' making its second appearance of the night, the carriages bursting with well oiled Pogues people, very uncool London tube behaviour, the way it should be, wonderful, even more so, as it takes my mind of the claustrophobia thing.

Over to see Oz in the morning, he took a shine to Teresa in an instant. We could sit in his café all day, his patter is just the best, and his Oz special is not good for someone trying to lead a modern, healthy lifestyle, but after the beer, it certainly does the trick, setting you up for the day.

The King's Cross area of London is, of course, where it all began to happen for the finest band that's ever played music. The place is steeped in Pogues history, just up the road a bit from Oz's and the Travelodge is a bar/live music venue called The Water Rats. This establishment was once called The Pindar of Wakefield, and it was here that Pogue Mahone played their first proper live gig. I'd never got round to checking the place out, but today was going to be the day. The three of us were in just after opening time, and of course had to order a round of drinks. This was not beneficial, to someone who was trying to embrace a modern, healthy lifestyle. The barman showed us through to the gig room and put the lights up for us; being in there felt nostalgic, and Keith and I were up on the stage in no time. The drum kit and microphones were already set up in preparation for the next live band. I pretended to be MacGowan for a moment, standing at the central mic, but I wasn't fooling anyone into thinking that I could write or sing like him. There's a lot of music memorabilia on the walls, of various artists that launched their live musical careers here. The barman told us Bob Dylan played his first British gig in this very place; disappointingly, there's nothing to be seen to mark The Pogues' performances here. I actually have an advertising poster, in my collection of Pogues items, for a gig at The Pindar – one day I'm going to try and sort something out, and get them to display my poster, which I would be happy to donate. There should be something to commemorate The Pogues at their old stomping ground.

Just across the road from the Water Rats is Cromer Street. Shane had a flat here, detailed in James Fearnley's book; there was a strong hint that he wasn't fond of housework. A little bit further up the road is Burton Street, where various band members actually met each other for the first time. The road was full of dubious squats. There is no evidence of anything like that there today – the street is very upmarket; a shed there would probably set you back £50k.

Later on after our silent 'gig' in the Water Rats, we went up to Knightsbridge, and met Philip at The Rib Shack. It was a surprise for Teresa and for Keith! I'd arranged it with Philip. We had a few beers and a big meal, which was not harmonious with someone who is trying to embrace a modern, healthy lifestyle. The Rib Shack is sadly no longer there nowadays. It was a smart bar and restaurant, not unlike Sticky Fingers, without The Rolling Stones theme obviously. It was Keith's round for dinner tonight, this place was anything but cheap, and he got stung. Of course, after a few beers, and suitably relaxed, we found this hilarious. I offered to pay at Oz's in the morning! If it's not your day Keith, it's not your day, and it didn't finish there!

A Pogues gig is not for Philip, but it was an opportune, enjoyable get together, and we said our farewells then treated Teresa to the overhead train from Victoria to Brixton, down the stairs at the dark railway station that strongly smelt of piss. Things were rowdier in the Academy balcony tonight, but I had a horrible feeling all through the gig, that this could be the end. I lapped up their every song, but suggested we went about halfway through 'Fiesta' – I didn't want to wish the band goodnight, maybe for the last time; we would get away quickly on the tube.

A rather boozy Keith was patting his pockets at the entrance to the tube station; the patting became frenzied. When trying to locate his Travelcard, to his horror, the realisation was hitting home that his wallet was gone. Keith wears his jeans around his knees – it's the worst case of workman's arse you've ever seen in your life, with full crack on view most of the time; it would be no problem to park a bike in there! I can't help thinking that some bastard helped himself to his wallet from his back pocket at the gig, it was pretty rowdy tonight, it would have been easy pickings right enough for some tealeaf twat. We turned around, back towards the Academy, fighting our way through The Pogues throng. The staff at the venue were very unsympathetic to poor old Keith's plight. The wallet hadn't been handed in. He could have lived with the cash being taken, but it's the cards and the mountain of inconvenience that hurts. It was a rather solemn tube journey back to King's Cross tonight, The Pogues public long gone, leaving us with the late birds of London town for company.

In the morning, I sorted Keith out with some emergency cash at Oz's, then it was back to Perth on the train. It was running three hours late with disruption caused by the weather, but we were lucky, as the day before there had been no trains whatsoever heading north from King's Cross due to frozen points and power lines.

So that was it, the end of The Pogues farewell Christmas tour – for us anyway. I sincerely hoped, prayed, that it wasn't the absolute end, when it came to seeing the best night out in town, live, and in all its glory.

A TERRIBLE TUESDAY MORNING

Early in January 2011, Mum fell over in her kitchen at home and broke her hip. It was a major setback as she had been doing all right, despite the cancer obviously still being present. As usual, she was trying to do too much. I guess there's a bit of that in us all when we're not well, to try and carry on as if everything is normal, prove you can do it. She ended up being confined to her bed in the same position, and in quite a bit of pain, hardly a bundle of laughs. This time though, we did have to get help in, there were carers that came four times a day to wash her and see to her everyday needs etc. She was seen weekly by some absolutely dreadful district nurses (I really really hope that this lot have retired if I need this sort of help one day!) and our most brilliant family doctor came to check on her regularly. Teresa and I were as ever present as much as we could be. It was a particularly bad time for Dad, because of his dementia he didn't really know what was going on but obviously knew something serious was up. It was just a really bad scenario and Mum hardly had a minute's peace.

It's natural, so they say, to take things out on the ones you love first and foremost. Mum was going through a hard time, and, due to her nature, she was always going to be a terrible patient. I got the sharp end of her tongue frequently, although nobody did more for her than me. I'm not for one second blaming her, but I was pushed to the max at the time trying to keep everything going, and getting it in the neck from your Mum when you're so tired is hard to take. There were a few times that we had 'words' – something I feel very bad about now, if you consider what she was going through, but it was difficult hearing her being nice to everyone else and being jaggy with me a lot of the time. We only live along the road from Mum and Dad, and, as always, a bit of humour is never far away even in difficult circumstances.

My mobile phone rang, it was about 4 am; she seemed distressed, so I told her I'd be along to see to her in two minutes. Mum was wide awake, but something was troubling her. "Where's that horrible dirty bloke?" she asked me. I told her that I couldn't see any bloke. "The bloke with the mucket military uniform, big black hat, he's drunk all my whisky and his cigars are stinking!" What could I say, except to reassure her that the bloke appeared to be gone now. "That's good," she said. Then came: "What time is it?" "Twenty past four in the morning, Mum." Her reply was fantastic: "What the hell are you doing up at this time of day? Get to yer bed!" The morphine she was on to numb the pain was starting to play tricks with her mind – some of the things she came out with and the manner in which they were delivered were priceless.

Sometimes, when it was just me and her in the house, I would sit with her in her bedroom. She got tired quickly if we were talking, so she used to tell me to go through to the living room, but said that it was good knowing I was in the house. There's only so much tidying up you can do. It was such a busy time, that sitting on my arse in the living room felt a bit alien. So, I decided that when I was red carded to the living room, I would start writing a book...

The staff at The Aviator were very supportive, and Teresa was a rock for us all. I was very fortunate to have such a caring wife. I really don't know how Dad and I could've got through this difficult time without her.

With all the care and support in place for Mum, and latterly for Dad too, our family doctor suggested that I back off a bit, and let the various people do their jobs, so me and Teresa decided to go through to Glasgow for a night, just for a break, hopefully to come back a little refreshed and more able for the tasks lying ahead of us. Mum's neighbour again said she would help by keeping an eye on both her and Dad, which was the assurance I needed to take a temporary back seat. When I told Mum we were going away for the night, she was surprisingly quite ok about it, which I didn't really expect. She didn't seem her usual self though. Although she was very ill, morphine excepted, she kept her wits about her all the way through; there just seemed something different about her on the day we left for Glasgow. I'm not suggesting she was glad to see the back of us, because I just know that wouldn't be true, but she seemed very happy with herself, it was just strange.

So through to Glasgow we went, on the train, with a couple of newspapers and a small beverage to hand. The relief was amazing. We checked into the Jury's Inn hotel, down by the river, where we had stayed the previous December to see the mighty Pogues. We had a cracking room this time, very high up, and you could see for miles right over Glasgow. When I was taking in the view, I kept looking towards the Glasgow Academy. I could see the building clearly, where the Pogues held their Christmas concerts, and every time I looked all I could think of was of James Fearnley throwing his accordion about, entertaining the audience, but sadly he was probably in America somewhere, not giving a second thought to Glasgow or its Academy. We just had a few drinks and a rest. After we went to bed, Mum's neighbour rang me, and indeed confirmed that Mum had been acting really strange, not settling at all in her bed, but far from being upset, she was deliriously happy.

We got back early afternoon next day, and I went to see her straight away, and indeed she was away with the fairies. We didn't understand what was going on with her, until one of the brilliant carers, Jackie, told us that this was a common thing that happened when time was almost up. What a thought. I didn't want Mum to suffer, I really didn't. But I didn't want to lose her either.

She deteriorated badly over the weekend. I had no choice but to work on the Sunday, but Teresa stayed with her, and looked after Dad. It looked ever more likely that she could leave us at any minute, so Teresa called me at work. I dropped everything and drove to the house like a madman. Mum wasn't really conscious as such, she knew we were there but she couldn't talk to us. I said to her that she was the best mum a boy could ever have, and that I was very grateful for my upbringing. She lifted her hand and stroked my face. It was a lovely, but heartbreaking moment. We stayed with her through the night, her mouth was constantly open so every now and again we had to put a wet swab into her mouth to help keep her comfortable. Her breathing was erratic and it was awful just watching her in the last throws of life. Every now and again, I would say to her, "Mum, it's ok, just go to sleep." There was an instant reaction to this whenever I said it: she vigorously shook her head. You just wonder where she mustered the energy from to do this, but her message was very clear – she was fighting. She made it through the night with little change.

The next day, Monday, Davo came up to see her and say his goodbyes. She couldn't react but I know she knew he was there. Davo was upset when he left. I'm so grateful to him for coming up to the house. The man is too busy for his own good these days, but he made time for Roselle. Laura from the Aviator also came up to see Mum on the Monday. For someone so young, she was an amazing support to the Bruces. She used to talk to me in the kitchen at work about Mum and was mature beyond belief at times.

Our doctor organised a Marie Curie nurse to come in on the Monday night to sit with Mum and keep her comfortable, so Teresa and I could sleep. We were exhausted and hadn't slept since the previous Saturday night. We slept in the house, in the living room; while it was good to close my eyes, I was also kind of aware of things at the same time, and I don't think I drifted off completely. I went to the toilet around 6 am, and the nurse told me that in her experience, the end was near. Teresa and I went through to Mum's bedroom and sat with her. Just before she took her last painful breaths she squeezed both our hands. And then my mother left us, and this world we still lived in, on this terrible Tuesday morning.

Of course it doesn't hit you, not really; it just doesn't sink in, the magnitude of the event that has just happened. By this time, Dad had been attending a day centre on weekdays, he really enjoyed it and it gave us a wee break. He didn't understand what was going on with his wife, and even when I tried to tell him, he just didn't get it. So he went to the day centre as normal.

The family doctor came round and certified Mum's death. Of course, she had most of her funeral arrangements organised – I can't help thinking that she knew her time was almost up before she became seriously unwell. Big Les had sent out some messages, as I mentioned in a previous chapter, and I've since heard a few cases of people doing things or holding heavy conversations with loved ones some time before passing away, almost as if they know. Two fellas from the funeral directors came up to the house, and dressed Mum in some clothes Teresa had selected for her. They made her look nice, and they made her look peaceful. We followed her out of her house, her family home for the past 35 years, for the very last time. That Tuesday morning, was the greyest, rainiest, most depressing day weather-wise we'd had for a long time, and it stayed like that all day, it was just so dark.

We had to go to town to register the death, it was all very difficult, but I wanted to be as organised as possible, because I wanted to get her funeral just right.

When Dad came home from the day centre, I think he twigged something awful had happened when he looked at Mum's empty bed. It was such a shame, he looked desperately under the duvet, under the bed, anywhere he could, but I still don't think he believed she was gone. We then had the task of phoning everyone to tell them the news; nothing was easy, but had to be done nevertheless. Mum was a very popular lady, and her funeral was going to be a big deal.

She lay in the funeral home, and the first time Teresa and I went to see her, it actually wasn't as bad as I expected. I got a tremendously strong feeling that my mother had gone somewhere else, and the body in the coffin just wasn't her. I took comfort from that, when I least expected it.

We set the date for her funeral for the following week, Wednesday afternoon. Cousin Scott was travelling from Dubai to attend, Keith and Philip from Surrey, so we thought this would give everyone time to organise themselves. Mum's wishes were to be buried at the local cemetery, about half a mile from the house. She wanted a humanist to carry out the service, as she wasn't religious, and this was to be done at the graveside. Then back to The Aviator, our restaurant, of which she was so proud, to celebrate her life.

There were many new emotions surfacing, I couldn't believe how Mum wouldn't need her possessions any more. Her hairbrush, her clothes, the phone; I didn't expect how sad I would feel regarding her stuff. On the Sunday before the funeral, I went back to the funeral home, by myself, to say goodbye for the last time. Dad just didn't want to go in, and I didn't push him, no one knew for sure how much of this he was understanding, so he and Teresa stayed in the car outside. We were going to Dundee, I had ordered a new suit for the funeral, and I was going to pick it up. There wasn't much happening in the way of conversation in the car, it's about a half hour journey, so I put 'If I should fall from grace with God' onto the CD player, and I cranked up the volume. Before you knew it, the three of us were singing along, Dad was clapping his hands, our feet were going, all in time to the most excellent music you've ever heard – the lift that The Pogues gave us that afternoon was close to a miracle. I was enjoying it so much I actually felt a little guilty. None of the three of us will forget how The Pogues made us feel that day, and give us a major bit of relief, during a very difficult time. That playing of that album will live with me forever. It was the first time our faces had broken into smiles since that terrible Tuesday morning; listening to the CD gave us a bit of renewed strength. The power of The Pogues' music within my family can never be underestimated.

We closed The Aviator on the day of Mum's funeral, and the night before we put large blown up photos of her, showing happy images of events and good times in her life, all over the walls of the bar. Teresa picked out one particular early photo of her; it was just passport size, and was a bit worse for wear, nevertheless it was simply stunning. She was quite a looker in her day – it would have been nice if she could have passed a bit of this on to me, but I think she forgot! This was the photo that we chose to make a card with, for the friends and family that were coming to pay their respects. A mate of mine, John McKinlay, ran a successful printing company in the town, and he organised the blown up photos and produced the card. What a brilliant job he made of it, it was perfect; he is a real master of his trade, no mistake. To take a small, scruffy old photograph, and turn it into what I thought was a work of art, was simply amazing.

The service was starting at 2pm. Keith and Philip arrived in Perth that morning, so there was just enough time to meet them briefly before we all had to get ready. I was particularly touched that they put their work aside, at the other end of the British Isles to pay their respects to Mum, and support me, Teresa and Dad. Cousin Scott travelling from Dubai, well what can you say about that? The hearse with Mum's coffin arrived at the house and we made the journey following her in another fancy car to her final resting place. I remember, as we travelled through the streets, an elderly gentleman stopping in his tracks, before removing his hat, as Mum's car passed him. The look on his face was one of extreme sorrow. The cemetery was packed with people, a lot of faces I was actually surprised to see – what a great effort everyone made.

The service itself was delivered beautifully by the humanist; he was an Irish chappie and his accent and manner was spot on, there was a bit of humour in his words – Mum would have definitely approved. A sales rep, a lady called Valerie who used to visit me at the restaurant, gave me some good advice on how to get through the part when we lowered the coffin into the ground, and it was highly invaluable advice, I can tell you. She told me that if I was starting to well up, to take deep breaths, and say to myself, "I'm a Bruce, and I'm proud of my family." Quite simply it worked, and I managed to hold it together, just. Teresa, Philip, Keith, Davo, cousins Scott and Kevin, my good friend Geoff and I slowly lowered Mum into the earth and it was over. In my favourite Pogues song, 'Lullaby of London', there's a wonderful Shane MacGowan lyric at the end. "May the angels bright, watch you tonight, and keep you, while you sleep." These words also gave me the strength to throw my red rose into her grave, and be able to walk away from her last resting place. I hope you had the angels briefed about my mother, Shane. And this is the song that I told you about earlier that I wanted played at my funeral, I wasn't thinking about it in regards to my mother's, but the support Shane's lyrics gave me personally, cannot be emphasised enough. The whole thing was surreal, it was difficult to take in and it went so quickly.

Back at The Aviator – again she had a really healthy throng – to have a wee glass of something, a sandwich and a sausage roll, as you do. We got everyone's attention and Davo gave us all a lovely speech about the character that was Roselle Bruce, and his personal experiences of their discussions and the odd playful bollocking he would receive from her. I asked Davo to do this, and I just knew he would not disappoint; his speech was perfect. At the end of his delivery, we both lit up a Berkley cigarette (neither of us smoke) and had a glass of her favourite sherry to toast her. The sherry was murder, and the cigarette didn't last long either. Yes, this was inside the building, therefore not allowed actually, but you'll remember that little fact never stopped Mum from sparking up inside The Aviator – her and Shane, fighting for the cause, to schmerk!

The rest of the evening was very pleasant. People started drifting away, until the 'heavyweights' that liked the bar were left. We played a lot of Mum's favourite music, she loved Buddy Holly and of course she loved The Pogues. We let loose a greatest hits album and we sang along, we had a dance, and we toasted the life of my dear mother; the Pogues always gets it going! At a social gathering of any kind, Davo and I are usually heard to say, "Get the fucking Pogues on!" The poor barman, Graham, was handling the pressure. "They ARE fucking on!" he would reply.

People have very differing views of how a funeral should be. I received many, many comments that Mum's family had done her proud from start to finish, and I know it's the way she would have wanted it. I do feel the day went well, some folks think that drinking and socialising after a funeral service is taboo and I respect that, but Mum was all about socialising, and if there were a few snifters involved, then all the better.

Teresa, Dad and I left The Aviator while there were still some people there; that's what I wanted to happen. When I said my goodbyes to Philip and Keith I completely broke down, then it was home, to sleep. Keith, as you'll expect by now, still had a hand to play, more of which later. I sometimes think I should have named this book, 'The adventures of Keith Clifford Williams'!

It was March, 2011. The year had started tragically, my mother gone. The rest of the year was, however, to get a bit better, thanks once again, to The Pogues.

Interview with Darryl Hunt

@ David Lally

One of the true unsung heroes of the greatest band that ever played a tune, is our Darryl, the bass man. He's kept his youthful looks over the years, and has been an ever present, right up until The Pogues called it quits, well after Shane's departure. His performances are solid, yet he keeps out of the limelight somewhat I feel. Darryl was actually around The Pogues long before he started plucking those thick steel strings on his guitar under the lights of the stage. In fact he was one half of the duo Pride Of The Cross, somewhat ironically with Cait O'Riordan at one point. Ironic as it was Darryl who eventually replaced Cait, when she hung up her plectrum to go and marry Elvis Costello. Before this, however, Darryl had many tasks to oversee with The Pogues. He would twiddle with the sound controls and generally organise the band, when they were on a circuit of live shows. One of Darryl's many tasks was to drive the van, taking the band to gigs. This may sound like a straightforward enough task, but when you consider the personnel involved, I'm quite sure it was anything but!

Word is that Darryl, when steering the van of refreshed musicians into a new town or city, would look for the football ground or grounds relating to where they were, the high floodlight pylons giving the driver an obvious clue. Quite right, Darryl, I think I speak for most of us football fans, when I say that it's one of the first things that comes into our football 'nuts' when visiting somewhere new that has a football club resident. Darryl's team is Nottingham Forest, something he had in common with Philip Chevron.

I had an idea that I put to Darryl, relating to his football way of thinking. Years ago, in 'Shoot', the popular football magazine, there was a page where a particular player was 'lightly grilled' on his likes and dislikes. I loved this page, finding out all kinds of essential information like favourite colours and food. Steak and Chips, if I recall correctly, was always to the fore. Nothing wrong with that by the way!

So here we are, dear reader, an insight into the world of Darryl Hunt, with some vital, and some not so vital, information on what floats his boat. As I expected, his answers are entertaining, but serious when it comes to the football based ones. It's all here, and I can't thank Darryl enough for his co-operation. Enjoy!

MOST MEMORABLE EVER POGUES SHOW?

Darryl: Manchester Central (2006/7?).

FAVOURITE POGUES SONG?

Worms.

FAVOURITE JAMES FEARNLEY STAGE MANOEUVRE?

The one he executed against the Russian lad in Iceland years ago – a very famous chess move it was!

DO YOU PREFER USING EMULSION OR GLOSS, WHEN PAINTING YOUR HOUSE?

Can't use either because I live in a submarine, strictly sonar deflecting stuff is all she'll take. Up periscope! ! !

FAVOURITE VENUE TO PLAY A GIG?

The Wag Club.

FAVOURITE ARTWORK ON ANY POGUES RELEASE?

Fall from Grace.

YOU'RE A NOTTINGHAM FOREST FAN. DID YOU EVER MEET CLOUGHIE?

Sadly not, but I think I saw him play for Middlesbrough once when I was nowt more than a nipper. I'll have to check my old programmes.

FAVOURITE ALL TIME FOREST PLAYER?

John Robertson.

ARE YOUR NIPPLES OR BELLY BUTTON PIERCED?

No, only by accident. Had a narrow escape in Dallas, Texas.

DO YOU HAVE ANY PRE-SHOW RITUALS OR SUPERSTITIONS?

Only eat venison boiled in Guinness before a show.

FAVOURITE SHANE MACGOWAN HABIT?

Laughing.

CUSTARD SLICE, CHOCOLATE ÉCLAIR OR JAM DOUGHNUT?

All together in one great melange.

BOXER SHORTS, THONG OR Y FRONTS (FOR YOUR FEMALE FANS)

Pantaloons, with special support for my gigantic balls.

ANY FEARS? CLAUSTROPHOBIA, HEIGHTS?... SPIDER?

Falling out of planes without a parachute.

WHAT CAR DO YOU DRIVE, WHEN YOU'RE ON DRY LAND?

A triumph amphibious car, i never know when i may run out of dry land.

FAVOURITE MUSIC / ARTIST?

Today it's Chuck Berry and Marcel Duchamp.

IF YOU CAME BACK AS AN ANIMAL, WHAT WOULD YOU CHOOSE TO BE?

A gorilla.

FAVOURITE LONDON TUBE STATTION.
This week it's Embankment.

YOUR SPECIALITY IN THE KITCHEN?
Today it's fish curry.

HAVE YOU EVER HAD A PUNCH UP AT THE FOOTBALL, DARRYL?
WERE YOU EVER A NOTTINGHAM FOREST SOCCER CASUAL?
I was always too casual to react.

AND FINALLY, ARE YOU GOING TO READ MY BOOK?
If I'm in it, then yes, for sure!

DAD

The moment my mother died, one of the first things that hit me was the fact that my father was now a widower, and that Teresa and I were directly responsible for him. It was almost as if we now had a child. We have never had kids – we did plan to when we got married, but it just didn't happen, without it being a problem for either of us – it's just the way things went. Poor Dad couldn't do much for himself, and we had in theory been looking after him for a while anyway during Mum's illness, but he had lost his wife of 49 years and needed round the clock support. Forty-nine years married: a real shame that they didn't see the 50. However, Mum got a bit confused near the end – their anniversary was in January and she told a couple of her cronies, wrongly, that it was indeed their 50th, and as a result there were a flurry of cards and flowers on the 15th January, so she did indeed experience a 'Golden wedding anniversary'. That was just like her, to pull a stunt like this, quite brilliant really. None of the well wishers were any the wiser.

Dad had enjoyed a more privileged upbringing than my mother had experienced in Aberdeen. His father was a successful fish merchant in the Granite City – I didn't realise how successful, until recently, when I came across an old black and white photograph of the fleet of fish vans he owned. Grandad Bruce was a bit of a boy by all accounts – he loved a drink, so much so, that he actually drank all his hard earned money, and pissed it against the wall. If I manage to make a few bob with this book, then in the interests of family progression, I promise only to drink half of the money! Dad and I were never particularly close. I'm not saying for one minute that we didn't get on – we did – but I was always closest to Mum. I'm hopeless at things like DIY. Dad was teasing me about this one day when I was home for a visit from the South. I defended myself by complaining that he'd never shown me any of that kind of stuff, so no wonder I was shit at odd jobs round the house. I thought no more of it. I was away to see The Hibees on the Saturday, it was an all day session, navigating my way to my bed around 2am. The next morning, around 6.30 am, Dad was in my room, curtains open, a wet cloth in my coupon, he was shaking me awake. I felt as rough as fuck. "What the fuck are you doing man?" I asked, more than a bit concerned for my own safety. "Oh, I just thought I'd show you how to cut the grass!" was his measured reply, a huge smile on his face, as he disappeared!

Mum had told him once to talk to his son about the birds and the bees. I overheard her telling him to get the job done. This sort of thing was awkward in our house, and I was thinking to myself that I could really do without any of that. When the moment came for our chat, I got in there straight away. "I know what you're up to, just forget it, we're not having this conversation, just tell Mum that we did!" He was both surprised and delighted. It turned out to be a brilliant deal for all parties, one of the best I've done. There was to be a twist though when, a few months later, I had been out, and on my return home, the house was in total darkness, the front door was unlocked. Very strange. I was met by various items of clothing spread around the house, most of which was on the floor. Even my old man's wallet was present, in amongst the trousers, shirts and, JESUS, a bra! The house was in total silence. I took to my bed in an instant. Next morning, when I rose, Mum (who was never up this early) and Dad were in the kitchen, looking sheepish. Mum started the conversation off with, "Last night, son..." I put my hand up, stopping her in her tracks, and told her that I now knew all about these things, Dad had explained everything to me recently, and that I really didn't want to know any more, thank you very much. Dad's face was a fucking picture – maybe the DIY skills are not there, but I'm sure he appreciated the way I had handled the two rounds of 'The Birds and the Bees'.

I was still looking at Mum's possessions, and just couldn't take in the fact that she didn't need them anymore. I thought to myself that she would never be phoning anyone ever again, never smoking a fag again, never visiting places she had been to in the past, ever again. The bed that she had died in was still made, I could still smell my mother, it was strangely comforting. One morning I bit the bullet, stripped the bed and fed the sheets and pillow covers into the mouth of the washing machine. Dad was in the kitchen, eating his breakfast; he was totally unaware of my heavy weeping and upset state. As I was clicking the washing machine into life, he came over to me. I thought that maybe he did understand what was going on, but he didn't. He was over looking for another piece of bread. It would have been so comforting to grieve a bit with him, but he just wasn't getting what had happened, and wasn't aware that things had changed forever. I wasn't blaming him, I felt sorry for him. Maybe though, it was a good thing that he didn't quite understand what was happening. There was to be a twist to that scenario though in later times.

One of the first things we arranged after Mum's funeral, was a wee trip for me, Teresa and Dad, a change of scenery, but somewhere where we had friendly faces to visit. So we booked a few days down South, travelling on, yes, the train, staying in the now named Savill Court Hotel, less of a tongue twister than The Anugraha. It was here of course that we had held our wedding reception, it was here that I'd worked with Philip for almost ten years, so it will always be a place close to our hearts.

Dad is a master blagger; he still is to this day. When he meets someone who knows him, but doesn't remember who they are, he can act out a scenario where he looks at total ease with the situation, even saying all the right things, "Oh it's great to see you, how are you?", then a little later, to me, "Who on earth was that?" We spent some time with Keith and Philip, and with Teresa's parents who still live about a mile from the Hotel, in Englefield Green. One night, they were good enough to look after Dad, so we could have a night at Sticky Fingers with Philip and Keith. The driver was hired again, and we had a great night. Keith and I usually have a bit of a carry on once we've had a few – Philip turns a blind eye to this – we try and crack each other's fingers, but tonight, there was an addition of full blown slaps to the head! Every now and again, out of nowhere, there'd be a "Whack!" followed by a "You Bastard!". We were both pissing ourselves laughing through the pain. We picked up Dad from Teresa's parents, and he was right in the thick of the horseplay; he loved a carry on like this, if it was cracking fingers and a bit of shoving, then Dad was yer man, although we didn't do the slap head thing with him.

We stayed at Keith's house one night, history repeating itself, Dad away for a wander, starting at 4 in the morning, somehow being drawn to Keith and Berrit's bedroom. Keith goes to work early, and no matter how I tried to tell Dad that he couldn't go in there, he just kept going back. Berrit was fine about it, but the mind boggles at what he might have walked in to! Dad was in a right sulk, right up until he was tucking into his poached smoked haddock, at The Savill Court later that morning, his bedroom breaking and entering long forgotten, as his breakfast hit the spot! The trip was not a total success, Dad didn't settle – we had tried to do something nice, the three of us, after Mum's passing, but we were learning that everything was getting narrower due to his illness.

We still had the restaurant to run. When I look back on it all now, I really don't know how we managed to keep everything going, but somehow we managed to get through things, day by day. We were still trying to get to grips with Dad's illness; we still didn't totally understand what all was going on with him, and his dementia.

We improvised things by taking Dad out to the restaurant with us regularly; he was quite happy pottering about in the kitchen with me. He dined in some style when he was there, the waiting staff always making a fuss of him with plenty of laughs never far away. One Sunday, it was me and Father on kitchen duties. I was quite busy with a steady stream of punters needing their lunch, when I got this order on for a table of two: 2 x soup, followed by 2 x haddock. No problems there, an easy one for me. I served the soup, and put two nice pieces of fresh breaded North Sea haddock beside the deep fryer – I would cook them when the soup was cleared, so they would be perfect and piping hot. When the waitress breezed into the kitchen and announced that Table 2's soup was cleared, I went to the fryer to place the fish in to cook. No sign of the haddock. I was quite busy, and thought to myself that I must have left the fillets of haddock elsewhere, so I started looking – still couldn't find them anywhere. Dad at this time seemed to be very 'industrious' over at one of the sinks. I went to see what had made him so obviously busy. He had the two aforementioned haddock fillets in the sink, with a good dose of detergent, hot water and a green scouring pad – well I'm sure you can imagine how that looked. I burst out laughing, with Dad following suit until there were tears in our eyes; it was a nice moment. I'm glad I managed not to get angry, and have a go at him, even if he was close to putting me, as they say in kitchen terms, of being in the shit.

Teresa and I stayed at Dad's house for a while – one thing that helps people with dementia is routine. There was never going to be a chance of Dad staying in our house, just along the road – he got restless if he was there for too long during the day, never mind stay overnight. He still craved independence from us, but he just wasn't able to be independent. We tried talking to him, to explain how things had changed since Mum had died, but sadly he couldn't understand that he couldn't look after himself, and was having none of it.

Saturday night at The Aviator was predictably our busiest time as a general rule, so Dad used to come out with us in the morning until late afternoon. During this time, I would do as much food preparation as I could, but when four o 'clock chimed or thereabouts, Dad had had enough and we had to go home, leaving Laura and Teresa to do the busy service at night. Not ideal, but they always managed. Teresa had never claimed to be a chef, but her starters and desserts were actually clinically excellent. Laura always delivered the goods, in whatever situation – she just thrived on pressure.

On one of the first Saturday afternoons that Dad and I went home, he was telling me in the car that he wanted to spend some time in his house on his own. I reluctantly agreed, so I got him settled in front of the television and told him that I'd be back in a couple of hours and we would have some dinner. No problem, so I went along the road to my own house to catch up on the glamorous task of the housework. This had been slipping lately with our new busier schedule and the house looked like Beirut High Street on market day. Anyway, music while you work, The Pogues on the stereo and off we go, dusting, hoovering, washing, cleaning the toilet and…my mobile phone goes. Number withheld. So I answer to a stern voice asking if they were talking to Calum Bruce. "Yes, that's me," I replied. "Who's this?" The voice tells me it's the police. They were with Dad, in his house, with the downstairs neighbour. So why were they phoning me is the question. Well! It turned out that the minute I left him in his house, Dad went for a wander, first down to Tesco to buy some bread to feed his beloved birds in the garden. On leaving the store, he got disorientated and walked a mile or two in the very wrong direction. The police actually found him wandering about, on the road, near the Broxden junction, a major roundabout, the busiest one in Perth, that links the city with routes both north and south – he really couldn't have chosen a busier road. He was clearly lost. A police car had passed him and the officers had sussed that he was in a state of distress, and thankfully picked him up. He managed to tell them his address and upon arrival to his house, the neighbour filled in the blanks, so to speak.

I was along to Dad's house like a whippet, and felt really guilty as I explained the situation to the sympathetic policemen. They took some details and were on their way, leaving me and Dad to have the biggest row that we'd ever had. If I still didn't fully understand his condition, we both nevertheless understood perfectly our uncomplimentary descriptions of each other that afternoon. I left my househusband chores, and hung around with an agitated father. Saturday night, with nothing much more to do except cook dinner and settle down to Saturday night TV for the first time in about 20 odd years. Fuck me, Saturday night TV really IS shite! Dad eventually went to bed, and when he was settled, I locked him in and went back to the restaurant to help with the clearing up after a busy service. Dad told me that the reason the police picked him up and took him home was because they thought he was a professional crook! Nothing I could say would persuade him otherwise. I made up my mind, there and then, that I would have to take his key for the house. This led to the very unfortunate but necessary situation of when I left him in his house, I had to lock him in at all times. I'm very aware that this was far from ideal for all sorts of reasons, and I received a lot of unwanted comments from various people because of it. But, there was definitely less chance of there being a fire in the house than him continuing his burglary hobby, and wandering the highways.

Eventually we settled into a pattern where Dad went to a day centre, for people with conditions similar to his own, from 10am until he came to my house around 3.30pm, Monday to Friday. This was great as Dad, for the most part, really enjoyed it, even reaching the dizzy heights of chief bingo caller! He had a good pal in the shape of Tom, who used to drive the minibus that took Dad back to ours. Tom would often say that if they could go back a few years, my father and he could have run the town of Perth with fear being their game, a bit like the Kray twins had in London in years gone by. Dad would puff his chest out when Tom spoke of this, and pull his best menacing, facial expression; it was brilliant, he was so serious. Whenever I saw Tom, I would sing to him, "Big Tom is still the king" a line that I borrowed from Shane MacGowan's track 'Rock n Roll Paddy'. When Dad was in the day centre, it freed me and Teresa up to go to work and see to our general chores, knowing he was safe and happy was a tremendous comfort. On his arrival at 3.30, he chopped up bread for the birds, then we had our dinner, and it was along to his house to settle down for the night. Dad would normally go to bed about 9 ish; however, sometimes he had no concept of the time of day we were at. This was a real nightmare. He would demand that I take him to his 'work' (the day centre), I would tell him it was shut, but always ended up driving him there so he could see for himself. The situation would escalate into him refusing to go to bed – this could go on until 3 in the morning.

It was obvious that Teresa and I needed more help with the situation. It was a really long haul but the appropriate authorities and a social worker arranged for Dad to go into care for a week, to ease our situation. The help that we received with Dad was good and we were very grateful, but it wasn't without endless meetings and very complicated paperwork so I couldn't help thinking an old couple on their own, wouldn't have a hope in hell. There must be some grim situations for old folks all over the place; it's a sad, sobering thought. The journey through the meetings and form filling included Dad being assessed by a doctor on the state of his mental health, with a part oral, part written examination. I accompanied him to this meeting and as usual with Dad, it wasn't without the odd touch of humour. The doctor asked Dad to write a sentence, so he wrote 'Write a sentence'. Technically, I think he was correct. There were lots of questions like what day of the week is it, or what county are we currently in, spelling words, some of them I think I would have struggled with. At the end of his test, Dad turned round to me, more than a wee bit pissed off, and said to me "That bloke didn't know hellish much about anything did he? I even had to tell him what day it was! Makes you wonder how he can get a job – what an idiot!" The sincerity of his outburst was priceless.

Something where there was no laughter whatsoever was a return to the dribbling. If you've digested my tale of learning to dribble, a wee while back, my point to the story is merely confirmed with this. Mum's estate wasn't complicated, there was only me and Dad left regarding immediate family, there were no disputes, but it was a bit of a journey still, to sort everything out. I had a power of attorney document, which was to save our bacon in lots of ways, both financially and regarding my say in welfare for Dad. I'm not going to bore you to death with the details, just make sure you have one of these present in your family affairs. That's probably the most important sentence you've read in my book.

However, we're now going back to the subject of dear old insurance, life insurance this time. When trying to sort out my mother's, after she had passed, yes, you've got it, I was connected on the phone to a young dribbler. We were getting nowhere, so I ended up, stereotypically, getting very angry with young dribbling Jim, who refused to put me through to someone who might have known how to handle my call. This went on for some time. His crowning glory was about to happen, when he started asking me some baffling security questions that were indeed stupid, cryptic and very annoying. I was just about to explode into more abuse, when, I kid you not, dribbling Jim said this to me. "If you're not sure of the answers to my questions, perhaps you could ask your mother!" There you are, that sums up the world of dribbling insurance firms in an instant. To be fair, it wasn't totally Jim's fault, he was not up to the task, and was feeling the pressure as our conversation went on. WHY do people like dribbling

Jim get to go 'live' in the call centre, especially with sensitive issues such as life insurance. If Jim and I were face to face that day, I would have been arrested, and it would've been a mess. Eventually, I spoke to dribbling Jim's supervisor, who sorted it all out very quickly; it wasn't complicated, it was not large sums of money we were talking about either. Insurance companies quite simply are the scum of this earth; it's actually getting worse as time goes on. I hear of more and more tales, that they'll try anything not to pay out claims, just so they can hire more people to dribble at their phones. Fucking Bastards!

I felt awful about Dad going to a care home for a week, but the home we chose, after visiting them all, we thought to be a good one. I had to think of Teresa, who supported me 100% with everything; we needed a break, especially her. Dad's week in the care home came and went, he was elated to get home, but once this wore off, it was all back to the usual routine. One weekend we had a real problem because Laura had booked some time off, meaning I had to be at The Aviator all day Saturday with Teresa, and with Dad. We were doing all right until about 6.45pm. Dad put his coat on and declared he was going home; he'd make his own way, six miles to the house no less, maybe fit in a bit of house breaking on the way. We had about 40 people booked for dinner, first table at 7pm, and always picked up more 'chance' diners on a Saturday night. I knew there was no persuading Dad to stay any longer, so I got into gear in a flash, and bundled him into the car for an express lift home where I would have to leave him, locked in, again. He was insisting on walking himself, so I had to force him into the car, which did not go down well. I drove like a madman, all the while Dad letting me know I'd made a big mistake in putting him into the car like that, and he was going to make me regret it. Thank fuck he was prone to forget the odd thing here and there! Once we arrived at his house, I got him inside, and then drove madman style again back to the Aviator, where we had a couple of orders on for food – talk about getting there by the skin of your falsers! Once we'd finished at the restaurant, I went back to Dad's; he was still up, and none the wiser of the evening's earlier events. I got him settled, and we all slept happily ever after, well, for the rest of that Saturday night/Sunday morning, which was very welcome as I think we were all exhausted.

Dad was 85 years old at this point, he had brilliant willpower. He had a dodgy time, when he was about 60, with his health, so he decided to stop drinking. He loved a red tin of McEwan's Export and a nip of Grouse whisky. He would use the old twin tub washing machine in the kitchen, as his bar. He would stand there and listen to that awful Scottish music I told you about. As the drink hit the spot, he would very gradually slip down the machine a bit further. This would escalate, if he was flush with cash, when he partook in a single malt, along with his McEwans. He gave all this up though, instantly and religiously when he decided the time was right. Earlier in his life he had smoked tabs, and this was given up too, as it did not complement his weak chest. A doctor told him to stop smoking, so he did, simple.

There wasn't anything he could do about his present condition though, just the cards he had been dealt, but in many ways, looking on as I was, this was a real cruel illness – nothing emphasised this more than the fact that he kept forgetting his wife had died, he would ask me where she was, and I would have to tell him. It was like he had to go through it again, time after time. I would take him to Mum's grave, and it would bring it all back to him; perhaps it wasn't the right thing to do looking back on it.

One sunny day though, again, he gave us some welcome amusement in the unlikely setting of the cemetery itself. There were lots of people out that day, tending to their lost loved ones' graves, as we were with fresh flowers. I always keep Mum's grave in tip top condition. Dad looked down at the ground, where Mum is buried and shook his head, "Well, she must be dead by now, nobody could survive under there for that long without air or water or anything!" I started laughing, Dad did the same, the woman next to us was absolutely horrified and hastily made an exit from the scene, which made Dad laugh even more. I was trying very hard to stifle my laughter by now. What a man!

I would visit my mother's grave daily, and still do. I often go for a walk to the grave, taking different routes, through woods and along those little lanes running through council estates that I haven't walked by since I was a kid. It brings back a multitude of memories, nearly all of them good. I was so lucky to have good parents. I often look at the kids today, and I would say that a lot of them don't have a hope in hell in this world, through no fault of their own. This fucked up country, combined with the unfortunate home environment they find themselves in, will see to that. Unlike when I was a kid, they can't go out and play football in the streets or in small areas of green grass anymore. There's too many dangers to do this now. No wonder we don't produce any Kenny Dalglishs, Joe Jordans, Pat Stantons, Archie Gemmills or, erm, Derek Rodiers any more (might have to google that last one, dear reader!).

Dad had been allocated four weeks a year in the care home, respite for me and Teresa; he was looked after, and he was safe, fed and watered. This was handy if work was hectic, or, if something was in the offing that took us away from Perth. That something was promising to be a fucking cracker – it didn't get any better than this!

SEA SHANTY IN GREENWICH

In the office at work one day, pissing about on the computer, the mouse took me to The Pogues website, to see what the latest was with the boys. They'd completed a ten date tour of America, and had summer dates scheduled for Europe. Wait a minute, what's that? Greenwich? Greenwich summer sessions, Saturday July 30th. I couldn't believe my porkies, oh how the internet is just wonderful.

Greenwich is always a place Teresa and I visit when we're in the smoke; we love it there, with its market, pie and mash shop, the Cutty Sark and a wonderful Wetherspoon's pub, The Clock Tower, where you can sit outside and watch the world go by in this very smart area of London. The views down by the River Thames are fantastic. There's so much going on in Greenwich – it's also home to The Royal Navy College, one of Greenwich's most famous landmark buildings, with its two golden domed towers. And this is where The Pogues were going to be playing, live in Greenwich, happy, happy, days!

Without further ado, I booked three tickets for the event. They were pushing those VIP tickets again, at inflated prices, and for what? Well it looked like the VIP bit was access to a bar! I did push the 'tea clipper' out a little bit though, when I bought tickets for the Grandstand, whatever that was – I thought that we would have the best seats in the house for this special gig. I researched the summer sessions thing a bit more; this was their second year of holding the event – it consisted of three or four dates during a week in the height of the summer. This year included Status Quo, Mark Ronson and Squeeze, with my old mate Glenn Tilbrook who played those two songs for me in the kitchen at The Bein Inn years ago. An added bonus was that The Buzzcocks would be supporting The Pogues, the session's headliners on the Saturday night.

After the trauma of what we'd been through lately, I was in the mood to spoil Teresa when I made arrangements for our summer trip to London. Teresa is a lot more fussy than me when it comes to hotels and accommodation, so I really went for it this time, swallowing very hard, and booked The Grosvenor Hotel in Victoria. My credit card almost combusted when I coughed up, then it told me to 'get tae' when I booked us on the train, first class. As you'll realise by now, we love getting the train to London. It was time to re acquaint ourselves with that corridor of purple foxgloves that lined the train track that would take us all the way down to the big smoke. I'd usually do a 'Darryl Hunt' on the train and pick out all the football grounds we would pass. For those of you interested, we passed Hearts, "Hibernian! Hibernian! Ra ra ra!", Berwick Rangers, Newcastle United, Darlington, Peterborough and Arsenal. I would point these grounds out to Teresa; she was not remotely interested.

The hotel staff at The Grosvenor really looked after us from the minute we walked through the door. We were treated to drinks on arrival, and were then shown to our suite! I didn't expect any of this; maybe the fact I had booked for five nights swayed the manager to give us a lovely room, right on the top floor. Teresa was impressed. We had a great build up to the Saturday, gig day; the weather was fantastic and we met Philip and Keith at Sticky Fingers and had a night at the dogs at Wimbledon. There's a bookmaker at Wimbledon, who Teresa and I always have a right carry on with. Of course, these days my stakes are a lot smaller than when I had my little problem with the gambling, and this jolly chap is forever taking the piss out of me, when I put my fiver or tenner on. He has an assortment of 'lines' that he addresses me with as I place my bet with him. "Oh no, I'm not going to eat for a week, now you've started betting with me", "I'm sending the boys round to sort you out, I know where you live" and a few others, all on the same subject, him being 'scared' of my bets. We have a load of really brilliant banter all evening, it never lets up; he's just so entertaining. For the record, I reckon I'm just ahead with him, but I'm very sure that he still eats very well indeed!

We paid Oz a visit, of course, and had a night in Highgate at The Boogaloo, where Shane had once hung out for a while, when he had a flat up there. They always had live music on, and it was always decent. There's a courtyard at the back, with written lyrics from songs on the white tiled wall. Shane has two sets of lyrics on the wall, one from 'The Broad Majestic Shannon' and one from 'Rain Street'. If there was a let up with the live acts, the jukebox is a cracker there too – apparently it was influenced by Shane and Spider.

The day before the gig, Teresa and I went down to Greenwich for a wee recce of the venue itself, The Royal Navy College. We spoke to a lovely lady called Karen, who was head of security – one got the impression that underneath the polite exterior, there was a person not to be messed with. She told us all about the format of the next day's events, and how it was all coming together; it was actually quite interesting to hear of the round the clock organising that went into something like this. We said our cheerios to Karen, telling her that we may bump into her again tomorrow. She warned me, playfully, that I should be on my best behaviour when Pogues time arrived.

Saturday comes, a beautiful thought, when my eyelids prised themselves open, realisation kicks in (slowly in my case) where am I? Oh yes, today we are going to Greenwich, a Naval theme was never too far away from The Pogues' catalogue of music.

Keith arrived in town, checked into his hotel in Victoria, and it was off to sea we went, catching the Boat Train to The Embankment, rather than Circular Quay. A quick starboard glance, up the river, when awaiting The Irish Rover to arrive, you would see The Albert Bridge, but with no Misty Morning to block the view. Captain Teresa Bruce, with her eyes as blue as the water in the, erm, Thames, and her two jolly men, boarded the craft that was said to be a Floating Hell – did she have Greenwich Whale Fisheries in her mind today? Probably not, the way she was quaffing her bottle of Becks! We were wary of previous deceased Captain's Corpses, throwing their arms around our necks – the thought of that might make me want to go for a crap, and become a bold shithouse poet, adding my regal scrawl. We heaved and hauled away, right round the Cape Horn of the Isle of Dogs, to South London, where I wasn't born. There was no sign of The Broad Majestic Shannon, but I had a feeling we'd be hearing about it later! We reached Greenwich and its unbarren land, we told Kitty the ticket collector that we must go ashore; we were early, and wondered if Thousands would be sailing, to dear old Greenwich, later in the day.

We settled outside The Clock Tower boozer, it was a beautiful summer afternoon, and life felt quite good again. I got the first round in at the bar, Keith had his usual 'Wreck the hoose juice' Stella, and after his first sip promptly spilled it all over me. I was soaking, but Keith was giving his almost empty stemmed glass a more concerned look, than he afforded drookit me! No matter, nothing could dampen the mood, not even Keith's beer. We slowly got ourselves into Pogues mode; during the afternoon, I thought to myself that I really wouldn't want to be anywhere else in the world, than outside this boozer, in Greenwich, with a small function at The Royal Naval College pending, fucking marvellous! On the next outside table to us were sat three, tasty, Souf London geezers. We ended up having a great crack with them; one of them was a Millwall fan. You wouldn't have wanted them as enemies, that's for sure, but we were having a great time in their company.

Meanwhile, Janice, from The Aviator, was attending her own music function that day, an absolutely horrendous event, called the Eighties Rewind festival, held in the grounds of Scone Palace. Such little treasures as Right Said Fred, Holly Johnson and Chesney Hawkes were the 'mercurial' artists hired to entertain the crowd. JESUS! What a thought. I'd rather scoop my own eyes out with a teaspoon! Having said that, we gave her a ring on her mobile. Her event had already started, and we asked a pissed Janice who was next up on the stage. Steady yourself for her reply, the one, the only... Mr Rick Astley! Can you believe that BLOKES that I know, actually attend this pish! As soon as I told the company that it was Rick Astley that was coming on, all of us, to a man (and captain Teresa) broke into a Millwallesque chorus of "Never gonna give you up, never gonna let you down..." and we all sang it word for word, in perfect harmony! And here's me slagging the fucking thing off! I think Janice was impressed, even though she could hardly string two words together.

It was almost time to navigate our way to The Royal Naval College; we reluctantly bade farewell to our new pals; they were great lads. I exchanged mobile phone numbers with one of them, but ultimately cocked it up. We've been back to the Clock Tower many times since that day, and unfortunately not run into the boys again – maybe one day; I really hope so! One permanent punter that is always in the Clock Tower though, is this charming old fella, who we always have a chat with. He's a war veteran, a lovely bloke; his stories are so vivid, that on your way out, you have to dislodge the shrapnel that's lodged itself into your body!

On arrival at the west gate of the college, we met head of security Karen again; she was well aware that we'd had a few – well I did warn her that The Pogues and a wee drink went hand in hand. She told us to enjoy ourselves, ok then Karen, really shouldn't be a problem. The Grandstand was as popular as The Pope leading an Orange Walk – it was a makeshift structure at the side of the stage, and was occupied mainly by people, I felt, who didn't really want to be there. I had tried to do the right thing by getting slightly 'better' tickets, but no matter, nothing was spoiling today. There was a healthy crowd in the Naval College grounds, The Buzzcocks appeared and played a solid set, everything I wanted to hear, lots of their excellent singles from days gone by. I really admire Pete Shelley, a no nonsense guitarist and vocalist, with his almost feminine voice. Only downside was I thought it could've been a bit louder with the volume buttons.

Teresa and Keith had joined the massive queues for the beer stall, and came back with fresh supplies of lager and Guinness, all set for The Pogues. The grandstand was less than half full, some of the attendees were up for the cup, but there were a lot of stiffs in there too, with long faces. Karen's security staff were more lively. There were two young girls 'looking after' the grandstand, they were lovely, and they themselves appeared excited to see The Pogues. 'Straight to Hell' comes over the PA, here we go, here we go, here we go!

There was a very healthy audience on the grass in front of the stage; it seemed to go a long way back. We did have a good view from the grandstand, at least we weren't stuck behind any skyscraper punters. I was past myself with excitement by now (just for a change), so much so, that when 'Streams of Whiskey' kicked in, I was up and over the barrier in front of us (with a certain degree of athleticism this time) and had a dance to myself on a 'no man's land' area of grass, in-between the grandstand and the main body of the crowd. I felt every pair of brown eyes from the grandstand were on me, but I wasn't embarrassed, I was going to enjoy myself, no matter what. I had a twirl with the security girls, to the most wonderful music, being amplified into one summer evening, drunk to hell, in Greenwich. Now and again, I was joined on the grass, with some like minded fans from the grandstand, and we had a jig, linking arms, going round a full turn, like you do, when dancing to The Pogues.

The band? Top drawer again, Shaney boy in particular. After they performed 'Kitty' Spider turned round to Shane and looked at him, before paying him a lovely compliment, "That was fuckin' brilliant!" which it was. As always, when yer man is on form, he plays a real maverick centre forward's role, and scores goals for fun. I had a wee break, back in the seats, just in time for 'Tuesday morning' with Spider to the fore. 'Tuesday morning' will, of course, be an emotional one for me from here on in; it will always remind me of my mother. If I get a chance, I'll ask Spider to dedicate a performance of the song to the memory of my dear mother one day, that would be really something. 'Waltzing Matilda' was still on the set list, the song reddened my eyes once again, just awesome. Keith and Teresa couldn't smoke their tabs in the grandstand, so they had to go onto the grass and into the main crowd as it were; a new security wifie was in tow by now, and she wasn't a fan of my dodgy dancing on 'no man's land'. She had her eye on me, in a very uncomplimentary manner. Well, I'd fucking well show her, wouldn't I? I was feeling very, very naughty, buoyed by the occasion and the river of Guinness I'd consumed. The concert was mind blowing; it was a shame though that it just wasn't quite loud enough – a few decibels louder would have been in order, but there might have been a limit in place for the good residents of Greenwich. Mind you, if I was one of those residents, I certainly wouldn't have minded this music being 'piped' into my back garden, on a summer's evening!

Anyway, back to the task in hand: I had decided that it was indeed time for a wee wander. I had no idea just how far my stroll would be, or even a definite destination, but I was up for seeing just how far I could progress in a certain direction. I very casually made my way up the side of the grandstand area, past the unmanned gate, along the side of the main crowd, and before you knew it I was at the very back of the stage area. It was very quiet; there was no one around, no activity at all. I pulled back a bit of tarpaulin, and there was Joey Cashman directly in front of me, rolling a dubious tobacco wrap; a young lady was also present. I went straight to Joey, who was neither up nor down at my sudden presence, shook his hand, and informed him that we had met years ago in Glasgow, at a Shane and The Popes concert. He still wasn't really paying attention to me, which was actually very convenient.

My wander continued, unchallenged – how fucking wonderful my little stroll was turning out to be. Up a small wooden ladder, another tarpaulin curtain, and hey, there were the Pogues from the back; they were blasting out 'The Irish Rover'. I'd been to many Pogues shows, but I'd never seen them like this before. Question is though, what do I do now? Amazingly, I resisted the temptation of running straight onto the stage – no mean feat considering how sociable I was feeling. I enjoyed my exclusive 'Executive box' view for the last few moments of the song, and then Shane was doing his "Goodnight, good luck" bit, meaning they were coming off stage, in preparation for an encore. Shit! What now? What else – I was out onto the stage, in front of 6000 punters, right up to Shane, as he turned to retreat to the back of the stage, I gave him a cuddle, and he hugged me back – he must've needed a love!

Joey Cashman was now very interested; in his thick Irish accent I heard him say, "You don't want to be doin' that!" That was my cue to get out of there, the way I had come in reverse. As I got to the side of the crowd, I received a few high fives; I felt semi-famous for about, oh, ten seconds! I was brought back to earth with a bang when I was reunited with Keith, and a concerned Teresa, in regards to my disappearance earlier. "Did yous see that?" I asked them. "See What?"

Fucking hell! They'd only both missed my unscheduled appearance on stage. For fuck's sake, I was only the ninth Pogue, just like Strummer, Earle, and Kirsty (oh come on, please pretend along with me) for ten seconds or so. An observant lady nearby was over to us, asking how I had managed to get myself in position for a hug with Shane; she was mighty impressed, even congratulating me on the success of the result of my mini expedition; she was vociferously telling Keith and Teresa about me being on the stage. Their faces were full of astonishment. I couldn't believe they hadn't seen me – what on earth were they looking at, when my 'moment' was unfolding?

It was time for 'Fiesta' which of course meant that this wonderful concert was coming to a close. I had a good Pogues jig with the observant lady, the one who *was* paying attention, the band wished us goodnight, and The Pogues, at Greenwich, concluded.

We saw Karen on the way out; thankfully she too was none the wiser regarding my breach of security. I gave her a kiss goodnight and we made our weary, but highly contented way back to central London on the Docklands Light Railway. The poor old dog, The Irish Rover, would have been drowned by now!

We had based our five night stay in London around The Pogues gig. We spent the whole of the next day, a sunny Sunday with Keith, on a rooftop garden bar in Lancaster Gate, reminiscing about the fantastic day we'd had at Greenwich. It was the height of summer, we were not in Siam, but it really didn't matter, it was really brilliant when a Pogues concert took you to different places and venues – this one will always be remembered as extra special, and it was a real tonic for myself and Teresa after losing my mother. The Pogues are just what the doctor ordered, in many, many ways. I'm quite sure they just don't realise just how good their musical medicine is!

THE END OF THE LINE

Dad's condition was one that would never improve, it would only get worse; he would become even more forgetful. You just couldn't take anything for granted regarding what you would imagine to be everyday things. For example, one day we were having a cup of tea in the house. Dad always liked a chocolate biscuit – it was a Kit Kat he was having today. I looked round, and the whole shooting match was churning in his mouth: wafer, chocolate along with the silver foil and the red wrapper! Of course, when I 'interfered' he wasn't for giving it back, so after a stramash it all went down the hatch! When we were out walking, he always walked behind me, rather than alongside. I would think he was lost sometimes, and tell him to walk beside me, but he wouldn't. He was using me as a guide, and if someone was approaching us in the opposite direction, he would just stop, until they had passed; he couldn't gauge the distance required to avoid a collision. Takes a while to suss all this out though, and we sometimes exasperated each other. Nowadays, he doesn't walk so well, and I hold his hand when we do walk together – he's fine with this, it works having a hand free, just in case we need to stick two fingers up to people who gawp at us from time to time. It's what is necessary, simple as that.

We really were struggling now. The Aviator, business wise, was not doing so hot – again, without trying to sound like I'm making excuses, I just think we were caught, like everyone else, with the economic depression. People couldn't afford to go out so often for a meal, we couldn't put our prices down, as our overheads were only going one way, it was a real Catch 22. Of course, there's always the jobsworths to go to for advice, but let's not. Teresa and I started talking, very seriously about the future, regarding both the business and Dad. Apart from anything else, Dad wasn't very happy being shunted from pillar to post – his house, the day centre, our house, The Aviator... it was a really hard time for everyone.

We needed to give The Aviator a lift, create a bit of interest about the place. Teresa is amazing at thinking outside the box, streets ahead of me, and she came up with a masterplan. We were going to have an X Factor competition, one Saturday night, right in the middle of a quiet period of business. Teresa is a fan of the show, I most definitely am not. In fact, on a Saturday, after a long working shift, we would arrive home, crack open a couple of cold ones, Teresa would put the X Factor on, and I would settle down reading the paper. But I would find myself glancing over the top of my poor quality tabloid, with the odd comment or two forthcoming, never complimentary, usually aimed at the judges. They got on my tits, fucking full of themselves, telling the poor hopefuls that they were the dog's bollocks, when in fact, (to me anyway) they were worse than pish! Teresa would pause the TV, turn to me with a scornful look and tell me to shut my puss or go to another room, I was spoiling her programme. "Sorry," I would say. Ten minutes later though, I was at it again, the red card would come out this time, and I was sent to the bedroom, to finish my paper, and usually succumb to big ZZs. It was usually the multi talented Cheryl Cole that would tip me over the edge. She's a stunningly beautiful woman, of that there's no doubt, but talent? Do me a fuckin' favour. Her accent only emphasised how thick she could come across at times: "Wor Ashley, he's only gannin' aboot shaggin otha whooers!" I love the Geordie accent, but she just had me in a regular rage. Good old Ashley! With me up the tunnel, Teresa could now enjoy the rest of the programme in peace. I'm quite convinced a similar scenario went on in many households on a Saturday night, regarding the X Factor. If however, the X Factor gig was to give us a much needed boost, then I was a fan. For one night only.

Teresa ensured all our staff would be off duty for the evening so they could attend with their friends. She had incentives in place to reward those who sold the most tickets for the event, the interest was immense, and selling the tickets was a walk in the park. She even employed three barmen for the night, who were clearly eye candy for the ladies, and, probably, for some of the men too!

Ironically, we started to get bookings through for dinner on the very night we were hosting the X Factor – one of those bookings we just couldn't refuse though; it was for a brass band of 50 people, wanting a buffet dinner, served late after their performance that evening at Perth Concert Hall. They had been to us last year, we didn't want to let them down, so they agreed to have their buffet in our private dining room – it would be a tight squeeze, but we'd take our chances.

The actual competition was based on competing candidates, both groups and individuals, singing their way through a chosen song, with the help of a karaoke screen if required. Pah! Shane MacGowan doesn't need one of them. Just a tumbler full of brew and a tab, and he's fine! There was a panel of three judges, it was very slick and well organised, and a lot of the performers were taking it very seriously indeed for the cash prize – winner was taking all. Our in house DJ, Stewart, even had the X Factor music, and he kept things moving along nicely. We must have had 150 bodies in that night enjoying themselves, the three stallion barmen were kept busy, and thankfully, the till was hotter than it had been for a wee while.

Laura and I entered the competition; we called ourselves 'The Kitchen Fannies'. There was no way we were murdering a Pogues song though, so we chose Blondie's 'Heart of glass'. I tried to sing as high pitched as I could – you'd have thought my bollocks were in a vice. We had a dance routine that we made up as we went along, and without doubt, received the best ovation from the audience so far! I assumed then, that we would be in the next round, so I had a word with the judges, asking if we could go on first, as we were due to serve up the buffet for the brass band. Laura and I had partaken in a few drinks by then, very unprofessional, I know, but we got into the kitchen, like a pair of fannies, and served the buffet, both hot and cold, quite efficiently I thought, under the circumstances. Right! Buffet served, punters in the dining room munching away, and we were ready for our song number two, The Clash, 'Should I stay or should I go?'. We were not going fucking anywhere, as we didn't make it into the second round. Fucking hell, whatever happened to giving the punters what they wanted, fucking ridiculous! STEWARDS' FUCKING ENQUIRY!

A young chap who used to come to the restaurant with his mother for lunch on occasions deservedly took the prize money. His first number, U2's 'With or without you', set the standard; he drew everyone's attention from that moment on, and the result was never in doubt really. Some of the acts, in true X Factor style, were both horrendous and hysterical. A very good mate of mine, Graham White, was on the panel of judges; someone had given him a Louis Walsh mask, which actually saved his bacon a few times. Graham likes to laugh; if the act was too much for him to remain respectfully composed, then the mask, resting on top of his head, was discreetly slipped down, to hide his laughing coupon!

Competition done and dusted, we had a big party; some of the brass band joined in, the night succumbed to early morning, and in true Aviator style, we partied on until about 7am. Well done Teresa, a brilliant, very original idea, happy punters, a happy cash register to pay those bills, and very tired Aviator staff for the Sunday, but we'd all get over it. There's always a million reasons not to do things that are a bit outside the box, but I really admire people that get on with it, and make it work. Everyone did their bit for the X Factor night, but Teresa's vision of the whole thing was, without doubt, one of The Aviator's finest moments.

On the big picture though, the X Factor's success was merely papering over the cracks. We had been there for five years, we'd had some great times, we'd worked hard and for long, long hours, but we'd no regrets. The combination of the family trauma, looking after Dad, and the fact we were forecasting a non-too-financially prosperous future, sealed our decision to finally call it a day. We had one last hurrah, yet another party at The Aviator, family, friends and customers celebrated with us once last time. A night like this was always a problem when it came to Dad. He had been in the care home when the X Factor was on, but not this time. I had to wait with him, keeping my fingers crossed that he would not have one of his

late night, disorientated 'marathons' and go to bed at the usual time.
Things did not look good when he said he was going to make himself a
sandwich. I said that I would do it for him, but he wasn't having it, so
through to the kitchen we went. What had I been doing at The Aviator
all this time? We had a sandwich menu, but there was nothing on it,
that compared with Dad's extravaganza that night! Between two pieces
of white bread, he crammed in the following: ham, cheese, hardboiled
egg, jam, honey, and I kid you not, broken up pieces of mint chocolate
Aero! If I had challenged his choice of sandwich filling, I'd have been
there all night, so I wished him, "Bon appetite!" and told him I'd see
him in the morning.

Later on in the evening, I sat alone in the Aviator kitchen, but I
wasn't sad – people thought I was, but I was actually reflecting on
what everyone had achieved there. Nothing lasts forever, the staff that
were with us at the end, each and every one of them, should be rightly
proud of what The Aviator was. They were the ones that could step up
to the plate; talk is cheap, but they could actually walk the walk. I'll
always love them all, that core of quality people, for our latter days at
the restaurant. We started the venture without a silver spoon in our
mouths, and I think we achieved a lot, many times against the odds,
but we couldn't have done anything without our wonderful, loyal staff.

We had a lot of loose ends to tie up, but eventually we did tie
them, and closed the doors of The Aviator for the last time. It was a
mixed emotion of sadness, but with relief. Of the staff's future, they
were all confident enough to look after themselves, and fix up new
employment. The one staff member that I was concerned about was our
Laura. She'd been on holiday, to Turkey, had met a kebab as usual and
was loved up. She was going over there, after The Aviator, to live with
Kebab in eternal bliss. I was upset, because I thought she was throwing
her career away. I'd always thought that I was grooming her! Just settle
yourself down now will ya? I'm talking about grooming her as a chef,
NOT what you were thinking, shame on you, to further her career
down in Surrey, at The Savill Court, with Philip Borthwick. I would
not recommend just anyone to Philip, oh no, but I knew Laura had
what it took to progress in his kitchen. I had many discussions with
Philip about this very subject. Laura did shack up with kebab, over in

Turkey, but, thankfully it was short lived. She returned to Scotland, and I managed to persuade her to do the right thing. She still works with Philip and Keith to this day, she has excelled in the Savill Court kitchens, and I, for one, could not be more proud of her. I'm just so glad she listened to my gentle persuasions; it wasn't easy convincing her, but what a happy ending. She is, quite simply, a very good chef – a rare commodity these days – and she's in good hands. A kebab is fine, tasty even, especially a holiday one, but there's no longevity, it turns to shite, usually quite quickly, I'm sure you'd agree!

Teresa, Dad and I soldiered on. Sure, we had more time now, but one week was just rolling onto the next, the social worker that was dealing with our situation was telling us that it was time to let go. We couldn't keep him locked up overnight in his house, he was hardly able to do anything for himself; I even had to help him when he took a bath. He hated me washing his hair, saying he was going to F'in kill me when he got out of the bath. Dad's case ticked all the boxes for him to go into permanent care. It had been nine months since Mum passed. I knew deep down it was the right thing to do, but I couldn't help thinking that I was failing him. I, in particular, was actually in denial about how bad he really was; everyone else could see it clearly. There was an added pressure to finally make the decision, when the social worker told us that there was a place available in the care home where he had been going for respite; this place may not have been available at a later date. He was always going to end up in care, but we might not have had a choice of establishment in the future. That was it then, decision made, and we all had to live with it.

As if this wasn't enough, The Pogues were true to their word, thus far. No Christmas tour was announced, the first time since 2004 that the Academies at Glasgow and Brixton would be Pogue-less at Christmas time. I fuckin' bet you that the respective bar managers had some explaining to do, regarding their figures for December! If ever there was a year that we could have done with the Pogues' Christmas tour, it was 2010.

LOOKING FOR JAMES

Dad was settling into his new surroundings; it was a real culture shock for us all. We felt lucky that he had got into the care home we had chosen, but it was hard letting go. We were sometimes rightly critical of the care he was receiving, and we were not slow at voicing our concerns. Of course, the staff at the care home had to get used to Dad too, and us getting used to the idea that he was in there for keeps; everyone got there, eventually. I'm not going to harp on about care homes – that's a humungous can of worms, nothing about it is ideal – it's just life, and that about sums it all up really.

Husband and wife had worked very well together at The Aviator, so we were keen to do something together again. A real change of direction saw us working for The Salvation Army, in the clothing recycling division. Basically we picked up donated clothes from clothing banks, transferred the clothes to a trailer and, once it was full, it would be taken away, and we'd start again. We had a big van to travel to the various banks, mainly in our local area but also up North in Aberdeen and along Royal Deeside, where we were fortunate to see some stunning scenery and wildlife. We worked six days a week, which was the downside of the work; it was reasonably rewarding though, financially.

I gathered a bit of momentum writing this book when The Aviator finished, as I obviously had more time. I had this fanciful idea that I would like James Fearnley, The Pogues' maestro accordion player, to perhaps give me his seal of approval, and maybe give me a few pointers on the way. Little did I know at the time that James was about to unleash his own book upon us Poguey people; I wasn't sure if it was a good thing or bad to be honest, in regards to me contacting him, as he would obviously be a wee bit busy with his own project. He could surely do without the likes of me hassling him.

Of course, when I first discovered James was doing a book, it was definitely something to very much look forward to. Previously there had been a few books published about the greatest band on Earth. Carol Clerk's publication 'Pogue Mahone, the story of the Pogues' is by far the best one on the market in my opinion, but we'd never had a Pogues book directly from a band member before. Shane MacGowan's girlfriend, Victoria, had published 'A drink with Shane MacGowan', which was actually a series of conversations between the two love birds that was recorded. It caused a lot of controversy at the time of publishing, as Shane said some very uncomplimentary things about various members of The Pogues. He apologises for this at the end of the book, and has since said that he was just rambling on to his missus about this and that. As you do. The book wasn't really a book about The Pogues though; there were lots of subjects covered, and I found Pogues subjects to be quite sparse throughout.

I personally think our James is a bit of an unsung hero in The Pogues story. He always gives 100% at gigs, and his book confirms what I've always suspected. James had made a considerable contribution in the early days of The Pogues regarding the instrumentation of the band, where, it's maybe fair to say, that his fellow band members' musical talent was still in its embryonic stages. He's a versatile member of The Pogues. This is evident in their live shows, where he usually plays three different instruments during the set. No singing though – with an accent like his, Northern industrial, it's maybe just as well! His book is actually very enjoyable, and comes across as very honest. I had a feeling that James' book would be full of flowery adjectives that would needed looked up in a dictionary and I wasn't wrong. There's more 'flowers' in his book than an adjectival large summer, blooming garden in Harrogate!

So, how exactly would I get to tell him about my book and see if he was at all interested in helping me? I didn't want to 'advertise' what I was up to on any of the forums on his or The Pogues' websites, just in case somebody else, with more flowers in their wordsmith skills than me, got in there first. It was on James' own website, however, that I discovered he was doing a few bits and pieces in Britain (he lives in the U S of A these days) to promote his book. This would surely be an ideal opportunity, to try and catch him for five minutes of his valuable time. There were a few dates listed; he was doing some readings from his book. The only date suitable for me would be at the weekend. It was to be his first date, he was appearing at The Laugharne weekend, a festival of sorts, that seemed to have a bit of everything going on, even a 'It's a Knockout' thing hosted by the actor Keith Allen, Lily's Dad. Give that one a swerve then! James was also doing readings in Leeds and London, which would have been easier geographically, but where was Laugharne? Fucking hell! No, it wasn't actually in hell, but on further investigation, I discovered Laugharne was in Carmarthenshire, south Wales. This would have to be it for me – the other dates were all midweek, getting time off work was not an option available to me at the time, so I would have some major shoehorning to arrange, to even manage to get to the Welsh leg of James' 'tour'. He was appearing in a small church, to do his readings, along with a geezer that used to be on The Old Grey Whistle Test. Apart from me wanting to speak to James, the event itself sounded really good.

Trying to organise my time, around the event with work, was proving to be a nightmare. I was beginning to think that maybe it just wasn't meant to be, when Teresa pointed something out to me. I'd 'met' James three times previously, each time outside the Glasgow Academy. On each of these aforementioned occasions I was pissed (surprise!) and if The Pogues were to play there again, history would probably repeat itself. James would not want to hang around too long, probably longing for the solitude of his hotel room, after hurling the squeezebox around all night. The Laugharne thing would offer a different atmosphere altogether, so decision made, I was bound for Wales.

I started work on the Saturday morning at 4am. My mate Graham White, of X Factor judge fame, had agreed to give me a lift to the airport; he was picking me up at noon. Graham is some man: he has recently built a most amazing house for his family to live in. If Graham built you a gaff, it would not fall down, no matter how big the wolf was that huffed and puffed! He went through some shit, building that house, a real case of pushing to extremes regarding human endurance, but it's all worked out for him. I truly admire this man's self discipline. So I knew he wouldn't let me down, he would not be late, everything was so tight for time, there was little margin for error. Graham was actually one of the few people that knew of my project; on the way to the airport I was 'filling him in' with what I was up to this weekend. We arrived at the airport in plenty time for my flight to Bristol, I bought us a coffee and a cake, and almost had to take out a mortgage to pay the bill. The day enhanced itself nicely, when I heard the news that Hibs had defeated Aberdeen, just down the road at Hampden Park, in the Scottish Cup semi final.

I was sat beside two young lads on the plane; they were both boisterous and loud, they were annoying everyone close by, but they had won me over, before too long. Their patter was simply superb, their one liners telling all and sundry that the plane was going to crash, but we just had to look on the bright side of this awful catastrophe that was about to unfold. We were all going to see Bon Scott, the long since departed singer with rock giants AC/DC, the plane was actually on the 'Highway to Hell' and a few of us were going to form a band with him. I was told, in no uncertain terms, that I was on bass! I'd have to learn quick for the gig commitments we had at The Devil's Tavern. We were all coming back as porn stars too, if we measured up! If we didn't, then the sharp shears were for the wee boys. I gave the lads a serious look that just may have saved me from a shearing! As you can imagine, they were upsetting some of the passengers, the banter went downhill (yes, it really did) and the more I laughed, well, it was if it was me that was egging them on.

On the clear descent to Bristol's airport, I started to pay attention to the landscape. I could see the Clifton Suspension Bridge, over The Avon Gorge – the view was amazing. I picked up a hire car at the airport, and my adventure continued, looking for James. I was travelling to Llanelli, a place about 30 miles from the remoteness of Laugharne. I drove over the Severn Bridge, principally on the M4, and fucking blasted the stereo out, "Going Transmetropolitan, yip ay aye!" I passed some lovely countryside, followed by the suburban industrialism of Port Talbot. It was a fantastic feeling to check into the hotel, and order up a cold beer, followed by a curry. I was fucking knackered, not quite as bad as the dudes that Rudyard Kipling's Gunga Din attended to in the First World War though. Ahh, a poem close to my heart, I think I must have used old Rudyard's brilliant work more than a few times in my English exams at secondary school, and in my English O'grade, which I got an 'A' for, by the way! I would bet, that you're scratching your bonce over that one, now that you are quite well on, in this book!

Knackered I say, I got my head down. And couldn't sleep! Probably thinking too much of what lay in store the next day – was it all going to be a waste of time, all that organising and expense for nothing? Time would tell. I was up, and down to breakfast for insomniacs bang on 7 am, me, myself and I in the restaurant, all the smug sleepers still tucked up in their kip, giving it big ZZZs. I went for a wee walk, to clear my head; it was a lovely day for April, back to the room for a shit, a shave and a shower, (but no half pint of Powers). Then it was time for the relatively short journey to Laugharne, that I had since been informed was pronounced "Larne". I travelled, armed with some very badly typed chapters from my book, a letter explaining who I was and my intentions for the book, and my contact details; I couldn't help thinking I was being far too presumptuous, but shy kids don't get many sweeties though. I also had a photo of me and James outside the Glasgow Academy, with his 'at, when I told him to look like he was enjoying himself.

Laugharne was remote all right, but it was also beautiful, a real charmer of a small town, overlooking the massive Taf estuary. There's a car park in the centre, with a sign warning the motorist that the water just may creep up on your vehicle unannounced, so unless harbouring amphibian tendencies, then beware. James was appearing at the Congregational Church around 3pm, so I had plenty of time for a wander; the views were just superb. Once again, The Pogues (indirectly) had taken me to a new, stunning environment, through chance circumstances. Laugharne is most famous for a boathouse belonging to Welsh poet and writer, Dylan Thomas. There's also a shed thing, where apparently he did most of his writing. Dylan Thomas doesn't mean much to me, through ignorance more than anything, but I went for a look at his gaffs anyway; they were both very popular with visitors.

It was time to make my way up to the church, it was about 20 minutes to three, but word was that James was now due at 3.30. I had a seat on a bench in the welcome sunshine, a small crowd were gathering and this bloke was paying me a bit too much attention. I was starting to feel uneasy, so I just said "Hello" to him, trying to sound friendly rather than hostile. "Are you Steve?" he asked. I replied, "Sorry, no, would you like me to be?" He just laughed, and he stopped staring. A few minutes later 'Steve' had clearly arrived, and off they went together. The way they greeted one another, it could well have been a blind date. I had a feeling that in the very near future a memory foam mattress was about to be given an extremely serious work-out. I wonder if the bloke was happy with the real Steve, or maybe he'd have preferred me – I guess I'll never know. Just as well, he wasn't my type, and I'm too fidgety for the memory foam!

Settle. It was time to go to Church, Sunday after all. The place was basic, it had rows of bench seats looking on to a raised 'stage' where minister James was about to do his preaching. Mark Ellen from the Whistle Test was first to appear. I turned round and there was the minister himself, just to my right. He was stood right next to me and I felt my throat dry up. "Hi James," I pathetically croaked. He looked at me for a second, before delivering "Yeaaahawrriiiiite?" He had a long 'Pogues of old days' coat on which defied the weather, his customary white shirt and a suit – he always seems to dress like this. Mark Ellen kicked things off, explaining that James was going to do some readings from the book and there would be time at the end for a question and answer session, sounded just great. He started by asking James some questions himself, and for the next hour or so, I found myself to be thoroughly entertained. One of the first subjects that was discussed was the state of Shane MacGowan's flat when James had visited in the early days; by all accounts, flea pit didn't even come close to a description. Mark Ellen suggested to James that we had all lived like that at some point in our lives, enter that James Fearnley quizzical look that I had experienced, when asking him about 'croissants' in Glasgow. "Speak for yourself," James snapped.

James commenced the readings by going for the jugular, talking about the prickly subject of Shane's sacking from The Pogues whilst on tour in Japan. I found myself hanging off his every word. On a lighter note, he recalled a night out with Shane in London. Shane wasn't fucking about when it came to ordering the drinks; Black Zombies were the order of the night, every clear spirit imaginable with a dash of coke. The two pals were paralytic, staggering their way home. Shane was bouncing off shop windows and was struggling, when James tried to help. "Fuck Off!" snarled Shane, but he wasn't finished there. "CUNT! CUNT! CUNT!" As James recalled this drunken night, his short lived career as minister came to a close, howling language like that in a church would be gross misconduct for sure – the look on Mark Ellen's face when the 'C' word was being shouted out was priceless. I actually felt quite good about James' colourful language in his book – there's plenty of choice words in mine too; it's the language of any industry, anyone who says they never swear is a fucking liar!

I really enjoyed James reading out the extracts from his book, then there were a few predictable questions from the audience at the end. One I found quite interesting. Someone asked if all the band members were happy with the book's content. James hesitated before answering that all were Ok with it, apart from two. He refused to say who they were, an educated guess can be mustered after reading the book itself. Mark Ellen brought proceedings to a close, and a queue formed to buy copies of the book, that James was personally signing. This was it then. I purposely went to the back of the line. When I handed over my sovereigns to James' female assistant who was flogging the books, I also asked if she would take my camera, and take a picture of me and the author; "no problem," she said. I started getting nervous again, dry throat syndrome returned, I could have murdered a pint of ice cold beer, with condensation running down the pre chilled, tall glass!

It was my turn, the end of the queue, we shook hands and James asked my name so he could do his signing. He wrote, "To Calum, love James xx." A good start then! I started warbling about why I was really there, emphasising how far I'd travelled, and told him that I was trying to write my own book, primarily about The Pogues from a fan's prospective, and the effect the music had had on my life over the years. I explained that I'd had lots of experiences around attending Pogues gigs, and wondered if the band themselves would be interested to hear what goes on at the other side of the stage as it were. James was generous with his reaction, he said the idea in principle was "Awesome". I handed him a folder, containing the chapters, a photo of me and him in Glasgow and my contact details. I asked him simply if he would tell me what he thought, and asked him to keep in touch. He promised he would, and in return I told him I would respect his privacy. I didn't want to overdo it. I was aware that James had just newly returned from a Pogues tour of Australia, so I kept it short. I took the camera back from his assistant, only to be informed by her, that she hadn't taken any photos yet! "Oh aye!" I felt my face redden, fucking hell, no half measures with me, either blootered or shy and nervous. I'm hardly ever shy or nervous, but this was a big deal to me, this was James Fearnley. The single photo shoot did indeed take place, we shook hands again, he wished me a safe journey home, then I and my face fire left the Church and it's 'C' wording minister/author.

I felt brilliant after meeting James. I somewhat reluctantly drove away from lovely Laugharne, and back to my hotel. I ordered that beer I'd been fantasising about, and bent Teresa's ear off, on the phone for about an hour, which is incredible considering I only spoke to James for five minutes. I also slept better that night, but it was a very early rise in the morning, 2.30am, back to Bristol Airport, for an early flight to Glasgow. Bristol's Airport was really busy, but things were moving along OK, when this absolute penis of a 'business man' bustled his way to the front of the queue on check-in, he almost knocked a poor girl to the ground, it was way over the top. A lot of people were watching him, but nobody said anything. The girl that checked me in said that all the flights were leaving around about the same time, and that penis had plenty of time, God only knows what his problem was. I went through security and after a short while, joined yet another queue, this time in the Gents' room. I suppose the majority of us blokes are quite 'regular' in the mornings, so this queue was for the cubicles. All of a sudden, in storms penis the business man, the tool from check-in, and again, right to the very front of the water closet queue too, fucking unbelievable! This time though, things didn't go quite his way. The bloke at the front was a heavy metal freak, and was the size of a Sherman tank. With a very thick Bristolian accent he gave out a warning to penis. "Here, cunt! If you wants to shit, go to the back of the line, or it's me who shits into the hole where your head used to be!" By the look on Dennis the penis' face, I think his bowels were no longer a problem he had to worry about, just, perhaps, an intense clean-up operation. As he scurried away from the scene, a murmur of appreciation went along the line of patient, wannabe shitters; I was quite happy to be one of those.

I had a smooth, if uneventful journey home, and was out for work at 10.30 am, knackered but very happy. It was an adventure with a difference, something to cherish, a memory to look back on fondly. I love travel, it's great to see new places, even better if you get to talk to a Pogue.

James took his time, and I wondered if I would hear from him at all. But I'm glad to say that I eventually did. First off, he emailed me, telling me that he was getting through the chapters, and that chapter 3, the taxi incident, when I was knocked arse over tit on the road, was hilarious. Charming! But he needed more time, then he would get back to me in more detail. A while later, I received an envelope in the post, all the way from Los Angeles, USA, James had typed a four page report on my writing, he was very thorough. He liked some of it, but gave me a bollocking for other parts. I didn't agree with everything he wrote, but there were a couple of really crucial bits of advice that really helped me tune up what I'd already written and for what I was still to write. He was touched that I'd travelled all the way to Laugharne to see him, and wished me well for the future. He thought my project was a worthwhile one, and he asked if I intended writing more about my family. I was grateful that he had taken the time to write to me; it was fantastic to get a letter from the accordion player from the Pogues.

GLORY TO THE GREAT HIBEES

When I was fourteen years old, I started negotiating with my folks for their blessing to do something that had been on my mind for a while. I wanted to start going regularly to see Hibs on a Saturday, and now I thought I would try and turn a tragedy into a bit of a result for me personally. Hibs had just been relegated from the Scottish Premier League, the first time they were not to play in the top league for donkey's years. They would be playing smaller teams this next coming season, and that was to prove to be the reason that my discussions with Ma and Pa were successful. They didn't fancy me going to see Hibs play Rangers or Celtic, but were cool with the prospect of Stirling Albion or Dunfermline Athletic. I worked right through the summer holidays, I had both a milk round, and went berry picking, and I managed to save up a load of cash that was going to take me to see my beloved Hibees on match day. I would need it, as every match was really an away day, with me living in Perth and Hibs playing in Edinburgh. Dad had taken me now and again to see Hibs; he was never keen though. I had to go on about it for an age, before he took me, to stop me nagging. Dad is an Aberdeen fan. We all have our problems. Live football matches were never really his thing to be fair though.

I had a great time that first season, coming back from the very first fixture, a desperate 1-0 home defeat by Raith Rovers. I met Jimmy, big Les, Mike and Whytey on the train. I'd no idea how close we were to become. Hibs won their league that season; a highlight for me involved the legendary, one and only, Mr George Best. George had turned out for Hibs during the previous season, his presence packed grounds out that might have been half full, at most, without him. He was carrying a bit of weight, and was past it really, but now and again you would still see a flash of genius, and he was playing in the green and white of Hibernian FC. And this season he was back for more. We were at Dunfermline, he was warming up before kick off, without pushing himself too much, taking shots at the Hibs keeper. Lots of fans were running on the pitch to get his autograph; by the time I'd got there, I think George had had enough. He told me to "Fuck off!" I had a rather embarrassed run back to the terraces autographless. The very next week, Ed the Gazelle and I were outside our own ground, Easter Road, waiting for George's arrival for the match. We were going to be successful this time, George appeared happy and was up to us, willing to do some signing. I said to him, "You told me to fuck off last week at Dunfermline!" He looked horrified, he went into the close by Hibs shop and came out with two cartoon poster caricatures of himself in the Hibs strip, signed them, apologised and gave one to me, the other to Gazelle. I forgave him.

I didn't miss many matches that season. I loved it. I started getting excited around the Thursday thinking about the match at the weekend. During the festive period, there are usually more matches scheduled than on normal weeks of the season, and on New Year's Day, 1981, Hibs were at Berwick. Whytey drove a few of us down in his electrician works van, and the Hibs fans showed the world just how talented, versatile and caring they could be. They were having a bit of a set to with the local constabulary, wishing them a happy new year, taking the piss out of their domed helmets, and singing them a song that was proving to be as popular as Hannibal Lecter holding classes for making black pudding. "TEN THOUSAND POLIS, AND ONLY ONE YORKSHIRE RIPPER!" The Hibs fans were relentless: "TEN THOUSAND POLIS..." Old Bill was most certainly not amused. The female population of Yorkshire had been terrorised for over five years by a serial killer, and Bill were proving to be less than useless at catching him. As you can imagine, the song had struck a nerve with plod at Berwick; they were lifting the Hibs supporters at will. The very next day, January 2nd, Peter Sutcliffe was arrested and charged. The Yorkshire Ripper was behind bars, all due to the Hibs fans' encouragement, telling Bill to get their finger out. Thanks to the green and white army, the good ladies of Yorkshire and Northern England could enjoy a safe night out at the bingo again – the Hibs support is just wonderful!

A few years later, with Hibs re-established in the Premier League, I was in the Hibs Supporters' Club one Saturday, before an eagerly anticipated derby match against Hearts. This geezer was sitting at a table, and had an urn with him. The bloke was from Canada, the urn contained his departed brother's ashes, whose wish was to be scattered on the pitch at Easter Road. Hibs were typically unhelpful to the poor bloke's predicament. I'm glad to say that these days the club is much more in touch with their fans, one of the very few things that have improved with time. But they weren't having any of this request, so the bloke took comfort with a few pints before the game, telling his and his brother's story to some very interested Hibs fans. Of course, in time of bereavement, the obvious soother is, "Would you like a drink?" When it was time to go to the match, the boy was blootered with whisky. He was standing in the old enclosure, just in front of the main stand, the Hearts fans were not too far away in the opposite enclosure, all the usual verbals and songs were to the fore, an Edinburgh derby is a passionate event. Just before half time, Hibs midfielder Paul Kane was through on the Hearts keeper, he did the business and put the ball into the Hearts net to open the scoring and send three quarters of Easter Road into a delighted frenzy. Drunk matey from Canada got caught up in the wild celebrations, the urn went up in the air, and a lot of us were treated to a literal taste of his brother's ashes – it was everywhere, it was even in my ears! Of course, no one minded one little bit, I think that the way his ashes were scattered could not have been more perfect, bang on scoring against Hearts, scattered over delighted Hibees. Wonder what bit of him was in my ear?

I was to meet Geoff Ford a little later than the other Perth Hibs lads; he has a brother Mike, who is a colourful character. He told us a brilliant story of when he worked as a porter in an upmarket London Hotel. He was asked to take a bottle of Jack Daniel's up to one of the suites on the top floor; on arrival, he knocked on the door. There was no reply. Eventually, he let himself in the room, placing the bottle of Jack's on a table with a couple of glasses. The television was on, and being screened was some of the hardest porn that worldly Mike had ever seen in his life. Mike sat on the comfy chair; he wouldn't be missed for five minutes! Out of the adjoining room, a figure came gliding towards him, fucking hell, if the shock of that didn't startle Mike, how do you think he felt when he saw Keith Richards of The Rolling Stones in front of him! Mike was spluttering through his apologies, but Keith was just shaking his head; he put his hand up and said, "It's all right man, you can watch, but have you got the Jack Daniels?" Mike handed him the bottle. "Thanks man," and Keith retreated, back to the other room. Mike didn't hang around, and didn't unzip either!

Davo and I were going to Tannadice, to see Hibs' away match at Dundee United. We'd had a good drink in us on the way up to the match from Dundee's town centre. They say that dogs can smell fear in people, well this huge fucking monster bounding down the hill towards me, must have smelt the shit in my underpants. Before you knew it, the bastard was standing on its hind legs, its paws resting on my chest; in between barking, the hound was licking my face, it showed mercy and left me unharmed. There must have been literally hundreds of fans walking up the hill towards the football ground that day, but I just knew that the slobbery canine was coming for me!

We had a habit around that time of going into the 'wrong end' at the Hibs games, into opposition supporter territory, with our green and white scarves tied round our waist, under our jackets, it was just a giggle rather than a macho battle cry. At Tannadice that afternoon, we were right in the middle of the United 'mob'; there was a segregation fence, on the other side the Hibs fans were stood. We received a few waves from boys in the Hibs end that knew us, a few of the locals were cottoning on to this. So we decided to tell Old Bill that we were Hibs supporters and accidentally went into the wrong end, and we were worried for our safety. Bill wasn't happy, (short fuckin' memories these coppers, the solving of The Yorkshire Ripper crimes springs to mind!) but they reluctantly opened a gate in the segregation fence, and allowed us to walk through. Timing is just everything, is it not? And I kid you not, just as we went through to friendly territory, our right back, Alan 'Cyclops' Sneddon hit a thirty yarder, right into the top corner of the bulging Dundee United net! FUCKING YYEEEEAAAAAAHHHSSS! Did Davo and I celebrate? You fucking bet we did, the United punters were up at the fence, baying for our blood, that fence helped our bravado no end, we gave them the wanker sign, and suggested that we would 'go ahead' with the lot of them any time they liked! Cyclops must have been aiming for a clearance towards the corner flag, but what a fucking goal he'd just scored. It's a wonder he didn't run into a wall whilst celebrating. The football used to be so much fun, it really did. All this before the sterility of all seated stadia, and don't you dare fart, or you're out, banned from every ground in Scotland for 120 years!

I was to meet my great friend Postie through Hibs as well. As his nickname suggests, Paul Smith delivers her Majesty's mail; I've never come across such a waste of talent in all my life. Postie's brain is a computer of the highest quality; he's amazing at remembering dates, times, events, details – he forgets nothing. Postie should be employed at NASA or out fleecing casinos.

One New Year we were playing Hearts at home, it was an evening kick off, and our crew were through in Edinburgh early doors. I had actually completed a small part of my journey back to London, having been home for a break, the Edinburgh derby was a welcome stopping off point before catching the overnight sleeper to the smoke. There were loads of us through that day, we spent all afternoon and early evening in Pierce's pub on Leith Walk, the limited jukebox doing its best to keep up with our state of high jinx. Aztec Camera came on the jukey, none of us were fans, except Postie – he stood, and treated us to a shameless vocal of the song; we all sat in a huddle, with our arms round each other, swaying from side to side in time with the music and Postie's singing. It was like something out of The Waltons, and ever since that day, Postie is associated with 'Somewhere in my heart' with absolutely no reference whatsoever to the Jambos who we were about to defeat that night at Easter Road. In a previous chapter you'll recall that he sung it at my wedding, and at Gazelle's, the latter with a full band behind him. The song just reminds the Perth Hibs boys of good times; it always will. After defeating Edinburgh's little team, it was a very difficult goodbye to all the boys, then I settled into my sleeper wondering who my companion was going to be that night. The train was still stationary in Edinburgh Waverley when I heard the next door berth's occupants arrive, a couple. As soon as I heard their door close, they were at it – the lady was a screamer all right, what a fucking racket. I was still in my berth on my own, the woman was shouting by now, "You're hurting me, you're hurting me, you're ssooooh big!" I couldn't resist it, I hammered my fist on the thin wall between us. "STOP HURTING HER, FOR FUCK'S SAKE, JUST PUT HALF OF IT IN!" All of a sudden there was total silence, seems that I had destroyed the moment. I could only imagine that things had gone a bit limp, but it wouldn't be sore no more, love, and I can report things did not continue thereafter. Noisy bastards!

When Paul Kane rose at the Hearts end of their Tynecastle ground, to bullet in a header, to the back of their net, we were so impressed that we decided to call our supporters' branch after him. The Perth Paul Kanos. We had our own song to mark that classic goal: "Leapt like a salmon! He only leapt like a salmon!" Ok, the lyrics are sparse, but you get the idea. We held two very memorable dinner dances in Perth, with 'Kano' attending both, along with his lovely wife Veronica, and some of their friends. At one of those dances, we presented to him a whole silvery and slippery salmon, quite a size it was, on a large shiny platter. I'll never forget the look on his face, as if to say, what the hell am I going to do with that. I'm not sure if the salmon shared the Kane hotel bed that night or not!

As I mentioned previously, the Perth boys would regularly meet up with Hibs fans from other towns on a regular basis, in particular, from Inverness and Glasgow. Three regulars from Glasgow had a common interest with big Les 'Reg' Rennie. They liked nothing better than a scrap on a Saturday afternoon, with opposing supporters who were like minded. Craig, Jamie and Johnnie were actually fearless when it came to this particular pastime. I'll never forget Craig running at and into Celtic supporters inside Parkhead, the odds monumentally stacked against him, and he did all right for a while, probably due to the sheer bewilderment on the Celtic fans' faces, to what he was actually attempting.

Wee Johnnie was mental; he was a really funny guy, who had a passion for Newcastle United as well as Hibs. I've not seen Johnnie for years, but I used to love his company and his patter. During an evening match at Easter Road v Aberdeen, he gave many Hibs fans a laugh and a moment to cherish forever. We were playing Aberdeen, who were wiping the floor with everyone at the time. They had a defender called Doug Rougvie. Let's just say that this lad was 'rugged'. If he was the only contestant in a beauty contest, Douglas would have come second! As the match ball went out of play, over to the enclosure where we were standing, the delectable Mr Rougvie came over to retrieve it, preparing to take a throw in. The problem was, Johnnie had hold of the ball, and before he handed it over, he commenced into a tirade of insults and a volley of very uncomplimentary vocabulary, directed at the not so meek and mild Douglas Rougvie. The big defender just stood there, letting Johnnie have his 'say'. When Johnnie was finished, Rougvie hung around for a while, it seemed like an age, just staring at Johnnie – he was so close, Johnnie would have been able to feel Doug Rougvie's breath, and all of a sudden, our hero had lost his tongue. The look on Johnnie's face was priceless. Mr Rougvie was to prove to be more than a formidable opponent, without even saying a word. Eventually, he turned and took the throw in, leaving us all in stitches, with a very visibly shocked Johnnie for company.

The lads from Inverness were certainly loyal to the cause, the mileage they clocked up was ridiculous when following the Hibs; their accents used to crack us up, they had a language all of their own. By the time we met them in Perth, they'd usually had a right good drink in them already and were up for a party. Bean would be literally pickled in Blue Nun wine by the time we had reached the destination of our match.

I've had so many great times following the Hibees over the years, and met some brilliant people through supporting them. It has to be said, for a club the size of Hibs, they have underachieved results wise. However, I wouldn't change my team for the world, they play in simply the best strip, in green and white colours, they play in an area of Edinburgh/Leith that is steeped in history, they're a cavalier type of club, never afraid to try something new, they were the first British side to compete in European competition, the first Scottish club to install undersoil heating, and the first to have advertising on their shirts – all of these things are taken for granted today. The late Tom Hart, the Hibs chairman at the time, livened up a dreadful relegation season, with having George Best turn out in the colours of Hibernian FC. They have been a big part of my life, and were the glue that kept the Perth Hibees' friendship together; a match usually gave us a really tremendous social occasion, but I would be a rich man if I had a pound for every time one of us said, "What a brilliant day that was, apart from the football of course!".

These days, I probably go to about five or six games a season; it's still great socially, and I still love being in the vicinity of our very smart modern stadium, but, like the dinosaur I am, I preferred our ground when it was crumbling, when we stood on the steps of the terracing, and when we scored a goal in a highly charged match – you might well end up on yer arse, in the middle of a delightful mêlée! However. One thing that I definitely don't miss are the barbaric toilet facilities of Easter Road stadium, as they were, when I first started going regularly to the matches. It was quite simple really. Thousands of Hibs fans at the dear old ground for a couple of hours, and no one, really, no one, will need to go for a shit! The facilities were almost non existent – as for fluffy, 3-ply toilet tissue to gently caress your steaming ringpiece back to respectability, well, you'd be disappointed! At the time, the Krypton Factor was the big, mainstream TV quiz show, for intelligent fuckers. I can see it now, "This is Gordon Burns presenting The Krypton Factor for you tonight. First challenge is a fusion of physical and mental ability, where one must take a dump at Easter Road on match day. It sounds a tall order, but the more imaginative contestant just might manage to empty their bowels cleanly and with dignity." Really?

We've had some fucking awful managers, Jim Duffy and Colin Calderwood instantly come to mind, and the game in Scotland generally is on its arse, in a non delightful mêlée. But I'm so glad I didn't up following the herd and falling into a predictable, narrow minded trap of alleging myself to one the old firm, Rangers or Celtic. I know so many people that 'support' these teams, telling any cunt that will listen to them that they are staunch supporters, yet have never been near Ibrox or Celtic Park in their lives – or maybe once or twice at the most. There's nothing worse than listening to these fuckers; if Hibs are under achievers as a team, then the old firm are currently a hundred times worse, with the riches they have at their disposal. I've no time for either of them. What I do have respect for however, are the fans who follow these teams week in week out, you always hear them backing their side, they're always loud, and they are properly loyal to the cause. You can't argue with that. It's like Man Utd in England. Their away support never stop singing at a match, they are the real diehards, the real fans, not the stay at home Sky Sports, replica shirt wearing, Wayne Rooney mask wearing, key ring collectors.

Nowadays, it's sometimes soul destroying, sitting in the West Stand at Easter Road, watching overpaid shite players, scared of making a simple pass, to a team mate, who doesn't look like he fancies receiving that pass. There've been too many players recently that are not prepared to sweat blood for the cause. Anything less is not acceptable. I was recently reprimanded, by none other than Jimmy 'train guard imposter' Duthie when we met at a local supermarket one fine morning. When discussing the limitations of some of our current players, Jimmy reminded me of an incident at Easter Road, where I was shouting at one of those 'culprits' who was definitely aiding nothing to the Hibs cause. He told me that I shouldn't be doing that, and we started to debate the issue. When I thought about it, I realised that he was absolutely right. When I first started attending Hibs matches regularly, I wouldn't have dreamt of shouting or roaring at one of our players. The Hibs fans, at home, can be really hard on the team, and it's actually little wonder that our recent home record is pish. It's not all down to me (honest!) but I will try and keep myself in check from hereon in, starting with my next visit to the Leith San Siro. After our discussion, Jimmy and I moved on to the even trickier subject of chocolate biscuits and eggs with extra bright yellow yolks – there's a first time for everything! Hibs are my team, they always will be, even if it's not very often the best afternoon or night out in town.

A certain Terry Butcher has recently been appointed manager at Easter Road. As a player, you couldn't help but admire him, even if he was playing for Rangers or England. Like thousands of fellow Hibees, I'm hoping he can steer our dear old football club back to something a bit more fluent and passionate. If I were a player, I would not fancy going in to see Mr Butcher after a shite performance!

The people I've met through supporting Hibs have been an experience in itself. The Perth Hibs boys are well documented throughout my story; however, over the years, meeting the Hibs fans from outside Edinburgh has seen some real bonds of friendship develop.

I'm talking about Big Craig Handyside from Lochgelly. Andy Blance from Rosyth, Lownie (now from Dundee), The Thomsons, Phil, Steve and Andy, Neil from Coupar Angus. Kenny from Pitlochry, Rabies from Arbroath, Gordon from Falkirk, Niall, Tony and Stewart from Dunblane. The legendary Inverness boys, enter Big Bean, Bleep, Woody, Kev, Rory and Freddie. The Glasgow branch, Jamie, Johnnie and Craig. And I must mention four Edinburgh dudes, Paul Kane, Chopper, Keith and Alfie Brodie. And here in Perth, some Hibees I've met in more recent times: George, Charley, James, Davey, John, Harrison, Jo Jo and Bruce. Sorry if I forgot anyone. Bless you all.

Glory, Glory To The Hibees!

A HOSE DOWN AND A
VISIT TO THE DOME

After the disappointment of a no show last Christmas, The Pogues
were, however, giving their fans opportunities to get a fix in the
summer. First up was The Stockton Weekender, a three day outdoor
festival, yet another opportunity to see the greatest band on Earth,
somewhere a little bit different from the norm. The Pogues were
headlining on the Saturday night, so we arranged to meet Keith
in Stockton the night before, booking a Premier Inn that had been
mentioned on The Pogues website as a good call for accommodation
if attending the gig. We travelled down on the train, changing at
Newcastle, going through Sunderland and Philip Borthwick's native
Hartlepool, before shunting into Stockton. Waye aye man! On arrival
at the station in Stockton, Teresa and I hit the nearest boozer, to grease
our throats and to order a taxi to the Premier Inn – we didn't have a
Scooby Doo of its location. I ordered a pint of the beer that the locals
were drinking. The barman took a pint glass that had been half poured
already, then pressed a button at the pump, and handed me a beer that
required a chocolate flake and a wafer! The locals were watching me,
and my somewhat surprised expression gave them a cause for laughter.
Our brief stay in the pub, before the taxi arrived, was brilliant – the
locals were very friendly, and the beer wasn't half bad either!

Keith arrived a little later. We were outside the hotel's pub waiting
for Monsieur Williams, when his white Carina appeared in the car

park. He was pushing his luck with that banger of a car, but he'd made it, his lips were now quivering with anticipated excitement at the thought of a cold Stella passing through them. During our evening, we were reminiscing about the old days, as we often did. An Abba song came on in the boozer, reminding me of a wonderful Keith story of yesteryear. They had an Abba tribute band playing at the hotel in Surrey, ticket sales were poor, so the management announced that the staff could attend to swell the attendance. Keith and I went along, it was an excuse for a drink. Once a few of those were had, Keith appeared agitated; he had something he wanted to get off his chest. After the group had finished, he made his way to the blonde bird that was singing as part of 'Abba'. The lady was heavily pregnant, and Keith told her he wasn't happy about this at all, it was in fact a major and personal disappointment to him. We were all waiting for an explanation, including poor blondie. Keith announced that he used to masturbate about her regularly, and seeing her now, with a huge belly was a fucking disaster, it had destroyed all those pleasant thoughts he had about her! What a silver tongued stallion, I couldn't believe what he had just said. The poor lady was speechless, only Keith could get away with saying something like that. Some of his chat up lines are legendary. "Can I drink yer bathwater?" or "Can I use yer shit for toothpaste?".

In the morning of gig day, smooth talking Keith drove us to nearby Middlesbrough for a mooch around, we followed Teresa into Primark, doing nothing but annoying her, as Keith and I tried on various garments and accessories. We visited a second hand bookshop, the bloke in the shop asked what our interests were, I told him that Keith's was masturbation. The bloke didn't bat an eyelid. He said, "Well, I've got a book on Kylie Minogue over there, and there's lots of pictures in it!" After a giggle, Teresa removed us both from the premises. Enough of this shopping lark, back to the hotel, ready for the concert, a few beers in the bar that was now populated by a number of Pogues fans.

A taxi was ordered to take us to the festival site, near the town centre, beside a river. Diane turned up in our taxi, her north east accent was so thick, it was a joy to hear. I love strong, different accents, one thing that makes the country's population a little bit more interesting.

Diane was the worst case I'd ever seen of mutton dressed as lamb, fuck
knows how old she was, but she was dressed as a teenage girl would
– it was almost a shame to leave her taxi, her patter was just brilliant,
and she really wished she was going to see The Pogues with us. The
Stockton Weekender was busy, 10,000 punters they reckoned, the low
price of the tickets working a treat, this was the organisers' method:
cheap tickets (£15 per skull) and cram them in, the way it should be.
The various artists and bands had been on all day, but we were in
time to see We Are Scientists – not bad, but not the reason we were in
Stockton.

We armed ourselves with liquid supplies, and were right down the
front; Teresa was shittin' herself, but was game. 'Straight to Hell' filled
our eardrums, superb, nothing beats it, it was Pogues time again. As
par for the course, the band members started appearing, Teresa was
christened with some flying beer in her hair, she was almost expecting
this, and handled it well. Fucking hell! When it was MacGowan's
time to enter the spotlight, he looked a million dollars, as if he'd had
a makeover in Hollywood or something. He's been hosed down, he
was clean shaven, had himself a Vidal Sassoon of a hairdo, a crisp
white shirt and a smart jacket was the garnish for male model Shane!
It was really good to see him like this – the way he was looking, you
just knew that tonight was going to see a great performance from him.
And we did. The sound was spot on, louder I'm glad to say compared
to Greenwich and the band were on the money, they were awesome,
treating the north east punters to an evening of unparalleled soul,
passion, emotion and pulse racing excitement. The set list didn't throw
up any surprises, but that was more than Ok. Teresa more than held
her own down the front, and Keith found plenty like-minded, willing
participants for his rough and tumbling shenanigans. I think it's fair
to say that the huge crowd at the Stockton Weekender's Saturday night
had a party with The Pogues to remember;, it was a monster gig. When
they get the sound levels right outdoors, it makes all the difference.
Silky smooth Shane and his comrades had come up trumps once again.
Teresa was NOT impressed with the toilets though; festival bogs have
never been the best. I thought Teresa was going to pass out as she
exited the stinking portaloo thing.

I awoke around 4 30 next morning, and could hear Keith talking to someone outside the hotel, he was up for his early morning cigarette, and had obviously met a fellow member of the exclusive early fag club We had breakfast later on, talking to some Pogues punters who were residents, all were delighted with last nights entertainment, the main topic of conversation was of course, about boy band, hearbreaker Shane!

The Pogues, as a band were thirty years old this year, 2012, and to mark the occasion they had two shows scheduled in Paris to celebrate. The shows were to be recorded, a live DVD and CD were in the pipeline. Paris. In September. Sounded amazing. The venue they were playing, The Olympia, looked really smart too, an old fashioned theatre with stalls, circle and balcony. Teresa and I talked about getting to Paris, a trip there on our favoured train to London, followed by the Eurostar across the channel was a really appealing thought. The trouble we were having was getting time off our work. The Paris gigs were mid-week, and we were really struggling to cover our commitments. After much discussion and permutational planning, we decided that we would have to miss Paris. When the dates of the gigs arrived, it was a horrible feeling, imagining what was going on over in the land of frog limb munchers. When the DVD came out, we realised what a big mistake we had made. What have I been harping on about, all the way through this story? When it comes to opportunities to see The Pogues, one must be ruthless and selfish. Because, there will come a time, when the live shows will stop. No more. Finished. When you're on your deathbed, reflecting on your life, I've got a feeling that one might think about a wonderful Pogues show or two in Paris, rather than a few mundane days at work.

The live DVD is an outstanding product; it really captures a quality Pogues show. There's no frills; it's a simple affair, in a most excellent way. It starts by showing the band (minus Shane at this point) in the wings of the stage, then entering their workshop for the evening to the delight of the frogs, and the sensible punters who had travelled from other countries! Shane, as standard, keeps everyone waiting a wee while longer, almost going the wrong way at the stage, eventually appearing in front of his adoring followers. They would see that he'd continued his boy band grooming, old Vidal was still in tow, trimming and combing his thatch! He looked so fit, he must have been swimming the length of the River Liffey, at least twice a day! The footage is the closest you can get, in my opinion, to capturing the best night out in town – far better quality than the live stuff released years ago at The Town and Country Club. If we're having a few beers at home, and we're feeling like we could do with some pogueing, then it's really handy to slap this DVD into the machine and enjoy the next best thing.

Speculation starts around September on the Pogues' website: are they doing Christmas or not? Philip Chevron was the man that fielded the enquiries – he usually hinted rather than confirmed anything – something might have been arranged, but he wasn't saying. The longer the time went on, I thought the worst. Sometimes the Academy websites can give you a clue, if they have free dates or even confirm things just before the Pogues' website does; however the trail this year had definitely gone cold.

We'd been down to visit Teresa's folks one weekend, and we found ourselves up in Camden one afternoon, enjoying a pleasant beverage, by the canal. I had a crazy idea. I had an almost uncontrollable urge, to press the buzzer on Carmel's flat, just up the road. We walked there, it really was like going back in time, and I pressed that buzzer. It had been twenty years, but I had a feeling, a really strong one, somehow, that Carmel would still be in residence. ZZZZZZZZ! I found, and I pressed that buzzer, the one that Shane had loved pressing for an age, all that time ago. "Hello," a lady's voice. "Carmel?" I enquired, "Yes" – she was still there; she very kindly invited us up. She was very welcoming, even if she only vaguely remembered me. She was in the middle of decorating her flat, and was glad to stop for a break as she put the kettle on. We talked about the old days, and laughed as we remembered her flat was like Euston Station back then, with so many people passing through. Of course Diesel had long departed, but she had a new pooch, 'Patch' and he was lovely, but he didn't take me to the off licence. We let Carmel get back to her paintbrushes; it was great to see her and we're now in touch.

We were on the train home from King's Cross. We're always armed with plenty of papers and magazines. As the train headed north, I opened up a London Time Out magazine, which tells you what events are coming up in the capital, and flicking through the pages, noticed a full page, green and white advert; the picture of the band was very familiar. I said to Teresa, "They ARE doing Christmas!" Teresa just looked at me, "WHO'S doing Christmas?" She was hopeful, grinning. I just smiled at her, and she knew. I handed her the magazine. I hadn't looked at it properly, and had assumed that it would be Brixton Academy, with other dates dotted around in the usual places. I couldn't have been more mistaken. Teresa enlightened me with the fact that it was the O2 Arena they were playing, the Millennium Dome of old, just round the corner from the Naval College in Greenwich. It was advertised as a Christmas tour, suggesting there would indeed be more dates.

Teresa fired up her iPad thing. I'd not been on the website for a few days. We discovered that it was a one off gig though. My first thoughts were that the venue was highly ambitious – I think the place holds about 20,000 punters. However, I was also very excited, again, this was something new, a different place to see The mighty Pogues, and we were grateful that we had something to look forward to again, to soothe the mistaken decision not to go to Paris. As soon as we got home, I booked everything up, train, hotel in Greenwich and tickets for the gig. I'd absolutely no idea how we were going to juggle this with work commitments during what would be a busy time, but I was not going to lose any sleep over it. Reaction to the gig on the Pogues forum from the fans was mixed. Some weren't happy with the choice of venue, some were complaining that they wouldn't be able to make it because of X, Y and Z, so I put my tuppenceworth in, telling the whingers to stop fannying about and get on with it, buy your tickets, get there by hook or by crook, and have a Christmas party with The Pogues, with a few stories to tell after. What could be more wonderful than The Pogues in London, at Christmas time? I received some welcome support on the forum to my tirade of sensibleness!

A friend was good enough to cover us for a few days at work – really, the situation regarding time off from this job we were doing was ridiculous in the extreme; our mate had to juggle his own work commitments as well as ours, but we were grateful, and ultimately found ourselves in London, Greenwich, and The Clock Tower, where we had sung a Rick Astley song in the summer. Tomorrow night was the big one, The O2, Keith was coming in of course, and we had a new companion about to lose her Pogues live show virginity (well, it wouldn't be any other kind of virginity!) in the shape of Laura 'kebab' Sundae. Laura had been getting curious with me and Teresa going on about The Pogues, had dipped her toe in the water, and guess what, she was now a fan, hooked! The Pogues were bridging that generation gap again. Laura liked all the usual young girl charts stuff, she had that in common with charts man Keith, but she had caught The Pogues bug, totally understandable, and she was gagging to see them in the flesh. Keith and Laura had booked into the same hotel as us, I was residing with Mick McManus, the girls in the other room, much to Mick's disappointment!

On gig day, I took Teresa to Harrods, a surprise for her birthday. She'd always wanted to eat in their steak bar, in the food hall. I emailed James Fearnley, told him he could join us if he liked. I had a folder for him with more chapters of my project for him to look over. He apologised saying he wouldn't be able to make Harrods, but thanked me for my kind invitation. You fucking bet it was kind. Our lunch was superb – the bill almost choked me though! Still, it was a good experience, and Teresa really enjoyed it.

After, we actually travelled to the O2 itself; it was mid afternoon, and I wanted to hand in my folder, for James Fearnley's attention. We also wanted a look to see what the place was like close up, and we'd some time to kill before the arrival of Mick and Laura. As we entered the massive complex, I really didn't think we'd get far with the folder – security appeared to be shit hot; it was a bit like going through the security check at the airport, and that was before even getting near where the actual concert arena was situated. I spoke to a staff member, outlining my intentions re the folder, and was shown to another security door, with a no nonsense geezer controlling everything. We really thought this would be the end of the line, but maybe he would take the folder and pass it through to the dressing rooms, or give it to a member of Pogues personnel. The Geezer was actually very accommodating; after checking that James Fearnley was on his clipboarded list, he told us to wait at the side for a few minutes as he spoke into his walkie talkie. The support band were arriving at the same security door, the musicians for Frank Turner. They had to wait at the side with us too. To our great surprise, the security man told us to 'go through' past the back of the stage and ask for Zoe. Fucking hell! We were right in the bowels of the O2; naturally we took our time, and had a right good look around. We were out in the Arena itself; it was huge, there were people twiddling with the instruments, plugs and wires on the stage, where all the equipment was congestedly together. We passed the Chef – he'd be busy preparing himself for the pampered popstars perhaps – I bet he's got a few stories to tell.

We met Zoe in a kind of control room. There was a chart on the wall, saying that the ground floor of the Arena, where all the seats had sensibly been removed, was 'Full'. Ticket sales must have gone well. She was expecting us after getting the nod on the walkie talkie. Even though she was clearly busy, she was really nice, and assured me that the folder would get to James, along with the bottle of Cairn o'Mohr Perthshire wine we gave him for his Christmas and as a thank you for him bothering with my project. We shared a laugh to keep it out of Shane's reach, and left her to be busy some more. I more than dragged my heels on the way back to our point of entry to the Arena. I found that seeing at first hand how a concert like the one we were attending all came together fascinating. There were people everywhere, but no one was really paying us any attention – I was very tempted to go for a two hour wander! Teresa was having none of it though, and 'persuaded' me it was time to go. Just as well, because matey at the security door was both waiting and looking for us to return. We thanked him warmly, wished him a good Christmas and were on our way. I wouldn't have liked to get on the wrong side of this fella, but he was a true gent to us both, allowing us to go where we did. It was an experience in itself really, to be in the O2, in the afternoon before The Pogues.

Keith and Laura appeared a little later in the afternoon, we had a few swallaes in the Clock Tower in Greenwich, before making our way back to the O2 for the real thing. James had emailed me earlier telling me that he'd received my folder and vino, and hoped we'd enjoy the gig. We got to our seats at the side as standard, we had a good view of the stage and got plenty of liquid supplies, also as standard ready for the off. The folks round about us were up for a party. I got talking to a bloke from Colchester – like Laura it was his first ever Pogues gig, and he almost looked nervous. The mass of the floor area in front of the stage appeared to go back for miles, and it was indeed full. The punters at the back would surely have seen very little, although there were large screens showing activity on the stage. The seats weren't full, but were not poorly populated either. We were on our toes as 'Straight to Hell', as standard, signalled the arrival of our heroes. When Shane trundled on to the huge stage, it was very clear that he'd given Vidal Sassoon his books – he was back to a more 'comfortable' look. He announced that he wasn't feeling well. Oh no! We needn't have worried about his performance though – he was spot on, as was the performance as a whole, the sound was good, I thought the venue was more than OK, it was miles better than The SECC in Glasgow, which actually needs fucking demolished! My new mate from Colchester was going nuts, at the end he was absolutely drenched in sweat, he could hardly speak, he looked like he'd just had the best sex of his life – for an hour and a half! Laura sang along word perfect, and Keith actually refrained from once, from vampire lusting after strangers' earlobes and beards, giving Teresa an easy night, keeping the troops in check. The Pogues had yet another venue cracked, we all had a very merry time, Christmas just isn't Christmas without the Pogues.

SHANE MACGOWAN, DUBLIN

Where on earth do you start with the subject of Shane Patrick Lysaght MacGowan? I'm so grateful to him; his mere existence has enhanced my life more than considerably. In James Fearnley's book, there's a very poignant few words near the end, when The Pogues part 1 with Shane was falling apart. James also said he felt so grateful to him, albeit in a different way from me I would expect. I loved reading those words.

The Pogues have given me so much in life, fabulous times that I've tried my best to document here, hours and hours of listening to their music, with literally hundreds of hairs up on the back of my neck moments. What I've written is my personal take on The Pogues, how I've enjoyed some shows more than others; the same could be said of their performance on vinyl. One thing is certain though. None of it would have been possible without one Shane MacGowan, and that is not an opinion, it's an obvious fact. As a group, they really have been to hell and back, they've been through so much together, I often tell Keith how lucky I am that I've managed to have the pleasure of seeing them so many times live, especially since the first reunion of 2001.

Keith has been with me to lots of these shows, he's a big part of my story... Oh yes, my mother's funeral! Keith and Philip were staying in a Perth hotel after the event, it had been a long day, and Keith maintained that the last pint of Stella he had quaffed was a strong one.

Philip had retired to his bed, but Keith went for a very disorientated cigarette first. After he'd stepped on the tab, Keith couldn't find his room. And he needed a piss. He mistook a room door for a urinal (easy mistake) and before you knew it there was a Steward's Enquiry at reception, with three of Old Bill's finest in attendance. There probably wouldn't be much on for Bill in Perth on a Wednesday night, and word was they were wanting to take Keith back to their own version of overnight accommodation, complete with piss pot. Philip was telephoned, and came down the stairs to try and resolve the enquiry. Keith was by now totally fed up with all this attention and was grumpy. Philip pointed out to the night manager and Bill that Keith had been to a funeral and was clearly upset. They should make an allowance or two, surely. Bill looked confused; one of them said: "He's just told us that he was at a WEDDING!" Somehow, Philip saved his bacon, appeased the night manager and Bill would still have at least one room still available in their quality accommodation block. Keith slept it all off, was none the wiser in the morning, and wondered why Philip was a bit 'off' with him during their long journey home. He's an awffy man. My dear mother would have loved to have heard that story about Keith; she had a lot of time for him, and his antics that night would have tickled her no end. It was almost a fitting finale to a highly emotional day; Keith never disappoints. Philip could've done without Keith's high jinx that night; he's a proud man, but long before they had reached Bracknell, things would have been back to normal. I don't think any of us would want Keith to change, and I don't think he will either.

I managed to get in touch with Shane's girlfriend, Victoria Clarke. The couple live in Dublin, and I spoke with Victoria about the days of Carmel's flat in Camden Town, and Diesel the dog. Apparently she and Shane couldn't remember the dog's name after talking about the very subject of Carmel a few days earlier, so I was glad to fill in the blank on that one. She very kindly invited me over to Ireland's capital city, to spend a bit of time with her and Shane, take a few pictures and have a chat with the great man. I couldn't believe my luck, but I didn't get my hopes up on too large a scale, as I knew that Shane could be unpredictable when it came to times and arrangements. Still, neither I nor Teresa had ever been to Dublin, but we now had time on our hands, as we'd given up the time noose round our necks with the Sally Army job. We booked a flight and city centre hotel, and were bound for Dublin.

The descent into Ireland's fair city afforded us a real good view of our destination, you could pick out the Aviva stadium, the new place that was once Lansdowne Road, and the very distinctive pair of tall pillars signifying the entrance to the docks. It felt really good to be visiting Dublin. We settled into our hotel, just up from the old main drag of O'Connell Street where we headed to a pub called Murrays. Straight into the lovely Guinness for me, a lager for Teresa, fuck me, it wasn't cheap, but the black gold slipped down a delicious treat. The pub was roasting hot; I was sweating so much, I had to scratch the Dublin Bay prawns that were playing havoc in my pants! People were talking to us, strangers, it was actually very refreshing – we were digging Dublin, right from the off. Back to the hotel, and we settled in the bar, met a couple of real characters that you felt could tune in to a conversation about any subject you could throw at them, they were both very staunch nationalists and told us some wonderful stories. We were very late to bed after a brilliant night.

Victoria had invited us to a dinner, at Andrew Rudd's Medley restaurant in Drury Street. The dinner had a theme, a 'Speaking Supper', tonight's subject being religion. After spending a very enjoyable day having a bit look at Dublin's town centre, where the thing that made Ireland stand head and shoulders above anywhere I've ever known was the wonderful people. We were in a shop, Teresa bought some make-up. As the change, receipt and bag were produced, we were treated to some friendly, non profiteering advice, on where to go, if we were looking for something to see, to do the touristy thing. I really thought that this was marvellous, and it happened in most of the places we went to that afternoon – the good souls of Dublin were really going out of their way to accommodate Jock and his missus!

We really didn't know what to expect from our dinner date, however; we were actually quite nervous. We sat in Murrays, having a beer, shaved, with clean, non itchy underpants on, contemplating what lay ahead of us with the Speaking Supper. It was pissing down with rain, so we hailed a taxi to take us to Andrew Rudd's. In Drury Street.

Taxi man didn't have a clue where we were talking about, but, assured us, we would get there. After an extensive tour of Dublin's central back streets, and after stopping to wind the window down to talk to half of Dublin's cabbies, we arrived, in Drury Street. Andrew Rudd's Medley was upstairs, where we were met by a very glamorous looking Victoria Clarke; it had been a while since we'd last met. She was charm itself, giving us a very warm welcome. We reminisced briefly of the days of Carmel's flat in Camden, and I produced a photo of me and Carmel, taken when we recently visited her. Victoria wanted to show Shane the picture. She had no recollection of Shane painting Carmel's carpet though!

With Victoria and her partner in crime Sarah holding court, attending to the arrival of their guests, it was time to get to the bar. "Two beers please, chieftain!" The suave geezer serving just shook his head and grinned. "There's no beer, just expensive wine." OK Teresa, over to you. She obtained a bottle of the pre warned, far too fucking expensive stuff, and fought a losing battle explaining to me that it couldn't be drunk in the same way as beer – the bottle didn't last long at all. Get the Euros out, we need another one! We were sat at a table with some really warm, friendly people; indeed, from the minute we touched down in Dublin, the people were actually immense. They were an absolute example to their counterparts across the short water, head and shoulders above what happens here, on the big island, I'm ashamed to say. Food was served, the wine bottle's contents were evaporating rapidly and Victoria was over to me and Teresa, asking if we were ok. "Fine," I reassured her, but, "is Shane coming tonight?" She looked at me, and said, "Oh yes, he'll be here".

By now, some of the company had been up to do their 'speeches' on religion. It was really entertaining, laced with plenty of bad language and more humour as the night went on; these people struck me as highly intelligent individuals, all very comfortable in each other's company. Teresa went out for a fag with Liz who was sat at our table. While she was away, a figure appeared to glide their way into the middle of the room. Dressed in a long, black leather coat, dark blue jeans and some awful pumps with no laces, stood the one, the only, Mr Shane MacGowan! A bloke that was sitting at our table asked me if I was 'starstruck'. "Yes," I was. Shane had a look around the room, then settled himself at a table in the corner of the restaurant, with what looked like some of his pals. Unbeknown to me, Teresa had exchanged "hellos" with Shane already outside! Shane looked comfortable, he was sooking the dear life out of one of those electronic cigarettes, having himself a little tipple and was nibbling on the food that was on his table. He certainly did not appear to be drunk, far from it, but he did look very tired and sleepy from time to time. My conversational skills with our new pals went downhill rapidly; I must have came across more ignorant than usual, but I was just fascinated with the goings on at yer man's table – I must have been staring! Victoria asked if I was going to take a turn of speaking for the company. I wanted to, I really did, but, of course, it would've been easier not to. I pathetically told her that I wasn't sure. She was good enough to take me over to Shane's table though and introduced me to him and his mates.

The Irish welcome was never more apparent, than at this precise moment. Before I knew it, a space was made available for me to park my arse, a glass was produced with a large Gin and Tonic and handed to me. I showed Shane the picture of Carmel and he laughed, his famous laugh. SSSSCCCHHHHHHRRRRRCCCCHHH! I was fortunate also to meet Mr Paul McCluskey and Mr Tom Creagh. Paul seemed a canny chap, he'd been the first up to do a speech that night; Tom was the total opposite, he had us all into a sing-song, the favoured numbers were The Skye Boat Song and Flower of Scotland, for the benefit of their new table guest, who Shane playfully was referring to as 'A Scottish bastard'! They made me feel like one of the boys, I can't emphasise enough how grateful I was to them for accepting the gatecrasher. I spoke with Shane about all sorts of random things. I asked him about his farmhouse in Tipperary, telling him that I'd love to see it one day, and also see the River Shannon that he sings about so passionately. Tom was right there, A Tipperary man himself, he told Teresa that he'd love to show us around. Maybe one day. I told Shane that I'd love to see him on 'Masterchef', involved in a cook off against Spider Stacy! He just shook his head as he was laughing. Here was my all time hero sat next to me, and I was genuinely having a lovely time in his company, along with a couple of his close pals. Paul told me that the well known saying, never meet your heroes, for fear of disappointment, did not apply to Shane. Paul was actually a big fan of Shane's too, as well as being his mate. Shane's friends could have been forgiven for being hostile about my settling at their table; they were anything but.

Up until now, I hadn't mentioned my book. Teresa, who was still sitting mainly at our original table, was over to me. If I wanted to 'Speak' then it was now or never, as the speeches were drawing to a close. She pushed me a bit, and I'm glad she did. Victoria was on the microphone, and announced that Calum was the next speaker. Fucking hell!

Unlike the previous, accomplished speakers, who spoke from the top of their heads, I found myself fumbling with little pieces of paper that I'd written on earlier in the day. I was also bucking the trend, because, as I told the company, I wasn't going to speak about religion, but about the effect, that Shane and The Pogues' music had had on my and my family's life. I said that I was currently writing a book, based on that very subject, and was both thrilled and delighted to be over in Dublin to spend some time with Victoria and Shane. I spoke mainly about my father, and told the story about burying my mother, with Shane's words keeping me right that day from 'Lullaby Of London', "May the angels bright, watch you tonight, and keep you, while you sleep". I was really nervous whilst talking, but I think I just about pulled it off. Amazingly, I wasn't really conscious of Shane's reaction to my speech, but that all changed when I heard him say "Yeah, yes" approvingly. I stopped talking and raised my hand towards him. I was thrilled that he appeared to be enjoying what I was talking about. When I finished, I was both glad that Teresa had encouraged me to talk and relieved that I'd got through it. The people that we had just met that evening were very generous with their reaction to this stranger from Scotland, spouting on about the book he was trying to write; they really were a touch of class – it was a pleasure to be part of their company.

On my return (to Shane's table of course) I had myself a big glug of my wine, and listened to a hilarious speech from Tom 'Tipperary' Creagh, who in turn introduced Shane himself to say a few words, bringing the speeches to a close. One of the first things Shane said was "Thanks to the gentleman from Scotland" and this brought a round of applause, which I couldn't help milking a bit. Victoria had told us that Shane hadn't slept for a good while (days?) and he was really struggling now, nodding off every now and then, but he fought it admirably enough. For anyone thinking that he wasn't aware of what was going on, they would've been mistaken. We took some photos and talked some more to the great man. Teresa had been fancying his expensive sunglasses, so Shane handed them to her and she wore them for a while, but did give them back! We spoke about all sorts of things, including X-Ray Spex – Shane wasn't aware that Poly Styrene had died, and he looked saddened by the news. He kept handing me his electric fag, offering me a drag, who was I to refuse? It was brilliant talking to his mate Paul – he told me to look at the roof of the restaurant. "Looks like a fucking car park roof," he said, and he had a point. He started taking pictures of Andrew Rudd's restaurant roof. "That's going on Facebook," said Paul.

It was almost time to leave, we were all stood up now, Shane was asking Tom where the toilet was, and he pointed in its general direction. Shane wasn't sure though, Tom was deep in conversation, so he looked at me, and I knew what he was saying. I guided Shane through to where the toilet was and showed him the correct door to go through. "Cheers," he grunted. Don't you fucking dare! I know what you're thinking! I let Shane have a piss, on his own, even I have a line! Shame on you! After a while, he reappeared, and we shuffled back into the restaurant.

Unbeknown to me, Victoria had invited me and Teresa to her and Shane's house the next day for a drink. Teresa had their address tucked away safely in her bag. Icing on the cake. A lot of the people as they were leaving told me that they had enjoyed my speech; one lady who was in the book publishing business gave me her card. We said our farewells, and Shane was gone, a driver had arrived to whisk him and his company away, and we hailed a taxi back to our hotel – the driver knew the way this time. Straight to the bar in the hotel, we were buzzing; some of the folk we'd met the night before were there, and a few Guinnesses were had before bedtime, it was really late now. What a night – I felt like the proverbial kid who'd been GIVEN the sweetie shop!

Teresa and I were struggling at breakfast; in truth we were very happy, but still drunk, and had to go back to kip for a while.

I was trying to take the events of last night in, my brain trying to compute what had happened. I was Shane's mate for a few hours, he had treated me as an equal, there was nothing 'superstar' about him whatsoever. Here was a man who had written songs that regularly had reduced me to tears, and I had to take him for a piss! Here was I, a 47 year old man, a very lucky one, to have met his hero, just another geezer actually, share a bit crack (not the substance!), a drink and a drag or two of an electric fag.

I was under no illusions whatsoever that the wee drink in Shane and Victoria's Dublin home was a long shot. Teresa kept telling me to check my emails, and I kept making excuses that I'd do it later. We got a few bits and pieces together and we were off, destination Chateau MacGowan/Clarke. This was an adventure in itself. I just love going to new places. Shane's neighbourhood was leafy and classy; the sun was shining. We walked up to the front door and rang the bell. No reply. One more ring. No one home. We hadn't arranged an actual time, just the afternoon. Teresa took things out of my hands by checking my emails herself; sure enough, Victoria had apologised that Shane had eventually succumbed to sleep and would be in bed all day, he wasn't feeling too good. She had to be somewhere, and couldn't guarantee she'd be in the house. It was really strange, amusing almost, to look up at the heavy curtains guarding what we imagined would be the bedroom, where yer man was probably tucked up in his kip. I wasn't disappointed at all, far from it, I was just so happy about last night, and quite enjoyed the short journey to Shane's house. We both felt honoured, that Victoria trusted us with such intimate details, as their actual address.

Paul McCluskey had emailed Teresa; he sent a picture he'd taken of me and Shane. That picture can be found on the back cover of this book. The words he wrote in his mail just blew me away. He said that he was watching Shane during my speech, he was listening intently and that he thought he was genuinely moved by what I was saying, about one subject in particular, which I'll tell you all about in the final chapter. It felt so good that I'd managed to explain, over a few minutes talking, what The Pogues meant, and felt even better that he'd 'got it'. Paul was very interested in my book, and we've been in touch ever since – he's a great man. A measure of him is the fact that when The Pogues play in Dublin, he buys a ticket and stands with the punters, despite Shane telling him that he doesn't need to. I'm so glad I met him. That trip to Dublin took a bit of digesting –, even when we got on a service bus from O'Connell Street back to the airport, the driver didn't charge us the fare, he was just pleased to be looking at Teresa's breasts rather than mucking about with Euros. When we got off at the airport, Teresa blew him a kiss. So did I. Friendly folk to the last. We'd had ourselves a simply fantastic few days; we had constant smiles on our faces.

So there you have it. I can only attempt to explain how good it felt, to be able to tell Shane MacGowan, in an environment amongst his friends, how I felt about his contribution to music. It was almost like a relief. He defies everything I hate about the music industry, with his uncompromising looks, and attitude to candy coated programmes like Top of the Pops, putting two fingers up to the programme that made Jimmy Saville famous. Shane was on the money there, the way that cunt ended up. A tart holding a microphone, showing a glimpse of fanny flap is all well and good, but it's not music – I thought that was soft porn. I don't think Shane would have got away with showing off his arse hairs alone! It sounds corny, I know, but that night in Andrew Rudd's Medley, in Dublin, was one of the best nights of my life – that's how damned good it felt.

I remember hearing an earlyish interview with Shane; the bloke asking the questions was French or something. He asked Shane a question on how he would feel, "Once the music has gone" implying that The Pogues were popular at the time, but wouldn't last, it would all become dated, and would fade. Shane hesitated, "Once the music's gone eh?" he said, as if he couldn't believe the journalist's question. That was never Shane's plan. Even then, I think Shane knew he was on to something massive, that would have appeal for both young and old, for generations to come. He's always modest about his work; he doesn't feel the need to tell people that the songs he's written are good. Songs like 'A pair of brown eyes' I don't think will ever be put in a box, and thrown in the loft. Shane is often contradictory about his work, but one thing that's very clear is his passion for his country. Shane's songs will be around forever; in particular, the good folk of Ireland alone, will take care of that.

Shane's life has been well documented over the years, both in books and on film. He must be sick to the back teeth (pun intended) of folk asking him about his habits, drugs and drinking in particular. Really. It just shows how narrow minded we've become, if that's the main focus of a man like Shane MacGowan. After the Pogues' Christmas show at the O2, I read an article supposedly reviewing the show. Here we go again! The prick that wrote this piece of shite was actually saying Shane should be dead, one got the impression that would've been Ok with this tosser. As many articles before, a lot was made of the fact that he left the stage a few times, when it was Spider's turn to sing or whatever. Shane was drunk again, out of his tree. Actually, he wasn't. These cunts just expect him to be. As a fan, at the concert, I know when he's drunk, and so do the majority of the other Pogues fans – it's not difficult. What that twat of a journalist failed to notice, was the thousands of happy souls, going mental to 'The Body of an American' or welling up at 'A Rainy night in Soho' – THAT'S what it's all about, not if Shane goes for a piss when it's not his turn to do vocals. Yet, you never hear of Shane, sharply biting back (pun intended); he's clearly comfortable and secure in his own skin, and I truly believe that he really doesn't give a fuck about any criticism that may come his way. Many of us say that we don't give a fuck about various things, probably half the time we don't mean it though. The way Shane has lived his life, he's conformed to very little in the way of what life is 'supposed' to be like; he does his own thing, something that I think, perhaps, a lot of us would like to be able to do, even if not in the same way as him. I truly admire him for this. I'm not for minute dismissing the fact that he's obviously difficult to work with. But, I would say to the other members of The Pogues, all your patience and the inconvenience he may have put you through, were well worth it, results wise, for what you've given to your supporters.

The chemistry of the Pogues as a band, has been essential – again, how many bands 30 odd years on have held the same personnel, bar one absentee, especially as there's eight of them! Lucky, lucky Pogues fans. Drummer Andrew Ranken, I feel deserves some special praise, when it comes to the dynamics of the band. Sometimes, most of the time actually, he looks like an undertaker, who's just been told that death is no longer compulsory. He rarely looks happy, he's had some shit in his life, and I don't believe he's had his troubles to seek health wise. If you listen closely and pay attention, the versatility of his drumming throughout the Pogues catalogue is fantastic. Check out the video for 'Dirty old town' and you'll see what I'm on about. Indeed they are all brilliant musicians, and contribute greatly to the cause; there are no passengers. Shane's voice is perfectly suited to the music these talented guys extract from their instruments, sometimes his voice is stronger than it is at other times, but he usually makes it work, and when he's on his game, well, I've told you all about that. Once or twice.

Interlude

I hate namedropping. When people engage in it I mentally rewrite the lyrics of Hal David. All together now: "Namedrops keep falling on my head". Anyway, for this anecdote I'm reduced to namedropping.

I was sitting opposite Shane MacGowan at a Speaking Supper last April. Speaking Suppers are the brainchild of Shane's partner Victoria Mary Clarke and her friend Sarah Leahy. The premise of them is that, over a three course meal, you have the opportunity to speak in public for three minutes. For some it's a fear conquering exercise, for others an ego massage, but for all a unique, fun, evening out.

Anyway, as I sat opposite Shane, a couple approached our table. They introduced themselves as Calum and Teresa Bruce. Calum, a genial Scotsman, explained he had a piece written about Shane. He was nervous about speaking to an audience. I wished him luck and after a while his turn came.

Calum, it transpired, is a longtime fan of Shane and his music. His speech mentioned this in passing. The crux of what he said will stay with me a long time. Calum explained his father has dementia. This cruel illness has robbed them of a typical father and son relationship. To counteract this Calum has found that bringing his father on car journeys, accompanied by Shane's music on the car stereo, is a source of joy for them. Mr Bruce senior is known to sing aloud, gesture, and, above all, laugh and smile, on these trips.

As Calum's speech unfolded, I looked across at Shane. He was visibly moved. Shane and I looked at one another. Words were not necessary. Music is a glorious thing.

Paul McCluskey, Dublin, October 2013

THE TIDE MAY
BE HIGH?

A sad announcement was made via The Pogues' website, delivering the news that band guitarist Philip Chevron was having problems again, with his damned cancer that he'd been in the wars with over the years. Everything was unfortunately pointing to the fact, that he didn't think he was going to be able to beat it this time. The website was filled with messages from fans in an instant, passing on their best wishes and stressing their general state of sadness and upset. Right enough, Philip hadn't been singing his famously penned song 'Thousands are sailing' of late, and he hadn't been looking so well. It was a nasty shock to hear this news though.

A testimonial concert for Philip was organised, scheduled to take place at The Olympia Theatre in Dublin, where a bill of artists were going to perform, to honour Philip. The concert was dated for August; I had a few trips booked already, and didn't think I would be able to go. Teresa's mother was also due to visit us in Perth, and would be here on the night the concert was taking place. Little did I know that my lovely wife was in touch with Paul McCluskey, he whom we had met at the dinner in Dublin with Victoria and Shane. Shane's pal. She had been telling Paul that she'd booked my flight and a hotel in Ireland's capital city, so I could be there to support Philip. What a diamond my darling wife is. Teresa would be staying at home, with her Mum. Teresa's Mum, Pauline, surprise surprise, has well and truly got The Pogues bug.

She can't get enough of their music, and is always asking me about them when she comes to visit. She sings along, often making up her own lyrics; she pretends to be shocked at the swear words (but loves it really) and is fascinated by Shane MacGowan and all his 'ways'.

The Philip Chevron testimonial concert was to be on a Saturday night. I travelled over late on the Thursday, and met Paul on Friday afternoon. He took me to some real proper bars; we almost needed a fork and knife to drink the Guinness, it was really delicious! We had a great night. Paul is a walking encyclopedia of all things Shane/Pogues/ Popes, he has an amazing memory, very similar to my mate Postie. I found myself loving his stories, and as we walked in Dublin, he pointed out some buildings and places that had some sort of connections to the subject of The Pogues or Shane. The time, it just flew by. He was meeting a chap from Stoke Newington, London the next day – another Pogues fan, named David Lally, who was also coming over for Philip's gig. We met at lunchtime, and instantly got on really well; we started drinking right away, and ended up in a bar called Bowes, where we met a few other punters with a liking for The Pogues. Paul was in the middle of everything, I call him 'The Captain' nowadays.

The Olympia is a fantastic venue. We were in the 'pit' downstairs, being issued with a wristband to get yourself in and out of the pit for drinks and a piss. The evening was one of mixed emotions really; there were quite a large number of artists performing, some of them doing Pogues numbers. The Radiators from Space, Philip's other band, were also in the house and played some songs for Philip and his supporters. Philip himself was sat right above us, in an alcove. He had a bright red, striking, tartan suit on. He appeared on stage; it has to be said that he looked really thin and unwell, and he was struggling to talk into the microphone. It was actually heartbreaking. And what of The Pogues themselves? The greatest group on earth were represented by Shane MacGowan, Spider Stacy and Andrew Ranken. Together, along with a geezer from Hothouse Flowers, they treated us to a version of 'Thousands are sailing'. Shane looked well, and sounded good.

Paul told me and David to follow him, we went through some corridors, and ended up outside the stage door where we met Victoria and Shane. It was great to see them and we chatted for a bit. They were a bit emotional with the evening's events. Suddenly, a car appeared. It stopped, right beside me, Paul and David. When I looked round, Philip Chevron was in the passenger side of the car. He was literally a couple of feet away. He just looked at us. I waved and he waved back. He looked so dreadfully ill. In a second, the car drove off, and he was gone. I will never forget the sight of Philip, at that moment, for the rest of my life. It was such a sad, poignant moment. I thought it was probably the last time I'd see him. The image of him in that car stuck in my mind, constantly, for days.

I'd very much enjoyed being in Paul's and David's company. We had a right kick of the ball with the bevvy, and I got to bed, in my hotel about 3.30am. I'm just glad that I was there, at Philip's concert. I'm sure it gave us all something to think about, in terms of life itself.

Word is, that Shane MacGowan is not keen to do any concerts with The Pogues for the time being. With that, and Philip Chevron's sad predicament, one can't help wondering if this indeed is the end of the road for The Pogues as a live act. I obviously hope and pray that it is not. However. If that's the way it is, then I thank them for the music; the sheer pleasure they have enhanced my life with; for all the adventures and scrapes I've found myself embroiled in due to being at their shows; for the goosebumps they've brought to my bare arms; for the exercise they've given the hairs on the back of my neck; for their green vinyl records; for the excitement they create, just before they appear on stage; for taking me to new venues and places; for helping me through the big things in my life, be it my wedding, or the saddest funerals; for Shane's mesmerising lyrics; for the songs he wrote that changed my world; for the rainbow of emotions his music brings along with it; for giving me a reason to write a bloody book; and for the pleasure of meeting special people, such as David from London, and Captain Paul McCluskey. I'm glad I went out of my way, and was selfish, regarding getting to the gigs. No regrets. (Apart from Paris.) A group's music has never intrigued me so much, even if I didn't 'get it' straight away. As the years go by and I listen to their music, I grow to love it even more. I didn't think this would be possible, but clearly it is. Writing this book has actually felt like a type of avenue to 'get it all out', the way I feel about the music of The Pogues.

But wait, what do I know? Maybe it really is fuck all about fuck all! The Pogues have just announced four UK Christmas shows, and, furthermore, they've promised to play their wonderful second album, 'Rum, Sodomy and the Lash' (you know, the one that I played for the neighbours, on that summer's day, many years ago) in its entirety! Shane must have relocated his mojo, absolutely wonderful news. Better start planning, no regrets...

My story is almost at an end. Almost.

Rum & Sodomy, at The Pogues' Christmas Bash!

We make our way, down the old main drag, where you've got to watch them Wild cats of Brixton, they'd be sure to kill Kenny, in their dirtiest of dirty old towns.

A car and a sat nav are definitely not required, there's an inbuilt navigator in my head, takes me straight to the academy, where I waltz past Matilda, the security dolly. Mind, she's looking bedraggled tonight, she's clearly been drilled up in the ticket box, by an ungentlemanly soldier. People heard them at it. Ra ta ta tat!

I've a bone to pick with Billy on the merchandise stall, why the fuck is my book not for sale? I'll turn his pair of brown eyes into black ones, the lazy drunken bastard.

I hook up with David Lally, better make the most of it. He's a man I don't meet everyday.

Jesse James is performed tonight, rising from its sickbed, no doubt persuaded by Paddy Garcia and his pistol, a visit to Sally MacLennane's being touted as a reward, it's the greatest little boozer. The brown is served by Bob, the grub by Charlie, both of them dirty little Fords.

It's all over, take a train home, one that sets the night on fire. No, we sail away on Medusa, bound for Circular Quay (via The Traitor's Gate) –who's at the wheel? Not Burgess, it's the Captain, Paul McCluskey! He's howling like a banshee, and he's going to turn that damned raft into a floating hell.

A FINAL THOUGHT

The last word goes to my father. As I explained earlier, his condition deteriorated so badly that he had to go into permanent care. It was a Sunday morning that he was scheduled to make the move. The day before, Teresa and I took him in the car to Aberdeen, to visit his two brothers, his niece and some old friends of his and my mother's. It was a busy day, getting round everyone; he hadn't a clue what was going on – in truth, the day proved to be a bit too much for him to cope with.

The next morning, he rose and had breakfast, just like any other day. But it wasn't long until Teresa and he left in a taxi, Dad stepping outside his home for the very last time. In an act of sheer cowardice, I remained in the house, twitching behind the curtains. Watching them leave, I'll never forget that precise moment, when the taxi pulled away.

It took a while, but he settled eventually, in the new environment he found himself in. At least he was safe, and wasn't locked in his own house any more, but I'm pleased that we managed to get him into the best (in our opinion) care home in our area. His few pleasures in life were whittling down; he's not that fussed for food these days, sometimes even seeing eating as a chore. He still likes his sweeties though, we make sure his daily supplies are delivered, he gets through quite a bit, and helps maintain the financial situation of Tate and Lyle – he certainly does his bit for them.

The other thing that he has in his life, still, is music. If there's someone playing live music in the home, which they do from time to time, Dad is right in there; he's not backwards at coming forward either

– if it's not up to scratch, he'll let the musicians know; equally, if he's digging it, then he'll be very enthusiastic, often standing a few feet directly in front of them, in his one man mosh pit!

Dad though, likes his music best, when he's in the car with me. He has something in common with Mr MacGowan, in that he sleeps when he feels like it; it can happen at any time. I go to see him almost every day, sometimes he's nodding off constantly; at others, he's as bright as his condition will allow him to be. He has been known to go for two or three days without sleeping properly...exactly like Shane.

This is what I was talking about in Dublin, the subject that I wanted Shane to know about, the subject I want The Pogues to know about. The car is the best place to play your sounds, as loud as you like, without really bothering anyone. My Dad likes his music as loud as I do. We've come a long way, in regards to The Pogues, since he was smuggling my records to tape onto his cassettes, without ever admitting that he actually liked the group. There's no holding back. He's as passionate now listening to Shane and The Pogues (or The Popes) as much as he's been about anything in his life. He claps his hands in time with the beat, sometimes aggressively, he stamps his feet, and he even sings along, remembering lyrics when I least expect him to. This is incredible, considering he really can't remember what happened two minutes ago. He asked me just the other day, whilst listening to The Pogues, "Is he still alive? I really hope he is." In between tracks he'll tell me that the music is just "magic", often with tears in his eyes. Oh my God, Messrs MacGowan, Fearnley, Woods, Hunt, Stacey, Chevron, Ranken and Finer: you make an old man, at the fag end of his life, so happy, that he cries. He laughs when he picks out Shane swearing, or roaring or maybe a lyric that he finds amusing. For a man that doesn't have very much in his life any more, there you have it again, the emotion of The Pogues summed up, in a nutshell. I really don't think that Led Zeppelin would stir such an emotion, or Haircut 100, or Mott the fuckin Hoople, Lieutenant Pigeon or even The Beatles. No fucking chance. Once The Pogues are in your bloodstream, then that's it, nothing comes close. At the moment, 'The Broad Majestic Shannon' is top of the William Bruce, real music chart. The other day, he took my breath away, when the song reached the dreamy instrumental part in the middle, when he 'conducted' the music, just like Shane does at a live show, if he's in the mood. He definitely has some kind of link with Shane, of that there's no doubt. As soon as I get him settled and seat belted in the car these days, he starts clapping, he knows what's coming. He fucking loves it!

When we finish our drive, I'll kill the engine and turn the stereo off. Dad will turn to me, with a determined serious face, and his 'Frank Murray moment' kicks in: "Me and you are going to make a fortune with that music!" I'm not sure how we're going to do it, but you can make a start for us, by recommending my book to a friend... Of course, I play other music in the car from time to time; Dad usually enjoys this too. I'll ask him if he likes it and he'll say something like, "Aye, very good, but not really what we're used to, not up to the usual standard, is it?" Once The Pogues are back on, I'll say, "Is this what you're meaning?" One of Dad's symptoms with his dementia is that he repeats himself, saying the same things over and over. To my question, he will always reply with "If you don't like that, you bloody well don't like anything!"

My story is no more than a ramble of things that have happened throughout my life since discovering the wonderful world of The Pogues. My literary hero, Irvine Welsh, can sleep safe in his bed, knowing that my book will not be challenging his in the charts of the bookshops. I humbly apologise to anyone who disagrees with my thoughts on the band, or opinions of certain live shows and situations I've written about. What is important is the sheer entertainment that The Pogues have brought to the Bruce house. That's the point.

Unfortunately, just before my book went into print, Philip Chevron sadly passed away. He died on a Tuesday morning. October 8th 2013. A part of the Pogues family has been broken. A thousand thoughts of fondness and love will sail your way every day Philip. May he rest in peace.

Thank you, for reading my book. I hope you enjoyed it. Be lucky. Cheers.

ACKNOWLEDGEMENTS

Thanks

Thanks, first and foremost, goes to my darling wife, *Teresa*, for the huge support and encouragement she has given me, right from the start, to getting over the finish line. She often gave me the 'push' I needed, when I sometimes doubted myself.

Thanks also to *Captain Paul McCluskey*, both for his contributions in this book and for his dedication, support and advice, which was given without condition from the moment I met him in Dublin. Paul, you're a diamond geezer!

And to *David Lally*. An unlimited wealth of ideas, for introducing me to Josie for THAT photograph, and for the pure enthusiasm he has shown for this book. Your efforts are appreciated. It's a pleasure to know you, sir.

Thanks to *Carmel Armstrong*, herself still going strong, in dear old Camden Town. Some great photos you allowed me to use, and it was fantastic reminiscing about "the old days" as you call them.

Thanks to *Paul Davidson* (*Davo*), my long term comrade, for introducing me to something that's given me so much pleasure for the past 28 years. You gave me The Pogues, and I introduced you to

Hibernian FC – you owe me big time (or perhaps not!)

And to my other Perth Hibs mates, *Geoff, Whytey, Foggie, Gazelle, Coupar, Bird, Mike, Postie, Jimmy,* the late *Les Rennie* and *Gavin,* for the fantastic adventures we have shared.

Thanks to *Josie Montserrat* from Canada, for providing and allowing me to use the perfect Pogues group photo. Not easy getting them all in one shot, but she is a real talent at her trade. Her gallery of Pogues pictures really are a pleasure to behold. It's well worth a visit to her website,
www.blackmoonphotography.com

A special thanks to *James Fearnley,* for taking the time to both write and email me throughout this project and for the foreword he very kindly submitted. Look out the dictionary!

To *Victoria Mary Clarke* for inviting me and Teresa to Dublin, and looking after us so well.

To big *Tom Craigh* from Tipp' and again *Captain McCluskey,* for welcoming us to your table, for an unforgettable night in yours and Shane's company.

To the editor *Ruth Lunn.* I was always worried she would stop speaking to me, as she got through my sometimes rude story, but she hasn't – thank you for your patience and understanding, Ruth.

To *Jason (Jay) Thompson,* the designer. When he's not reheating other people's King Prawns, his skills in his trade are truly magnificent. It's been a pleasure to work with you both, I think of you as friends, let's go and get drunk!

To *Mr Keith Clifford Williams,* in many ways the 'star' of this book, and to Philip Borthwick, for being there, whenever I've needed you, and for always spoiling my mother.

To my uncompromising friend, *Graham White,* one of the few people
I confided in when writing this book, thanks for listening to me
whittering on, and on, and on...

To The Pogues manager, *Mark Addis,* for his kind words of support.
Talking of support... a HUGE thank you to *Darryl Hunt* for that
revealing interview containing vital information about his balls...

Sorry for all the trees I've destroyed. I've had bits of paper everywhere,
even in the toilet, with a pen, in case I forgot something – multi-
tasking in the toilet can be tricky!

And of course, I thank the greatest band that ever played music; your
story is a truly remarkable one. To *Spider Stacy, Terry Woods, Cait
O'Riordan, Andrew Ranken, Jem Finer, Darryl Hunt,* the late *Philip
Chevron* and again, *Mr James 'maestro' Fearnley.*

Thanks to you, *Shane MacGowan.* Some man, for one man.

Lightning Source UK Ltd.
Milton Keynes UK
UKOW06f1552100416

271850UK00003B/16/P